OXFORD MONOGRAPHS ON LABOUR LAW

General Editors: PAUL DAVIES, KEITH EWING,
MARK FREEDLAND

The Labour Constitution

OXFORD MONOGRAPHS ON LABOUR LAW

General Editors: Paul Davies, Fellow of Jesus College and Allen and Overy Professor of Corporate Law in the University of Oxford; Keith Ewing, Professor of Public Law at King's College, London; and Mark Freedland, emeritus Research Fellow in Law at St John's College and emeritus Professor of Employment Law in the University of Oxford.

This series has come to represent a significant contribution to the literature of British, European, and international labour law. The series recognizes the arrival not only of a renewed interest in labour law generally, but also the need for fresh apptroaches to the study of labour law following a period of momentous change in the UK and Europe. The series is concerned with all aspects of labour law, including traditional subjects of study such as collective labour law and individual employment law. It also includes works that concentrate on the growing role of human rights and the combating od discrimination in employment, and others that examine the law and economics of the labour market and the impact of social security law and of national and supranational employment policies upon patterns of employment and the employment contract. Two of the contributing authors to the series, Lucy Vickers and Diamond Ashiagbor, have received awards from the Society of Legal Scholars in respect of their books.

TITLES PUBLISHED IN THE SERIES

The Legal Construction of Personal Work Relations
Mark Freedland FBA and Nicola Kountouris

A Right to Care? Unpaid Work in European Employment Law
Nicole Busby

Regulating Flexible Work
Deirdre McCann

Welfare to Work: Conditional Rights in Social Policy
Amir Paz-Fuchs

EU Intervention in Domestic Labour Law
Phil Syrpis

Towards a Flexible Labour Market: Labour Legislation and Regulation since the 1990s
Paul Davies and Mark Freedland

The European Employment Strategy: Labour Market Regulation and New Governance
Diamond Ashiagbor

The Law of the Labour Market: Industrialization, Employment, and Legal Evolution
Simon Deakin and Frank Wilkinson

The Personal Employment Contract
Mark Freedland

International and European Protection of the Right to Strike: A Comparative Study of Standards Set by the International Labour Organization, the Council of Europe and the European Union
Tonia Novitz

Freedom of Speech and Employment
Lucy Vickers

Women and the Law
Sandra Fredman

Just Wages for Women
Aileen McColgan

Justice in Dismissal: The Law of Termination of Employment
Hugh Collins

The Right to Strike
K. D. Ewing

The Labour Constitution

The Enduring Idea of Labour Law

RUTH DUKES

OXFORD
UNIVERSITY PRESS

Great Clarendon Street, Oxford, OX2 6DP,
United Kingdom

Oxford University Press is a department of the University of Oxford.
It furthers the University's objective of excellence in research, scholarship,
and education by publishing worldwide. Oxford is a registered trade mark of
Oxford University Press in the UK and in certain other countries

© R. Dukes 2014

The moral rights of the author have been asserted

First Edition Published in 2014

Impression: 1

All rights reserved. No part of this publication may be reproduced, stored in
a retrieval system, or transmitted, in any form or by any means, without the
prior permission in writing of Oxford University Press, or as expressly permitted
by law, by licence or under terms agreed with the appropriate reprographics
rights organization. Enquiries concerning reproduction outside the scope of the
above should be sent to the Rights Department, Oxford University Press, at the
address above

You must not circulate this work in any other form
and you must impose this same condition on any acquirer

Crown copyright material is reproduced under Class Licence
Number C01P0000148 with the permission of OPSI
and the Queen's Printer for Scotland

Published in the United States of America by Oxford University Press
198 Madison Avenue, New York, NY 10016, United States of America

British Library Cataloguing in Publication Data
Data available

Library of Congress Control Number: 2014943656

ISBN 978–0–19–960169–1

Printed and bound by
CPI Group (UK) Ltd, Croydon, CR0 4YY

Links to third party websites are provided by Oxford in good faith and
for information only. Oxford disclaims any responsibility for the materials
contained in any third party website referenced in this work.

For Dominic and Francesca

Series Editors' Preface

The characterisation of the books in this series as 'monographs' on labour law carries some implication that each volume will confine itself to some special and particular part of the field. Nevertheless, more than one of the previous contributions have amounted to or come close to being a general survey of the state of the art as a whole, and this present volume has again ascended to those heights from which such an over-view can be taken. In this case the author sits on the shoulders of giants to obtain that vantage-point. She first goes back to the writings of two of the founding fathers – arguably *the* two founding fathers – of the discipline of labour law, Hugo Sinzheimer and Otto Kahn-Freund, drawing upon their respective foundational ideas of 'the labour constitution' and 'collective *laissez-faire*'. She then goes on to turn that set of historical insights into a critical searchlight upon what she views as a composite genre of writings by a group of authors who, she feels, have between them strayed from the path marked out by Sinzheimer and Kahn-Freund into a different place identified as 'the law of the labour market'.

Those authors, two of these Series Editors among them, will have the opportunity to make their rejoinders if they so choose, and we anticipate that many others will be drawn into the ensuing debate. This, however, is not the moment for that discussion, but rather for the celebration of the vigour and capacity for self-renewal of labour law scholarship which this work – a *tour de force* in its own right – represents. This book richly deserves to join our series, and we are confident that it will sustain and even enhance its existing reputation.

Paul Davies, Keith Ewing, Mark Freedland
July 2014

Acknowledgements

I have worked on this book for several years and incurred many debts along the way. First and foremost, I would like to thank the editors of the *Oxford Monographs on Labour Law* series, Paul Davies, Keith Ewing, and Mark Freedland, each of whom has offered very kind and constructive support since the inception of the project. I also owe a debt of thanks to Natasha Flemming at OUP for her patience and advice on the completion of the manuscript. I'm grateful to the *Modern Law Review* for permission to reproduce material previously published as R Dukes, 'Otto Kahn-Freund and Collective Laissez-Faire: An Edifice without a Keystone?' 72(2) *Modern Law Review* 220–46.

At the School of Law, University of Glasgow, I have been generously supported by colleagues over the years and would like to thank, in particular, Rosa Greaves, Mark Furse, Jane Mair, Maria Fletcher, Alison Craig, Lindsay Farmer, Adam Tomkins, James Sloan, Gavin Anderson, Mark Godfrey, and Claire La Hovary. In 2011/12, I benefited from a sabbatical as an AHRC Early Career Fellow, and from a term spent at the University of Edinburgh as a MacCormick Fellow, where I had very fruitful discussions with Neil Walker. Outside Glasgow, I've had the good fortune to be welcomed into a remarkably supportive community of labour law scholars. At the risk of omitting someone inadvertently, I'd like to express my gratitude to the following, who have each helped in one way or another with the research and writing of the book: Harry Arthurs, Tonia Novitz, Eric Tucker, Richard Mitchell, Achim Seifert, Makoto Ishida, Karl Klare, Kerry Rittich, Guy Mundlak, Dagmar Schiek, Simon Deakin, Brian Langille, Ron McCallum, Lizzie Barmes, Bob Simpson, Douglas Brodie, Bob Hepple, Wanjiru Njoya, Florian Rödl, David Cabrelli, Hugh Collins, Michel Coutu, Sandra Fredman, Virginia Mantouvalou, Kenji Arita, Anne Davies, Harry Glasbeek, and Alain Supiot. Thanks are owed, for the same reason, to Richard Hyman, David Kettler, Gunther Teubner, and Nina Fishman.

Since beginning work on the book, I've been involved in a number of collaborative projects which have advanced my thinking considerably. In 2012, I participated in a seminar on the emerging discipline or methodology of an 'economic sociology of law' organized by Diamond Ashiagbor and colleagues at SOAS. I benefited greatly from the discussions that took place at the seminar, and with Diamond on other occasions. In 2012, I co-authored a paper with Alan Bogg which was later published as 'The European Social Dialogue: From Autonomy to Here' in N Countouris and M Freedland (eds) *Resocializing Europe in a Time of Crisis* (Cambridge 2013). The fruits of that collaboration helped to shape the argument advanced in the final part of chapter 6, 'The Question of Autonomy', and I'm grateful to Alan, and to Mark Freedland and Nicola Kountouris for organizing the Resocializing Europe project. In Glasgow, I've benefited enormously from sharing research interests with Emilios Christodoulidis, and from working with him to organize two series of workshops on the 'Constitutionalisation of Employment Relations' (2009), and 'Social Rights and Markets' (2013). Discussions with Emilios and with the workshop participants have been incredibly useful in helping to direct my research and inform my argument. I would also like to thank him together with Judy Fudge and Paul Davies for very kindly finding time to read large parts of the finished manuscript, and for offering constructive comments and support throughout. Finally, I wish to express my gratitude to Gilian Dawson for her generosity over the years, to Dominic for his unfaltering love and patience, and, of course, to my mother and father for so much; not least instilling in me, from an early age, the importance of the historical view.

Ruth Dukes

Edinburgh
9 April 2014

Contents

List of Abbreviations	xiii
1. Introduction	1
The Idea of Labour Law	1
The Idea of the Labour Constitution	3
Labour Constitution, Collective Laissez-Faire, and the Law of the Labour Market	7
2. Hugo Sinzheimer and the Economic Constitution	12
Introduction	12
Labour Law as the Law of Dependent Labour	14
The Economic Constitution	17
State and Autonomy	23
Conclusion	30
3. The Labour Constitution in the Nation State: Germany and the Institutionalization of Codetermination	33
The Labour Constitution of the Weimar Republic	33
The Labour Constitution of the Federal Republic	45
The Postwar Labour Constitution in Decline	57
Conclusion	65
4. A Labour Constitution Without the State? Otto Kahn-Freund and Collective Laissez-Faire	69
Introduction	69
Collective Laissez-Faire	72
Labour Law and the British State: 1890s to 1950s	84
Conclusion	89
5. From Collective Laissez-Faire to the Law of the Labour Market	92
The End of Consensus	92
Towards a Law of the Labour Market	95
The Labour Market and the State	111
Conclusion	119
6. The Labour Constitution of the European Union: The Social Dialogue	123
Introduction	123
Maastricht and the Constitutionalization of the Social Dialogue	125

Paris and Rome	130
Rome to Maastricht	137
The Question of Autonomy	145
Conclusion	155

7. A Plurality of Labour Constitutions? — 158

The Question of Harmonization	158
Upward Harmonization of National Labour Constitutions?	162
Labour Rights as Fundamental Rights: A Defence against Negative Harmonization?	173
Conclusion	190

8. Labour Law or the Law of the Labour Market? — 194

Introduction	194
Approaches to Labour Law Scholarship	197
Reassessing the Old Approaches	207

Bibliography 223
Index 239

List of Abbreviations

BDA	*Bundesvereinigung der Deutschen Arbeitgeberverbände*
BIS	Department of Business, Innovation and Skills
CAP	Common Agricultural Policy
CBI	Confederation of British Industry
CDU	*Christlich Demokratische Union*
CEEP	European Centre of Employers and Enterprises Providing Public Services
CISC	International Federation of Christian Trade Unions
CJEU	Court of Justice of the European Union
CSU	*Christlich Soziale Union*
DGB	*Deutsche Gewerkschaftsbund*
ECB	European Central Bank
ECFTUC	European Confederation of Free Trade Unions in the Community
ECSC	European Coal and Steel Community
ERO	European Regional Organization
ETUC	European Trade Union Confederation
ETUF	European Trade Union Federation
ETUI	European Trade Union Institute
EU	European Union
EWC	European Works Council
FDP	*Freie Demokratische Partei*
ICE	Information and Consultation of Employees
ICFTU	International Confederation of Free Trade Unions
ILO	International Labour Organization
IMF	International Monetary Fund
JIC	Joint Industrial Council
KPD	*Kommunistische Partei Deutschlands*
MNC	Multinational Corporation
LSE	London School of Economics
NAFTA	North American Free Trade Agreement
OMC	Open Method of Coordination
SNB	Special Negotiating Body
SPD	*Sozialdemokratische Partei Deutschlands*
TEEC	Treaty establishing the European Economic Community
TFEU	Treaty on the Functioning of the European Union
TUC	Trades Union Congress
UNICE	Union of Industrial and Employers' Confederations of Europe
USPD	*Unabhängige Sozialdemokratische Partei Deutschlands*
WERS	Workplace Employment Relations Study
WFTU	World Federation of Trade Unions
WTO	World Trade Organization

1

Introduction

The Idea of Labour Law

The broad intention behind this book is that it should serve as a contribution to current debates regarding the idea of labour law.[1] The question of the idea of labour law—of its scope, and its defining purpose or paradigm—is one which has exercised scholars since the birth of the subject as a distinct and coherent legal discipline at the beginning of the twentieth century.[2] For much of that century, there was a broad consensus among scholars that labour law could rightly be defined with reference primarily to its *protective* function: labour laws were those laws which protected working people from unfair and unjust treatment at the hands of employers, either through the creation of individual labour rights, or by allowing or encouraging unionization and the collective negotiation of workers' terms and conditions. In the 1980s and 1990s, this consensus began to show signs of fracture. Trends towards significant reductions in union membership levels and collective bargaining density, the implementation by governments of policies directed at encouraging such trends, and changes in the organization of work and production including the marked feminization of the workforce were each understood by scholars to call into question the central assumptions upon which the study of labour law had until then rested.[3] In as early as 1989, and with reference especially to the legislation of the Conservative government in power in the UK since 1979, Keith Ewing raised the question whether scholars were then witnessing the 'death of labour law'.[4] In 2007, Cynthia Estlund asked the same question, focusing on three interlocking tales of decline in the USA: the 'ossification' of federal labour law, the growing 'irrelevance' of trade unions and collective bargaining to the vast majority of private sector workers, and the ailing state of labour law scholarship.[5] At the same time, these and many other scholars

---

[1] 'Labour law' is used throughout the book in its broader sense to refer to both collective labour law and to individual labour—or 'employment'—law.
[2] For discussion, see Lord Wedderburn, 'Labour Law: From Here to Autonomy?' (1987) 16 *Industrial Law Journal* 1–29.
[3] See eg J Fudge, *Labour Law's Little Sister: The Employment Standards Act and the Feminization of Labour* (Ontario 1991); J Fudge and R Owens (eds) *Precarious Work, Women, and the New Economy: the Challenge to Legal Norms* (Oxford 2006).
[4] KD Ewing, 'The Death of Labour Law?' (1988) 8 *Oxford Journal of Legal Studies* 293–300.
[5] C Estlund, 'The Death of Labor Law?' (2006) 2 *Annual Review of Law and Social Sciences* 105–23; C Estlund, 'The Ossification of American Labor Law' (2007) 102 *Columbia Law Review* 1527–2002.

turned their attention to considering how the study of labour law could best be revived in the new post-Reagan and post-Thatcher world: a world where even political parties of the centre-left—parties with strong ties historically, organizationally, and financially to the union movement—could not be relied upon, in government, to lend state support to the objectives of unionization and union involvement in decision-making; of the improvement of workers' terms and conditions through the conferral upon them of statutory rights, for example, to a living wage or job security.[6]

Inherent in such scholarly attempts to redefine or re-imagine labour law was a rejection of what were often referred to as the 'old ways' of thinking about the subject. For some, the changed political landscape, and, in particular, the acceptance across party political divides of a market logic forcefully resistant to regulatory 'interference', appeared to render futile any attempt to remain tied to old notions of labour law as state intervention to guarantee fair terms and conditions of employment.[7] More realistic and more useful, it was argued, were conceptions of labour law that worked *with* and not against the logic of markets: labour law as regulating for competitiveness or flexibility; labour law as increasing access to labour markets. For others, the centrality of the contract of employment to the 'old ways' was especially problematic, specifically the traditional focus on inequalities of bargaining power in employment relationships. Under conditions of globalization, it was argued, it was no longer the case (insofar as it ever had been) that the majority of working people work under a contract of employment, and could expect to do so until retirement. Even those in stable employment were not always directly subordinated to their employers in the sense that was paradigmatic of Taylorist and Fordist systems of production.[8] Rather than being directed by management as to how and when to work, many workers enjoyed a measure of freedom in work comparable with independent entrepreneurs. Performance was measured (and wage rates set) according to results, and there was an expectation that employees would apply themselves not only to getting the job done but also to developing new and better ways of doing it.[9] The notion of an inequality of bargaining power between an individual employee and her employer no longer served, then, to capture the experience of working people today—to identify the wrong in their lives that needed to be righted.

Notwithstanding the persuasiveness of such arguments, the starting point for the research project that has resulted in this book was the identification of a tendency, in some of the writing on the subject, to reject the old ways as outdated and unhelpful without appearing to delve very deeply into the question of what

---

[6] See eg A Supiot, *Beyond Employment: Changes in Work and the Future of Labour Law in Europe* (Oxford 2001); G Davidov and B Langille (eds) *Boundaries and Frontiers of Labour Law* (Oxford 2006); C Arup et al (eds) *Labour Law and Labour Market Regulation* (Annandale 2006); G Davidov and B Langille (eds) *The Idea of Labour Law* (Oxford 2011).

[7] A Hyde 'What is Labour Law For?' in G Davidov and B Langille (eds) *Boundaries and Frontiers of Labour Law* (Oxford 2006); B Langille, 'What is International Labour Law For?' (2009) 3 *Law & Ethics of Human Rights* 47–82.

[8] M Castells, 'Informationalism, Networks, and the Network Society: A Theoretical Blueprint' in M Castells (ed) *The Network Society: A Cross-Cultural Perspective* (Cheltenham 2004).

[9] Castells, 'Informationalism, Networks, and the Network Society'.

those ways were; of why, *precisely*, it was that they had now lost their utility. The aim of the project, then, broadly stated, was to give detailed consideration to the old ways of studying labour law and to the question of their outdatedness, or—more positively stated—their potential usefulness still today. The old ways focused upon were, firstly, the idea of the labour constitution as developed by the German scholar, Hugo Sinzheimer, in the 1910s and 1920s, and, secondly, the principle of collective laissez-faire elaborated by Sinzheimer's one-time student, Otto Kahn-Freund, in England in the 1950s. Having explored in some depth what these ideas were, and how they related to the labour laws in force and the government policy of the time, consideration would then be given to their currency today. The question would be asked, in other words, whether and how the ideas of the labour constitution and collective laissez-faire could be abstracted from the political, economic, and social contexts within which they had been developed so that they might still usefully be applied to the study of labour law. In recognition of the increasingly international and transnational nature of production and employment relations, this question would be addressed not only with reference to the labour law of nation states, Germany and the UK, but also to the labour law of the supranational European Union (EU). While the choice of geographical contexts would follow fairly straightforwardly from the choice of the labour constitution and collective laissez-faire as points of focus, it was hoped that the conclusions drawn might be instructive in jurisdictions beyond the borders of Germany, the UK, and the EU.

The Idea of the Labour Constitution

As is suggested by the subtitle, *The Enduring Idea of Labour Law*, the central argument of this book is that the idea of the labour constitution *can* be developed so as to provide a useful framework for the analysis of labour law today. The argument is made in respect, primarily, of the labour constitution, and not collective laissez-faire. As is argued in the course of the book, collective laissez-faire can best be understood as the expression of two political principles to which Kahn-Freund remained committed throughout his life: that labour ought to be collectivized, and that, in respect of their interactions, negotiations, conflicts, and conflict resolution, trade unions and employers ought to enjoy a very wide measure of autonomy from the state. Even abstracted from the particularities of 1950s England, the idea of collective laissez-faire implies an insistence upon the importance of union and employer autonomy which does not fit very readily with the changed circumstances of the late twentieth and early twenty-first centuries. Used nonetheless as a framework for analysis, the principle brings with it a danger of encouraging a misleading appraisal of current labour laws and institutions, and a misguided set of recommendations for reform.

The idea of the *labour constitution* was first developed by Sinzheimer in the immediate aftermath of the First World War, as he participated as a scholar and politician in efforts to create out of the 1918 November Revolution a new, social democratic state.[10] Politically, Sinzheimer was positioned to the non-Marxist right of the SPD (*Sozialistische Partei Deutschlands*) of the time. In common with others—Hermann Heller, Franz Neumann—he theorized social democracy as involving the extension of democracy from the political to the economic sphere and, thereby, the emancipation of the working class.[11] A democratized economy was a capitalist economy with guaranteed property and contract rights, but it was an economy governed by capital and labour acting together in furtherance of the public good. Within such an economy, the labour constitution (or economic constitution as he originally termed it[12]) figured as the body of law that allowed for the collective regulation of the economy by the 'economic organizations'— trade unions, works councils, employers, and employers' associations. It was, in Sinzheimer's terms, the body of law which called labour into a community with 'property' (ie capital); which created a community of labour and property that existed for the furtherance of the common good; and which guaranteed the right of labour to participate, on a parity basis, in the administration of the means of production. Through its participation in the regulation of the economy, labour was freed from its subordination to capital; workers were freed from employer efforts to dictate the social and economic conditions of their existence, and, at the same time, became free to participate in the formation of those conditions.

Sinzheimer's use of the term labour, or economic, constitution can be contrasted, therefore, with the notion of the economic constitution developed by the ordoliberal school of economists and more familiar, perhaps, to English-speaking scholars by reason of its application to the constitutional order of the EU.[13] Like the English-language term 'constitution', the German *Verfassung* has two meanings: 'constitution' in the legal and/or political sense, and, alternatively, the 'state' or 'condition' of a thing (eg 'she is in no fit state to work'). When applied to the economy rather than the political sphere, either—perhaps both—of these meanings may be apposite. As used by the ordoliberals, the term 'economic constitution' reflected the belief that the economy had an inherent *order* which should not be disturbed by concepts originating from other orders.[14] The economic constitution was the legal framework necessary to protect the 'natural' economic order from disturbances—to guarantee 'fair' competition, private property rights, etc.[15] And this was so irrespective of whether the laws in question were formally entrenched

---

[10] O Kahn-Freund, 'Hugo Sinzheimer' in R Lewis and J Clark (eds) *Labour Law and Politics in the Weimar Republic* (Oxford 1981).

[11] D Schiek, 'Europe's Socio-Economic Constitution ("Verfasstheit") after the Treaty of Lisbon' in T Dieterich, M Le Friant, L Nogler, K Kezuka, H Pfarr (eds) *Individuelle und kollektive Freiheit im Arbeitsrecht—Gedächtnisschrift für Ulrich Zachert* (Baden-Baden 2010), 172–3. D Kettler and T Wheatland, *Learning from Franz Neumann: Theory, Law, and the Brute Facts of Life* (London forthcoming).

[12] Sinzheimer's use of the term 'economic constitution' is compared at length with his use of the term 'labour constitution' in chapters 2 and 3.

[13] C Joerges, 'What is Left of the European Economic Constitution?' (2004) *EUI Working Paper Law* No. 2004/13; ME Streit and W Mussler, 'The Economic Constitution of the European Community: From "Rome" to "Maastricht"' (1995) 1 *European Law Journal* 5–30.

[14] D Schiek, 'Europe's Socio-Economic Constitution', 170–1.

[15] Schiek, 'Europe's Socio-Economic Constitution', 170–1.

within a written (political-legal) constitution or bill of rights. In contrast to this essentially conservative understanding of the desired role of the economic constitution, social democrats including Sinzheimer emphasized the potentially transformative nature of constitutionalization. 'Constitutional norms [were] purposive norms, charged with the mission to mould society';[16] and the state was potentially the architect, the overseer, the agent, of social progress. With this emphasis, both the constitutive and limiting functions of the law were highlighted.[17] Through labour law, the state recognized—'announced'—the economic actors; it empowered them to act (for example, to create legally binding norms through processes of collective bargaining and codetermination); and it set limits to their powers.[18]

In the course of what follows, the focus lies primarily with the notion of the labour constitution as developed by Sinzheimer.[19] The term 'labour constitution' is used, as he used it, to imply a concern with questions of state ordering of the economy: with the role that law (and especially labour law) plays and could play in ordering, or constituting, the economic sphere, economic institutions, and economic actors. Normatively, the idea of a *constitution* is understood to imply, of itself, a concern with democracy and with the objective of identifying and achieving more democratic ways of doing things. As applied to the economy and the status of labour within the economy, the notion of the *labour* constitution is understood to suggest a concern, more specifically, with democratic participation as a means of emancipating workers. In terms of subject matter, then, the field of enquiry is taken to extend beyond questions of constitutionalization and constitutional rights in the narrow sense, to encompass all laws and legal frameworks that allow for, encourage, constrain, or prohibit worker participation in decision-making.[20] As it was in Sinzheimer's writing, the term 'state' is used as more or less synonymous with 'government', broadly understood.[21]

The argument that the framework of the labour constitution remains useful today is constructed against a critique of the work of a group of British

---

[16] Schiek, 'Europe's Socio-Economic Constitution', 173.
[17] I take the terms constitutive and limiting from Teubner: G Teubner, *Constitutional Fragments: Societal Constitutionalism and Globalization* (Oxford 2011).
[18] H Sinzheimer, 'Eine Theorie des Sozialen Rechts' (1936) XVI *Zeitschrift für öffentliches Recht* 31–57; reproduced in H Sinzheimer, *Arbeitsrecht und Rechtssoziologie: gesammelte Aufsätze und Reden* (Frankfurt, Cologne 1976), especially 36–7 and 54–5.
[19] Taking inspiration as I do from Sinzheimer, Florian Rödl and Dagmar Schiek have each developed the idea of the labour constitution and applied it to an analysis of the constitutional order and labour law of the EU. Both have developed the idea to have a wider meaning than I suggest, however, so that it does not retain its core focus on worker participation as a question of democracy: F Rödl, 'Labour Constitution' in A von Bogdandy and J Bast (eds) *Principles of European Constitutional Law*, 2nd ed (Oxford 2011); Schiek, 'Europe's Socio-Economic Constitution'; D Schiek, *Economic and Social Integration: The Challenge for EU Constitutional Law* (Cheltenham 2012).
[20] On the limitations of human rights as a means of advancing workers' rights see eg H Arthurs, 'Labour and the "Real" Constitution' (2007) 48 *Les Cahiers de Droit* 43–64; J Fudge, 'Constitutionalizing Labour Rights in Europe' in T Campbell, KD Ewing, A Tomkins (eds) *The Legal Protection of Human Rights: Sceptical Essays* (Oxford 2011).
[21] That is, as referring not only to the executive but also to the legislature, judiciary, civil service. For criticism of Sinzheimer's understanding of 'the state', see Kahn-Freund, 'Postscript' in Lewis and Clark (eds) *Labour Law and Politics*, 201–3.

scholars—Paul Davies, Mark Freedland, Hugh Collins, Simon Deakin, Frank Wilkinson—who have argued during the course of the last ten to 15 years that labour law scholarship ought to be reoriented to align more closely with the functioning of labour markets; that labour law as a field of scholarship ought to be reconceived as the *law of the labour market*.²² In part, it is suggested, such proposals have been born of a wish, on the part of the authors concerned, to remain relevant: to engage in forms of scholarship which track quite closely the policy and legislative concerns of the government of the day, and which stand a chance, for that reason, of informing and influencing policy debates. Engagement with questions of market functioning, market access, market segregation, etc, and with economic methodologies and discourses, should allow, so the authors argue, for the construction of arguments which meet head-on the neoclassical or neoliberal objection to certain types of labour law: that they constitute barriers to optimal market functioning and, as such, are likely to generate higher unemployment and depressed rates of growth.

The critique of the work of these scholars builds on arguments made, in particular, by Wolfgang Streeck in recent years, in his case with respect to scholarship in the fields of institutional theory and comparative political economy.²³ Finding fault with the way in which markets are often conceived in those fields—in the abstract, as politically neutral institutions—Streeck has argued persuasively that there is a need to 'bring capitalism back in' to the analysis; to understand markets instead as firmly embedded in capitalist political economies, and as highly politically contentious.²⁴ Not only questions of market regulation or configuration are contested, but also the prior question of the inherent utility of markets and the desirability of their extension into ever wider fields of social life. Considered in the light of Streeck's argument, the question is asked of the 'law of the labour market' approach, whether it tends to underemphasize the existence of conflicts of interest—in working relationships and in questions more generally of the ordering of the economy. In underemphasizing conflict, moreover, does the labour market approach tend towards the implication or suggestion that good economic policy—and good labour law—are non-political by definition; that the evaluation of particular labour laws or institutions involves nothing more than a scientifically grounded assessment of their capacity to facilitate 'optimal' market functioning?

Against this line of criticism, the primary claim made for the usefulness of the framework of the labour constitution is that it highlights the inherently political

---

²² As is explained in chapter 5, the term 'law of the labour market' is suggested by Deakin and Wilkinson, and not by Collins or Davies and Freedland. Further differences between the approaches of the authors are identified in chapter 5.

²³ W Streeck, *Re-Forming Capitalism: Institutional Change in the German Political Economy* (Oxford 2009).

²⁴ Chapter 17 of *Re-Forming Capitalism* bears the title 'Bringing Capitalism back in'. Similar arguments have been made by Eric Tucker and Harry Glasbeek: E Tucker, 'Renorming Labour Law: Can We Escape Labour Law's Recurring Regulatory Dilemmas?' (2010) 39 *Industrial Law Journal* 99–138; H Glasbeek, 'Book Review: S Marshall, R Michell, I Ramsay (eds) *Varieties of Capitalism, Corporate Governance and Employees* (Melbourne 2008)' (2008) 22 *Australian Journal of Corporate Law* 293–304.

nature of labour laws and institutions, in addition to their economic functions. As viewed through the framework of the labour constitution, trade unions appear as political as well as economic actors; labour laws and institutions can be seen to have political as well as economic significance. Though it certainly allows for the study of labour markets and labour market institutions—for consideration to be given to questions of market functioning, market access, market segregation—it does so without tending to assume or imply the existence of essentially non-political, win–win, answers to these questions. It does so, then, without narrowing the capacity of labour law scholarship to retain its critical edge, ie to develop lines of critique and discourse aimed at identifying the injuries and injustices done to workers by particular forms of economic organization, and at proposing means of transforming existing institutions and relationships in a more democratic, participatory, and egalitarian direction.[25]

Labour Constitution, Collective Laissez-Faire, and the Law of the Labour Market

The first half of this book is devoted to an exploration of three ideas, or approaches to the study, of labour law: the labour constitution, collective laissez-faire, and the law of the labour market. In each case, consideration is given to the matter of how the idea or approach was shaped by the circumstances of the time and place of its development, and, in addition, by the author's particular understanding of the purpose of labour law scholarship. What did the author wish to achieve with his analysis or commentary or criticism of the law; whom did he wish to persuade? A second point of focus lies, in each case, with the desired role of the state in industrial relations, and in the regulation of labour markets, as understood by each of the authors and implied by his approach. Building on the exploration of these ideas, an attempt is made, thereafter, to develop the labour constitution as a framework for the analysis of labour law today. In chapter 3, attention is given to the labour constitution of Germany, and in chapters 6 and 7, to the labour constitution of the EU. With respect to these later chapters, the intention is to begin to test the applicability of the framework to the supranational institutions of the EU; to understand how it might map on to the Union's 'split-level' constitution, and to spaces falling outside the regulatory reach of the nation state. In the concluding chapter, the question of the usefulness of the labour constitution as a framework for scholarly analysis is addressed directly, and the case made for regarding the labour constitution as an enduring idea of labour law.

The book begins by introducing the figure of Hugo Sinzheimer and his idea of the economic, or labour, constitution. Chapter 2 seeks to position the labour constitution in relation to Sinzheimer's wider understanding of the meaning of labour

---

[25] K Klare, 'Horizons of Transformative Labour Law' in J Conaghan, RM Fischl, K Klare (eds) *Labour Law in an Era of Globalization: Transformative Practices and Possibilities* (Oxford 2002), 3.

law and in relation to the political and industrial relations context of the time. It explores, at some length, the question of the role of the state in the labour constitution, comparing Sinzheimer's conception, here, with Kahn-Freund's Weimar writings, and with contemporaneous articles by the scholar Ernst Fraenkel. In part explanation of differences in thinking between the three, it is suggested that Sinzheimer had in mind a very particular notion of the state as he drafted his commentaries and prescriptions: specifically, a *social democratic* state, defined as one which functioned in furtherance of the common good. When the governments of the Republic acted contrary to his expectations, throughout the 1920s, he was slow to admit it, slow to acknowledge the failure of the social democratic project.

Chapter 3 addresses the question of similarities and differences between the labour constitution as theorized by Sinzheimer, and the terms of the labour legislation enacted in the Weimar Republic, and in the postwar Federal Republic. In addition to shedding further light on the intended meaning of the labour constitution, this allows for consideration to be given to the broader matter of the relationship between labour law scholarship, on the one hand, and labour law as a distinct body of legislation and legal principle on the other. The title of chapter 3 refers to 'codetermination', which is used here in its broadest sense to include collective bargaining and workplace works council relations, as well as company board labour representation. With an eye to assessing the significance of the state to the German labour constitution, discussion extends beyond collective labour law and industrial relations to include the question of trade union and employers' association participation in the administration of social welfare: their assumption in this field of 'para-public' roles, and the implications thereof for the nature of their relations with one another, and with the state.

On the basis of the analysis contained in chapters 2 and 3, the conclusion is drawn that Sinzheimer's notion of the labour constitution was closely informed, like all of his legal scholarship, by a fundamental belief that law could be used as a tool to achieve social justice. This led him to read the labour legislation in its best light, as social democratic labour law. If his depiction of the labour constitution thereby underemphasized the sometimes problematic nature of state intervention in industrial relations in the Weimar Republic, it captured well the core principles that could be read from the provisions of the Constitution and collective labour legislation: that the overarching purpose of labour law was to free workers from their relation of subordination to the owners of capital, securing for them freedom to participate meaningfully in the regulation of the economy, and the material conditions of their existence; that, in furtherance of that aim, the state should take steps to 'order' the economy and the process of its regulation by economic actors, while at the same time respecting the autonomy of those actors. In the decades following the Second World War, the German model of industrial relations or collective labour law could, again, be understood with reference to Sinzheimer's work. Then, as in the Weimar Republic, the legislation could convincingly be read as creating a framework for the autonomous regulation of terms and conditions of employment by the workers and employers. By reason of the system of 'welfare corporatism' that developed after the war, the state was in a position to wield some influence over the 'autonomous' processes, while the unions and employers' associations enjoyed positions of authority beyond the sphere of industrial relations narrowly conceived.[26] In recent decades, the question has arisen, whether use of the term 'labour constitution', in the sense intended by Sinzheimer, is now less appropriate than it once was. Notwithstanding the continued stability of the legal framework, trends towards decentralization and disorganization in industrial relations and the economy have meant that it is, perhaps, no longer accurate to imply the same degree of state support and oversight of a coordinated system of labour participation as Sinzheimer originally advocated.

The focus of chapter 4 lies with Kahn-Freund's principle of collective laissez-faire. The title of the chapter refers to 'a labour constitution without the state', but, in fact, the argument here is that collective laissez-faire was not intended to denote a complete absence of the state, and of law, from the field of industrial relations. If, at times, Kahn-Freund was guilty of overemphasizing the extent to which the British collectivist system functioned independently of government, a careful reading of his work reveals that he was in no doubt that the labour legislation then in force was supportive of the creation and maintenance of that system in very significant respects.

In explanation of the meaning of collective laissez-faire, its strengths, and its shortcomings, it is suggested that Kahn-Freund and Sinzheimer adopted a similar approach to labour law scholarship. As legal scholars, and not historians, neither was concerned, primarily, to provide an accurate account of the origins of the legislation in force at the time of writing—of the policy priorities of the government responsible for its drafting, for example, or the political compromises necessary to secure its adoption. Instead, the aim was to identify the principles which could be read or abstracted from the terms of the legislation and used, having been made explicit, to make sense of various provisions or statutes as a single, coherent body of 'collective labour law'. In undertaking the task of the identification or abstraction of the relevant legal principles, both Kahn-Freund in 1950s England and Sinzheimer in Weimar Germany succeeded in reading the then current legislation in a way which aligned with his own political convictions. As a result, legal analysis and normative argument were combined very closely in their writings.

Chapter 5 engages with an influential strand of British labour law scholarship which argues that labour law ought to be reconceived as the 'law of the labour market'. The chapter focuses on a body of work published by Davies and Freedland, Collins, and Deakin and Wilkinson during the period in office of the Labour Party under Tony Blair (1997–2007). Through a close reading of this work, it seeks to shed light on the nature of the approach to labour law scholarship adopted by the scholars; on the methodologies used and advocated by them;

---

[26] The term 'welfare-corporatism' is taken from Streeck: W Streeck, 'Industrial Relations: From State Weakness as Strength to State Weakness as Weakness. Welfare Corporatism and the Private Use of the Public Interest' in S Green and WE Paterson (eds) *Governance in Contemporary Germany: The Semi-Sovereign State Revisited* (Cambridge 2005).

and on the set of policy objectives—the new normativity—identified by them as lying at the heart of the law of the labour market: as providing a paradigm against which to define or rationalize the new, more widely drawn subject of scholarship. Though emphasis is given to the sometimes significant differences that exist in the work of the scholars, it is suggested that, for the purposes of the discussion, there are similarities enough to justify treatment of their arguments as constituting a single school of thought.

Following the exposition of the work of the 'law of the labour market' scholars, the chapter seeks to highlight some potential difficulties with their approach. It is in respect, primarily, of the work of Deakin and Wilkinson, and of Deakin writing alone, that doubts are raised regarding the tendency of a market-focused framework to underemphasize conflicts of interest. At the core of the labour market approach as expounded by Deakin and Wilkinson lies the notion of the 'well-functioning labour market', defined as one which allows for the utilization of all of society's resources to the benefit of all. Inherent in this notion is the suggestion that markets can be judged, quite objectively, as functioning well or badly, that labour institutions and norms can be evaluated objectively as desirable or undesirable, in accordance with their propensity to help markets function 'better'. The weakness of this conception, it is argued, is that it can cause the authors to underemphasize the extent to which particular forms of economic organization (labour market institutions, laws, normative frameworks) can have quite different consequences for different sections of society. It can cause them to underemphasize, for that reason, the inherently political nature of labour laws and labour market institutions, and to disregard or overlook the case for worker voice as *a question of democracy*.

In chapters 6 and 7, attention is turned to the EU. The idea of the labour constitution is adopted as a framework through which to analyse the history of the Union and, in particular, the question of worker participation at different levels of economic organization—different sites of decision-making—within the Union: workplaces, companies, national government, supranational government. In the first instance, consideration is given to the European social dialogue at the supranational, cross-sectoral level, and to its precursors in the Economic, and Coal and Steel, Communities. Viewed through the framework of the labour constitution, the key question to be addressed is taken to be that of the potential of the dialogue to function in a way comparable with the collective bargaining and corporatist arrangements of the (old) member states: to democratize the EU economic order, and to deliver improved substantive outcomes for European workers. With that question in mind, the chapter seeks to assess the social dialogue as it is embedded in the constitutional or institutional structure of the EU, and influenced by the nature and motivations of the parties to the dialogue: the 'state', the 'trade unions', and the 'employers'.

In chapter 7, the focus of concern lies with the relationships between the different economic constitutions, or orders, of the Union, supranational and national. As a starting point for the discussion, the founding logic of the Union is explained to have relied upon the premise that market integration would be compatible with the continued existence of a plurality of such orders. As advocated by the Ohlin and Spaak Committees, and as reflected in the terms of the Treaty of Rome, the guiding principle of the EEC was that the creation of the common market would not require the harmonization of national social welfare systems and labour laws. In order to examine this logic further, the chapter considers the possibility of both the positive and negative harmonization of national labour constitutions as they have figured throughout the history of the Union. In terms of subject matter, discussion focuses, first, on the only body of EU legislation to deal specifically with questions of collective labour law, namely, the several directives providing for employee rights to information and consultation. The question to be addressed here is that of the extent to which the directives were intended to achieve, and did in fact achieve, the upwards harmonization of national labour constitutions. As a second point of focus, the chapter examines the gradual recognition of certain labour rights as 'fundamental' in the legal order of the EU and the capacity of such rights to constitute a defence against downwards harmonization, or 'social dumping'.

Chapter 8 is the concluding chapter. In seeking to argue for the continued usefulness of the idea of the labour constitution as a framework for scholarly analysis, the chapter builds in the first instance on a comparison of the scholarship of Sinzheimer and Kahn-Freund with the approach of the 'law of the labour market' scholars. In a second section, it aims to reassess the old approaches, and to consider their applicability in the light of globalization and the many changes implied by that umbrella term to production, distribution, finance, and work that have occurred during the course of the past half century. Drawing on the discussion of the European Union in chapters 6 and 7, the question is addressed as to how the idea of the labour constitution might be abstracted sufficiently from the particularities of the historical and geographical context in which it was developed so as to render it applicable to current conditions, while holding on still to the normative principles at its core. In contexts where it is not possible to ascribe to the 'state' the role of architect and overseer of the labour constitution, as was proposed by Sinzheimer, the framework of the labour constitution is argued to emphasize, still, the critical nature of the link between labour law and democracy. And it is argued, on that basis, to frame the subject of labour law in a way that allows for important questions to be asked, and important arguments to be made: questions regarding the consequences for workers of the continuous expansion of markets insulated from democratic control; arguments which re-assert the importance of democracy and worker participation.

2

Hugo Sinzheimer and the Economic Constitution

Introduction

In his discussion of the political significance of labour law for the Weimar Republic, Ernst Fraenkel made the point, later echoed by Kahn-Freund, that the development of labour law in any country was contingent on the labour movement enjoying a significant measure of political strength. Until the point in time when the movement was stronger politically than it was socially and economically, it was likely to rely on its industrial might to force concessions from employers. Only when industrially weak and, at the same time, represented in Parliament, would labour leaders think to utilize law as a tool for the advancement of their interests.[1] In the course of this discussion, Fraenkel highlighted a second precondition of the emergence of labour law, namely the 'preparatory work' of developing socialist legal concepts and modes of legal reasoning. 'There have long been legal relations which we would now characterize as institutions of labour law. But it was not until the peculiarity of labour law relations was recognized, not until the employment relationship was disconnected from the abstract rules of the law of obligations. . . that labour law as such was discovered.'[2] Private law concepts were not up to the task of reflecting the economic and social reality of employment relations, or of regulating those relations justly. The individual employment relationship, for example, was only formally a legal contract; substantively, it was a relation of dictatorship of the economically strong employer over the economically weak employee. In bargaining collectively, employers and trade unions did not enter into contractual relations but rather engaged in the autonomous creation of norms governing the relations of third parties.[3]

In Germany, the emergence of 'labour law as such', as Fraenkel put it, came with the birth of the Weimar Republic. Responsible in no small part for the preparatory work of analysing employment relations and inventing appropriate legal

---

[1] E Fraenkel, 'Die politische Bedeutung des Arbeitsrechts' in T Ramm (ed) *Arbeitsrecht und Politik: Quellentexte 1918–1933* (Neuwied am Rhein 1966), 249; P Davies and M Freedland (eds) *Kahn-Freund's Labour and the Law*, 3rd ed (London 1983), 52.

[2] E Fraenkel, 'Die politische Bedeutung des Arbeitsrechts', 248, my translation.

[3] E Fraenkel, 'Die politische Bedeutung des Arbeitsrechts', 248.

concepts was the legal scholar and practitioner Hugo Sinzheimer. Writing before and during the First World War, Sinzheimer developed several of the key ideas that came to shape labour legislation in Germany and beyond.[4] As a parliamentary representative, in 1919, he delivered speeches in parliament, and was personally involved in drafting parts of the Weimar Constitution. Having failed in a bid to become the Minister of Labour of the Republic in 1919, he continued to work until 1933 as a barrister at the court of appeal in Frankfurt, and as an honorary professor of labour law at the then newly founded University of Frankfurt. As a Jew, he was stripped of his chair in that year and moved to the Netherlands, where he worked until 1940 at the universities of Amsterdam and Leiden. Following the German invasion of Holland, he spent the remainder of the war in hiding, surviving only barely to die of exhaustion some weeks after VJ Day.[5]

The idea of the 'economic constitution' was first developed by Sinzheimer in the aftermath of the November Revolution of 1918, as the constitution of the new German Republic was debated and fought over. In substance, the economic constitution referred to the various laws that allowed for the participation of labour, together with other economic actors, in the regulation of the economy: not only terms and conditions of employment, but also production—what should be produced and how. Use of the term 'constitution' here was intended to emphasize the democratic function that Sinzheimer believed that such laws fulfilled. Time and again, he emphasized that the economy was a public and not a private matter; a sphere of activity that required to be regulated in furtherance of the common interest. Time and again, he rejected the possibility of straightforward legal regulation of the economy by the state, on pragmatic as well as principled grounds. His concern, then, was to conceive of a 'constitution' that would allow for a satisfactory balance between the autonomous regulation of the economy by the economic actors themselves on the one hand, and state oversight or guardianship of the common interest on the other.

The precise substance of the economic constitution as initially proposed, and then described and analysed by Sinzheimer, changed over the course of the years as legislative innovations were debated and adopted or forgotten. The normative principles that informed the idea were not tied to the specific circumstances of the immediate postwar period, however, so, at the level of principle, there was a marked degree of continuity in Sinzheimer's thinking over time. In his prewar studies of collective agreements, as much as in his expositions of Weimar labour law in the late 1920s, he was concerned with the distinction between autonomous 'social' law and state law; with the importance of the former for the achievement of democracy; and with the potential of the latter to frame a space for its creation

---

[4] For a detailed discussion of Sinzheimer's influence, see O Kahn-Freund, 'Hugo Sinzheimer 1875–1945' in Lewis and Clark.
[5] For further biographical detail see: E Fraenkel, 'Hugo Sinzheimer' (1958) *Juristen-Zeitung* (JZ) 457–61; S Knorre, *Soziale Selbstbestimmung und individuelle Verantwortung. Hugo Sinzheimer (1875–1945). Eine politische Biographie* (Frankfurt 1991); K Kubo, *Hugo Sinzheimer—Vater des deutschen Arbeitsrechts* (Nördlingen 1985); in English: O Kahn-Freund, 'Hugo Sinzheimer' in Lewis and Clark.

and implementation. Most striking of all, perhaps, in his work, given the history of the Republic, was his unerring belief in the capacity of the people to construct a better and fairer way of life for themselves, harnessing the power of the state and 'constitutive' state law in order to do so.[6] His work was imbued, even as late as the 1930s, with the sense of a search for a new type of justice.

The question of the relationship between the theory of the economic constitution on the one hand, and legislation and industrial relations practices on the other is addressed in the following chapter. Here the intention is simply to explore in greater detail what Sinzheimer meant by the term 'economic constitution', and what he intended, through its use, to imply about the role of the state in the regulation of labour relations and the economic sphere. Reference is made primarily to key texts written between 1919 and 1939, and also to the work of Sinzheimer's students Fraenkel and Kahn-Freund. The following section explores the preliminary matter of what labour law meant for Sinzheimer: how he conceived of its scope and its fundamental principles, or aims.

Labour Law as the Law of Dependent Labour

In common with other scholars of the late nineteenth and early twentieth centuries, Sinzheimer conceived of labour law, in essence, as a corrective to private law.[7] In doing so, he was directly influenced by a number of authors, including Karl Marx and Karl Renner, but above all perhaps by Otto von Gierke.[8] Writing towards the end of the nineteenth century, Gierke argued in favour of the creation of a body of law to be known as 'social law', which would address the inequities arising from the formalistic separation of private and public law that was embodied in the German Civil Code.[9] In a famous speech delivered in 1889, he criticized the first draft of the Code in the following terms: 'We also need a private law, which—notwithstanding all sanctification of the inviolable spheres of the individual—embodies the idea of the community. In short: a breath of natural law freedom should waft through our public law, and our private law should be permeated with a drop of socialist oil.'[10]

Social law, then, was conceived of by Gierke as a means of protecting the economically weak by ensuring a greater degree of 'balance' in private law transactions through tempering the power of the economically stronger party.[11] Though

---

[6] On the question of Sinzheimer's and, more particularly, Franz Neumann's adherence to a kind of 'lawyers' socialism' see D Kettler and T Wheatland, *Learning from Franz Neumann: Theory, Law, and the Brute Facts of Life* (London forthcoming).

[7] After 1918, at least: A Seifert, '"Von der Person zum Menschen im Recht"—zum Begriff des sozialen Rechts bei Hugo Sinzheimer' (2011) 2 *Soziales Recht* 62–73; Kahn-Freund, 'Hugo Sinzheimer', 75.

[8] For Sinzheimer's own acknowledgement of the influence of Gierke on him, see H Sinzheimer, 'Otto Gierke's Bedeutung für das Arbeitsrecht: Ein Nachruf' (1922) in H Sinzheimer, *Arbeitsrecht und Rechtssoziologie: gesammelte Aufsätze und Reden* (Frankfurt, Cologne 1976).

[9] Seifert, 62–73.

[10] O von Gierke, *Die soziale Aufgabe des Privatrechts* (Berlin 1889), cited Seifert, 63–4.

[11] Seifert, 64; Kahn-Freund, 'Sinzheimer', 78–9.

his arguments were of only limited influence in the redrafting of the Civil Code, they were taken up and developed by others in the later part of the nineteenth and early twentieth centuries, including the labour lawyers Sinzheimer and Philipp Lotmar.[12] In the Weimar Republic, they found expression in the Constitution,[13] which recognized social and labour as well as civil and political rights, and in labour and social welfare legislation.

In Sinzheimer's writing, no very clear distinction was drawn between social law—*soziales Recht*—and labour law—*Arbeitsrecht*; indeed, in places, he seems to have used the terms almost interchangeably.[14] In the comprehensive exposition of labour law contained in his 1921 text, *Principles of Labour Law*, he defined both the scope and the aims of labour law broadly, with reference to the idea of dependent labour.[15] According to Sinzheimer, labour law was the body of law that regulated the relationships of workers (*Arbeitnehmer*).[16] Workers were those who belonged to the social class that could only find a material basis for its existence by performing dependent labour. It followed that labour law extended in its scope beyond the contract of employment. 'Workers' were not only those who worked under a contract of employment, but also civil servants, apprentices, home workers, and the unemployed.[17] Labour law encompassed laws regulating workers' relationships with employers, individual and collective (the law of dismissal, collective bargaining, works councils, and the like), and also their relationships with the state and state agencies (the law of unemployment benefit, work permits, and social insurance).[18]

In defining the key concept of dependent labour, Sinzheimer began with a description of 'labour as human activity', which he took from Marx.[19] As human activity, he wrote, labour fulfilled an individual and a social function: active man fulfilled his own material needs and those of others, and the whole was one big social workplace, in which the production of life proceeded through the cooperation of all. As he worked, man exercised a power of control over his work, granted to him by nature. Active man was the natural prerequisite of his own life and of social life. Dependent labour, in contrast, was labour under the—legally constituted—control of another. From the point of view of the worker, such labour fulfilled no individual or social function, but only an external function. In the

---

[12] Seifert, 64.
[13] The 1919 Weimar Constitution, or *Constitution of the German Reich*.
[14] For further discussion of the meaning of the former in Sinzheimer's work see Seifert.
[15] H Sinzheimer, *Grundzüge des Arberitsrechts* (Jena 1921; 2nd ed Jena 1927; all references to the *Grundzüge* in this chapter are to the 2nd ed). In Lewis and Clark, this volume is referred to as 'Basic Outlines of Labour Law', 74. For discussion see Lewis and Clark, 77–9.
[16] The discussion in this paragraph, and in the remainder of the chapter, is taken from the second edition of *Grundzüge*, 8–11. I translate *Arbeitnehmer* as worker, rather than employee, for the reason that its meaning is rather wider than 'employee' in English law. That said, *Arbeitnehmer* was used by Sinzheimer to denote a group within the wider class of *Arbeiter* (worker); this wider class included self-employed workers.
[17] Ie unemployed workers. The category workers did not include the self-employed: *Grundzüge*, 34.
[18] *Grundzüge*, 5–6.
[19] *Grundzüge*, 8–10, citing K Marx: 'Estranged Labour' in *Economic and Philosophical Manuscripts* (Moscow 1959 [1844]).

natural relationship to himself and to the whole in which the worker had stood, another appeared, separating him from himself and from the whole. The 'other', of course, was capital or, as Sinzheimer tended to refer to it, 'property' (*Eigentum*). Whereas labour was man himself, capital consisted of things that were external to man. Whereas labour belonged to man naturally, capital was only legally connected to man. Capital was the material basis of human life. It belonged in the world of things, which had no aims of their own, except the purpose of serving men as means. Labour was the personal basis of human life. It belonged to the world of spiritual things, which had their own aims and whose purpose could not be reduced to that of serving as a means to the ends of another. 'In the kingdom of ends everything has either a price or a dignity.' Man had dignity.[20]

In a 1928 article on the 'democratization of the employment relationship', Sinzheimer situated the notion of dependent labour historically through a description of the legal status of labour in times of feudalism, bourgeois society, and social democratic society. Throughout history, he explained, the legal status of the worker had been defined by the relationship between labour and property.[21] In feudal societies, the worker himself could be the object of property rights, so that working relations were regulated primarily by the rules of property law. The labouring person was treated in law as a 'thing', as an object of property at the disposal of the property owner, rather than as a 'person', a legal subject with rights and legal capacity. Moreover, since ownership under feudalism entailed public as well as private law powers, the property owner exercised not only the private-law right of ownership over the worker, but also full public-law jurisdiction. The worker was disappropriated in his private and public spheres. In bourgeois society, the notion of owning the worker was abolished and replaced with the language of freedom of contract. Because the contractual regulation of labour presupposed a free individual, with rights and legal capacity, the worker now existed in law as a person rather than a thing. The employer, who had previously exercised private and public law authority over the worker, now related to the worker only as a private person. The public sphere as it pertained to the labourer was taken out of the employer's control and placed under the exclusive purview of the state.

Again citing Marx, Sinzheimer identified the injustice latent in the 'freedom of contract' conceptualization of working relations as the fact of the employer's continuing domination over the employee.[22] It was true, he wrote, that with the contractual regulation of labour, property lost its direct legal domination over working people. It continued, however, to be a means of domination over those who were dependent on things that belonged to others. Property was not only a legal concept but also a social power. Since property entailed the means of living and working, the worker was obliged to 'turn to property' in order to work

---

[20] *Grundzüge*, 8, citing Kant, *Grundlegung zur Metaphysik der Sitten*, § 434 (my translation).

[21] 'Private ownership of the means of production': H Sinzheimer, 'Demokratisierung des Arbeitsverhältnisses' (1928) in H Sinzheimer, *Arbeitsrecht und Rechtssoziologie: gesammelte Aufsätze und Reden* (Frankfurt, Cologne 1976), 115.

[22] 'Demokratisierung des Arbeitsverhältnisses', 116–17, citing K Marx, *Capital: A Critique of Political Economy Volume 1* (Moscow 1959 [1844]).

and live. Though the 'free' contract of employment negated legal compulsion to work, it did not address social compulsion. The contract of employment released the worker from his attachment to one particular employer but not his attachment to property generally. Moreover, since the right of command was inherent in the ownership of capital, property controlled labour power. In a relationship of dependent work, the worker was subordinated to the control of the owner of the means of production. Within social democracies (or, specifically, within the Weimar Republic), the status of the worker was regulated primarily not by property law or contract law but by a collection of *labour* laws developed especially for that purpose.[23] Labour law answered the objections of the labour movement to the injury done to the worker by (bourgeois) private law and its complete lack of regard for the social conditions of the worker's existence. The task of labour law was to emancipate the worker from the relationship of subordination to the owner of capital, 'to temper the employer's power to command'.[24] Acting not to replace private law, but to supplement it and to limit its application, labour law recognized the social condition of the worker and restricted the exercise of the social power inherent in private property. Through protective labour laws, social insurance, and codetermination laws, labour law gave expression to the social existence of the worker. Just as law had been used in bourgeois society to elevate the worker from thing to legal person, so it was used now to elevate him from legal person to human being.[25]

The Economic Constitution

The economic constitution and economic ('industrial') democracy

The idea of the *Wirtschaftsverfassung* or economic constitution was first developed by Sinzheimer in 1919 in the context of impassioned political debate and violent street battles between workers and the military over the question of the future role of the revolutionary workers' and soldiers' councils in the new constitutional settlement.[26] In speeches and publications of that year, he advocated the accommodation of the revolutionary councils in a new 'councils system', which itself would form the basis of a new economic constitution.[27] With reference to the political debates of the time, he offered his vision as an alternative to the two 'extremes' advocated by others: the creation of a 'council dictatorship' along the lines of Soviet Russia or alternatively the 'reactionary' sidelining of the councils and of the working class in a secondary parliamentary 'labour chamber'.[28] In contrast to these extremes, the institution of an economic constitution would be intended, argued Sinzheimer, as an integrated supplement to the already existing

---

[23] 'Demokratisierung', 117–23.   [24] 'Hugo Sinzheimer', 79.
[25] 'Demokratisierung', 124.   [26] See chapter 3.
[27] 'Über die Formen und Bedeutung der Betriebsräte', 'Das Rätesystem', 'Die Zukunft der Arbeiterräte', all 1919, all reproduced in H Sinzheimer, *Arbeitsrecht und Rechtssoziologie: gesammelte Aufsätze und Reden* (Frankfurt, Cologne 1976).   [28] 'Über die Formen', 321.

political constitution. Its purpose would be to meet the need for the organization of economic life, to put an end to the anarchy of so-called 'economic freedom', and to ensure that the economy was run so as to fulfil social ends. As a prerequisite for the achievement of those purposes, it would serve as a means of ensuring the necessary aggregation of all economic forces, including the revolutionary workers' councils.[29] Just as the Parliament was and would remain the organ of political democracy, so the councils would become the organs of economic democracy.[30]

In writings from the late 1920s, Sinzheimer developed the notion of economic democracy further, advocating it then more explicitly as a means of emancipating working people. Without economic democracy as a supplement to political democracy, he wrote, the vast majority of the people remained unfree, subject to the control of a minority-wielding economic power.[31] Despite democratization of the political sphere, there was still government of the masses by the minority. Only with economic democracy—the elimination of despotism at the workplace, of the control of the markets by capital, and of the state by the propertied classes—could true democracy be achieved.[32] Like political democracy, economic democracy was depicted by Sinzheimer as holding the promise of both *freedom from* abuses of power and *freedom to* participate in the exercise of power. Political democracy aimed not only at guaranteeing individual rights vis-à-vis the sovereign, but also at seizing political power from private hands and transferring it instead to a 'public community' (*öffentliches Gemeinwesen*) in which all citizens participated in the creation of a political common will. The same went for economic democracy. On the one hand, it involved the emancipation of individuals vis-à-vis the bearers of economic power, and on the other, it was directed at transferring such power from private persons to a 'community of the economy' in which all economic actors could participate in the creation of an economic common will. In an economic democracy, workers should be free from employer efforts to dictate the social and economic conditions of their existence and, at the same time, free to participate in the formation of those conditions. It was for this reason that the role of labour law was not exhausted by rules directed at securing fair wages and working hours, and at providing social insurance against periods of sickness or unemployment. It had also to provide a means of worker participation in government of the workplace and of the economy as a whole.[33]

The first use of the term economic, or industrial, democracy in German language scholarship is sometimes attributed to Fritz Naphtali, a trade unionist and politician who worked between 1927 and 1933 as the director of research on political economy for the confederation of free trade unions, the ADGB.[34] In 1928, Naphtali edited a collection of essays entitled *Wirtschaftsdemokratie: ihr Wesen, Weg und Ziel*, which was intended to be a programmatic manifesto for

---

[29] 'Über die Formen', 321–2. [30] 'Das Rätesystem', 327.
[31] Grundzüge, 207–13; 'Demokratisierung', 118–23.
[32] *Arbeitsrecht und Rechtssoziologie*, 16–17. [33] 'Demokratisierung', 118–23.
[34] *Allgemeiner Deutscher Gewerkschaftsbund*.

the confederation.³⁵ Sinzheimer contributed a chapter to the collection and referred in it, like Naphtali, to *Wirtschaftsdemokratie*; however, he had used a very similar term—*wirtschaftliche Demokratie*—in the 1919 speeches and publications.³⁶ Though it cannot perhaps be known for certain, it seems highly likely that Sinzheimer originally took the idea of industrial democracy from the Webbs.³⁷ Their two volumes on *Industrial Democracy* were translated into German in 1898, and according to Kahn-Freund, Sinzheimer 'must' have read them.³⁸ For the Webbs, of course, industrial democracy was synonymous with collective bargaining, a term which they themselves coined to describe the collective negotiation of workers' terms and conditions of employment by trade unions representative of the workers and employers or employers' associations. In the final chapter of *Industrial Democracy*, they wrote of the idea in terms which strongly foreshadowed Sinzheimer's later exposition. The experience of trade unionism and collective bargaining in the UK was said by them to have revealed that a proper understanding of democracy must extend to economic as well as political relations.³⁹ The democratization of the latter alone (as effected under the US Constitution or the French Declaration of the Rights of Man and of the Citizen) left the majority of the population, the manual-working wage-earners, unemancipated. 'To them, the uncontrolled power wielded by the owners of the means of production, able to withhold from the manual worker all chance of subsistence unless he accepted their terms, meant a far more genuine loss of liberty, and a far keener sense of personal subjection, than the... far-off, impalpable rule of the king.'⁴⁰ In demanding freedom of association and factory legislation, workers demanded, in effect, a 'constitution' in the industrial realm. The legal recognition of collective bargaining and the gradual elaboration of a labour code signified the concession of a 'Magna Carta' to the entire wage-earning class, and the extension of the values of liberty and equality from the political into the industrial sphere.

In Sinzheimer's 1919 expositions, as we have seen, it was workers' councils rather than trade unions which, together with representatives of the employers and others involved in production, were posited as the primary organs of economic democracy. On the question of the role of the unions within the economic constitution, or of their relationship to it, and to the councils, the work suggests

---

³⁵ F. Naphtali, *Wirtschaftsdemokratie: ihr Wesen, Weg und Ziel* (Berlin 1928). See also the ADGB Resolution of 1928 on 'Die Verwirklichung der Wirtschaftsdemokratie', reproduced in M Schneider (ed) *Kleine Geschichte der Gewerkschaften* (Bonn 1989), 436–7.

³⁶ Sinzheimer's contribution to the Naphtali collection was 'Die Demokratie des Arbeitsverhältnisses', reproduced in *Arbeitsrecht und Rechtssoziologie*. The term 'wirtschaftliche Demokratie' was used by Sinzheimer in eg 'Rätesystem', 327. In 'Zukunft der Arbeiterräte' he referred to 'soziale'—social—rather than 'wirtschaftliche' democracy.

³⁷ 'I know [that Sinzheimer] was very much influenced by the Webbs': O. Kahn-Freund, 'Postscript' in Lewis and Clark, 196.

³⁸ *Industrial Democracy* was published in translation in two volumes as *Theorie und Praxis der englischen Gewerkvereine* (Stuttgart 1898). *The History of Trade Unionism* was published in German in 1895 as *Die Geschichte des britischen Trade Unionismus* (Stuttgart 1895).

³⁹ S and B Webb, *Industrial Democracy* Volume II (London 1897), 840–2.

⁴⁰ Webb, *Industrial Democracy*, 841.

that he experienced a change of heart.⁴¹ In a short publication from February 1919, he envisaged that trade unions should eventually become fully integrated into the councils' system.⁴² Since the workers' councils were intended to be representative of *all* workers, such integration would require the creation of a legal duty on the part of workers to join a trade union of their choosing. Unions should become public-law rather than private-law bodies, concerned primarily not with industrial conflict but with furtherance of the common interest. At the end of the following month, however, Sinzheimer argued to the contrary that trade unions should be the principal representatives of the workers.⁴³ In an address to the SPD, he made efforts to emphasize that trade unions would be largely unaffected by the institution of the councils' system.⁴⁴ It was of particular importance, he suggested, that unions should continue to bear primary responsibility for the negotiation of terms and conditions of employment: unions and not workers' councils had the necessary overview of economic conditions throughout each sector; unions, and not workers' councils, were capable of industrial action.

The economic constitution of the Weimar Republic

As an SPD representative in the National Assembly and SPD spokesman on labour and social policy, Sinzheimer had the opportunity to present his vision of the economic constitution to Parliament, and eventually to convince his fellow politicians of its merits.⁴⁵ In part 5 of the Constitution of 1919, provision was made for a 'councils system' along the lines advocated by him. Article 165 referred to workers' councils (*Arbeiterräte*), representative of the workers social and economic interests, and to industrial councils (*Wirtschaftsräte*), charged with 'accomplishing the overall tasks of the economy'. The former were to be organized in pyramid form at workplace, district, and national levels. The latter were to be made up of representatives of the district workers' councils, the employers, and other participant groups, and organized, too, at district and national levels. According to the terms of Article 165, the national industrial council would coordinate decision-making in the smaller councils, and would have some limited influence in the political sphere, with rights to propose legislation and to comment on draft legislation.⁴⁶

As interpreted by the *Reich* Court in a decision of 1926, Article 165 was eventually ruled to have only 'programmatic effect'.⁴⁷ As such, it was not legally binding

---

⁴¹ GA Ritter, 'Die Entstehung des Räteartikels 165 der Weimarer Reichsverfassung' (1994) 258 *Historische Zeitschrift* 73–111, 94–5; M Martiny, *Integration oder Konfrontation? Studien zur Geschichte der sozialdemokratischen Rechts- und Verfassungspolitik* (Bonn–Bad Godesberg 1976), 98.
⁴² 'Zukünft der Arbeiterräte', esp. 353–4. Ritter gives the date of publication of the piece as February 1919.   ⁴³ Martiny, 98.   ⁴⁴ 'Rätesystem', 332–3.
⁴⁵ 'Hugo Sinzheimer', 86. The National Assembly was the first elected government of the Weimar Republic, led by the SPD leader, Friedrich Ebert. See chapter 3.
⁴⁶ Sinzheimer, 'Über die Formen und Bedeutung der Betriebsräte' in *Arbeitsrecht und Rechtssoziologie*, 321.
⁴⁷ Decision of the *Reichsgericht* of 11 February, 1926, cited G Flatow and O Kahn-Freund, *Betriebsrätegesetz vom 4. Februar 1920 nebst Wahlordnung, Ausführungsverordnungen und Ergänzungsgesetzen* (Berlin 1931).

without further legislative implementation. In fact, no legislation was ever passed on the establishment of district industrial councils, or workers' representative councils at district and national levels. A decree of May 1920 made provision for the creation of an interim national industrial council but this never developed into a body of significant power or influence, and no permanent council was set up.[48] The only part of Article 165 to be effectively implemented—in the Works Councils Act of 1920—was that which referred to the formation of worker representative councils at *workplace* level. Together with a Collective Agreements Decree of 1918, which predated the Constitution, the Works Councils Act made provision for what would later be called a 'dual channel' system of collective worker representation. Both trade unions and works councils were granted rights to represent workers, and both collective agreements (concluded by trade unions and employers) and works agreements (concluded by works councils and employers) were given legal primacy over the individual contract of employment.[49] In the Works Councils Act, the relationship between trade unions and works councils was clarified with the establishment in law of a general priority of trade-union policy and organization over the decisions and activities of the works councils, and the guarantee of union rights to influence matters arising inside the workplace.[50]

Of the plans for an economic constitution contained in Article 165 little could be discerned. In content, the 1920 Act was rather similar to earlier legislation regulating workplace committees, providing for the establishment of works councils with rights to represent workers' interests at the workplace level vis-à-vis the employer.[51] The idea that the councils should function as part of a wider system of autonomous regulation of the economy survived, on the face of it, in the form of the duty placed upon councils to act in furtherance of the *Betriebszweck*, or 'works objective'.[52] The original intention behind this provision was that each workplace in the Republic should be assigned an objective by the district and national industrial councils, working together with the government, in line with an integrated national economic plan.[53] The existence of such an objective would serve 'to limit the freedom of the employer to control the use of the means of production'.[54] Without the institution of the industrial councils and any form of national planning for furtherance of the common good, the provision lost its meaning. Instead of ignoring it as a lame duck, however, the labour courts came to interpret the

---

[48] HA Winkler, *Von der Revolution zur Stabilisierung: Arbeiter und Arbeiterbewegung in der Weimarer Republik, 1918 bis 1924* (Berlin 1984), 238.
[49] Flatow and Kahn-Freund, 306.
[50] R. Dukes, 'The Origins of the German System of Worker Representation' (2005) 19 *Historical Studies in Industrial Relations* 31–62.
[51] The Auxiliary Service Act 1916 and the Collective Agreements Decree of 1918. Fraenkel called the new Act, 'a codification of the works committees that developed autonomously in the pre-war and wartime periods'. E Fraenkel, 'Zehn Jahre Betriebsrätegesetz' in T Ramm (ed) *Arbeitsrecht und Politik: Quellentexte 1918–1933* (Neuwied 1966), 108.
[52] Kahn-Freund 'The Social Ideal of the *Reich* Labour Court' in Lewis and Clark; Fraenkel, 'Zehn Jahre Betriebsgesetz'.
[53] Kahn-Freund, 'The Changing Function of Labour Law' (1932), in Lewis and Clark, 185–6.
[54] Kahn-Freund, 'Social Ideal', 113.

works objective as co-extensive with the employer's aim of maximizing production and profit.[55] Moreover, pointing to the fact that the works councils' two duties were given equal weight within the legislation, the courts ruled that the duty to act in furtherance of the *Betriebszweck* could, in some circumstances, prevent the council from furthering the interests of the workers. As Kahn-Freund explained, writing in 1931: 'What was originally intended as a starting point in a move towards the socialisation of the economy [was] gradually transformed by the *Reich* Labour Court into a limitation on the really fundamental task of the works council: the representation of the interests of employees.'[56]

Reviewing the labour legislation of the Republic in 1929, and the courts' interpretation of the legislation throughout the 1920s, Fraenkel made the following assessment.

If one compares Article 165 with the social and political realities, one must draw the conclusion that the construction of the economic constitution was not only not completed—since 1920, it has not even been seriously contemplated. When one reads in Article 165 that district works councils and a national workers council should be responsible for the achievement of socializing legislation, that workers should participate on a parity basis in the regulation not only of wages and working conditions but the entire economic development of productive forces, one must smile a weary smile. The attempt, in Article 165, to weaken the absolute sovereignty of the political parliament has not been successful.[57]

Read together with Kahn-Freund's and Fraenkel's bleak appraisals, Sinzheimer's later work is all the more striking for its continued use of the term 'constitution' in application to labour law throughout the 1920s. In the 1927 edition of *Principles of Labour Law*, he used the term 'labour constitution' to refer to what would otherwise be called the collective labour law of the Republic: the law regulating works councils, trade unions, collective agreements, industrial action, and arbitration. Referring directly to Article 165, he described the labour constitution in terms very similar to earlier descriptions of the economic constitution.[58] Article 165, he wrote, could *not* be understood merely as a programmatic declaration: it called labour into a community with property; it created a community of labour and property that existed for the furtherance of the common good; and it guaranteed the right of labour to participate, on a parity basis, in the administration of the means of production. The most obvious difference between this and earlier conceptions of the economic constitution lay simply with the concrete form that the constitution was now said to take. Instead of a pyramid structure of councils with the national industrial council at its peak, the labour constitution was now described as comprising the organization of workers into trade unions and works councils, and the activities of these bodies as supported by the state: 'organization, industrial action and arbitration'.[59]

---

[55] 'Social Ideal', 116, 135.   [56] 'Social Ideal', 116.
[57] Fraenkel, 'Kollektive Demokratie', 86.   [58] *Grundzüge*, 207–13.
[59] *Grundzüge*, 213; see also Fraenkel, 'Kollektive Demokratie', 89.

State and Autonomy

To one schooled in the British voluntarist tradition the use of the term 'constitution' in application to collective labour law and industrial relations is initially surprising. Well-versed in the language of Kahn-Freund's collective laissez-faire, one is met with a theory of labour law that seems at first entirely foreign, based apparently not only on the presumed presence rather than absence of legal regulation but also on the notion of *constitutional* law with all that implies: fundamental, entrenched norms and public rather than private law; the involvement in some very important respect of government. When one delves a little deeper into the detail of what Sinzheimer advocated under the banner of the economic constitution, the initial impression of foreignness wanes.[60] For Sinzheimer, as for Kahn-Freund, the primary goal of labour law could rightly be described as the facilitation of the autonomous regulation of employment relations and working life by collectivized labour and employers or employers' associations. For Sinzheimer, as for Kahn-Freund, the means of achieving this could rightly be said to lie primarily with the removal from the economic sphere of the otherwise inequitable consequences of the functioning of private law: the sanctioning of the collectivization of labour and the withdrawal of labour power in enforcement of collectively reached agreements. Where the two authors did differ significantly was in their opinion of the role of the state in industrial relations, their opinion, in other words, of the measure of autonomy that ought to be enjoyed by economic actors in the course of regulation.[61] According to the principle of collective laissez-faire, collective bargaining was a process decidedly private to the collective parties engaged in it. The parties should enjoy the freedom to decide on the content of negotiated agreements, and on the methods of their negotiation and enforcement, without 'interference' from government. In contrast, Sinzheimer was quite explicit in his belief that the liberal 'bourgeois' notion of the economy as a private domain was false and had to be rejected together with the liberal legal separation of private from public law.[62] The economy was a public (*Gemeinschafts-*) and not a private matter and should operate for the achievement of public and not private aims.[63]

That Sinzheimer and Kahn-Freund took rather different views of the desirability of state intervention in industrial relations was discernible already from their respective analyses of the labour law of the Weimar Republic. In Sinzheimer's work, the importance of the autonomy of the economic constitution from the political constitution, and of the economic actors from the state, was certainly emphasized time and again. According to his proposals, regulation of the

---

[60] R Dukes, 'Constitutionalizing Employment Relations: Sinzheimer, Kahn-Freund and the Role of Labour Law' (2008) 35 *Journal of Law and Society* 341–63.
[61] R Dukes, 'Otto Kahn-Freund and Collective Laissez-Faire: An Edifice without a Keystone?' (2009) 72 *Modern Law Review* 220–46.   [62] See eg 'Die Fortbildung des Arbeitrechts'.
[63] Sinzheimer, 'Das Rätesystem', 334

economy was to proceed autonomously of the state insofar as was possible. The power of the economic actors to create and to enforce law autonomously was to be recognized (for example, it ought to be recognized that the normative parts of collective agreements had 'automatic compulsory normative effect'[64]). Furthermore, it was to be recognized that within the economic sphere, 'state' legislation was of secondary importance to autonomously created norms, since only the latter had sufficient flexibility and 'immediacy' to guarantee their effectiveness.[65] That said, however, Sinzheimer also proposed that autonomous norms should be subsidiary to state law in the last instance. Autonomous law was dependent on the state: it could only rightly be judged 'law' where the state had allowed for autonomous law creation, and where that creation proceeded within the boundaries and according to the forms prescribed by the state.[66] As a matter of law, then, the economic actors were autonomous from the state but at the same time dependent upon it as the ultimate source of their legislative powers. The economic constitution, in other words, was legally subordinate to the political constitution.

At the same time as Sinzheimer argued for the importance of autonomy, he also emphasized that it was undesirable that economic actors should be afforded *absolute* freedom of action. He contrasted the economic constitution with 'collective liberalism', depicting the latter in terms similar to those later used by Kahn-Freund to describe collective laissez-faire.[67] Collective liberalism, Sinzheimer noted, was informed by the same belief as individual liberalism, namely, that the public interest would best be served by the unmitigated emancipation of economic actors. Where parties were free of every state obligation to reach agreement, the common interest would be furthered as if automatically. State intervention in free collective bargaining could serve only to damage the community between labour and property.[68] According to Sinzheimer, experience had shown that this was not the case. A wholly free economy did not result in collective regulation by means of collective bargaining, but rather in the reassertion of employers' control through the 'free' negotiation of individual contracts of employment.[69] In any case, collective regulation was of itself no guarantee of furtherance of the common interest. The participation of all in the framing of that interest did not exclude the possibility of certain interest groups having a defining influence, nor did the existence of collective actors exclude the possibility of controlling individuals, the emergence of oligarchies.[70]

It was for these reasons that it was vital, in Sinzheimer's opinion, that the state should assume the role in the economy of the ultimate guarantor of the public interest. The (social democratic) state's interest in the economy was not exhausted with the freeing of the collective economic actors.[71] The state itself had a direct

---

[64] 'Hugo Sinzheimer' 82. According to Kahn-Freund, 'the "normative effect" was Sinzheimer's most individual contribution to the practical realization of the principle of autonomy in labour law'. 'Hugo Sinzheimer', 82.   [65] *Grundzüge*, 46.   [66] *Grundzüge*, 46.
[67] Sinzheimer, 'Die Reform des Schlichtungswesens' in *Arbeitsrecht und Rechtssoziologie*, (n 30) 243.   [68] 'Reform des Schlichtungswesens', (n 30) 243.
[69] 'Zur Frage der Reform des Schlichtungswesens' in *Arbeitsrecht und Rechtssoziologie*, (n 4).
[70] 'Eine Theorie des sozialen Rechts' in *Arbeitsrecht und Rechtssoziologie*, 178.
[71] The role of the state is discussed at length in 'Zur Frage der Reform', (n 14); 'Reform des Schlichtungswesens', (n 10); 'Eine Theorie des sozialen Rechts'.

interest in the social and economic conditions of the existence of working people and, more widely, in the efficient functioning of the economy. It had an interest, too, in ensuring that economic decisions were not reached with reference solely to economic considerations: economic interests were not the only interests of the people, and the economy as life sphere should not be isolated such that it functioned without reference to other life spheres. The terms of the economic constitution should allow for state intervention to further these various interests. The state should be able, for example, to take and implement decisions where the 'economic community' was unable to do so, to intervene where industrial action threatened the public interest, and to protect individuals from harm at the hands of powerful economic actors.[72] Ultimately, it was up to the state to ensure that the common interest was furthered, rather than simply the economic interests of the (strongest) economic actors. 'An economy which was entirely independent of the state would be able to preclude any regulations which were not based on economic considerations.'[73] A balance had always to be struck, however, between the autonomy of the economic actors (fundamental to democracy), and state intervention in furtherance of the public interest. The state should not assume the task of regulating the economy, and collective actors should not be regarded as instruments of the state. Therein lay the path to totalitarianism.

For all that Kahn-Freund had been Sinzheimer's doctoral student, for all that he remained throughout his life a great admirer of Sinzheimer's work, it is striking that he made no mention whatsoever of the economic constitution in his commentary on Weimar labour law.[74] In both his 1931 monograph and 1932 journal article, the intention behind the Weimar legislation was said, instead, to be the introduction of 'collectivism' as the dominant ideology in labour law.[75] Collectivism was then defined so as to emphasize the desirability of only a limited measure of state involvement:

The characteristic feature of the collectivist ideology of law is that it transfers the main emphasis in social policy from the political to the social sphere . . . The state recognises as law the result of the social conflicts between collectively organised employees and collectively organised employers, and makes available all its resources of power in order to enforce the law thus created . . . The state relinquishes any claim to determine the legal situation as it affects social policy; on the contrary, it gives full scope to the social development of the law and endorses its outcome at any given time.[76]

In writing these pieces, Kahn-Freund's primary intention was to reveal how the function of the originally collectivist legislation had changed while the content of the 'written law' remained the same. Throughout the 1920s, the Weimar courts had misinterpreted the legislation, suppressing class struggle and severely limiting the collective parties' autonomy. Instead of recognizing the freedom of the collective parties to negotiate collective agreements as a means of furthering their

---

[72] 'Eine Theorie', 180.   [73] 'Eine Theorie', 181.
[74] O Kahn-Freund 'The Social Ideal of the *Reich* Labour Court' and 'The Changing Function of Labour Law' in Lewis and Clark.   [75] Kahn-Freund, 'Changing Function', 167 ff.
[76] 'Changing Function', 168.

interests, the judiciary had come to regard the parties as a 'particular kind of state body' existing to further the interests of the state. 'The state no longer leaves a large area of working life to the autonomous regulation of the [class] organisations . . . on the contrary the organisations enter into the service of the state in the very process of carrying out their autonomous role.'[77] Through the mechanism of compulsory arbitration, the state had even become directly involved in fixing the content of collective agreements. Where the collective parties were unable to reach agreement, the state arbitration authorities were given freedom to impose their own view of what was 'equitable on a fair balancing of interests'. Instead of a true compromise reached in the furtherance by the collective parties of their interests, collective agreements increasingly gave legally binding effect to the 'aims of state social policy'.[78]

For Kahn-Freund, then, the principal flaw in the Weimar system of labour law was characterized as a problem of too much involvement of the state. With reference to aspects of the legislation that had been intended to herald the institution of the economic constitution, the courts had decided legal disputes so as to further the professed interests of the state. These interests had been identified by the courts as lying with the maintenance of industrial peace and continued production. In deciding cases in this way, Kahn-Freund argued, the Weimar courts had acted according to a 'social ideal' identical to that of the fascist courts in Italy. Specifically, they had ascribed to industry and to the workplace a unitary aim defined in accordance with the state's interest in production and industrial peace, they had encouraged collective worker and employer organizations to act in furtherance of this aim, and they had proscribed industrial action.[79] In the hands of the courts, labour law, originally 'an instrument to assist the rise of the suppressed class', had been transformed into 'an instrument of the state to suppress class contradictions'.[80]

Though Kahn-Freund was not explicitly critical of Sinzheimer's work, his reservations regarding the idea of the economic constitution were nonetheless clear. It was the perversion of collectivism that he bemoaned and a return to collectivism that he advocated: respect must be accorded, *above all*, to the rights of the parties to act in furtherance of their own interests. In discussing the courts' misinterpretation of the *Betriebszweck*, for example, he recommended that the idea of works councils as the guardians of the 'works objective', or the public interest, should simply be forgotten and works councils recognized by all as the representatives of the interests of the employees.[81] And in emphasizing the dangers inherent in the courts' 'statist' approach, he described fascist industrial relations in terms that implied at least some measure of similarity to the economic constitution.[82] '[T]he most likely road to fascism in our social conditions is not through force, but

---

[77] 'Changing Function', 180.   [78] 'Changing Function', 174.
[79] Kahn-Freund, 'Social Ideal', 110–11, 124.   [80] 'Social Ideal', 152.
[81] 'Social Ideal', 113.
[82] When Kahn-Freund used the term 'fascism' here, he had in mind the Italian fascist model, in particular the model of labour relations as determined by the *carta di lavoro*.

through the veneration of peace and order, of discipline and welfare provision, and *above all through the ideological integration of the organisations of struggle into a hierarchically-ordered national community.*'[83]

In later years, Kahn-Freund was more directly critical of Sinzheimer's work and in particular his understanding of what 'the state' meant and represented. In line with a German tradition articulated above all by Hegel, Kahn-Freund wrote, Sinzheimer had conceived of the state (*der Staat*) as a unitary entity quite separate from society embodying the common interest. 'At many points in his work the state seems to be a kind of "corpus mysticum", a living being, which has things brought to its notice, which takes an interest in events.'[84] Thus, ministers and members of parliament who made and applied the law were regarded by Sinzheimer not as individuals and members of society but as bearers of a will distinct from that of society.[85] To this it might be added that Sinzheimer also postulated a strict division between the state and the economic organizations (the trade unions, works councils, and employers' associations) that did not exist in reality.[86] At the time of the November Revolution, and during its immediate aftermath, the revolutionary workers' councils wielded significant political power within the Republic. The question of whether they would perform some kind of formalized political role within the new state was not finally settled until 1920, with the introduction of the Works Councils Act and the final bloody suppression of the revolutionary councils' movement.[87] Fearing the power of the councils, the leaders of the trade unions and employers' associations had come together days after the Revolution to negotiate an agreement confirming their respective roles as the rightful representatives of the two sides of industry. Since the resulting *Stinnes-Legien* agreement then formed the basis for the Collective Agreements Decree of 1918, this provided an unambiguous example of the involvement of the 'autonomous organizations' in the 'state' legislative process. Famously, the trade unions also played a central role in defeating the attempted Kapp Putsch in 1920, giving their full support to the calls of the government for a general strike. Finally, during the late 1920s and early 1930s, union leaders looked increasingly to the government to provide political support for the promotion of union interests as their industrial strength was further weakened by mass unemployment.

Reflecting, much later in life, on questions of labour relations and the state, as well as on differences of opinion with Sinzheimer, Kahn-Freund explained that he had come to the study of labour law at a time when the plans for an economic constitution contained in Article 165 had already been abandoned.[88] He had never regarded the implementation of those plans as a real possibility: 'I always read

---

[83] Kahn-Freund 'Social Ideal', 155, my emphasis.
[84] Kahn-Freund 'Hugo Sinzheimer', 80; see also 'Postscript', 201.
[85] 'Hugo Sinzheimer', 80.   [86] This is not a point made directly by Kahn-Freund.
[87] On 13 January 1920, workers demonstrated against the Works Councils Bill outside the Reichstag. The peaceful demonstration quickly escalated into violence and attempts were made to storm the Reichstag building. The police retaliated with gunfire, causing 42 deaths and 105 injuries. Winkler, *Von der Revolution zur Stabilisierung*, 288–90.
[88] Kahn-Freund 'Postscript', 201.

paragraphs 2, 3, 4 and 5 of Article 165 [referring to the institution of industrial and workers' councils] a little bit the way one reads *Alice in Wonderland*.'[89] In a lecture given in 1975, Kahn-Freund described the economic constitution as utopian.[90] Sinzheimer had had 'high, perhaps too high, hopes' for the bipartite regulation of the economy.[91]

If . . . we still today read Sinzheimer's essays, and especially his speeches on these matters, with rapt attention, this is because of the coherence of his plan and above all the visionary power and conviction of his words. We read his stirring exposition on the 'economic constitution' in the same way as we read the great utopian books and political novels of the European past.[92]

Perhaps this is one way in which we might begin to account for the different opinions of the two authors: Kahn-Freund was simply the more pragmatic, Sinzheimer the more romantic.[93] It is certainly the case that they reacted very differently to the political and legal developments of the late 1920s. Compare, for example, their commentary on the increased use of compulsory arbitration, and the growing tendency of the state arbitrators to substitute their own 'collective agreements' for those of the trade unions and employers.[94] Whereas Kahn-Freund criticized what he identified as the negation of the principle of autonomy in industrial relations, Sinzheimer continued as late as 1930 to give a measure of approval to compulsory arbitration, holding to the belief that it might provide some kind of political support for weakened trade unions.[95] The state had a direct interest in the conclusion of collective agreements, he wrote in 1929, and in the development of employment and social norms.[96] For that reason, state involvement in the setting of those terms could be regarded as legitimate.[97]

In their excellent introduction to a translation of Kahn-Freund's Weimar writings, Roy Lewis and Jon Clark argued that the course of German history in the 1930s and 1940s must be understood to have proven Kahn-Freund right.[98] There could be little doubt, they suggested, that Kahn-Freund's analysis was vindicated by 'the tragic spectre of union leaders kowtowing to Hitler and participating in his May Day celebration . . . the immediate prelude to the total destruction of the German labour movement'. As Gerard Braunthal, expert in the history of the SPD, explained:

---

[89] 'Postscript', 201.
[90] The lecture was published as 'Hugo Sinzheimer 1875–1945' in 1976; this was reproduced in English in Lewis and Clark.   [91] 'Hugo Sinzheimer', 91.
[92] 'Hugo Sinzheimer', 88.
[93] In the German context, romanticism was linked very strongly to conservative political opinion. I do not intend to use 'romantic' in this sense, nor, of course, to imply any conservatism on the part of Sinzheimer.
[94] 'Hugo Sinzheimer' 85–6; Sinzheimer, 'Zur Frage der Reform des Schlichtungswesens' and 'Die Reform des Schlichtungswesens'. See also the correspondence between Clemens Nörpel (a leading trade unionist) and Kahn-Freund, reproduced in Lewis and Clark, 226–32.
[95] J Clark, 'Towards a Sociology of Labour Law' in Lewis and Clark, 98.
[96] Sinzheimer, 'Zur Frage der Reform des Schlichtungswesens', 226.
[97] 'Zur Frage der Reform des Schlichtungswesens', 226.
[98] Lewis and Clark 'Introduction', 50.

[T]he increased intervention of the state in the economic realm, especially during the Depression years, and labour participation in public administrative bodies, accentuated the problems faced by the unions in their relationship to the state. As a result, the unions increasingly lost their independence of action and their militancy. Ironically, this trend occurred after the unions had openly or tacitly welcomed government intervention in the labour field as a means of improving their own position. Since the survival of democracy in Germany depended on the strength of the organisations committed to its defence, the position of the trade unions vis-a-vis the state was of crucial importance. If a proper balance in their relationship to it had been established, such as less reliance on its services, then they would have enjoyed more autonomy and freedom of action. This might have resulted in a greater degree of militancy against the fascist menace.[99]

This is not the place to delve any further into the question of trade union culpability in the rise of Nazism. Nor, in fact, is that a matter which speaks directly to the merits of Sinzheimer's work on the economic constitution, though it may tell us something about the reasonableness, or otherwise, of his optimistic appraisal of industrial relations at the end of the 1920s. Sinzheimer was quite firmly in agreement with Kahn-Freund that too much intervention by the state would result in totalitarianism; they differed only on the question of how much amounted to too much. More relevant to an assessment of Sinzheimer's work is a point made by Fraenkel, and acknowledged elsewhere by Kahn-Freund, regarding the *type* of state that Sinzheimer had in mind when elaborating the idea of the economic constitution.[100] Throughout his work, Sinzheimer presumed the existence of a specifically *social democratic* state, defined as a state which functioned in furtherance of the common good. As Fraenkel pointed out, the labour legislation of the Weimar Republic was drafted on the basis of this same presumption of a social democratic state and a democratized economy. So, for example, when the Works Councils Act placed a duty on works councils to support the employer in the pursuit of the works objective, it did so on the understanding that a works objective would be assigned to the workplace by bipartite councils, determined in line with the wider goals of the economy and, ultimately, the goal of meeting the needs of all. Without the institution of the economic constitution, the works objective was interpreted by the courts, almost inevitably, as coterminous with the employer's wish to increase profit; in other words, with the state's interest in the efficient functioning of the economy.

When Fraenkel bemoaned the perversion of Weimar labour legislation, he referred, then, not to a problem of too much state intervention, but rather to a problem of the wrong kind of state. In his view, the 1920 Act had been based on a flawed understanding of the economy, on the erroneous belief that the private capitalist economy would quite quickly be transformed into some kind of socialized economy (*Gesamtwirtschaft*).[101] The drafters of the Constitution and

---

[99] G Braunthal, *Socialist Labor and Politics in Weimar Germany* (Hamden 1978), 154, cited Lewis and Clark, 29–30.
[100] Fraenkel 'Kollektive Demokratie', 87; Kahn-Freund 'Social Ideal'.
[101] Fraenkel 'Zehn Jahre Betriebsrätegesetz', 98–9.

the Works Councils Act (the latter being intended to implement the former) had overestimated the speed of the transformation of the economy. They had designed the roles of the works council to correspond to economic conditions amounting to the replacement of the private economy with the socialized economy. Within the private capitalist economy, to demand that works council members support the employer in the achievement of the works objective was to demand something that was to a great extent sociologically and psychologically impossible.[102] In a social democracy as envisaged by Sinzheimer, the interests of the state would have been interpreted by the courts to be identical with the interests of all. In the bourgeois state, they were interpreted as identical with the interests of the employer.

Conclusion

Looking back on Sinzheimer's work at the end of his own long career, Kahn-Freund suggested that the former's primary concern had been with human liberty. His whole work was 'dominated by the motif of freedom', 'a call to the emancipation of man'.[103] If this is true, it is true, of course, only with quite specific reference to Sinzheimer's socialist understanding of the meaning of human freedom.[104] The overarching aim of labour law, according to Sinzheimer, was the emancipation of working people from their subordination to capital. The means of emancipation lay with the democratization of the economy and the guarantee to workers of economic freedom. Like political freedom, economic freedom had to be understood to consist both of freedom from abuses of power at the hands of others and freedom to participate in the exercise of power. As a matter of law, it was possible to articulate freedom from abuses of power in terms of individual legal rights, for example to fair wages and working conditions. The guarantee of freedom to participate in the regulation of the economy, on the other hand, necessarily invoked the idea of workers acting collectively.

> The existence of the individual worker is tied up with collective living conditions. These collective living conditions involve, firstly, relationships at work . . . secondly, the general social relations that take effect above and through all workplaces . . . A change in the living conditions of the worker is, therefore, only possible through a change of the collective living conditions.[105]

If we talk of emancipation and freedom in connection with Sinzheimer, then, we do not talk solely, or even primarily, of the emancipation of the individual and of individual freedoms. The economic or labour constitution was intended to guarantee to workers freedom to participate *collectively* in the regulation of the economy, to act collectively to effect an improvement of their collective working

---

[102] Fraenkel 'Kollektive Demokratie', 87.   [103] 'Hugo Sinzheimer', 103.
[104] As Kahn-Freund wrote elsewhere: 'Human freedom and the dignity of man were, for Sinzheimer the socialist, as for ever true socialist, the alpha and omega of intellectual and political life': 'Hugo Sinzheimer', 74.   [105] 'Demokratisierung', 121, my translation.

and living conditions. In the course of the process of regulation, it was necessarily the case that the individual will would be subordinated to some extent to the collective will.[106] Indeed, this necessary subordination provided one reason for the involvement of the state in the economic constitution: where powerful economic actors were able to gain control, the state might have to act to protect individuals from possible 'violations'.[107] (Here, concern was expressed quite explicitly by Sinzheimer for the rights and interests of the individual.) If we suggest, moreover, that emancipation was understood by Sinzheimer to be the primary aim of labour law, then we must also recognize that he viewed emancipation both as an end in itself, and as a *means* to achieve the improvement of the economic and social existence of the working class. If Sinzheimer's whole work was a call to the emancipation of man, it was also a call for greater substantive equality between the social classes.

In proposing the economic constitution as the vehicle for the emancipation of workers, Sinzheimer suggested parallels between the institution of economic democracy and the institution of political democracy. Both involved the creation of a legal framework which served at once to limit the power of the sovereign/employer to govern/manage and to guarantee the right of the citizen/worker to participate in the exercise of power. By using the term constitution in this context, Sinzheimer also implied a rejection of the characterization of the economy as private, and of economic law as private law. This rejection was fundamental to his whole understanding of the role of labour law. In declaring the economy to be a matter of public or common concern, Sinzheimer made the case for the legitimacy, and even the necessity, of state involvement in its regulation. If the economy was to be managed in furtherance of the common good, then it followed as a matter of democratic principle that the economic constitution should be subsidiary to the political constitution: the economy should be subject, in other words, to the control of the people. In a fully autonomous economy, in which economic actors enjoyed absolute freedom from state control, the common good would not be furthered. It would not be furthered in a bourgeois laissez-faire economy, which would be run instead according to the interests of the owners of capital, and it would not be furthered in a collective liberal economy. The common good could not be understood simply as an amalgamation or reconciliation of competing economic interests.

Economic interests are not the only interests of the people. The economy as life sphere should not be isolated such that it functions without reference to other life spheres. Economics as a science may have the right to observe economic events in an isolated manner; but it does not have the right to insist that only those laws which correspond to an economy conceived in isolation are appropriate. The economy must put up with competition from other life spheres. And who can apprehend the interests of all life-spheres? Either the state, or an organization created by the state.[108]

---

[106] 'Hugo Sinzheimer', 83.   [107] 'Eine Theorie', 181.
[108] 'Reform des Schlichtungswesens'.

Over the years, Sinzheimer has been criticized, most notably by Kahn-Freund, for regarding the state, as a matter of course, as representative of the interests of the people. As Kahn-Freund pointed out, this definition of *der Staat* followed the dominant German tradition of state theory articulated by Hegel. But it is fair to say, I think, that it was also tied up with Sinzheimer's hopes for the new social democracy of the Weimar Republic. 'We held the naive belief that the Weimar Constitution, with its elaborate and very complicated scheme of political decision-making was the ultimate, not only as an ideology, an idea or a plan, but as a reality: it was postulated to be a reality.'[109] When Sinzheimer assumed that the state would act in furtherance of the common interest, that the state's interest was co-extensive with the common interest, he had in mind, quite specifically, the new social democratic state. When the state acted contrary to his expectations, throughout the 1920s, he was slow to admit it, slow to acknowledge the failure of the social democratic project. When we consider the strengths of the work he bequeathed to us, we can surely forgive him that. In Sinzheimer's writings, we find a theory of labour law built around the recognition of the importance of work to the individual and to society as a whole, a theory which takes as fundamental the humanity of the worker and the urgency of the workers' demands for emancipation. Most important of all, perhaps, we find a vocabulary of concepts with which we can conceive of labour law and labour relations beyond the constrictions of private law and economic theory; a vocabulary which thus allows us to give full expression to the importance of the social as well as the economic, the collective as well as the individual.

---

[109] 'Postscript', 202. The 'we' that Kahn-Freund refers to are: Sinzheimer, Kahn-Freund, Franz Neumann, and Ernst Fraenkel: 'Postscript', 202.

3
The Labour Constitution in the Nation State
Germany and the Institutionalization of Codetermination

The Labour Constitution of the Weimar Republic

In his 1927 text, *Principles of Labour Law*, Sinzheimer used the term 'labour constitution' to refer to the collective labour law of the Weimar Republic: the law relating to collective bargaining and industrial action, works councils, workplace agreements, worker representation on company boards, and arbitration.[1] In doing so, he distinguished the labour constitution from individual labour law, but also from the body of law which he called the *Arbeitsstand*, or 'labour status', comprising social security law, and freedom of association.[2] He defined the labour constitution, as we have seen, in terms that closely echoed his earlier descriptions of the economic constitution.[3] Article 165 of the Weimar Constitution called labour into a community with property, Sinzheimer wrote. It created a community of labour and property that existed for the furtherance of the common good, and it guaranteed the right of labour to participate, on a parity basis, in the administration of the means of production. The labour constitution was the body of law that regulated this community of labour and property. In contrast to the *economic* constitution advocated in the first years of the Republic, based upon a 'councils system', the labour constitution 'took effect' through worker organization (workplace organization and trade, or sector, organization), industrial action, and arbitration.

Throughout the 1927 text, Sinzheimer used this notion of the labour constitution to explain the relevant terms of the Weimar Constitution and collective labour legislation.[4] Workplace organization as regulated by the Works Councils Act of 1920 was characterized by him as 'a state arrangement' and classified quite straightforwardly as part of the—state-supported and circumscribed—labour

---

[1] H Sinzheimer, *Grundzüge des Arbeitsrechts*, 2nd ed (Jena 1927). All references to the *Grundzüge* in this chapter are to the 2nd ed.
[2] Together with individual labour law, the labour constitution involved the regulation of the relationship of the worker with the employer. The *Arbeitsstand*, in contrast, was the body of law which guaranteed to the worker the powers and means necessary to be human through acts of autonomous social determination (freedom of association) and state social determination (social welfare). See further below.   [3] Chapter 2; *Grundzüge*, 207–13.
[4] Articles 159 and 165 of the Reich Constitution, Part 1 of the Collective Agreements Decree of December 1918 (the remainder of the Decree having been repealed), the Works Councils Act 1920, and the Arbitration Decree of 1923.

constitution.⁵ The law that regulated works organization was said to be public law, and workplace worker representation was described as obligatory as a matter of public law.⁶ By way of legislation, Sinzheimer wrote, the state regulated the election and internal procedures of the works councils, the role of the councils within the workplace in terms of their rights and duties, and the duties of the employers in respect of the councils. It granted works councils the capacity to reach works agreements with employers, and ruled that the normative terms of such agreements should have the force of law. It provided that two council members should have the right to participate in every meeting of the supervisory board of the employing company, with the same voting rights as existing board members. In the absence of a council right to strike, the state ensured adherence to works agreements, and made provision for the settlement of workplace disputes, by instituting a system of labour courts and arbitration boards.⁷ Lastly, with a view to the creation of a comprehensive system of autonomous regulation of the economy, it instituted a hierarchy between works organization and trade organization, ensuring the priority of the latter. It was explicitly provided, for example, that the creation of works councils would not affect the role of the unions in representing their members. A duty was conferred upon the councils to ensure the execution of relevant collective agreements, and union representatives were granted a right to participate in works council meetings in an advisory capacity. The aim behind these latter provisions, according to Sinzheimer, was to subordinate tendencies of *Betriebsegoismus* (works egoism) and capitalist competitiveness between workers to the trade unions' promotion of the interests of all.⁸

Arbitration was also straightforwardly explained in *Principles* with reference to the labour constitution, and the idea that it invoked of the state acting to support and circumscribe collective employment relations.⁹ Arbitration was an administrative process, the purpose of which was to assist in the conclusion of collective agreements and works agreements where the parties were unable to reach agreement themselves, by normal processes of negotiation. Provision could be made for arbitration by the parties to a collective agreement or works agreement, and where no such provision had been made, 'state arbitration' would be available. In the case of state arbitration, the *Reich* Labour Minister and the *Land* authorities played a coordinating and supervisory role, issuing general guidelines, appointing arbitrators, and supervising their actions. The minister was also authorized to submit a dispute to arbitration (even against the will of those involved in the dispute), as was each of the collective parties. Arbitrators had a duty to attempt to assist the parties in reaching agreement, but where agreement was not possible, the arbitrator could make its own award, which would be legally binding on the parties as a 'compulsory collective agreement' or 'compulsory works agreement'.

---

⁵ *Grundzüge*, 214.   ⁶ *Grundzüge*, 214.

⁷ Works councils were not allowed to call or organize strikes. Individual works council members were not prohibited from striking.

⁸ *Grundzüge*, 222 and 232; see also H. Sinzheimer, 'Das Rätesystem', 332, 'Die Rätebewegung und Gesellschaftsverfassung', 358–60.   ⁹ Grundzüge, 299–304.

By reason of the importance accorded by Sinzheimer to the principle of trade union autonomy, the integration of collective bargaining and industrial action into the theory of the labour constitution was not quite so easily achieved.[10] Sinzheimer conceived of trade unions as voluntary organizations with their foundations in the act of 'social self-determination' or free association. They were not called into existence by the state, he reasoned, but were created by the people in opposition to the state.[11] It followed that freedom of association fell outside the labour constitution. When unions acted to represent workers, however, they acted in a public capacity. They did not act as agents of a principal but rather in their own name, representing the workers' collective interests (as opposed to the sum of the interests of the individual workers). The capacity to represent workers in this way was granted to the unions by the state.[12] When they concluded collective agreements, trade unions entered into private law contracts which had public law consequences, namely, the creation of new (autonomous) law. The capacity to create legally binding contracts and autonomous law was also granted to the unions by the state.[13] According to Sinzheimer's analysis, then, trade unions were private law bodies which performed public services by reason of public law.[14] The state did not create trade unions or collective bargaining but rather 'announced' the already existing bodies and collective relations.[15] It did not require that workers form or join trade unions but guaranteed their right to do so within the constitution. And in line with the state's own interest in the institution of economic democracy, it gave its support to the participation of the unions in the administration of the economy, granting them a constitutionally protected right to bargain collectively and freedom to take industrial action.[16] Where collective agreements were reached, the state ruled by way of legislation that the normative terms of the agreements should have the force of law. Where they could not be reached, the state made provision for the imposition of a substitute 'collective agreement' in the form of an arbitration award.

In Kahn-Freund's opinion, the integration of the trade unions into the economic, or labour, constitution was highly problematic, because it was necessarily compromising of the unions' autonomy.[17] In his 1975 lecture on the life and work of Sinzheimer, he criticized his old *Doktorvater* for having muddied the waters with regard to the 'private-law' as opposed to the 'public-law' status of trade unions. As Sinzheimer himself had often emphasized, trade unions were 'organizations of conflict' whose independence was paramount. They were better thought of, according to Kahn-Freund, as strictly 'private law' bodies.[18] In

---

[10] Kahn-Freund, 'Hugo Sinzheimer', 90. Cf Sinzheimer's earlier work where he insisted upon the wholly private law nature of trade unions and collective bargaining: Kahn-Freund, 'Hugo Sinzheimer', 75.   [11] *Grundzüge*, 68.
[12] *Grundzüge*, 72.   [13] *Grundzüge*, 273–5.   [14] *Grundzüge*, 79–81.
[15] Article 165 Weimar Constitution: 'Die beiderseitigen Organisationen und ihre Vereinbarungen werden anerkannt.'
[16] Freedom of association—'Vereinigungsfreiheit'—was protected in Article 159 of the Weimar Constitution. There was no explicit reference to freedom to take industrial action, but this was implied in the terms of the Article. M Kittner, *Arbeitskampf. Geschichte, Recht, Gegenwart* (Munich 2005), 410–11, 431–2.   [17] Kahn-Freund, 'Hugo Sinzheimer', 90.
[18] 'Hugo Sinzheimer', 90.

Principles of Labour Law, in contrast, there is not the slightest hint of any controversy or difficulty surrounding the definition of the role of the unions in the labour constitution, their relationship with the state, and with the works councils. Indeed, reading that text alone, one could be forgiven for assuming that the collective labour legislation of the Weimar Republic was passed in accordance with a pre-existing blueprint by a government united in its support for the institution of economic democracy, and that the relationships between the state, the trade unions, and the works councils were clearly defined both in principle and in the legislation, and agreed upon by all.

The reality, of course, was far messier and more complicated. The labour legislation of the Weimar Republic was passed over a period of several years and resulted not only from the ambitions of the November revolutionaries for the establishment of a new socialist state, but also from the slowly unfolding disappointment of those ambitions: the murder of Karl Liebknecht and Rosa Luxemburg and the bloody suppression of the revolutionary workers' and soldiers' councils; the failure of the SPD and the other left-wing parties ever to form a majority government; the recurring financial crisis and the high levels of unemployment and industrially weakened trade unions brought with it; and the growing strength of right-wing, anti-democratic factions with no loyalty to the Republic, its constitution, or its laws.

The labour constitution and the state: 1918–1933

On the morning after the revolution, everything seemed possible. On 9 November 1918, the Kaiser abdicated and the foundation of a new republic was declared from a balcony of the Reichstag building. A provisional government was formed comprising three representatives of the SPD and three of the left-wing USPD.[19] Within a week, that government had agreed an armistice with the allies and declared its intention to govern in a purely socialist manner, in fulfilment of a socialist programme.[20] Among the very first laws to be adopted were a Decree of 23 November introducing the eight-hour day, and the Collective Agreements Decree of 23 December. The latter contained important legal advances for the unions, including a right to bargain collectively and provision for the creation of workers' committees in all workplaces with at least 20 workers. It introduced the two key mechanisms of state support for union organization and collective bargaining that were to become lasting features not only of Weimar labour law, but also of the labour law of the Federal Republic—a rule which rendered the normative parts of collective agreements legally binding and a mechanism for the

---

[19] The *Rat der Volksbeauftragten*, or Council of the People's Representatives. The USPD, *Unabhängige Sozialdemokratische Partei Deutschlands*, was established in 1917 as the result of a split in the SPD between left-wing members and the majority.

[20] In its 'Aufruf des Rates der Volksbeauftragten an das deutsche Volk' reproduced in Kittner, 397.

extension of collective agreements to apply *erga omnes*.[21] In part, the terms of the Collective Agreements Decree were taken from the Stinnes–Legien agreement, concluded by the leaders of the trade unions and employers' associations some weeks before.[22] In that agreement, the employers had consented to recognize the unions as the legitimate representatives of the workers, and to negotiate terms and conditions of employment collectively with the unions. They had also agreed to the institution of workers' committees in workplaces with at least 50 workers, with the role of ensuring that workplace relations were governed according to the terms of the relevant collective agreement. The Collective Agreements Decree echoed this provision, conferring upon workers' committees a duty 'in community with the employer, to see that the relevant collective agreements are adhered to'.[23] Only where there was no collective agreement were the committees to participate in the regulation of wages and other working conditions.

At the time of issue, this latter part of the Decree must have read like little more than wishful thinking on the part of the trade unions and their supporters within the provisional government. The workers' councils of the revolution had little in common with the workplace representative committees envisaged by the Decree and by its wartime and prewar precursors.[24] During the last months of the war, workers' councils had assumed the authority to act as the representatives of labour, organizing industrial action and putting the workers' demands to the employers, and the increasingly unpopular government. Given the close cooperation of the union leaders with the government for the duration of the war, many workers had been willing to transfer their allegiance from the unions to the workers' councils. In November, it was the workers' and soldiers' councils that spearheaded the revolt against the Kaiser and the military leaders. In the immediate aftermath of that revolt, calls were made for the councils to play a central role in the new socialist state, to be constructed, soviet-style, on the basis of council representation. 'From the uppermost summit of the state down to the tiniest parish, the proletarian mass must . . . replace the inherited organs of bourgeois class rule—the assemblies, parliaments, and city councils—with its own class organs—with workers' and soldiers' councils.'[25] Indeed, it was the very existence of the so-called councils' movement that motivated German industrialists to negotiate the Stinnes–Legien agreement, hoping to bolster the position of the trade unions as a bulwark against more radical alternatives.[26] Notwithstanding the terms of that agreement and the pursuant Collective Agreements Decree, however, the question remained open in

---

[21] That is, to all workplaces in a specified geographical and industrial area, including those in which the workers were not union members, and the employers were not members of the relevant employers' association.
[22] Concluded 15 November 1918, and named after Carl Legien and Hugo Stinnes, the leaders, respectively, of the workers' and employers' delegations.   [23] Section 13, my translation.
[24] Provision was made from 1891 for the establishment of workplace workers' committees. See S Braun, W Eberwein, J Tholen, *Belegschaften und Unternehmer: Zur Geschichte und Soziologie der deutschen Betriebsverfassung und Belegschaftsmitbestimmung* (Frankfurt, New York 1992).
[25] R. Luxemburg, 'What does the Spartacus League Want?' first published in *Die Rote Fahne*, 14 December 1918. Reproduced in R. Luxemburg, *Selected Political Writings of Rosa Luxemburg* (New York, London 1971), 368–9.   [26] Kittner, 401–4.

the latter part of 1918, and on into 1919, what the role of the workers' councils within the new Republic should be; how the councils and trade unions could be reconciled.

Initially, the integration of the workers' councils into the state's political and administrative structures was opposed by the SPD and by the coalition government elected in January 1919, consisting of SPD, centre, and centre-left representatives. Those political parties that had actively supported the councils' movement, the USPD and KPD, fared badly in the January election and were not represented within the coalition.[27] In February 1919, the government declared that 'no member of the Cabinet contemplates the incorporation, in any form, of the council system into the constitution'.[28] Enraged by the prospect of their exclusion from government, and still enjoying the support of many thousands of workers, the councils responded with mass demonstrations and strikes.[29] In retaliation, the SPD-led coalition ordered troops to use military force to crush the demonstrations. At the same time, it negotiated an agreement with the Berlin workers' and soldiers' council, declaring on 5 March its intention to legislate after all to ensure the involvement of workers' councils in the administration of production.[30] After weeks of impassioned debate regarding the detail of such legislation, the government agreed to proposals based on Sinzheimer's conception of economic democracy by way of a councils system.[31] These were then incorporated into the Constitution of the Republic in Article 165. With the intention of delaying decision-making yet further on the question of the precise role of the councils and their relationship with the trade unions, the terms of the Article were kept deliberately vague on that point.[32] By the time that the Works Councils Bill came to be drafted, later that year, the councils had been significantly weakened.[33] In Parliament, it was agreed that the Bill should be used to allow the trade unions to establish control over the workers' councils, quashing their revolutionary tendencies once and for all.[34] As finally enacted, in February 1920, the Works Councils Act was wholly unrevolutionary in nature, designating the works councils simply as representatives of the workers' interests at workplace level, subordinate to the trade unions and to union-negotiated collective agreements.[35] The only significant

---

[27] The KPD, or *Kommunistische Partei Deutschlands*, was founded in December 1918 by a group of revolutionary socialists who split with the USPD, claiming that the latter was no longer actively pursuing revolutionary socialism.

[28] Cited in Ritter, 'Die Entstehung des Räteartikels', 78.   [29] Kittner, 415–18.

[30] Ritter, 81.

[31] Sinzheimer presented to the SPD and the Parliament in March, June, and July 1919: Ritter, 82–102.   [32] Ritter, 102.

[33] Council supporters mounted a final demonstration of strength in January 1920, protesting against the Works Councils Bill outside the Reichstag. When attempts were made to storm the Reichstag building, the police retaliated with gunfire, causing 42 deaths and 105 injuries. Winkler, 288–90.

[34] 'The compromise reached by the three competing factions [the supporters of the councils, other socialists, and social-reformists] was the recognition of the predominance of the unions and the acceptance of social-reformist thinking': K Brigl-Matthiaβ, *Das Betriebsräteproblem* (Berlin, Leipzig 1926), 15.

[35] According to Fraenkel, it was 'a codification of the works committees that had developed autonomously in the pre-war and wartime periods': 'Zehn Jahre Betriebsrätegesetz', 108.

memento of the political power of the workers' councils, and of the bloody street battles of 1918 and 1919, was a change in nomenclature: under the new legislation workplace representative committees would be known as 'works councils' (*Betriebsrat*) rather than 'worker committees' (*Arbeiterausschuss*).

Notwithstanding the terms of Article 165 of the Weimar Constitution, then, it is quite clear that the government of the Republic was never truly committed to the introduction of a system of works council and industrial council administration of the economy. Article 165 represented a 'formal compromise' that belied the deep-lying disagreement existing among and within the political parties on the question of the councils.[36] Within the SPD, most were minded, in line with the party's long-standing allegiances to the trade unions, to be wary of the councils and the threat that they posed to trade union organization. As for the USPD/KPD proposals for the introduction of a system of government by workers' councils, these were rejected by the majority of SPD members as thoroughly undemocratic, tantamount to a dictatorship by a minority.[37]

The opposition of the SPD to the councils' movement contrasted starkly with its resolute support for the trade unions. The party was, as Kahn-Freund later put it, 'desperately serious in all matters of trade-union rights and of social reform'.[38] This was apparent, already, in the speed with which the SPD/USPD provisional government acted to legislate to introduce individual and collective labour rights in the first days and weeks after the revolution.[39] After the general election in January 1919, the SPD was restricted in its actions by the need to negotiate further labour policy and legislation with its non-socialist coalition partners. In the first months and years of the Republic, however, even the centre and right-wing factions within Parliament were keen to support the trade unions, if only as a means of defence against the perceived threat of soviet-style socialism. Part I of the Collective Agreements Decree was allowed to remain in force, together with its mechanisms for state support of collective bargaining (the compulsory normative effect of collective agreements and the extension of collective agreements *erga omnes*). And the Works Councils Act, which replaced Part II of the Decree, was framed so as to support the integration of works councils into the trade unions.

Such efforts on the part of government to bolster trade union organization were, on the face of it, broadly successful. Between 1918 and 1920, union membership rose significantly from around 3.5 to 9.2 million members.[40] A determined campaign by the unions to 'unionize' the works councils resulted, by 1922, in 75–80 per cent union membership among works councillors.[41] In time, the works councils came to be viewed quite generally not as rivals of the trade unions but as the representatives of the unions at workplace level: the unions' *verlaengerte Arm*.[42] Notwithstanding this impressive consolidation of grassroots support, however,

---

[36] Ritter, 108.
[37] A Rosenberg, *A History of the German Republic* (London 1936), 25.
[38] Lewis and Clark, 36.   [39] See above.   [40] Lewis and Clark, 27.
[41] That is, membership of the socialist 'free' trade unions: Braunthal, 168.
[42] Extended arm: Kahn-Freund, 'The Changing Function of Labour Law', 185.

the unions were not well placed in the first years of the Republic to protect their members' interests and, in particular, to achieve increased rates of pay. In part, this was due to the hyperinflation of 1921–3, which wiped out cash reserves leaving the unions without strike funds. But it was also due to the relative strength of the employers at this time, better able to defend themselves against the effects of hyperinflation and, through cooperation within cartels, against the losses that they would otherwise have incurred as a result of strike action.[43]

Having decided to take the matter of wages into its own hands, the government acted in 1923 to pass the Arbitration Decree providing for compulsory arbitration at the request of either party in an industrial dispute or at the initiative of the arbitration board itself.[44] (Provision had been made for state arbitration some years before, in part 3 of the Collective Agreements Decree; however, it had not been possible under the old rules to render an arbitration order legally binding without the consent of the parties.) Through the issue of strict guidelines to arbitration boards, the government was henceforth able to impose wage levels as it saw fit, if necessary against the will of the relevant trade union and/or employers' association. Indeed, given the practice of so-called 'one-man arbitration', according to which a 'neutral' chairperson had a deciding vote, the government was even able to dictate wage levels *without* the agreement of the union and employer representatives on the arbitration boards. In the period to 1927, the wages of around 50 per cent of workers were set by arbitration orders.[45] By the following year, wage levels had increased such that the government felt able to curtail its policy of intervention.[46] When economic crisis struck again in 1929, however, the new policy of non-intervention proved to be short-lived. For the last years of the Republic, arbitration was used by increasingly authoritarian governments as a mechanism for *lowering* wages (in order to combat inflation), and for undermining the system of collective bargaining more directly.[47]

In the earlier years of the Republic, intervention in collective bargaining so as to ensure higher wage levels was not the only use to which arbitration was put. From 1923, it was also the main weapon in the state's armoury in the suppression of industrial action.[48] Given the destruction that the country had suffered during the war, and the demands of reconstruction and reparation, the efficient and uninterrupted course of production was regarded as a priority. In furtherance of this goal, the government placed strict controls on industrial action from the outset, even invoking the emergency powers provision of the Constitution to legislate to bring specific disputes to an end.[49] In theory, at least, there was a freedom to strike under Weimar law, and to take other forms of industrial action including

---

[43] Kittner, 462–7.   [44] Kittner, 459–60.
[45] Kittner, 472–3. There is no official record of how many of these orders were imposed without the agreement of one or both of the parties.   [46] Kittner, 480–1.
[47] See further Lewis and Clark 17–19.
[48] Even before 1923, compulsory arbitration was used to control industrial action under the terms of the Demobilization Decree (*Demobilmachungsverordnung*) of 1919.
[49] Between 1918 and 1925, President Ebert issued 135 orders under Article 148: Kittner, 410.

the lockout; however, this so-called freedom was severely restricted by a panoply of private- and public-law measures.[50] From the point of view of a striking worker, for example, participation in industrial action amounted to a breach of the contract of employment, which left the worker vulnerable not only to dismissal, but also to suit in tort for losses suffered by the employer.[51] For the trade unions, too, industrial action could involve a breach of contract and, more specifically, of the 'peace obligation' implied into all collective agreements. This was a contractual term which bound the parties to an agreement not to take industrial action aimed at changing the terms of the agreement.[52] Where a comprehensive collective agreement was in force, in other words, the peace obligation rendered all industrial action unlawful for the duration of that agreement. That being the case, it was the peace obligation which made compulsory arbitration such an effective weapon in the suppression of industrial action. By reason of the implication of the peace obligation into *all* collective agreements, including arbitration orders, the government was able both to prohibit industrial action before it began, and to intervene to bring specific disputes to an end.[53]

Such were the limitations of the freedom to take industrial action under Weimar law, that it has been doubted whether it is appropriate to talk in connection with the Republic of the existence of 'freedom of association'.[54] Where industrial action was understood by the government to be politically motivated, it was routinely brought to an end with the help of the army and para-militaries.[55] Where it was thought to threaten the provision of goods and services to the population, it could be undermined by the strike-breaking 'Teno', a division of the army sponsored by the state to fill the posts of striking workers.[56] In essential industries, industrial action was prohibited unless or until the underlying dispute had been referred for arbitration.[57] For all civil servants, it was prohibited outright.[58] In the remainder of cases, individual participants in industrial action had either to quit their employment beforehand or assume personal liability for losses caused to the employer. And all trade unions had either to comply with the restrictive 'peace obligations' implied in collective agreements and arbitration orders, or themselves become liable for such losses. Even industrial action that complied with the relevant peace

---

[50] *Grundzüge*, 283–98; Kittner, 429–53.

[51] Liability in tort could be avoided if the worker gave notice of his intention to strike, in the form of notice of an intention to quit, but of course in that case the worker still lost his job.

[52] Industrial action could only lawfully be taken, in other words, when negotiating the terms of a new collective agreement, or in connection with a matter that had not previously been the subject of an agreement. Breach of the peace obligation entitled the other party to all the usual private law remedies for breach of contract including interim injunctions.

[53] Kittner, 454. Despite the government's efforts to suppress industrial action, the Weimar Republic had the highest levels of industrial action of any period in Germany's history: Kittner, 500.   [54] Kittner, 454.   [55] Kittner, 397–8.

[56] *Teno* was short for *Technische Nothilfe* ie technical emergency help: Kittner, 435–42; Sinzheimer, *Grundzüge*, 285.

[57] Ie in workplaces providing the country with water, gas, electricity: *Grundzüge*, 87–8.

[58] Kittner, 442.

obligation could be declared unlawful if the courts regarded it as *sittenwidrig* or 'immoral'—a term defined remarkably widely by the Weimar judiciary.[59]

With hindsight, it may be wondered why the trade unions did not put up greater resistance to such infringements of their freedom of association. Though they voiced some objection to the use of compulsory arbitration, for example, they consistently complied with its use, often requesting themselves that disputes be referred to the arbitration boards.[60] In part, such compliance was due simply to pragmatic considerations of the benefits that compulsory arbitration could bring, especially in districts or sectors where union organization was weak.[61] In part, it was due to the unions' and the workers' allegiance to the Weimar state as a hard fought for and won social democracy. 'Today's state is no longer the trade union-hostile state of the pre-war era', stated Clemens Nörpel, leader of the federation of socialist unions, in 1929. 'The trade unions participate in this state, they wield significant influence within its institutions, they can reconfigure those institutions, have reconfigured them to a great extent. This new state must have the right, within certain limits, to place restrictions on the freedom of action of the trade unions and the employers' associations.'[62] Having welcomed the creation of the Republic and the end to the *Kaiserreich* so passionately, many were reluctant to admit the often undemocratic nature of action taken by their ostensibly democratic government. In explanation of the unions' acquiescence, Michael Kittner has drawn attention, finally, to the lack of conceptual clarity that existed at the time, in respect of the semi-public status of the unions and the system of collective bargaining.[63] Though the principle of autonomy was emphasized in labour law theory, and in Article 165 of the constitution, it was never translated into a clear set of rules establishing and safeguarding the desired relationship between the unions and the state. Some, including Sinzheimer, tended to conceive of collective bargaining as one part of a greater system of state-supported social self-determination. Others (for example, the young labour law scholars Kahn-Freund and Hans Carl Nipperdey) criticized this approach for blurring the dividing line between state support and state edict, arguing for their part that compulsory arbitration was irreconcilable with the principle of trade union autonomy. Notwithstanding the tragic fate of the Weimar Republic, the matter was by no means settled in the period to 1945.

The labour constitution and the welfare state

Germany's system of welfare provision was introduced, famously, by Otto von Bismarck at the end of the nineteenth century.[64] In the textbook explanation of the

---

[59] 'Immoral' industrial action was unlawful by reason of para 826 of the Civil Code: *Grundzüge*, 294–8. In respect of industrial action, the paragraph was interpreted so widely that *any* instance of industrial action could be declared unlawful if the courts so wished: Kittner, 607.
[60] Kittner, 455–6, 468–70.   [61] Kittner, 455–6, 468–70.
[62] Cited Kittner, 470. My translation.   [63] Kittner, 470–2.
[64] Bismarck was Chancellor of Germany 1871–90.

political motivations that informed the move, the metaphor of the stick and carrot is often employed: in an attempt to halt the rise of the labour movement, Bismarck wielded the carrot of social welfare and the stick of repressive anti-socialist laws. Appropriate though this may be as an illustration of Bismarck's own intentions, the metaphor has the disadvantage of obfuscating the fact that the welfare state served in due course to *strengthen* the trade unions, reinforcing their legitimacy and authority as the representatives of workers' interests at a time when they had not yet otherwise been recognized as such in law.[65] Contrary to Bismarck's plans, the new welfare system was financed, in essence, directly by employer and worker contributions. The organizational structure of the system was built upon existing forms of collective self-help, such as workers' mutual funds, and new administrative bodies were constructed out of worker, employer, and state representatives.[66] On the part of those in power, the aim was to integrate the trade unions into the administrative apparatus of the state and thereby to defuse the workers' potential for radicalism, encouraging them to greater order.[67] Seen from a rather different point of view, however, the process of integration of the unions and employers could be described with Sinzheimer as a process of constitutionalization; by way of legislation, the state acknowledged and circumscribed the role of the interest group representatives in the 'self-administration' of welfare, and bestowed upon them legal authority to act in the necessary ways. In the field of accident insurance, for example, special 'liability associations' were created by law and granted legal authority to create and enforce safety standards—to set the standards, to inspect factories, and to levy fines against firms that breached the standards. In order to minimize conflict between labour and management over liability for industrial accidents, bipartite arbitration committees were created with authority to decide contentious cases.[68]

For Sinzheimer, as we have seen, the law of the welfare state in the Weimar Republic was quite clearly part of labour law. As such, a discussion of rights to welfare and to participate in the administration of welfare was included in *Principles of Labour Law*. According to the scheme set out in the book, however, the involvement of trade unions and employers' associations in the administration of social policy and the fulfilment of further public functions fell outside of the labour constitution.[69] Together with freedom of association, the law that regulated such participation was classified as part of the law of the *Arbeitsstand*: the law, in other words, that related to workers as members of a social class, rather than as parties to a particular social relationship (ie the relationship, individual and collective, with the employer). The law of the *Arbeitsstand* was the body of law that determined workers socially, that guaranteed to workers the powers and means that they required in order to classify as human beings, rather than merely as legal

---

[65] See P Manow, 'Welfare State Building and Coordinated Capitalism in Japan and Germany' in W Streeck and K Yamamura (eds) *The Origins of Nonliberal Capitalism* (Ithaca, NY 2001), 110–18, esp. 113–14.   [66] Manow 2001, 111.
[67] G Steinmetz, 'Workers and the Welfare State in Imperial Germany' (1991) 40 *International Labor and Working Class History* 18–46, 30.   [68] Manow 2001, 112–13.
[69] *Grundzüge*, Book I, chapter 4.

persons. It encompassed the law of *autonomous* social determination (freedom of association) and the law of *state* social determination (the law regulating the right to work or to unemployment benefit, rights to sickness and incapacity benefit, and rights to participate in the fulfilment of public activities or functions insofar as these related to the rights or interests of workers).[70] The labour constitution, on the other hand, was the body of law that regulated the community of labour and property that was created for the purposes of setting terms and conditions of employment and administering production.

In discussing these two areas of law quite separately, Sinzheimer did not address the question of the ways in which the role of the trade unions and employers' associations in the industrial sphere might be influenced by their participation in the administration of social policy and other public functions. Pre-dating by several decades the emergence of the labour law of the Weimar Republic, the 'proto-corporatist' system of social welfare administration served in a number of respects to lay the ground for the 'fully-fledged corporatism', or economic constitution, of later years.[71] In 'constitutionalizing' the social welfare system, the state acted not only to shape and support that system, but also to influence the nature of interest representation more widely.[72] Given its wish to secure control over social welfare for itself rather than the *Länder*, for example, the federal state lent its support in particular to national, centralized interest representatives, providing them with a measure of defence against the growth of enterprise unions and syndicalism. In some cases, it bestowed privileges directly upon the large industrial unions, defining them exclusively as the representatives of labour. Indirectly, it encouraged the growth of local craft unions into centralized, bureaucratized unions by introducing centralized rather than local methods of social policy provision and administration. More generally, the system of social welfare was influential in illustrating the potential benefits of attempting *collective* solutions to different aspects of the social problem. In the case of accident insurance, for example, the pooling of risks across whole industrial sectors allowed companies to overcome certain collective-action problems, working together to reduce risks, to share state-of-the-art safety techniques, and to agree on common organization and technological standards of production.[73] Finally, the system was influential in lending the trade unions and employers' associations a significant measure of authority over and above the authority that they had by virtue of their membership. This relieved them both, in part, from the otherwise constant requirement to mobilize members' support and enabled them to engage in long-term, cooperative relations with one another.[74]

Because of the involvement of the trade unions and employers' associations in the participation of state functions, and because of the ways in which such involvement influenced the nature and practices of those organizations more

---

[70] *Grundzüge*, Book II, Part 1.
[71] G Steinmetz, *Regulating the Social: The Welfare State and Local Politics in Imperial Germany* (Princeton 1993), 44, cited Manow, 114.   [72] See generally Manow, 114–16.
[73] Manow, 112–13.   [74] Manow, 99–100.

widely, the system of social welfare was arguably much too important to be omitted from a discussion of the labour, or economic, constitution. If this was not explicitly acknowledged by Sinzheimer, it was recognized, at least, by certain of his disciples. Providing a less formalist and more functionalist analysis of the various branches of labour law and social welfare law, Ernst Fraenkel argued that the integration of trade unions and employers' associations into social welfare and state bureaucracy more generally could be regarded as constituting the first steps towards a *real* economic constitution (as opposed to one that was merely posited by the terms of the Constitution). Such integration represented the 'extension of political democracy through the economic forces within the state. Functions which were to be fulfilled, under Article 165, by the district and national works councils are fulfilled, in fact, by the autonomous organizations—the unions and employers' associations.'[75] Here, again, the question of the autonomy of the interest group representatives raised its head—the possibility that such autonomy might be compromised by close relations with the state. According to Fraenkel, writing in 1929, the integration of the representatives into state bureaucracy did *not* herald a progression towards fascism. Collective democracy made sense only insofar as it was built upon collective autonomy. This was the basic difference between fascist state ideology and the emerging collective democracy of the Weimar Republic.[76]

The Labour Constitution of the Federal Republic

During the years of Nazi rule, the Weimar system of collective industrial relations was dismantled. Trade unions and employers' associations were dissolved, works councils abolished and collective bargaining, industrial action, and workplace agreements prohibited. In place of the old system, the *Führerprinzip* was introduced, positing a unity of interests between workers and employers, and charging the employer alone with management of the workplace. Through the institution of so-called 'trustees' to replace arbitration boards, the state assumed the authority to set wages and working conditions directly for whole sections of industry. Collectively, workers and employers were 'represented' together in the same organization, the *Deutsche Arbeitsfront*, the main role of which, according to law, was to ensure industrial peace.[77]

The end of the Second World War and the Nazi regime saw a gradual reintroduction of collective industrial relations in practice and then in law. As things turned out, the collective labour legislation enacted by the new Federal Government in the period 1949–52 reintroduced much from Weimar law. One significant innovation was the provision of rights to parity or one-third worker representation

---

[75] Fraenkel, 'Kollektive Demokratie', 89, my translation.
[76] Fraenkel, 'Kollektive Demokratie', 89, my translation.
[77] See further eg M Becker, *Arbeitsvertrag und Arbeitsverhältnis während der Weimarer Republik und in der Zeit des Nationalsozialismus* (Frankfurt am Main 2005); T Ramm, 'Nationalsozialismus und Arbeitsrecht' (1968) 1 *Kritische Justiz* 108–20.

on the supervisory boards of large companies. Another was the decision to leave the matter of arbitration to the trade unions and employers' associations and to make no provision whatsoever for state involvement therein. These changes aside, the terms of the legislation regulating trade union and works council organization were very similar to those in force during the Weimar Republic. Freedom of association was guaranteed within Article 9 of the constitution, paragraph 3 of which closely mirrored the terms of Article 159 of the Weimar Constitution. Like its forerunner, Article 9 did not refer to a right or freedom to take industrial action, leaving the existence and limits of such a right to be established in time by the courts.[78] Trade union organization and collective bargaining were regulated in the Collective Agreements Act 1949, which reintroduced the key features of the Collective Agreements Decree of 1918, including the rule regarding the compulsory normative effect of collective agreements, and the mechanism for the extension of collective agreements *erga omnes*. Works councils were regulated in the Works Constitution Act 1952. Worker representation on company boards was regulated in that same Act and, in respect of coal and steel, in the Codetermination Act 1951. After 1952, this body of legislation was amended only in the detail, most extensively in the 1970s, following the election of the first postwar SPD-FDP coalition government.[79]

Insofar as it had been possible to explain Weimar labour law with reference to Sinzheimer's conception of the labour constitution, so the law of the Federal Republic could also be explained in those terms: the 'community of labour and property' now extended to encompass the management of individual companies, and the labour constitution now took effect through organization and industrial action alone.[80] In fact, the idea of the labour constitution was explicitly invoked in the name of the new works council legislation—the Works Constitution Act—and the term 'labour constitution' came to be used, quite generally, to refer to the body of law regulating collective employment relations.[81] As with Weimar law, however, it would be entirely misleading to suggest that the postwar labour legislation was implemented by a government intent on the achievement of economic democracy. Indeed, for a period of four years following the end of the war, there was no German government to form or implement any such plans. Instead, the country was governed by the four allied powers, each sovereign in its own

---

[78] As interpreted by the courts of the Federal Republic, the right to strike was subject to fewer limitations than in the Weimar Republic; see further below at 52. Since 1968, Article 9 has referred explicitly to industrial action in a third sentence, added by way of constitutional amendment, which provides that certain emergency measures taken by the government 'may not be directed against industrial disputes engaged in by associations within the meaning of the first sentence of this paragraph in order to safeguard and improve working and economic conditions'.

[79] In 1972 and 1976, steps were taken to strengthen the rights of works councils, and to extend rights to parity representation on company boards beyond coal and steel to all companies with more than 2000 employees. See further below.

[80] Ie no longer through arbitration. Cf Sinzheimer's depiction of the Weimar labour constitution outlined above.

[81] Eg Kittner uses the term throughout and not only in reference to the Weimar Republic. The central piece of labour legislation in Austria bears the name Labour Constitution Act (*Arbeitsverfassungsgesetz*).

zone. With the steady worsening of US–Soviet relations and the beginning of the Cold War—but *before* a new state constitution had been drafted or a government elected—the future of West Germany was decided. At the wishes of the USA, West Germany would be constituted as a liberal, free market economy, a frontier state at the furthermost reaches of the new West. Following the American model, independent trade unions would be permitted to act as the representatives of the interests of workers in negotiations with employers, but there would be no greater role for labour in the administration of the economy, and no nationalization of industry. With a coalition of centre and right-wing parties elected to power in the first elections of 1949, those with an alternative, socialist vision of the new Germany found themselves and their proposals overruled. In that respect, the postwar history of the Federal Republic echoed that of the Weimar Republic: the extensive reordering of the economy along democratic lines was planned but never achieved.

The 'obstructed reconstruction' of the West German state: 1945–52

As told by Eberhard Schmidt in his 1970 history *Der verhinderte Neuordnung*, the story of the institution of a new political and economic order following the collapse of the Third Reich is one of the failure of the trade unions and those on the left to have their demands met for a new economic democracy, first by the occupying allies and then by the Federal Government.[82] The failure is in part attributed by Schmidt to the unions themselves, to their hesitancy to act and, ultimately, their lack of preparedness to take industrial action to force the government's hand. But it is also attributed to those who acted to obstruct the efforts of the unions and other supporters of the institution of economic democracy: the US and British military governments and, following the elections of 1949, the coalition government led by the CDU and Konrad Adenauer.[83]

Schmidt's story begins with a missed opportunity on the part of the trade unions to catch the worm and take an early lead in shaping the political economy of the new German state.[84] In the first months of peace, there was a power vacuum in German society: the political regime and the majority of leaders of industry had been disgraced, factories destroyed, and employers arrested. Despite having been decimated by the Nazis, with many of their leaders exiled, imprisoned, or even murdered, trade unions were quick to re-form. Immediately on the occupation of Germany by allied forces, organizations of workers were established

---

[82] E Schmidt, *Die verhinderte Neuordnung 1945–1952: zur Auseinandersetzung um die Demokratisierung der Wirtschaft in den westlichen Besatzungszonen und in der Bundesrepublik Deutschland* (Frankfurt am Main 1970). Kittner argues against Schmidt and others that in the years after 1945 there was never any real chance of the development of a German politics independent of the allied powers: Kittner, 554. For a discussion of the period 1945–52 in English, see A Markovits, *The Politics of West German Trade Unions* (Cambridge 1986), 61–83.
[83] *Christliche Demokratische Union Deutschlands*, founded in Berlin and the Rheinland, June 1945.
[84] Schmidt, 67. Böckler was the first president of the DGB 1949–51.

at many hundreds of workplaces, usually through the efforts of surviving unionists and social democrats.[85] To the burgeoning union leaders, it appeared that the end of capitalism had come, that the choice of a new economic order lay ahead, and that the choice would be theirs to make.[86] Believing themselves to be in command of the country's destiny, however, the unions took some time in formulating concrete plans, so it was not until early 1947 that their policy programme was complete.[87] By then, they had missed the boat. Capitalist forces had begun to regroup and old power relations to be consolidated. With the steady worsening of US–Soviet relations, the Americans had made the decision to encourage the growth of a liberal market economy in West Germany as a bulwark against the Soviet-sponsored spread of communism.

A fear of the communist threat in Germany was discernible from the outset in the US and British Military governments' handling of the trade unions. With the aim of minimizing the chances of communist control of the unions, the British and Americans acted from 1945 to create a number of obstacles to the re-establishment of union structures at any level above the workplace, introducing an authorization requirement for the formation of new trade unions, and taking steps to prohibit the creation of one single union for the whole of Germany, as many German unionists wished.[88] Following the failure of the Moscow Conference of Foreign Ministers in April 1947, anti-communist attitudes hardened. If the British had been initially more sympathetic to the wishes of the trade unions, they were by 1947 increasingly dependent on the Americans financially, and in no position to challenge US plans. In contravention of the policy agreed by the allies in July 1945, aimed at the de-Nazification and decentralization of German industry, moves were made in the unified American-British bi-zone to bolster production levels and to begin the reconcentration of industry.[89] In breach of earlier pledges that sequestered concerns would never be returned to their private owners, former owners were allowed to exchange their old shares for participation in the re-formed companies.[90] Attempts made in a number of *Länder* to legislate for state ownership of certain industries, and to guarantee to works councils rights to codetermination in economic matters, were vetoed by both the Americans and the British, ostensibly on the grounds that such important and far-reaching political-economic decisions should be taken only by an elected *federal* government.[91]

On the German side, too, the restoration of a liberal market economy was increasingly supported, from 1947, by various groups and, most importantly, the bi-zone's economic council.[92] Formed by the US and the British, and made up of representatives elected by the parliaments of the relevant *Länder*, the council came to be highly influential in shaping the economic order of the future Federal

---

[85] Schmidt, 25, 27.   [86] Cited Schmidt, 66.
[87] By a 'political-economy' committee which delivered its conclusions to the inaugural meeting of the British Zone DGB in April 1947: Schmidt, 66–70.   [88] Schmidt, 31–3, 36–45.
[89] The British and American zones were unified at the beginning of 1947.
[90] Schmidt, 176–81.   [91] Schmidt, 163–5.   [92] Schmidt, 169–70.

Republic. Like its successor, the *Bundestag*, it split along CDU/FDP and SPD/KPD lines, and within the council, as within the Federal Parliament, the SPD found itself side-lined as part of the opposition. Under the leadership of the CDU and Ludwig Erhard, the council pressed for the guarantee and restoration of old power relations, including private ownership of industry.[93] The priority was to set a new economy in motion with a maximum of market freedom and capitalist initiative.[94] Regarding the matter of worker representation, CDU policy was based on a belief that the role of the trade unions and works councils should be limited to participation in the regulation of employment relations, and that the unions should be excluded from political decision-making and from participation in company board decision-making. It favoured a strict separation of works councils and unions in law, and the ousting of the unions from the workplace: works councils should be more independent of the unions than had been the case in the Weimar Republic.[95]

Following the success of the CDU at the first elections to the Federal Parliament in 1949, the now national federation of trade unions, the DGB, met to decide its policy programme.[96] Like the list of demands agreed in 1947 by the British Zone federation, the so-called Munich Programme was heavily influenced by the conception of economic democracy developed by Sinzheimer some 30 years previously.[97] Again, the unions called for the democratization of the economy as a necessary supplement to the democratization of the political sphere. Trade unions should regulate industry together with the employers through the institution of a comprehensive system of parity codetermination at all levels of industry (workplace, company, sector etc). Works councils should be defined in law as trade union bodies, as the representatives of the workforce and of the unions at workplace level, and the unions should have increased rights in the functioning of the works constitution. A number of key industries should be nationalized, together with the national bank.

Given the cooperation of German industry with the Nazi regime, codetermination within companies was a top priority for German unionists and workers: industry must never again provide political support and a material basis for militarism.[98] When it became clear that the old owners of industry were to be allowed to take repossession of the companies, the need for a worker presence on company boards was felt to be even more pressing. In 1947, rights to parity representation on supervisory boards had been introduced in the coal and steel sectors in the British zone.[99] Now the unions were demanding that these rights

---

[93] Kittner, 556–7. Erhard was Director for the Economy within the economic council, and later served as Minister of the Economy (1949–63) and Chancellor (1963–66).
[94] W-D Narr, *CDU-SPD: Programm and Praxis seit 1945* (Berlin 1966), 94.
[95] Schmidt, 206.   [96] Kittner, 597.   [97] Schmidt, 66–70.
[98] The trade unions explained the rise of fascism on the basis that the state and the owners of industry had joined forces against the democratic labour movement: C Dartmann, *Re-distribution of Power, Joint Consultation or Productivity Coalitions? Labour and Postwar Reconstruction in Germany and Britain, 1945–1953* (Bochum 1996), 99–102.
[99] The British had encouraged codetermination, partly motivated by an attempt to win labour support for deconcentration measures. But the scope of union involvement and the precise form that it took were down to the efforts of the German trade unionists. Dartmann, 105–21.

be secured and extended to all new companies in those sectors.[100] The intention of the government, however, was to abolish such rights.[101] Wishing nonetheless to avoid outright conflict with the unions, Adenauer invited the DGB and the main employers' association to meet in November 1949 with the aim of brokering an agreement on the issue.[102] When agreement proved impossible, the metal and coal mining unions prepared for strikes to defend their existing rights, with over 90 per cent of the membership voting in favour of strike action.[103] At a meeting between Hans Böckler, the president of the DGB, and Chancellor Adenauer, Böckler was able to state convincingly that a compromise over the matter of parity codetermination in coal and steel would not be possible.[104] Following talks between the unions and the employers, a Bill guaranteeing such rights was drafted and passed in April 1951.

Notwithstanding the terms of the 1951 Codetermination Act, the question of representation on company boards in industries other than coal and steel remained unanswered. The trade unions were determined that rights to parity representation should be extended to all sectors of the economy, and Adenauer and his government were equally determined that they should not. Seizing the initiative, the government drafted a Works Constitution Bill that provided for one-third worker representation on supervisory boards only. In respect of works councils, the Bill reflected the wishes of the CDU outlined above, that works councils should be independent of the trade unions, an intermediary between the employer and the unions, rather than a body representative of the workers and the unions in opposition to the employer. It did not guarantee any trade union rights to influence the establishment of the council or to direct the council in its work.[105] On publication of the Bill, the DGB made no move to call a strike. According to Schmidt, this hesitation was due to disagreement among the union leadership over the aims and appropriate methods of their opposition to the Bill.[106] Some were reticent to go out on strike because they believed that strike action would constitute an undemocratic threat to Parliament's sovereign right to regulate the economy. Others doubted their ability to halt the passage of the Bill, particularly in light of the apathy of the majority of the membership.[107] Agreement on a campaign of industrial action was not reached until it became clear that the government's intention was to regulate public and private sector workplace relations separately, a move which the union leaders vehemently opposed.[108] A series of strikes carried out in May 1952 induced the government to delay the second reading of the Bill and Chancellor Adenauer to offer to meet with the unions. At the subsequent meeting, however, union leaders were quick to promise an end to strike action, rendering themselves in effect powerless to block the government's

---

[100] Schmidt, 182–3.   [101] Bundeswirtschaftsminister Erhard cited: Schmidt, 183.
[102] Kittner, 598.   [103] Schmidt, 184–5.   [104] Schmidt, 186.
[105] Schmidt, 206–7; W Herschel, 'Der Betriebsrat—damals und heute', in F Gamillscheg (ed) *Im memoriam Sir Otto Kahn-Freund* (Munich 1980), 116.
[106] Schmidt, *Die Verhinderte Neuordnung*, 201 ff; Markovits, 81.   [107] Schmidt, 206.
[108] Schmidt, 209.

plans. The Works Constitution Bill had its second and third readings, and was passed in July 1952.

Economic democracy or interest representation in a market economy?

Having moved to London as a political refugee in 1933, Kahn-Freund made the decision not to involve himself again in the study of German labour law and industrial relations.[109] Had he chosen instead to comment on the policies and actions of German trade unions in the aftermath of the Second World War, one can well imagine that he would have expressed surprise or even dismay at the failure of the union leaders to learn the lessons of the Weimar Republic, as he understood them.[110] The tragic flaw of Weimar labour law, in Kahn-Freund's opinion, was the degree of state involvement in industrial relations for which it had allowed. During the years of the Republic, trade unions came to rely increasingly on state support to achieve their desired outcomes in collective bargaining and to identify their own interests, rather unquestioningly, with those of the state. This weakened the unions and compromised their ability to mount a defence against the rise of Nazism.[111] Despite this recent history, however, union leaders in the postwar period did not fight, first and foremost, for legal or other guarantees of their autonomy and freedom of association.[112] Influenced still by the work of Sinzheimer, and Fritz Naphtali and others, the policies of the trade unions in the formative period to 1952 focused around demands for the institution of a new state-supported economic democracy.[113] Specifically, it was desired that the unions should regulate industry together with the employers through bipartite administrative committees and parity worker representation on company boards, and through participation in the comprehensive state planning of the economy. Within such a 'controlled' economy, it seemed clear to the unions that they would not act straightforwardly as the representatives of the interests of workers entirely free of the state. Instead, they would act in the public or common interest, sacrificing some measure of their autonomy and freedom in collective bargaining in exchange for a leading role in the administration of industry.[114] As the SPD representative and trade unionist Erich Potthoff put it in 1948: 'in a controlled or planned economy, autonomy in collective bargaining will only be possible within limits set out in advance'.[115]

---

[109] Kahn-Freund, 'Postscript', 201.
[110] For a similar line of argument see Kittner, 560–9.
[111] See eg Kahn Freund, 'Labour Law and Industrial Relations", 39.
[112] Kittner, 560–2.
[113] Naphtali led the Research Centre for Political Economy of the German TUC (ADGB) from 1927 to 1933. Together with Sinzheimer and others he developed a policy programme for the unions published in 1928 as Naphtali 1928.   [114] Kittner, 562–3.
[115] Kittner, 562, my translation. Potthoff (1914–2005) served as an SPD representative in the government of the USA/UK bizone, 1947–8, and as the leader of the economic science institute of the trade unions from 1946 to 1949 and 1952 to 1956.

When it came to the drafting of the new German state constitution, a lack of conviction regarding free collective bargaining and industrial action as central elements of the unions' future role was much in evidence.[116] Within the CDU-dominated Parliamentary Council responsible for the creation of the constitution there was cross-party support not only for the constitutional guarantee of freedom of association, but also for the explicit constitutional recognition of a right to strike. When disagreement arose within the Council as to the specific wording of such a right, however, it was decided instead to omit all reference to it within the constitution and leave the question of its nature and extent to a future judiciary. What is remarkable about these events is that neither the trade unions nor the SPD fought hard at any point to have the right to strike included in the terms of the constitution. On the part of the SPD, this was part of a wider strategy to leave as many policy decisions as possible until after the first general election, which it felt confident of winning. On the part of the trade unions, it seems that the right to strike was simply not regarded, straightforwardly and across the board, as important enough to fight for. Writing at the time, Fritz Tarnow, a leading unionist in the Weimar Republic and the Federal Republic, described the unions' position as follows: 'We declared our agreement to the omission of the right to strike from the constitution or basic law. *Of itself, this issue is of little importance.*'[117]

In the union debates of the time a lone but influential voice was that of the labour lawyer Hans Carl Nipperdey.[118] In the Weimar Republic and again at the war's end, Nipperdey argued against the prioritization by the unions of participation in the management of the economy *above* rights to free collective bargaining.[119] In his role as the chief adviser to the unions on matters of labour law and constitutional law in the years 1947–9, he had a direct influence on the terms of the Collective Agreement Act of 1949, drafting the trade union Bill that was later introduced to Parliament by the SPD and passed almost without amendment.[120] In the early 1950s, he was personally responsible for framing the analysis of the law of industrial action which came, by way of adoption by the labour courts, to form the basis of the new law of the Federal Republic.[121] Though it was not fully appreciated at the time, Nipperdey's analysis afforded a much wider and more clearly defined right to take industrial action than had existed under Weimar law, based around the rule that such action was lawful provided that it concerned a dispute with the employers' association (or trade union) regarding matters capable of being regulated by collective agreement.[122]

Even though union efforts were concentrated in the period 1947–52 on the introduction of a system of economic democracy based on union and employer

---

[116] Kittner, 566–9.
[117] Cited Kittner, 569, my translation and my emphasis.
[118] Professor for Civil Law, Commercial Law and Labour Law in Jena und from 1925 in Cologne. First President of the Federal Labour Court in Kassel from 1954 until 1963. During the Nazi years, he remained in post and was a member of the Nazi *Akademie für Deutsches Recht*.
[119] Kittner, 470–2, 563.   [120] Kittner, 563–4.   [121] Kittner, 605–9.
[122] Kittner, 605–9.

involvement in the regulation of a 'controlled' economy, what they eventually got was a right to free collective bargaining and a constitutionally protected right to strike. A right to collective bargaining was guaranteed in the Collective Agreement Act of 1949, and in 1955 it was held by the new Federal Labour Court, of which Nipperdey was President, that a right to take industrial action could be derived from Article 9 of the constitution and the express guarantee of freedom of association contained therein.[123] With the decision taken not to introduce any system of state arbitration of industrial disputes, there was furthermore no possibility of direct state involvement in wage-setting or dispute resolution. On union demands for the right to involvement in the regulation of a controlled economy, on the other hand, little was ever achieved. No industries were nationalized and no comprehensive system of codetermination was instituted. On company supervisory boards, rights to parity workforce representation existed only in respect of the iron, coal, and steel industries, and then only in companies with at least 1,000 employees. In all other industries, companies with at least 500 employees were required to have only one-third of supervisory board members elected by, and representative of, the workforce.[124] In respect of works councils, none of the unions' proposed innovations had been implemented. There had been no extension of council codetermination rights to economic matters, and no increase in the role of the trade unions in the works constitution. The Works Constitution Act of 1952 applied to workplaces with at least five, rather than 20, employees, but at the same time its scope was restricted to the private sector.[125] Otherwise, it was broadly similar to the 1920 Act, providing for council rights to information, consultation, and codetermination; requiring employers to finance the council system; giving councils a dual role both representing workers' interests to the employer and cooperating with the employer to the good of the workplace; and, in line with this cooperative model, prohibiting industrial action.

Judged against the unions' demands for the extension of parity codetermination beyond the coal and steel industries, for more extensive works council and union rights, and for greater integration of the latter two bodies in law, the Works Constitution Act was condemned by union leaders as representing a 'dark moment for democratic development in the Federal Republic'.[126] Battling employer efforts to manipulate works councils to their own ends (securing employee loyalty to the organization and excluding the trade unions from the workplace), the unions fought successfully throughout the 1950s and 1960s to ensure the 'unionization' of the councils through the election of only union members to works council office.[127] At the same time, they continued

---

[123] BAG AP number 1 on Article 9 Basic Law of January 28, 1955, discussed Markovits, 45.

[124] See further W Däubler, 'Co-Determination: the German Experience' (1975) 4 *Industrial Law Journal* 218-28.

[125] Separate provision was made for the public sector by the *Länder* and in the Federal *Personalvertretungsgesetz* of 1967. [126] DGB cited in Markovits, 81.

[127] R Hoffman, 'Einleitung', in R Crusius, G Schiefelbein, M Wilke (eds) *Die Betriebsräte in der Weimarer Republik* (Berlin 1978), v–iv. By 1957, 80 per cent of works councillors in the steel and metal working industries were union members, and by 1968, the percentage of all works councillors

to campaign for legislative reform.[128] By the time of the publication of the DGB's *Düsseldorf Programme* in 1964, the policy aims of the unions were no longer directed towards the institution of economic democracy. Demands were made instead for the extension of codetermination within a Keynesian capitalist economy, and for the maintenance of rights to bargain collectively and to resolve industrial disputes without the involvement of the state.[129] Following the election of the Republic's first SPD-led coalition government, the law was amended along such lines, though not as extensively as the unions had hoped. The 1972 Works Constitution Act strengthened the position of works councils in relation to management and formally institutionalized greater links between works councils and trade unions (guaranteeing, for example, the rights of union officials to take part in works council meetings and to enter the workplace without prior notification of the employer).[130] And the 1976 Codetermination Act extended parity codetermination beyond coal and steel to all companies with at least 2000 employees.[131]

The labour constitution and 'welfare corporatism'

Commenting on the German system of worker representation in 1984, Wolfgang Streeck concluded that one of the consequences of the legislative amendments of the 1970s had been the erosion of the traditional legal distinction between workplace and company codetermination (a distinction that had anyway been difficult to maintain).[132] In his view, supervisory board codetermination, works councils, and trade unions were best regarded as three elements of an integrated system of worker representation. Within large companies (those falling under the regulation of both the Works Constitution Act and the 1976 Codetermination Act), the unions used the works council system and works constitution legislation as an institutional framework and major source of support for union activities and union recruitment at workplace and company levels. As a result, works councils had become de facto union bodies, and union density ratios had generally increased. Given that a large number of workforce representatives on the supervisory boards were works councillors, the legal separation of company codetermination and works councils had also become blurred. Company codetermination had served to strengthen the position of works councils, since council members on supervisory boards had greatly improved access to information: according to law, a right of access to any information at all that management might have. Although

---

who were union members climbed to over 80 per cent, at which level it remained until the late 1990s: K Thelen, *Union of Parts: Labor Politics in Postwar Germany* (Ithaca, NY 1991), 80.

[128] DGB *Vorschläge zur Änderung des Betriebsvefassungsgesetzes*, 1968 and 1970 cited: H Gester, 'Zur Stellung der Gewerkschaften im Betrieb nach dem neuen Betriebsverfassungsgesetz' (1972) *Gewerkschaftliche Monatshefte* 19, 20, 23.   [129] Markovits, 93–106.

[130] See further Gester.   [131] See further: Däubler.

[132] W Streeck, *Social Institutions and Economic Performance* (London, Newbury Park, New Delhi 1992), 137.

much of that information might be declared confidential, the works councillor could hardly be expected, when engaged in works constitution business, to forget what she had learned in her capacity as a supervisory board member.[133]

Notwithstanding the integration of worker representation across different levels of economic organization—and the picture this suggested of a united body of representatives working to further the interests of workers across the board—a second important feature of the system of codetermination identified by Streeck was the significant measure of cooperation between worker representatives and *employers* at workplace and company levels for which it allowed.[134] With the negotiation of wages centralized at industry level, worker representatives in individual workplaces and companies tended quite readily to perceive a shared interest with the employer in the survival and success of the enterprise. In general, worker representatives did not oppose management proposals for modernization or rationalization, provided that these did not involve involuntary dismissals or wage reductions. In recognition of the requirements of technological change, they were consistently committed to continuous retraining and redeployment of the workforce. And where a company or workplace faced economic difficulties, worker representatives would usually cooperate with adjustment measures such as early retirement schemes or financial incentives for voluntary redundancies. From the point of view of management, the readiness of works councils and worker representatives on company boards to cooperate with management strategies counted in favour of a general acceptance of codetermination. In many workplaces, works councils were even positively welcomed by managers as a useful means of communicating with the workforce and encouraging workers to accept change.[135] From the point of view of the trade unions, in contrast, cooperation between worker representatives and management could only be regarded with a measure of ambivalence.[136] On the one hand, it was clear that codetermination increased the employment security of workers who were already employed, and guaranteed to them an important voice in the management of workplaces and companies. At the same time, however, it raised the possibility of real conflicts of interests between workers employed at different workplaces and companies, and between employed and unemployed workers. As such, it undermined the influence of the centralized industrial trade unions, hindering their efforts to exert control and concertation, and to further the interests of workers as a social class.

A third important feature of the German system of worker representation, discussed elsewhere by Streeck, was the relatively close intertwining it involved of the state and the 'autonomous' trade unions and employers' associations.[137] Insofar as the terms of the postwar labour constitution suggested a strict separation of

---

[133] On the integration of trade unions and works councils, see further: B Bösche and H Grimberg, 'Die deutschen Gewerkschaftsgesetze', in T Klebe, P Wedde, M Wolmerath (eds) *Recht und soziale Arbeitswelt: Festschrift für Wolfgang Däubler zum 60. Geburtstag* (Frankfurt am Main 1999).
[134] Streeck, *Social Institutions*, 143–63; W Müller-Jentsch, 'Germany: From Collective Voice to Co-management' in J Rogers and W Streeck (eds) *Works Councils* (Chicago 1995), 65–72.
[135] Müller-Jentsch, 66–7.   [136] Streeck, *Social Institutions*, 164, 166–7.
[137] Streeck, 'Industrial Relations'.

the state from industrial relations, with the trade unions, works councils, and employers' associations acting straightforwardly as the representatives of their members' interests, they were misleading. While it was true that the principle of *Tarifautonomie*, enshrined in law, precluded the state from direct intervention in wage-setting, it was equally true that the trade unions and employers could best perform their wage-setting function only in cooperation with one another *and with the state*.[138] For the duration of the 1970s, 1980s, and early 1990s, such cooperation proceeded in tandem with the administration of social security. In the early 1970s, the *Bundesbank* introduced a non-negotiable monetarist policy which precluded the kind of Keynesian demand management practised at the time in other industrialized states. Together with the government, trade unions and employers' organizations learned to use welfare provision as the functional equivalent of demand management. If demanding and agreeing to higher wages was to lead necessarily to more unemployment, then so be it—the welfare state could compensate by providing generous pensions and unemployment benefit.[139] For as long as it lasted, this 'welfare-state consensus' brought benefits to the unions, the employers and the government alike, allowing for the egalitarian wage structure associated with centralized collective bargaining, securing 'social peace' between capital and labour, and lessening the likelihood of political discontent over unemployment levels.[140] As such, it provided all three parties with a clear incentive to cooperate and not to rock the boat too far in any direction. Well into the 1990s, wrote Streeck, 'union wage demands . . . met with limited resistance from employer associations, while trade unions and works councils could afford to tolerate industry-wide workforce reduction carried out in the name of international competitiveness'.[141]

In reality, then, the state was in a position to wield more influence on industrial relations than the legal framework suggested. According to the terms of the law, unions and employers' associations were autonomous organizations, which negotiated with one another autonomously to create legal norms, and which bore sole responsibility for the resolution of union–employer disputes. Having been instituted by CDU-led governing bodies with the encouragement of the American occupying forces, this framework implied a model of free interest representation well suited to a liberal market economy. As negotiated by a wide variety of interest groups and powers in the late 1940s and early 1950s, however, the political economy of Germany could not rightly be described as a liberal market economy. It was characterized rather by the existence of a whole range of social institutions which served to organize and regulate markets, and to shield certain areas of social life partially or even completely from the influence of market principles.[142] During the 1950s, the 'enabling'[143] or 'semi-sovereign'[144] German state had developed a

---

[138] Streeck, 'Industrial Relations', 139.   [139] Streeck, 'Industrial Relations', 139–43.
[140] W Streeck, *Re-Forming Capitalism: Institutional Change in the German Political Economy* (Oxford 2009), 58.   [141] Streeck, *Re-Forming Capitalism*, 59.
[142] W Streeck, 'German Capitalism. Does it Exist? Can it Survive?' (1997) 2 *New Political Economy* 237–56, 239–41.   [143] Streeck, 'German Capitalism', 241.
[144] 'Semi-sovereign' is the term famously used by Peter Katzenstein to describe the German state: *Politics and Policy in West Germany: the Growth of a Semi-Sovereign State* (Philadelphia 1987).

remarkable capacity for delegating to civil society organizations governance functions that would otherwise be performed by the state or left to the market. Having delegated these functions, it would then support the organizations in the performance thereof by, for example, awarding legal status to the outcome of collective negotiations, or providing for obligatory or quasi-obligatory membership.[145]

What this model of governance meant for the trade unions and the employers' associations was, first and foremost, the creation of bonds of mutual dependence with each other and with the state. The state was reliant on the interest groups to perform the wage-setting function effectively and responsibly—that is, with an eye to the general public interest, and the interest of the government in retaining the support of the electorate. In turn, the trade unions and employers' associations relied on the state for the maintenance of the legal and administrative framework that acknowledged their role in industrial relations and social security provision, and conferred upon them authority and law-making powers. And they relied upon each other not to oppose too often or too aggressively the outcomes and courses of action that they each respectively desired. With a view to explaining the motivations of the trade unions and other interest groups, Streeck has drawn attention to the two 'logics' that shaped their priorities: the 'logic of membership' and the 'logic of influence'.[146] In the 'welfare corporatism' of the postwar German state, the actions of trade unions and employers' associations (and other interest groups) were determined by the wishes of members but, at the same time, by the conditions and strategic imperatives of interaction with other organized interests, and with the public power.[147]

The Postwar Labour Constitution in Decline

Until the reunification of Germany in 1990, it was possible, without much distortion, to talk of a German model of worker representation or industrial relations. For four decades, the model was characterized by the existence of sectorally organized trade unions and workplace works councils, a comprehensive system of codetermination at workplace and company level, sectoral collective bargaining with some inter-sectoral coordination, and almost universal coverage of collective agreements.[148] As such, the model was widely regarded as integral to the success of the German social market economy, delivering remarkably low wage dispersion for such a large country, and supporting (through cooperative workplace and company codetermination) the highly competitive 'diversified quality production' characteristic of the economy at that time.[149] During the 1980s, the model drew attention outside Germany for the reason that it appeared

---

[145] Streeck, 'German Capitalism', 242–3.
[146] Streeck, *Re-Forming Capitalism*, chapters 3–4.
[147] Streeck, *Re-Forming Capitalism*, 54.
[148] See generally Streeck, *Re-Forming Capitalism*, chapters 2 and 3.
[149] Streeck, *Re-Forming Capitalism*, 38, 57.

largely resistant to the pressures causing the disintegration or dismantling of collective industrial relations in other industrialized countries, including prominently the US and the UK.[150] Since the 1990s, however, the continued existence of the German model has appeared increasingly unlikely, at least in its traditional form.[151] Trade unions and employers' associations have experienced falling membership levels[152] and the coverage of collective agreements has contracted.[153] There has been a significant and apparently long-term decline in the number of workplaces with works councils[154] and a slow but steady increase in the number of non-union works councillors, suggesting a weakening of the unions' control over workplace employment relations.[155] Finally, the number of firms failing to honour collective agreements has increased steeply. With ever-greater regularity, managements have chosen simply to breach collective agreements, without fear of reprisal, apparently, at the hands of the weakened trade unions.[156] Alternatively, firms have made use of so-called opening clauses, negotiated at industry level and included in the industry collective agreement, to allow for derogation from that agreement at workplace level.[157] In the past five years or so, the financial and economic crises and the unions' and employers' responses to them do not appear to have affected these longer-term trajectories of change.[158] Instances of cooperation between the unions, employers, and the state—for example, to avoid dismissals by reducing working time—have been tied to the particular circumstances of the crises, and cannot be taken to suggest any longer-lasting revival of traditional corporatist relations.[159]

---

[150] T Haipeter, 'Erosion, Exhaustion or Renewal? New Forms of Collective Bargaining in Germany' paper presented at the LLRN Conference, Barcelona, 2013, 6.

[151] See K Schmierl, 'Wird das deutsche Modell der Arbeitsregulierung die Umschichtung in der Arbeitsgesellschaft überleben?' *WSI Mitteilungen* 11/2003; J Abel and P Bleses, 'Eine Variante unter vielen?—Zur Gegenwart der dualen Struktur der Interessenvertretung' *WSI Mitteilungen* 5/2005; R Bispinck, 'Kontrollierte Dezentralisierung der Tarifpolitik—Eine schwierige Balance' *WSI Mitteilungen* 5/2004; Haipeter, 'Erosion, Exhaustion or Renewal?'.

[152] From 1950 until 1990, union membership stood at or around 30 per cent of the workforce. In 2003, it was estimated to stand at 19.7 per cent. Streeck, *Re-Forming Capitalism*, 46–7.

[153] Between 1995 and 2012, the share of West German workplaces bound by sectoral collective agreements fell quite dramatically from 53 per cent to 32 per cent. The share of workers covered fell from 72 per cent to 53 per cent. Streeck, *Re-Forming Capitalism*, 39; P Ellguth, 'Tarifbindung und betriebliche Interessenvertretung: Ergebnisse aus dem IAB-Betriebspanel 2012' WSI-Mitteilungen 3/2013.

[154] One set of figures shows a drop in the number of private sector workers represented by a works council from 50 per cent in 1981 to less than 40 per cent in 1994. A second set shows a drop from 50 per cent (West Germany) and 41 per cent (East Germany) in 1996 to 46 per cent and 39 per cent in 2005. Streeck, *Re-Forming Capitalism*, 40. The most recent IAB figures suggest that in 2012 in West Germany 43 per cent and in East Germany 36 per cent of workers worked in workplaces with a works council.

[155] In 2009, Streeck estimated that union representation on works councils had fallen from roughly four-fifths to two-thirds of works councillors during the preceding 25 years: Streeck, *Re-Forming Capitalism*, 40.

[156] Available figures show that in 1997–8, 18 per cent of firms breached the industrial collective agreement 'occasionally' or 'repeatedly': Streeck, *Re-Forming Capitalism*, 40.

[157] Streeck, *Re-Forming Capitalism*, 40–1.   [158] Haipeter, 22.

[159] Haipeter, 22.

Viewed through the lens of the labour constitution, with its emphasis of the importance of the role of the state in supporting collective industrial relations, the first thing to note about the weakening or erosion of the traditional model is that it has occurred, to date, despite the continuing stability of the encompassing legal framework. Since the formative period 1949–52, the letter of the collective labour law of the Federal Republic has remained broadly constant. Where amendments have been made, they have been aimed at strengthening rather than weakening collectivism, and have anyway not affected the overall character of the law. While it is true that more significant 'deregulatory' amendments were proposed by the CDU in the early part of the last decade, there is for the moment little likelihood of law reform.[160] Decollectivization and decentralization in industrial relations have occurred, then, despite the numerous ways in which the legal framework supports collective organization, centralization, and the participation of labour in managerial decision-making. In some respects, the legal framework has influenced the manner in which change has occurred and, in others, it may have acted as a brake on change; however, it has not been up to the task of preventing it.

In his 2009 book, *Re-Forming Capitalism*, Streeck presented the developments in the field of industrial relations as one thoroughly integrated element of a more general and irreversible trend towards 'disorganization' across the German economy. Disorganization, according to Streeck, means 'a loss of centralized control, towards decentralization, individualization, segmentalism, competitive pluralism, and the like, with market forces slowly taking the place of political decisions'.[161] Looking at patterns of change in collective bargaining, collective organization via trade unions and employer associations, social policy, public finance, and corporate governance, Streeck's argument was that, since the 1990s, there had been a 'decline in centralized control and organized regulation and an increase in competition in labor markets; in the collective articulation of interests; in the promotion of class cooperation and social peace by state intervention; and in the relationship between the state and the economy, between large firms, and between them and the banking system'.[162] Moreover, the state had been anything but a neutral or passive bystander in these mutually reinforcing processes of disorganization.[163] To the contrary, it had actively contributed to the disorganization of the tripartite administration of social policy, to the privatization of public enterprise, and to the dissolution of the institutional complex of German corporate governance and of what Streeck calls the German 'company network', all of which had previously served in important ways to prop up the collective organization of labour and capital and the collective bargaining system.[164]

---

[160] In 2003 and again in 2004 the CDU/CSU introduced a bill intended to facilitate derogations from collective agreements at workplace level, even in the absence of an opening clause. The bill was dropped in 2005 as part of the CDU/SPD Coalition Agreement.
[161] Streeck, *Re-Forming Capitalism*, 33.   [162] Streeck, *Re-Forming Capitalism*, 23.
[163] Streeck, *Re-Forming Capitalism*, 35.
[164] Streeck, *Re-Forming Capitalism*, 35 and, more generally, 33–89.

Decentralization and the collectivist legal framework

In describing developments in German industrial relations over the past twenty years or so, some authors have emphasized that pressures towards decentralization and 'flexibilization' have not played out in a uniform way across the whole economy.[165] In the case of small and medium-sized workplaces, in particular, there has been a rise in the number of workplaces with no works council and no trade union presence, and a corresponding growth in the individual negotiation of employment terms. Individualized employment contracts are especially common in the service sector and 'new industries', where collective agreement coverage is low and a large proportion of employees are highly qualified.[166] In industries in which companies tend to be organized into large workplaces, in contrast, there is evidence of some persistence of traditional forms of bargaining and codetermination.[167] And there is evidence too of what might be called a 'renewal' or 're-institutionalization' of industrial relations, involving experimentation with new forms of collective negotiations.[168] Notwithstanding variations of this type between and within sectors, however, it seems fair to say that there has been a general and widespread shift in emphasis from the sector to the workplace, or plant, as the key site of collective negotiations. The majority of German firms have not reacted to the new more market-driven economy and corporate governance regime by seeking to individualize employment relations.[169] Instead, they have sought to strengthen collective employment relations at workplace level, negotiating sufficient derogations from sectoral collective agreements to allow for continued participation in the collective bargaining process. From the workers' point of view, this has had the advantage of allowing them, nevertheless, a collective voice through representation by works councils. In comparison to the old model, however, it has the disadvantage of replacing obligatory with 'voluntary' localized arrangements much more susceptible than sectoral bargaining to market pressures.[170] There is evidence that wage differentials have increased as a result, affecting low wage earners most of all.[171] In recent years, trade unions and others have campaigned for the introduction of a national minimum wage, especially in weakly organized sectors.[172]

In the Federal Republic it is provided in law, as it was in the Weimar Republic, that a works agreement may not regulate remuneration or other conditions of

---

[165] Eg Haipeter, 10–19. [166] Abel and Bleses, 262; Schmierl, 654–6.
[167] For three case studies which support the view that traditional forms of worker representation are proving resistant to globalization, see A Börsch, *Global Pressure, National System: How German Corporate Governance is Changing* (Ithaca, NY 2007).
[168] Haipeter; M Behrens and W Jacoby, 'The Rise of Experimentalism in German Collective Bargaining' (2004) 42 *British Journal of Industrial Relations* 95–123.
[169] Streeck, *Re-Forming Capitalism*, esp. 85–7.
[170] 'Voluntary' because the works council may not lawfully organize industrial action: Streeck, *Re-Forming Capitalism*, 86, 87. [171] Streeck, *Re-Forming Capitalism*, 41–2.
[172] Streeck, *Re-Forming Capitalism*, 54. In 2013, the Bundesrat called upon the Government to introduce a minimum wage of at least 8.50 Euros: see resolution of the *Bundesrat* of 3 May 2013, *Gute Arbeit—Zukunftsfähige und faire Arbeitspolitik gestalten* (Drucksache 343/14). In November 2013, the CDU, CSU and SPD undertook as a term of their coalition agreement to introduce a minimum wage of 8.50 Euros during the term of the next Parliament: <http://www.spd.de/linkableblob/112790/data/20131127_koalitionsvertrag.pdf>.

employment that have been or are usually fixed within the relevant collective agreement, unless the collective agreement expressly authorizes this.[173] In other words, either party to the collective agreement has a right of veto over workplace derogations.[174] In principle, at least, this should allow the trade unions and the employers' associations a significant measure of control over processes of decentralization. Because the authorization of any workplace derogation must be agreed, according to law, by *both* parties, they should be encouraged to work together, aiming over time to find new structures and outcomes that are mutually beneficial, and that allow both sides to hold on to members. Behrens and Jacoby have spoken in this context of an 'experimentalist logic in collective bargaining': by reason of the legal rule ensuring their ultimate authority, trade unions and employers' associations are uniquely placed to experiment with new forms and combinations of collective bargaining and workplace negotiations, aggregating what is learned and diffusing it to other parts of the sector or the economy.[175] What this narrative assumes, however, is the existence of strong trade unions and employers' associations, with high membership levels and a good measure of authority over their members. It assumes that individual companies, as members of the employers' association, are bound and for the most part wish to remain bound by the sectoral collective agreement, and it assumes that whenever an individual company considers defecting from the association and the collective agreement, the threat of industrial action will be enough to make it think again.

One of the principal trends evident since the 1990s, as we have seen, is a decline in trade union and employers' association membership levels. In the case of employers' associations, the loss of membership has been accompanied, and greatly exacerbated, by the intensification of internecine conflicts between, in particular, small and large firms.[176] Differences in the priorities and interests of members were always a feature of employers' associations, but were rendered more acute in the 1990s as a consequence of the larger firms' reactions to increased pressures to be more—globally—competitive. For example, (large firm) manufacturers of goods, especially cars, began to demand significant price reductions from their (small firm) suppliers to offset the increasing labour costs which resulted, in part, from the same collective agreements that the suppliers were also obliged to respect.[177] Understandably, perhaps, small and medium-sized firms began to defect from sectoral collective agreements in increasing numbers. As the coverage of collective agreements contracted, membership of employers' associations and trade unions fell yet further—on the employers' side, because firm-specific arrangements became more commonplace, and therefore a more likely option for disgruntled firms, and in the case of the unions, because their accelerating loss of

---

[173] Works Constitution Act, s 77 para 3.
[174] Where either party withholds its consent, the terms of the collective agreement remain legally binding and any terms of the workplace agreement that purpose to derogate therefrom are void.
[175] Behrens and Jacoby.   [176] Streeck, *Re-Forming Capitalism*, 49–51.
[177] Streeck, *Re-Forming Capitalism*, 49.

control over wages made membership less attractive.[178] On the unions' side, meanwhile, a further tendency towards decentralization or disorganization emerged with the creation of small, independent unions of professional or highly skilled workers such as hospital doctors and airline pilots. Such unions seek to represent their members' interests quite aggressively in opposition to the industrial unions affiliated to the DGB, making it more difficult for the industrial unions to engage in wage levelling.[179]

As more and more firms expressed dissatisfaction with existing collective bargaining arrangements, and even took the step of defecting from the employers' associations, the associations reacted in two ways.[180] First, they created new so-called 'OT'—*ohne Tarif*—divisions, consisting of members who would henceforth not be bound by collective agreements.[181] Second, they began to demand much more regularly of the unions that opening clauses be included in collective agreements, allowing for deviations at firm level.[182] In light of their own decreasing membership levels, unions are for the most part no longer in a position to prevent firms defecting from collective agreements (whether by joining OT divisions or by resigning their membership altogether) by means of industrial action or mobilization.[183] In such circumstances, the legal requirement for the agreement of both parties to the inclusion of an opening clause is of scant consequence. Forced onto the defensive, unions are left with little choice but to agree, hoping thereby to retain at least some measure of influence over the negotiation of terms and conditions. Again, the picture is not a uniform one, and in some cases it seems that the legal requirement for opening clauses *has* supported union efforts to exercise control over workplace derogations. In a recent paper, for example, Thomas Haipeter describes how unions in the metal and chemical industries have been able to turn instances of workplace derogation to their advantage, in some measure at least, wringing significant concessions from employers at firm level and attracting new members.[184] The more general conclusion to be drawn from the experiences of the past 20 years or so is nonetheless that legal protections and legal supports may be of little use to trade unions which have been significantly weakened by falling membership levels.[185]

The logic of membership and the logic of influence

Over and above the enactment and enforcement of the postwar legal framework, the German state was constructed, and acted, in the decades following the end of the war in a way that lent support to the German model of industrial relations. In the large public sector, for example, collective bargaining

---

[178] Streeck, *Re-Forming Capitalism*, 52. [179] Streeck, *Re-Forming Capitalism*, 53–4.
[180] Haipeter, 8–9. [181] Streeck, *Re-Forming Capitalism*, 47–8.
[182] Streeck, *Re-Forming Capitalism*, 41; Haipeter, 8–10. [183] Haipeter, 9.
[184] Haipeter.
[185] Haipeter appears to agree with this conclusion: the 'precondition' for unions managing to use opening clauses as a means of improving control over collective bargaining and attracting members is that the unions in question, 'are still powerful enough'. Haipeter, 19.

was highly centralized and the coverage of collective agreements more or less comprehensive.[186] In the private sector, state support for a dense networking of firms and financial institutions (through cross-shareholdings of capital and interlocking directorates) helped to insulate firms from short-term competitive pressures, allowing greater scope for cooperative relations with the unions and works councils.[187] The DGB and the umbrella employers' association, the BDA, meanwhile, had seats on the administrative boards of public sector industries, such as the Federal Post Office and Federal Railways, and were otherwise represented in numerous ministerial advisory committees and quasi-governmental institutions.[188] Through such participation they were able to wield a direct influence on the formation of government policy and legislation. In the field of social policy, in particular, they participated as equals with the government, with one-third of the seats on the governing bodies responsible for the various social insurance programmes (unemployment, sickness, and retirement funds) assigned each to the DGB and BDA.[189]

In scholarly literature, the participation of the DGB and BDA in government and state bureaucracy has most often been discussed as an element of German-style corporatism rather than 'economic democracy' as such or the economic constitution. Streeck, as we have seen, used the term 'welfare corporatism' to highlight the ways in which trade unions, employers' associations, and governments colluded from the 1970s to use social security as a prop for centralized collective bargaining. Because the economy was focused on diversified quality production, it had only a limited capacity to absorb the country's labour supply. By virtue in particular of the *Bundesbank*'s strict monetarist policy, this meant that the high wages resulting from free collective bargaining came with the threat of further unemployment. Wary of provoking unmanageable industrial or political conflict, however, German governments did not seek to intervene directly in wage-setting or attempt a Thatcheresque suppression of trade union power, but instead took steps to limit the labour supply, expanding opportunities for early retirement and paying generous unemployment benefits.[190]

As a means of stabilizing the postwar class compromise, welfare corporatism bore the disadvantage of being expensive and ever more so. Because social security contributions added to the cost of labour, rising contributions resulted, in turn, in more unemployment, which resulted in still higher contributions, and so on, in an upward spiral of costs. Between the 1960s and the 1990s, the aggregate rate of contributions to pension, health and unemployment insurance rose from about 25 per cent to over 40 per cent of gross wages.[191] For the government's part, the share of the federal budget spent on social security increased dramatically from roughly

---

[186] In essence, one single collective agreement has determined the pay of all public-sector workers from rubbish collectors to university professors: Streeck, *Re-Forming Capitalism*, 72 and note 5.
[187] Streeck, *Re-Forming Capitalism*, 77–8.
[188] *Bundesvereinigung der Deutschen Arbeitgeberverbände*, or Federal Confederation of German Employers' Associations.   [189] Markovits 29, 15.
[190] Streeck, *Re-Forming Capitalism*, 56–9.
[191] Streeck, *Re-Forming Capitalism*, 59.

17 per cent of total federal spending in 1989 to a staggering 35 per cent in 2004.[192] During the 1990s, and against a background of rising public debt, it became clear that the government could no longer afford to support corporatist collective bargaining in this way. Helmut Kohl, and Gerhard Schröder after him, attempted to address the problem in a concerted fashion by way of tripartite 'alliances' for employment. When these failed, by reason of a lack of consensus among the three parties, the Schröder government changed tack and opted instead to exert unilateral control over social policy. In 2003 and 2004, it implemented the so-called Hartz reforms, tightening requirements for the unemployed to accept job offers, shortening the duration of unemployment benefits, and introducing means testing. In 2006, the Grand Coalition government extended the legal age of retirement from 65 to 67 without even informing the trade unions of its plans.[193]

The move to unilateralism in the field of social policy reflected and greatly contributed to what has been called the 'secular restructuring' of inter-organizational relations in the administration of social policy.[194] Beginning in the 1990s, the corporatist system of self-administration of social policy was 'disorganised' piece by piece, and replaced with an increasingly pluralist and competitive set of arrangements.[195] Within the social policy arms of both political parties, traditional ties with the unions and employers' associations were loosened. Organizations such as the Bundestag's Standing Committee for Labour and Social Policy underwent a striking change of membership, with career politicians and political generalists taking the place of politicians who had had strong ties to the unions and employers' associations.[196] At the same time, the bodies responsible for the administration of social policy were restructured, with the tripartite 'self-administrative' elements significantly reduced in terms of size and influence.[197] According to Streeck, as we have seen, all of this occurred against the backdrop of a much wider strategy of disorganization deliberately employed by governments from the end of the 1990s in an effort to reduce public spending.[198] In the face of ever-increasing public debt and a mounting fiscal crisis, governments acted to privatize parts of the economy, selling off state property, contracting out state activities, and inviting in private competition to put remaining public sector service providers under increased competitive pressure.[199] This resulted in a significant reduction in the influence of the trade unions and employers' associations, putting an end to the comprehensive coverage of collective agreements characteristic of publicly owned sectors (such as the postal service, telecommunications, railways) and expanding instead the number of private sector employers intent on

---

[192] Partly by reason of a government undertaking to keep the aggregate rate of contributions below 40 per cent: Streeck, *Re-Forming Capitalism*, 60.
[193] Streeck, *Re-Forming Capitalism*, 60–2.   [194] Streeck, *Re-Forming Capitalism*, 62.
[195] C Trampusch, 'Postkorporatismus in der Sozialpolitik: Folgen für die Gewekschaften' (2006) *WSI-Mitteilungen* 6/2006.
[196] C Trampusch, 'From Interest Groups to Parties: The Change in the Career Patterns of the Legislative Elite in German Social Policy' (2005) 14 *German Politics* 14–32.
[197] Trampusch, 'Postkorporatismus in der Sozialpolitik'.
[198] Streeck, *Re-Forming Capitalism*, chapter 5.
[199] Streeck, *Re-Forming Capitalism*, esp. 71–5.

operating outside the collective bargaining system using casualized, non-unionized, low-wage labour.

From the point of view of the employers' associations and even more so the trade unions, these strategies of disorganization have meant a significant weakening of their position of power within the political parties and within government. Having enjoyed a state-guaranteed monopoly as interest representatives in the field of social policy for several decades, they have been reduced to a position more akin to that of lobbyists—one voice among many competing to influence the policy and actions of government. As Streeck has put it, their ability to act according to the 'logic of influence' has decreased. And as a direct consequence, they have become more dependent on 'the logic of membership'—on the support of their members, and on the legitimacy, authority, and industrial or economic power which that support confers upon them. They have been forced to listen more closely to members, and to act as their members have instructed, catering more directly to members' *perceived immediate* interests. This, in turn, has made it much more difficult for the unions and employers' associations to impose a common definition of interest upon members, and to control and direct from the centre. Internal conflicts have intensified, and sectional secession has become a more common occurrence.[200] With no suggestion that the temporary resort to corporatist concertation occasioned by the economic crisis is likely to result in any more lasting rehabilitation of the unions and employers' associations within government and state bureaucracy, unions are having to come to terms with the increased importance of the 'logic of membership'—with the trend away from corporatism towards interest representation—learning from the experiences of US and UK unions, for example, about recruitment strategies.[201]

Conclusion

Sinzheimer's approach to scholarship and legal analysis was closely informed by his fundamental belief that law could be used as a tool to achieve social justice.[202] In the prewar era, his critical analysis of legislation was always undertaken with an eye to constructing arguments in favour of legal reform. During the years of the Weimar Republic, his intention was rather to read the existing law in the best possible light—to read it as 'social democratic' labour law, designed to emancipate workers by allowing labour to participate in the definition of its own social conditions of existence. As such he was not primarily concerned to explain the nature of the political compromises involved in the drafting and adoption of the legislation or the policy priorities of government. He wished instead to analyse the provisions of the legislation such that they fit with his pre-existing idea of the economic constitution and with the constellation of state, trade unions, works councils and

---

[200] Streeck, *Re-Forming Capitalism*, 64.   [201] Haipeter, 20.
[202] Kettler and Wheatland.

employers which that idea implied. It may be that Sinzheimer was influenced in this respect by his own legal practice and daily experience of advocacy before the labour courts; analysis and argument were closely combined in his writing in a manner suggestive of legal advocacy.[203] It may be significant, furthermore, that in Germany, scholarly analysis can figure as authoritative in the courts, with received opinion (*herrschende Meinung*) functioning as a kind of common law.[204]

In fact, Article 165 of the Weimar Constitution—which purported in such striking terms to call workers 'to participate on a parity basis with employers in the regulation of . . . the overall economic development of the forces of production'—did not result from a concerted political will on the part of Parliament to democratize the economy. It represented rather a temporary and unstable political compromise born of a perception shared across party divides of the threat to democracy posed by the revolutionary workers' councils. Declared by the *Reich* Labour Court to require further implementation by legislation, and with no such legislation forthcoming, the Article eventually became something of a dead letter. While it could not rightly be judged to have implemented Article 165, however, the collective labour law of the Republic was notable for the breadth of rights that it accorded to trade unions, and to works councils as the workplace representative of the trade unions. It was notable too for the system of compulsory arbitration that it introduced, allowing the state to intervene directly in wage-setting and dispute resolution.

With respect to the role of the state in the regulation of industrial relations, the relevant provisions of the Weimar Constitution, Collective Agreements Decree, and Works Councils Act all suggested that the state should perform functions that aligned more or less closely with Sinzheimer's prescriptions. The state should recognize the collective actors and their norm- or law-making authority; it should circumscribe the sphere in which they could exercise that authority; and it should make provision, while respecting the actors' autonomy, for furtherance of the common interest. State involvement in arbitration, in contrast, was arguably more problematic than Sinzheimer's analysis suggested. In the 1920s and early 1930s, the state used arbitration in ways that restricted very significantly the autonomy of the unions and employers' associations, seeking to exercise direct control over wage levels, and to prohibit or put an end to instances of industrial action. Though it wasn't perhaps fully acknowledged by Sinzheimer, the relationship between the state on the one hand, and the trade unions and employers' associations on the other was also influenced by the involvement of the latter in the administration of social welfare. In sanctioning and fixing the terms of such involvement, the state conferred a significant measure of authority upon the unions and employers, and at the same time expressed a—necessarily influential—preference for particular types of organization and modes of action.

---

[203] Kettler and Wheatland.
[204] See further: *Schluss der Debatte mit zwei Buchstaben: 'Das ist hM und kann nicht angezweifelt werden'* in Legal Tribune Online, 23 October 2011 (<http://www.lto.de>).

Conclusion

In the late 1940s, plans laid by the trade unions for the institution of an economic democracy built upon a comprehensive system of trade union/employer codetermination were heavily influenced by the earlier work of Sinzheimer and others. As such, they implied a partial sacrifice of autonomy on the part of the trade unions in exchange for state support of their taking a leading role in the administration of industry. Because the plans failed to win the approval of the occupying military powers and the first provisional and elected governments of the Federal Republic, however, they were never implemented. Only in the coal and steel industries were unions granted rights to parity representation on the supervisory boards of companies; at workplace level, works council rights to codetermination were no more extensive than they had been before the war. The legal framework created in the years 1949–52 shared much with the law of the Weimar Republic. With the absence of any provision for the involvement of the state in arbitration, however, and with a more clearly delineated and protected right to take industrial action, there was now far greater emphasis on the collective parties' right to free collective bargaining, or *Tarifautonomie*, than had previously been the case. In line with the image of trade unions and industrial relations propagated by the allies and later by the CDU-led government, the legal framework appeared to suggest that unions should act first and foremost as the representatives of the interests of their members, negotiating with employers to set terms and conditions of employment, and not at all as the agents of government or the bearers of public office.

In the decades following the end of the Second World War, the legal framework remained essentially unchanged. The realities of German industrial relations contradicted the expectations raised by the legal framework in a number of respects. Notwithstanding the promulgation in law of the principle of *Tarifautonomie*, trade unions and employers' associations were closely involved with the state, bound to it by bonds of mutual dependence, and acting themselves to fulfil a variety of state or public functions. Germany was not a liberal market economy but a corporatist, or 'welfare corporatist' state; trade unions and employers' associations were not, straightforwardly, interest representatives but rather para-public organizations, working at times in furtherance of public, not private, aims. Looking back to the Weimar Republic, Streeck's discussion of welfare corporatism brought to mind the suggestion made by Ernst Fraenkel that the participation of trade unions and employers in public administration could be understood as constituting steps towards a real economic constitution, as opposed to one that was merely posited by the terms of the labour legislation or constitution. Whereas the organizational scheme of a 'council constitution' provided for in the Weimar Constitution had not been realized, in Fraenkel's opinion the functional idea behind the scheme had been implemented to some extent by the assumption, on the part of the unions and employers' associations, of regulatory and administrative roles. In this way, workers had become involved in the 'regulation of wages and conditions of employment as well as in the overall economic development of the productive forces'.[205]

---

[205] Art 165, Weimar Constitution.

In the past 20 years or so, the importance of state support for the German model of industrial relations has been illustrated by the emergence of a trend towards decentralization or 'disorganization'. The removal of state support for collectivized, centralized industrial relations has not taken the form of labour law reform, as it did in the UK. It has occurred less directly through state orchestration or encouragement of the privatization of public enterprise, the dismantling of the system of tripartite administration of social policy, and the dissolution of the institutional complex of German corporate governance. Because all of these had functioned in important ways as props to the collective organization of labour and capital, and sectoral collective bargaining, their disorganization has contributed directly and indirectly to decreases both in the membership of employers' associations and especially trade unions, and in collective bargaining density. At the same time, it has meant the reduction of the status of the unions and employers' associations from state-sponsored national interest representatives with important 'para-public' functions to a position more akin to that of lobbyists. As a result, the ability of the organizations to act according to the 'logic of influence' has decreased, and they have become more dependent on 'the logic of membership'. If the term 'labour constitution' is understood to retain anything of the sense in which Sinzheimer used it, implying a significant measure of state support and oversight of a coordinated system of labour participation in the administration of the economy, then the question arises whether its application to Germany today is less appropriate than it once was.

4
A Labour Constitution Without the State? Otto Kahn-Freund and Collective Laissez-Faire

Introduction

The system of industrial relations that existed in Britain in the first half of the twentieth century is often described as 'voluntarist' or 'abstentionist'. In substance, the system involved industry-level collective bargaining between trade unions and employers' associations. The implication of the description voluntarist or abstentionist then is that industry-level collective bargaining proceeded for several decades independently of the state without, or with only minimal, legal regulation.[1] In the 1950s, Otto Kahn-Freund famously coined the term 'collective laissez-faire' to describe what he understood to be the particularities of the British system at the time. Like voluntarism and abstentionism, the label 'collective laissez-faire' appeared on the face of it to imply a system somehow insulated from government intervention: a sphere of action which the state left alone.

The principle of collective laissez-faire was first developed by Kahn-Freund in a trilogy of works published in 1954 and 1959.[2] In terms of a definition, Kahn-Freund juxtaposed the notion of *collective* laissez-faire with laissez-faire approaches to economic regulation. In the UK, collective bargaining was promoted by government as the preferred means of setting terms and conditions of employment and of settling industrial disputes. Rather than intervening directly in industrial relations, government left it to trade unions and employers to negotiate the rules that would govern working lives, and the rules that would govern collective dispute resolution. Instead of allowing for 'the free play of the laws of a market between individuals assumed to be equal', as Kahn-Freund put it, government policy in industrial relations was directed at promoting 'free play to the collective forces of society . . . the forces of organised labour and of organised management'.[3] In the 1960s, he used the term as descriptive still of the British

---

[1] C Howell, *Trade Unions and the State: The Construction of Industrial Relations Institutions in Britain, 1890–2000* (Princeton 2005), 7–14
[2] O Kahn-Freund, 'Legal Framework' in A Flanders and HA Clegg, *The System of Industrial Relations in Great Britain* (Oxford 1954); O Kahn-Freund, 'Intergroup Conflicts and their Settlement' (1954) 5 *British Journal of Sociology* 193–227; O Kahn-Freund, 'Labour Law' in M Ginsberg (ed) *Law and Opinion in England in the 20th Century* (London 1959), 215–63.
[3] 'Labour Law', 224.

approach to regulating industrial relations, and as desirable still in policy terms. During the 1970s, he amended his analysis and prescriptions for labour law in line with his changing perceptions of industrial relations in the UK, concluding in 1979 that collective laissez-faire as a normative principle was in urgent need of 'adjustment'.[4]

Commensurate with the measure of its influence on the development of the law and on legal scholarship in the UK and beyond, the principle of collective laissez-faire has been the subject of a great deal of academic comment over the years, not all of it wholly positive.[5] Some have questioned its adequacy as an explanation of the historical development of labour law, concerned that it encourages a disregard for the real struggles of workers and trade unions to have a variety of legal rights recognized by Parliament.[6] Others have cast doubt upon its normative value, Hugh Collins arguing, for example, that it is predicated on a false assertion of the impotence of law to regulate most aspects of industrial relations.[7] As the years have passed, it has increasingly been described as offering a framework for analysis that has become outdated.[8]

With the aim of assessing the usefulness of collective laissez-faire as an analytical framework or paradigm, the first part of the chapter seeks to read the collective laissez-faire works of the 1950s as one part of a much broader contribution to the study of labour law, spanning the Weimar writings of the 1930s and the last published work, *Heritage and Adjustment*, from 1979. When considered with reference to Kahn-Freund's later and earlier work, collective laissez-faire figures more clearly, it is argued, as just one episode in a life-long series of efforts to advocate a particular conception of social and economic justice. Throughout his life, Kahn-Freund adhered to the belief that the employment relation must be characterized with reference primarily to the imbalance of power between the employer and employee; that in order to right this imbalance, and so to place employees in a position to secure for themselves fair terms and conditions of employment, labour must be collectivized. Throughout his life, he remained consistent too in the belief that trade unions and employers' associations ought to enjoy a wide

---

[4] O Kahn-Freund, *Labour Relations: Heritage and Adjustment* (Oxford 1979), 88. See also Kahn-Freund, 'Labour Law and Industrial Relations in Great Britain and West Germany', 2: 'very many Britons ask themselves if the autonomy of the collective bargaining parties does not go too far.'

[5] Alan Bogg discusses such criticism and mounts a sustained defence of the theory of collective laissez-faire in A Bogg, *Democratic Aspects of Trade Union Recognition* (Oxford 2009), chapter 1.

[6] R Lewis, 'Kahn-Freund and Labour Law: an Outline Critique' (1979) 8 *Industrial Law Journal* 202–21, 217–18; KD Ewing, 'The State and Industrial Relations: "Collective laissez-faire" Revisited' (1998) 5 *Historical Studies in Industrial Relations* 1–31; N Fishman, '"A Vital Element in British Industrial Relations": A Reassessment of Order 1305, 1940–51' (1999) 8 *Historical Studies in Industrial Relations* 43–86.

[7] H Collins, 'Against Abstentionism in Labour Law', in J Eekelaar and J Bell (eds) *Oxford Essays in Jurisprudence* (Oxford 1987), 79–101.

[8] See eg 'Editors' Introduction' in P Davies and M Freedland (eds) *Kahn-Freund's Labour and the Law* (3rd ed) (London 1983). Brian Langille, among others, doubts the continued relevance of even the fundamental premise upon which the principle was based: the need for labour law to address the inequality of bargaining power in the contract of employment: B Langille, 'Labour Law's Theory of Justice' in G Davidov and B Langille (eds) *The Idea of Labour Law* (Oxford 2011), 105.

measure of autonomy in the regulation of industrial relations.[9] For Kahn-Freund, these were questions of democratic principle. The existence of trade unions and of mechanisms for the bipartite regulation of industry meant the extension of democracy from the political to the economic sphere.[10] The defence of the autonomy of trade unions and employers' associations was a defence against the possibility of pernicious levels of centralized state power, and the possibility, ultimately, of a descent into totalitarianism. Collective laissez-faire was the embodiment of these core principles as applied in the context of 1950s Britain.[11] What was particularly attractive about British labour law to Kahn-Freund, and what he sought to emphasize by referring to the idea of laissez-faire in this context, was the way in which a system of collective industrial relations was achieved and maintained without the kind of state intervention that would compromise too greatly the collective parties' independence and freedom of action. Legal intervention in industrial relations in the UK tended to be *indirect*, aimed at reinforcing the autonomy of the collective parties in respect both of the negotiation of terms and conditions of employment and the resolution of collective disputes.[12]

In emphasizing the degree of independence from the state which the collective parties enjoyed, the extent to which they met and bargained outside the reaches of the law, Kahn-Freund—a master of comparative law—sought to make the case both for the uniqueness of the British system and for the benefits of that system over others.[13] In doing so, he was capable at times of overstating or exaggerating certain features of the law or system of industrial relations in order to give force to his arguments. It is for that reason, it is suggested, that certain phrases or passages from the 'collective laissez-faire' trilogy can seem, when taken out of context, to suggest that the principle was intended to denote a complete absence of law or state intervention: 'the retreat of law from industrial relations and of industrial relations from the law'.[14]

On the basis of this interpretation of Kahn-Freund's work, the second part of the chapter considers the adequacy of collective laissez-faire as an explanation of the historical development of labour law in the UK. Here it is suggested that while collective laissez-faire may be understood to provide a reasonably accurate description of the type of state intervention in industrial relations typical of the first half of the twentieth century, as an account of the origins and persistence of the British 'system', it is less satisfactory. In particular, the idea of collective laissez-faire tends, misleadingly, to suggest that British trade unionists were united in opposing the use of legal rights to further members' interest, and that it is this opposition, first and foremost, which explains the 'non-interventionist' nature of the British system. It tends, misleadingly, to underemphasize or obscure

---

[9] See below 6–8, 13–15.   [10] See eg Kahn-Freund, 'Legal Framework', 49–51.
[11] This is particularly clear in O Kahn-Freund 'Industrial Relations and the Law—Retrospect and Prospect' (1969) 7 *British Journal of Industrial Relations* 301–16.
[12] See eg Kahn-Freund, 'Legal Framework', 65–6.
[13] For a similar reading of the principle of collective laissez-faire see S Deakin and F Wilkinson, *The Law of the Labour Market: Industrialization, Employment and Legal Evolution* (Oxford 2004), 200 ff.   [14] Kahn-Freund, 'Labour Law', 225.

the importance of employer preferences and economic arguments in shaping government policy. Perhaps it can be concluded that Kahn-Freund, like Sinzheimer, was not immediately concerned to explain the nature of the political compromises involved in the drafting and adoption of collective labour legislation or the policy priorities of the governments of the time. His concern was rather to analyse the provisions of the legislation such that they fit with his normative vision of collectivized labour bargaining collectively with management, free from state control.

Collective Laissez-Faire

Weimar collectivism

Kahn-Freund was born in Frankfurt-am-Main in 1900. As a young man, he studied law under Sinzheimer at the University of Frankfurt. Having completed a PhD on the normative effect of collective agreements, he worked between 1928 and 1933 as a judge in the Berlin labour court.[15] During the latter period, he published two works which addressed the question of the role of the Weimar state in the regulation of industrial relations. These were *Das Soziale Ideal des Reichsarbeitsgerichts*, a short monograph from 1931, and 'Der Funktionswandel des Arbeitsrechts', an article from 1932, published in translation as 'The Social Ideal of the Reich Labour Court' and 'The Changing Function of Labour Law'.[16] As has been discussed in chapter 2, both of these publications are striking for the extent to which they evidence a growing suspicion of an overly zealous state—an awareness of the potential dangers of a system which, as Kahn-Freund saw it, allowed for state interference in the rightful autonomy of the collective parties. Behind the scholarly and measured tone of the pieces, it is not difficult to imagine the strength of feeling that must have informed their writing. In describing the weakening of the collectivist system of industrial relations through the interventions of the state, Kahn-Freund was describing nothing less than the weakening of the Republic's democratic defences against the rise of fascism.[17]

For present purposes, the most interesting aspect of the Weimar writings is Kahn-Freund's identification of 'collectivism' as the basic underlying principle of collective labour law. In 'The Changing Function of Labour Law', he discussed collectivism in a way which highlighted the desirability of a limited measure of state intervention in industrial relations.

> The socio-political system of collectivism is characterised by a particular attitude of the state towards the class struggle. The legal system does not negate the class struggle or suppress it, but it does not allow it unlimited freedom; it rather attempts, within the framework of the capitalist system, to determine the way it is conducted by the establishment of legal norms and, over and above this, to utilise the results of each individual stage of conflict for the further development of the law.[18]

---

[15] For further biographical detail, see M Freedland, 'Otto Kahn-Freund' and 'Introduction' in Lewis and Clark.   [16] In Lewis and Clark.   [17] Clark, 98.
[18] O Kahn-Freund, 'The Changing Function of Labour Law' in R Lewis and J Clark (eds) *Labour Law and Politics in the Weimar Republic* (Oxford 1981), 172.

What was envisaged here was that the state should allow the trade unions and employers' associations freedom to regulate social policy through the autonomous negotiation of collective agreements, and should give its support to that regulation by guaranteeing the agreements' 'compulsory normative effect'. When, in fact, the state used the system of arbitration to give legal effect to its own policy aims; when it treated the unions and employers' associations as existing to further its own interests, then it acted, in Kahn-Freund's opinion, quite contrary to the principle of collectivism.

The belief that the undermining of collective institutions contributed to the rise of Nazism was something that stayed with Kahn-Freund throughout his life.[19] So too did his experiences of living in and being forced to flee the Weimar Republic for England, of learning from there of the horrors of Nazi rule. The opening sentence of an autobiography, which he began but never finished, read: 'The most important single fact of my life is that I am a Jew.'[20] Asked in 1979 about his decision to remain in England after the war, and to devote the remainder or his life to the study of English, and not German law, he replied:

Did I consider going back after the War? I'll answer with Goethe: *In demselben Flusse/ Schwimmst Du nicht zum zweitenmal.* It won't do. Whatever I say about present conditions in Germany is conditioned by my own past and by the impossibility of seeing things in Germany today in the same way in which I could see things in another country. The past is too strong, the emotional influence of the past is too strong.[21]

The break with Germany was, in one sense, final. In another, it was to prove a significant and lasting influence on his life's work.[22] In the words of Thilo Ramm, it was 'the most decisive experience of his life'.[23]

On arriving in London in 1933, Kahn-Freund embarked upon a period of study at the London School of Economics (LSE), completing an LLM in 1935 and qualifying as a barrister in the Middle Temple in 1936. He was appointed as an assistant lecturer at the LSE in 1936, promoted to professor in 1951, and remained there until 1964, leaving eventually to take up the Chair of Comparative Law at the University of Oxford.[24] In his earliest works on English labour law, published in the 1940s, Kahn-Freund applied his existing knowledge of German collectivism quite straightforwardly to the industrial relations and labour legislation of the UK. This was apparent in his emphasis of the notion of the individual contract of employment as a mask for the subordination of the employee,[25] of the potential for conflict between the judiciary and a more progressive legislature,[26] and,

---

[19] See eg 'Preface' to O Kahn Freund, *Arbeit und Recht* (Cologne, Frankfurt 1979) published in translation as 'Labour Law and Industrial Relations in Great Britain and West Germany' in Wedderburn, Lewis, Clark, 7.
[20] T Ramm, 'Otto Kahn-Freund und Deutschland' in F Gamillscheg (ed) *In Memoriam Sir Otto Kahn-Freund* (Munich 1980), xxi.   [21] Kahn-Freund, 'Postscript', 201.
[22] Kahn-Freund, 'Postscript', 199.
[23] Ramm, 'Otto Kahn-Freund und Deutschland', xxi.
[24] Freedland, 'Otto Kahn-Freund', 306–8.
[25] A 'command under the guise of an agreement': O Kahn-Freund, 'Introduction' to K. Renner, *The Institutions of Private Law and their Social Functions* (London 1976), 28.
[26] O Kahn-Freund, 'The Illegality of a Trade Union' (1944) 7 *Modern Law Review* 192–205.

most particularly, in his analysis of collective agreements.[27] During the 1950s, he re-evaluated parts of this early work, rejecting the method of applying German law principles almost unquestioningly to English circumstances. In the course of the discussion that follows, it is argued that the experience of living and working in the Weimar Republic continued nonetheless to influence Kahn-Freund's writing, helping in particular to shape the explanation of the desirable role of the state and legislation in industrial relations which found expression in the idea of collective laissez-faire.

From 'war legislation' to 1950s 'collective laissez-faire'

Kahn-Freund's first work on collective labour law in the UK was published in the *Modern Law Review* in 1943.[28] The aim of the article, it explained, was to subject the British collective agreement, and the wartime legislation that had given it its 'new legal status', to rigorous legal analysis.[29] Reflecting on the work in 1979, Kahn-Freund recalled that his tendency at the time had been, 'to try and inflict my ideas on English law, that is to legalize the whole collective bargaining process and the [collective] agreement'.[30] Indicative of this tendency was the contrast drawn at the beginning of the article between the 'contractual' and the 'normative' functions of collective agreements. This corresponded exactly to Sinzheimer's distinction between an agreement's obligatory and normative functions.[31] The substance of the distinction was that collective agreements functioned as a 'contract' between the collective parties that agreed it, and as a source of rules (terms and conditions of employment) between the members of the collective parties, the employers and their employees. In applying the distinction to British collective agreements, Kahn-Freund concluded that such agreements were contractual in the legal sense: that the trade unions and employers or employers' associations party to them were legally bound to abide by their terms.[32] This was the 'legalization' of the collective bargaining process that he referred to in 1979.

The 'War Legislation' of the title of the 1943 article was the Conditions of Employment and National Arbitration Order 1940 (Order 1305).[33] With the intention of reducing the incidence of industrial action and ensuring uninterrupted production, the Order instituted mechanisms for the 'compulsory arbitration' of industrial disputes, the 'compulsory effect of collective terms as between Members of Contracting Parties' (compulsory effect), and the 'extension of the effect of collective terms to outsiders' (extension effect).[34] From Kahn-Freund's

---

[27] O Kahn-Freund, 'Collective Agreements under War Legislation' (1943) 6 *Modern Law Review* 112–43.   [28] Kahn-Freund, 'War Legislation'.

[29] Kahn-Freund 'War Legislation', 112–13.

[30] O Kahn-Freund, 'The Study of Labour Law—Some Recollections' (1979) 8 *Industrial Law Journal* 197–201, 200.

[31] H Sinzheimer, *Grundzüge*, 252. The analysis was attributed to Sinzheimer explicitly in later work: Kahn-Freund 'Intergroup Conflicts'.   [32] Kahn-Freund, 'War Legislation', 114.

[33] Made on July 18 1940, under powers conferred by the Emergency Powers (Defence) Act 1940. See further Fishman.   [34] Kahn-Freund, 'War Legislation', 119–22.

analysis of the relevant provisions, and from the terminology he used to describe them, it may be readily surmised that he had in mind the corresponding provisions of the Weimar Collective Agreements Decree of 1918. Moreover, in judging compulsory arbitration 'an undesirable institution', he explained his opinion with explicit reference to his Weimar experiences.[35] 'The present writer attempted to demonstrate the disastrous consequences of compulsory arbitration in Germany in [his Weimar publications]. It is still his conviction that compulsory arbitration is incompatible with voluntary trade unionism, and that it has a close affinity to Fascist legal institutions.'[36]

If in Kahn-Freund's first work on English labour law he tended to interpret what he saw through the lens of his prior knowledge of German law and Sinzheimer collectivism, the 'collective laissez-faire' writings of the 1950s revealed a change of heart.[37] No longer were collective agreements to be regarded as legally binding contracts between the collective parties. Now the emphasis was on the extent to which industrial relations in the UK were practised beyond the reaches of the law. 'There is, perhaps, no major country in the world in which the law has played a less significant role in the shaping of these relations than in Great Britain and in which to-day the law and the legal profession have less to do with labour relations.'[38] Contrary to what he had earlier thought, collective agreements were *not* legally binding contracts for the reason that the parties to them lacked contractual intent: 'They are intended to yield "rights" and "duties", but not in the legal sense; they are intended, as it is sometimes put, to be "binding in honour" only, or (which amounts to very much the same thing) to be enforceable through social sanctions but not through legal sanctions).'[39] Though it was possible for the normative parts of collective agreements to be made legally binding through incorporation into individual contracts of employment, the matter of incorporation was consensual and non-compulsory.[40] In comparison to Weimar Germany, no legal rule existed in the UK which rendered the terms of collective agreements legally binding as a matter of course.[41]

The significance of the reappraisal of the legal nature of collective agreements was considerable: if the agreements were not legally binding, then it was for the collective parties, and not the courts, to *interpret, apply*, and *enforce* them.[42] From a comparative point of view, this informed the conclusion that, in Britain, trade unions enjoyed a greater measure of autonomy from the state than was the case

---

[35] Kahn-Freund, 'War Legislation', 120–1.
[36] Kahn-Freund, 'War Legislation', 121, note 30.
[37] Kahn-Freund, 'Legal Framework'; Kahn-Freund, 'Intergroup Conflicts'; Kahn-Freund, 'Labour Law'. [38] Kahn-Freund, 'Legal Framework', 44.
[39] Kahn-Freund, 'Legal Framework', 57–8.
[40] Kahn-Freund, 'Legal Framework', 58–61.
[41] From 1940 until 1980, a variety of statutory provisions were in place that allowed for collective agreements to be given compulsory effect, and for the extension of that compulsory effect to employers and employees who were not members of the parties to the agreements: Kahn-Freund, 'Legal Framework', 83–101.
[42] Kahn-Freund, 'Legal Framework', 44. See also Kahn-Freund 'Intergroup Conflicts', especially 202–10.

in other countries.⁴³ 'British industrial relations have, in the main, developed by way of industrial autonomy . . . [E]mployers and employees have formulated their own codes of conduct and devised their own machinery for enforcing them.'⁴⁴ For that reason, the British system could be regarded as more mature than other systems: trade union organization and collective labour-management relations had developed in this country to the point where there was little need for legal sanctions.⁴⁵ That was not to say, however, that there was *no* legal regulation of trade unions and collective action in the UK. At the end of the nineteenth and the beginning of the twentieth centuries, a series of legislative steps had been taken to create a legal freedom to organize and take industrial action. Limitations had been placed on that freedom, signifying 'the limits within which the community is willing to tolerate warfare and peacemaking by the autonomous forces of industry'.⁴⁶ In addition, a wide variety of legal and non-legal methods had been used, since the turn of the century, to encourage employers and unions to enter into collective bargaining arrangements with one another.⁴⁷

It is during the course of Kahn-Freund's long and detailed discussion of such legislation that it becomes clear that collective laissez-faire could not have been intended to imply an *absence* of law or state intervention.⁴⁸ The point was, rather, that legal intervention in the UK tended to be indirect and not direct, aimed at persuading rather than requiring trade unions and employers to negotiate terms and conditions of employment and to resolve disputes peacefully.⁴⁹ For Kahn-Freund, it was highly significant, for example, that the question of whether or not to submit an industrial dispute to conciliation, mediation, or arbitration was, as a matter of law, almost always for the unions and employers' associations themselves to decide.⁵⁰ Similarly, the 'extension effect' provisions, designed to extend the terms of a collective agreement to employers and employees not party to it, could not be invoked by the government, but only by the relevant union or employers' association. '[T]he groups themselves are the exclusive guardians of the intergroup standards, and it is . . . for no one else to decide whether the machinery of the law should be invoked for their enforcement.'⁵¹ Moreover, where industrial disputes were referred to external bodies (the Industrial Court or Industrial Disputes Tribunal), those bodies were 'completely independent' from the Minister of Labour. If the bodies gave effect to government policies within the terms of their orders, they did so because they regarded them as justified and not

---

⁴³ Kahn-Freund 'Legal Framework', 45.   ⁴⁴ Kahn-Freund, 'Legal Framework', 45.
⁴⁵ Kahn-Freund, 'Legal Framework', 43; Kahn-Freund, 'Intergroup Conflicts', 195.
⁴⁶ Kahn-Freund, 'Intergroup Conflicts', 215.
⁴⁷ Kahn-Freund 'Legal Framework', 101. In 'Legal Framework', there is discussion in particular of compulsory arbitration (83–101), of a range of statutory provisions intended to make the terms of collective agreements legally binding (58–65), 'Minimum Wage legislation' (65–75), fair wages clauses (75–83).
⁴⁸ In 'Labour Law' he describes the volume of statute law and subordinate legislation passed during the first half of the twentieth century as 'gigantic', and proceeds to explain why it was nonetheless 'subsidiary' to collective bargaining: 245, 250.   ⁴⁹ See eg 'Legal Framework', 65–6.
⁵⁰ Kahn-Freund 'Legal Framework', 91.
⁵¹ Kahn-Freund, 'Intergroup Conflicts', 212.

because they were legally bound to do so.[52] In British labour legislation and administrative practice, the notion of autonomy was 'fundamental'.[53]

As he developed the principle of collective laissez-faire in this way, Kahn-Freund was of course wholly conscious of the fact that the new analysis represented a partial rejection of earlier views. [54] Later in life, he described his realization that 'the whole method of legal analysis to which I had been used in my previous life just did not fit conditions in this country'.[55] The change of heart was attributed to contact with other academics at the LSE and Cambridge, and to his growing knowledge of the reality of industrial relations in the UK.

> The crisis in my thinking came towards the end of the War. I saw a great deal of Harold Laski, and of people like Lance Beales who had a tremendous knowledge of the history of industrial relations. It was probably the constant contact with these men that made me see that there was something wrong in my approach. The result is the totally different attitude shown in the 1954 contribution.[56]

A review of contemporary authorities reveals that Kahn-Freund's re-classification of collective agreements as not legally binding followed, in the words of Hugh Clegg, the 'generally accepted account of the working of British collective bargaining at that time'.[57] In his 1959 article on 'Intergroup Conflicts', Kahn-Freund cited the Ministry of Labour's 1953 *Industrial Relations Handbook* and Walter Milne-Bailey's 1929 *Trade Union Documents* as authority for the re-classification.[58] The latter text in particular was quite clear on the point: 'The Agreement itself ... is a "gentlemen's agreement" only. It is not legally binding, as such, though its terms may expressly or by implication become the terms of the individual contract of employment.'[59] Though he was not referenced in this context by Kahn-Freund, it is interesting to note that Allan Flanders, Kahn-Freund's friend and co-author, also confirmed 'the generally accepted account'. In his 1952 work, *Trade Unions*, Flanders explained, in terms which echoed Milne-Bailey, that 'voluntary negotiated agreements ... have not even the legal force of a business contract, although their provisions may expressly or by implication become the terms of the individual contract of employment.'[60] More generally, Flanders' 1952 chapter on 'Collective Bargaining' is notable for the similarity of coverage and tone which it shares with Kahn-Freund's 1954 and 1959 works 'Legal Framework' and 'Labour Law'.[61]

---

[52] Kahn-Freund, 'Intergroup Conflicts', 215–22; Kahn-Freund 'Labour Law', 239.
[53] Kahn-Freund, 'Legal Framework', 45.
[54] Kahn-Freund, 'Legal Framework', 56, note 4.
[55] Kahn-Freund, 'The Study of Labour Law', 200.
[56] Kahn-Freund, 'The Study of Labour Law', 200. See also R Lewis 'Collective Agreements: The Kahn-Freund Legacy' (1979) 42 *Modern Law Review* 613–22, 617–18.
[57] H Clegg, 'Otto Kahn-Freund and British Industrial Relations' in Wedderburn, Lewis, Clark, 24. Compare, though, F Tillyard and WA Robson, 'The Enforcement of the Collective Bargain in the United Kingdom' (1938) 48 *Economic Journal* 15–25, discussed by Lewis, 'The Kahn-Freund Legacy', 615–17.   [58] Kahn-Freund, 'Intergroup Conflicts', 210, note 68.
[59] W Milne-Bailey, *Trade Union Documents* (London 1929), 212.
[60] A Flanders, *Trade Unions* (London 1952), 77.
[61] According to Alan Bogg, Kahn-Freund was closer in thinking to Hugh Clegg than to Flanders: Bogg, chapter 1.

It seems significant then that in explaining the development of his thinking in later life, Kahn-Freund did not refer to the industrial relations experts Milne-Bailey and Flanders but rather to the political scientist, Harold Laski, and the historian, Hugh Beales. The suggestion is that there was rather more to the development of the principle of collective laissez-faire than a realization that collective agreements were not, after all, contractually legally binding. A comparison of Kahn-Freund's work on Weimar law and Order 1305 with his description of collective laissez-faire reveals that the latter also involved an adjustment of Kahn-Freund's wider understanding of the desirable role of the state in industrial relations. In his work on Weimar collectivism, Kahn-Freund had argued against state intervention to decide the outcomes of collective bargaining and dispute resolution processes, but had, at the same time, acknowledged the role of the state in creating the framework within which the collective parties bargained and negotiated. 'The legal system does not negate the class struggle or suppress it, but it does not allow it unlimited freedom; it rather attempts . . . to determine the way it is conducted by the establishment of legal norms and, over and above this, to utilise the results of each individual stage of conflict for the further development of the law.'[62] In his work on collective laissez-faire, there was a rather greater emphasis on the capacity of the collective parties to define for themselves the rules of the game. Comparing shop steward representation of workers in the UK with the 'elaborate legal system of works councils' in France and Germany, for example, Kahn-Freund wrote: 'it is, in the writer's opinion, an illusion to think that the law can guarantee a functioning system of workers' representation or of joint consultation. It is much better to leave these matters, including the rules applicable to grievance procedures, to collective bargaining.'[63]

What had informed this change of emphasis, I think, was Kahn-Freund's growing apprehension—developed through discussions with Laski and Beales, perhaps through a study of their work—of the pluralist nature of British society.[64] As Kahn-Freund himself now observed, there was an increasing tendency in the British society of the twentieth century for interest groups to participate in a variety of 'governmental' functions. 'The line between "State" and "society" has been blurred very deliberately, or to put it differently, the "pressure" of the pressure groups has been so organised as to work inside the legislative, administrative, judicial and policy making processes.'[65] This 'growth of "pluralism"' was of particular significance for labour relations.[66] At the time he was writing, trade unions and employers' associations participated, in the UK, in legislation, in administration, in the judicial process and 'above all' in policy making. Not only the Houses of Parliament and the Ministry of Labour, but also the General Council of the

---

[62] Kahn-Freund, 'Changing Function of Labour Law', 172.
[63] Kahn-Freund, 'Legal Framework', 51.
[64] The influence of English pluralism on Kahn-Freund is examined at greater length in Bogg, chapter 1, and in Lewis, 'Collective Agreements'.   [65] Kahn-Freund, 'Labour Law', 226.
[66] Kahn-Freund, 'Labour Law', 226.

TUC, the employers' associations and the trade unions were rightly regarded as 'part of the British Constitution'.[67]

It is easy to appreciate why the young Kahn-Freund should have embraced with enthusiasm the notion of England as a peaceful, pluralist society, governed not by a centralist, all-powerful 'State' but by a variety of self-governing associations: trade unions, churches, voluntary bodies. Describing his arrival, with his wife, in London, he explained: 'Consider the situation of two still fairly young people moving from the Germany to the England of 1933. Can you understand the admiration we felt for the civilized way things were conducted here?'[68] Whereas the German state and its representatives were, by 1933, something to be feared, England struck the Kahn-Freunds as a place where people discussed and did not shout, a place with 'an inherited political and social culture in which everyone participated, including the workers in the unions'.[69] Whereas the Weimar state had been too interventionist in industrial relations, limiting the autonomy of the collective parties and suppressing the expression of their interests, the British state was mercifully absent.

The Donovan Commission and beyond

Between 1965 and 1968, Kahn-Freund served as a member of the Royal Commission on the Reform of Trade Unions and Employers' Associations (the Donovan Commission). The Commission was called by a Labour government in the midst of a crisis in industrial relations of constitutional proportions, and was tasked with making recommendations for the improvement of 'relations between managements and employees'.[70] Reflecting in the 1980s on his own experiences of working on the Commission, Hugh Clegg suggested that by the mid 1960s Kahn-Freund's perception of British industrial relations had changed quite radically from that which had informed his development of the idea of collective laissez-faire. In the 1950s, Kahn-Freund, 'had followed, perhaps a little too readily, the generally accepted account of the working of British collective bargaining at that time in order to draw his illuminating comparisons with systems of collective bargaining overseas'.[71] Further study of trade unions and collective bargaining had revealed that 'intergroup relations' were not as central to the regulation of industrial relations as Kahn-Freund had once thought. Centralized union leaderships and employers associations acting at industry level were not always responsible for formulating terms and conditions of employment; by the 1960s, such institutions had been undermined by the development of informal and uncontrolled workplace-level collective bargaining and industrial action. They did not deserve the description 'mature' so much as 'decaying'. In recognizing the current

---

[67] Kahn-Freund, 'Labour Law', 226. Kahn-Freund cites Ferdinand Lassalle, 'On the Essence of Constitutions'. [68] Kahn-Freund, 'Postscript', 199.
[69] Kahn-Freund, 'Postscript', 199.
[70] Davies and Freedland explain the nature of the crisis: *Labour Legislation and Public Policy*, 242–3. [71] Clegg, 24.

state of industrial relations in the UK and by becoming involved, through participation in the work of the Donovan Commission, in the efforts to remedy its weaknesses, Kahn-Freund had 'fallen out of love with the British system'.[72]

How did this altered view of the realities of industrial relations affect Kahn-Freund's analysis of the potential role of labour law? In work written in the late 1960s and early 1970s it is possible to discern a less uncompromising attitude towards the use of direct legal intervention in industrial relations than that implied by the principle of collective laissez-faire. In a 'Note on the Legal Enforceability of Collective Agreements' prepared for the Donovan Commission, for example, Kahn-Freund proposed the involvement of the Minister of Labour in referring matters for compulsory arbitration, and the use of legal sanctions to ensure compliance with arbitration orders.[73] The note suggests a marked change in attitude from that expressed in earlier work. In his Weimar publications, and in the 'Collective Agreements' article of 1943, Kahn-Freund strongly disapproved of the use of compulsory arbitration to impose terms and conditions on collective parties which had been set externally by a third party body. This type of compulsory arbitration, he concluded, was incompatible with voluntary trade unionism and had a close affinity to fascist legal institutions.[74] In the 1950s, he examined the nature of arbitration and mediation in the UK in rather more depth and concluded that it had not, in this country, 'killed voluntary bargaining. On the contrary, in some cases [it] may have stimulated voluntary negotiation'.[75] What he was then concerned to emphasize, however, were the differences between compulsory arbitration in the Weimar Republic and in the UK. In the latter country, it was almost always for the collective parties themselves to decide whether a matter should be dealt with by arbitration. Where arbitration was undertaken by a third party, that party's independence from the government was guaranteed. In the 1968 note, Kahn-Freund recommended the introduction of a second mechanism to allow the submission, *by the Minister of Labour*, of a procedural dispute to arbitration. He suggested, furthermore, that in certain circumstances the procedural parts of collective agreements as determined by the arbitrator should be made legally binding and that in the case of violation of those parts trade unions and individuals should be liable to pay damages.[76]

Read in connection with further writings from the period, it seems that the change in attitude regarding compulsory arbitration may have been informed by Kahn-Freund's perception of the need to bring 'order' back to industrial relations—one of the key concerns of the Donovan Commission.[77] In line with earlier writings, he continued to insist that 'the main object of labour law has

---

[72] Clegg, 23.
[73] Prepared for the Donovan Commission. O Kahn-Freund, RC/P/224, 1–3.
[74] Kahn-Freund, 'War Legislation', 121, note 30.
[75] Kahn-Freund, 'Legal Framework', 96.
[76] For a fuller discussion see Dukes, 'Otto Kahn-Freund and Collective Laissez-Faire', 238–9.
[77] Lord Wedderburn, 'Otto Kahn-Freund and British Labour Law', in Lord Wedderburn, R Lewis, J Clark (eds) *Labour Law and Industrial Relations: Building on Kahn-Freund* (Oxford 1983), 48.

always been, and we venture to say will always be, to be a countervailing force to counteract the inequality of bargaining power which is inherent and must be inherent in the employment relationship'. He now added to this, however, the arguably contradictory statement that 'the principal purpose of labour law, then, is to regulate, to support and to restrain the power of management and the power of organised labour'.[78] In a 1970 article, meanwhile, he wrote that the opposition of trade unions to legal intervention in their internal affairs was not a sign of strength or maturity but a 'dead hand of history . . . at a time when their power in society was not comparable to what it is now'. Now it was time to remove the dead hand, albeit 'with caution and a realisation that the distrust of the unions against the courts and the lawyers is well grounded'.[79] Though this was not a widespread problem, it was true that some trade unions were controlling access to some sections of the labour market in a way that was morally reprehensible.[80] Legal intervention could act to remedy this.[81] In 1972, Kahn-Freund strongly criticized the types of picketing practised during the miners' strike of that year.[82] In recognition perhaps of the change of emphasis in his own writing in this respect, he concluded: 'Perhaps those who have with so much justification always argued against legal intervention beyond the point of absolute necessity should now consider the need for emphasising the role which the law still has, and will always have to play in industrial relations.'[83]

In 1977, Kahn-Freund published an article in which he argued strongly against the introduction of worker representation on company boards in the UK, as recommended in that same year by the Committee of Inquiry on Industrial Democracy (the Bullock Committee).[84] Kahn-Freund's analysis in that article revealed a continued adherence to pluralist values and to the belief that conflicts of interest in industrial relations were inevitable. Proposals for employee representation on company boards were rejected by him primarily for their potential 'to prejudice the very clear divide in the pluralist analysis between the management function to manage effectively and the trade union function to oppose independently'.[85] Industrial democracy through collective bargaining was preferable, he argued, because it was pluralistic and therefore realistic and ideologically sound.[86] In explanation of his preferences, Kahn-Freund made explicit reference to the

---

[78] O Kahn-Freund, *Labour and the Law* (London 1972), 8 and 5.

[79] O Kahn-Freund, 'Trade Unions, the Law and Society' (1970) 33 *Modern Law Review* 241–67, 241. [80] Kahn-Freund, 'Trade Unions', 243.

[81] 'In the area of the behaviour of trade unions to their members or potential members the law can play a role': Kahn-Freund, 'Trade Unions', 242.

[82] O Kahn-Freund, 'The Industrial Relations Act 1971—Some Retrospective Reflections' (1974) 3 *Industrial Law Journal* 186–200. [83] Kahn-Freund, 'Industrial Relations Act'.

[84] O Kahn-Freund, 'Industrial Democracy' (1977) 6 *Industrial Law Journal* 65–84. The Committee was charged with investigating the representation of the employees of companies in the private sector on the companies' boards of directors, 'accepting the essential role of trade union organizations in this process'. *Report of the Committee of Inquiry on Industrial Democracy* Cmnd. 6706, 1977.

[85] Lewis 'Outline Critique', 216. For further comment see P Davies and Lord Wedderburn, 'The Land of Industrial Democracy' (1977) 6 *Industrial Law Journal* 197–211.

[86] Lewis 'Kahn-Freund and Labour Law', 216.

original, 'ineffective' provisions for employee representation on company boards contained in the Weimar labour statutes.[87] 'My scepticism towards employee representation in the corporate organs of business enterprise goes back to the time of the experiment made in this direction more than half a century ago under the Weimar Republic.'[88] Indeed, there is a clear parallel between his scepticism about the Bullock Committee's notion of 'the interest of the company' and his scepticism 40 years earlier about the usefulness of the German law concept of the *Betriebszweck*.[89] Now, as then, Kahn-Freund thought it illusory to postulate a single unified interest of a company or workplace when, in fact, these organizations embodied groups with necessarily competing interests.

In his last book, *Labour Relations: Heritage and Adjustment*, published in 1979, Kahn-Freund addressed, at some length, the changing nature of labour relations in the 1970s and the 'adjustments' to policy that those changes necessitated.[90] In contrast to the labour relations of the immediate postwar decades, industrial organization in the late 1970s was notable for the significant growth of the service and white-collar sectors. This development, Kahn-Freund wrote, had resulted in changes in collective bargaining, in the role of legislation, and in the nature of industrial disputes.[91] With respect to collective bargaining, the growth in the service and white-collar sectors had meant the supplementation of voluntary recognition with statutory recognition. Since the 'vital concern' here was to ensure the extension of institutions of collective bargaining, the use of legislation was judged a reasonable response to employer reluctance to recognize unions voluntarily.[92] With respect to the use of legislation more generally, the changed composition of the labour force had caused a 'much enlarged sphere of legislation applicable to the individual relations between employer and employee'.[93] This too was judged a reasonable response to changing circumstances, reflecting both the late growth in collective bargaining in the white-collar and service sectors and the growing political power of the unions under any government.[94] Rather more troublesome for Kahn-Freund was the changed nature of industrial action or, more accurately, the 'social effects' of such action. Changes in the composition of the labour force had meant that the consumer, and not the employer, was now the primary target of industrial action. Where service industries were the site of industrial action, consumers suffered. But the problem extended beyond the services industry: 'The centralization not only of the supply of services but also of some essential goods means that any stoppage or delay or slowing down is likely to expose to serious hardship masses of people who do not have the slightest influence on the outcome of the dispute.'[95] Moreover, since 80–90 per cent of consumers were workers, the result was that the victim in many strikes was the working class itself.[96]

---

[87] Kahn-Freund, 'Industrial Democracy', 72.
[88] Kahn-Freund, 'Industrial Democracy', 83–4.   [89] See chapter 2.
[90] Kahn-Freund, *Labour Relations*.   [91] Kahn-Freund, *Labour Relations*, 73.
[92] Kahn-Freund, *Labour Relations*, 70.   [93] Kahn-Freund, *Labour Relations*, 71.
[94] Kahn-Freund, *Labour Relations*, 72–3.   [95] Kahn-Freund, *Labour Relations*, 76.
[96] Kahn-Freund, *Labour Relations*, 77.

What was to be done to remedy this situation? According to Kahn-Freund, it would have been wrong to attempt to limit the right of workers and trade unions to strike—this was a fundamental right, intrinsic to the maintenance of democracy.[97] In any case, legal intervention could be of only limited use in this context. 'The machinery of the law ... cannot be enforced so as to change the social mores of a large section of the people, establish rules at variance with such mores.'[98] The best hope for bringing more order to industrial relations, for ensuring a decrease in levels of industrial action, and in the types of harm caused to non-striking workers lay with the development of more centralized forms of collective bargaining. Some decision-making power should be devolved upwards, to the TUC and CBI negotiating at the national level, and some devolved downwards to the shop floor. Meanwhile the TUC and the CBI should take greater control of their members, imposing order through the mechanism of centrally negotiated collective agreements. The trade union movement itself must take steps towards this, recognizing that its role was not only to protect workers as producers 'but also as consumers', and, moreover, 'that it can discharge this function only centrally'.[99]

The analysis of industrial relations and the blueprint for their reform presented by Kahn-Freund in *Heritage and Adjustment* exhibited both an adherence to the principle of industrial self-government and, at the same time, a recognition that problems had been caused, at least in part, by adherence to that principle. '[C]ollective laissez-faire may be in need of adjustment more than any other part of the British heritage.'[100] In line with earlier publications from the late 1960s and 1970s, Kahn-Freund's proposals for the reform of collective laissez-fare were framed in terms that acknowledged the potential benefits of legal intervention in industrial relations in some limited respects. Characteristically, they also included an emphatic denial of the ability of law to address either the high incidence of industrial action or the 'internecine' character of its consequences. The solution that Kahn-Freund proposed was built, instead, on a continued belief in the potential of the collective parties (conceived of now in more centralized terms) to regulate industrial relations *autonomously* as they ought to be regulated.

It is true, of course, that in approving the use of legislative intervention to support trade union recognition, to guarantee minimum terms and conditions to workers not covered by collective agreements, and to control the 'misuse of trade union power',[101] Kahn-Freund also gave his approval to a measure of state intervention in industrial relations. But such approval remained implicit. Like earlier works, *Heritage and Adjustment* was notable for its lack of any discussion of the role of the state or the government in regulating industrial relations. In his treatment of the problem of industrial action and the hardship which it could cause to the worker-as-consumer, it is striking above all that Kahn-Freund declined

---

[97] Kahn-Freund, *Labour Relations*, 77.   [98] Kahn-Freund, *Labour Relations*, 79.
[99] Kahn-Freund, *Labour Relations*, 80–4.
[100] Kahn-Freund, *Labour Relations*, 88. See also Kahn-Freund, 'Labour Law and Industrial Relations', 2: 'very many Britons ask themselves if the autonomy of the collective bargaining parties does not go too far'.   [101] Kahn-Freund, 'Trade Unions', 242.

to acknowledge a role for government in protecting consumers from harm and identified instead the *employer* as the representative of consumer interests! '[T]he employer is in such a situation no more than the agent of the consumer, the instrument of the public (in the sense of the amorphous mass of the consumers) for maintaining or regaining the supplies and the services on which they depend.'[102] Thus, Kahn-Freund arrived at the remarkable conclusion that it was the employer who represented the consumer and who embodied the public interest. As a result of the refusal to confront head-on the possibility of a role for government in the regulation of industrial conflict, the consumer interest, the employers' interest, and the national interest were conflated.[103]

Labour Law and the British State: 1890s to 1950s

It has been argued in this chapter that collective laissez-faire was not intended by Kahn-Freund to denote a complete absence of the state and the law in industrial relations, that it was a comment on the quality rather than the quantity of collective labour legislation in force in the UK in the first part of the twentieth century. Much of the discussion in the three 'collective laissez-faire' works of the 1950s was devoted to the very question of how the development of 'mature' collective bargaining arrangements had been supported by labour legislation.[104] There was mention too of the indirect support afforded by full-employment and other economic policies, and of the need for more direct legal intervention in jurisdictions which differed from the UK.[105] In developing the idea of collective laissez-faire, Kahn-Freund sought to give expression to his long-held conviction that trade unions ought to enjoy a wide measure of autonomy, and that too much state intervention was inimical to democracy. In the England of the 1950s, this seemed to chime well with the realities of society as he encountered them—with the liberal preference for small government and with the pluralist 'tradition' of allowing all interested parties a say. In later life, Kahn-Freund adjusted his analysis and prescriptions for labour law in line with his changing perceptions of British industrial relations. For example, he advocated the involvement of the Minister of Labour in compulsory arbitration in some limited circumstances, and the imposition of legal sanctions for breach of arbitration awards. In adherence to his old suspicion of too much state intervention, however, he remained committed throughout his life to a pluralist belief in the potential of the trade unions and employers' associations to regulate industrial relations, for the most part independently of the state, with satisfactory results.

It was mentioned at the outset of this chapter that the principle of collective laissez-faire has been criticized over the years for providing an inadequate

---

[102] Kahn-Freund, *Labour Relations*, 76.
[103] R Lewis, 'Review: Labour Relations: Heritage and Adjustment. By Sir Otto Kahn-Freund' (1981) 44 *Modern Law Review* 239–42, 242. [104] Kahn-Freund, 'Legal Framework'.
[105] Kahn-Freund, 'Intergroup Conflicts', 202, 199.

explanation of the historical development of labour law in the UK. Both Roy Lewis and Keith Ewing have drawn attention, in particular, to the way in which it encourages a disregard for the real struggles of workers and trade unions to have a variety of legal rights recognized by Parliament.[106] For Lewis, this was symptomatic of Kahn-Freund's tendency to overemphasize equilibrium and consensus in industrial relations. In Lewis' opinion, 'the idea of the State maintaining equilibrium between the social forces through legal abstention was simply a myth'.[107] For Ewing, the greater difficulty was the way in which collective laissez-faire underemphasized the measure and importance of state intervention in industrial relations. With its focus on the nature of *legal* intervention in industrial relations, collective laissez-faire tended to underemphasize, in particular, the extent and the practical importance of non-legal methods of intervention. 'Contrary to received wisdom, what we have in the British system is in fact active and legally grounded intervention by the state.'[108]

In assessing the validity of these criticisms, a distinction may usefully be drawn between the question of whether collective laissez-faire provides a reasonably accurate *description* of the realities of British labour law from the 1890s until the 1950s, and the rather different question of whether it provides an accurate account of the origins and persistence of the British system.[109] On a careful reading of Kahn-Freund's work, it would be difficult to argue that it does not provide an adequate description of the type of state intervention in industrial relations typical of the first half of the twentieth century.[110] The system of industrial relations in place at that time was focused around the collective negotiation of wages and the collective resolution of disputes at industry level.[111] From the end of the nineteenth century, legislation guaranteed trade unions freedom to act without incurring legal penalties and without making themselves vulnerable to suit in tort. With the passing of that legislation, the attitude of the law to collective bargaining and industrial action could rightly be said to have moved from suppression to abstention.[112] Over and above these liberalizing measures, however, successive governments took steps actively 'to support the principles of collective bargaining and collective regulation', as Ernest Bevin put it in 1943, speaking as Minister of Labour.[113] Some of these steps were of general application, others were directed at specific industries; some took the form of legislation, others were administrative in nature. As a rule, government intervention was aimed at encouraging rather

---

[106] Lewis, 'Kahn-Freund and Labour Law', 217–18; Ewing, 'The State and Industrial Relations', 1.
[107] Lewis, 'Kahn-Freund and Labour Law', 218.
[108] Ewing, 'The State and Industrial Relations', 2.
[109] Cf Deakin and Wilkinson, 202–3.
[110] With the important caveat, rightly emphasized by Ewing, that state support was largely withdrawn in the period 1922–34: Ewing, 'The State and Industrial Relations', 21–6. Lewis acknowledges that collective laissez-faire provides a fair description of collective labour law until the 1950s or 1960s: Lewis, 'Kahn-Freund and Labour Law', 217. Ewing agrees, at least, that the 'central tenets of the principle... cannot readily be gainsaid': Ewing, 'The State and Industrial Relations', 31.
[111] For a recent account see Howell.
[112] Kahn-Freund, 'Legal Framework' 102–3; Ewing, 'The State and Industrial Relations', 3–5.
[113] Hansard (HC) 386, 9 February 1943 c. 1196.

than (legally) requiring the collective parties to act in the desired ways: employers to recognize unions, or to pay collectively agreed rates; unions and employers together to establish permanent machinery for negotiation and dispute resolution.[114] Kahn-Freund's principle of collective laissez-faire served well as a concise and memorable characterization of this type of intervention: 'The law seeks to stimulate collective bargaining and the application of collective agreements by indirect inducements in preference to direct compulsion, and, where this fails, to provide substitute standards enforceable by legal sanctions.'[115]

When it comes to explaining the emergence and the persistence of the collectivist system of labour law, Kahn-Freund's elucidation of the principle of collective laissez-faire was arguably rather less convincing. Writing perhaps with a comparatist's rather than an historian's pen, he sought on a number of occasions to emphasize the strength of British trade unions, their proud independence from the state, and their reluctance to rely on legal rights in furtherance of their members' interests. 'Trade union "recognition" was achieved in this country by purely industrial as distinct from political and legislative action . . . The proud edifice of collective labour regulation was built up without the assistance of the "law".'[116] Trade unions did not campaign to be granted positive legal rights, so the argument seemed to go, because they preferred to rely on their own industrial strength to be recognized by employers, and to negotiate with employers improved terms and conditions of employment, and methods of dispute resolution. They were 'traditionally disinclined to put their trust in legislation to be applied by courts of law'.[117] When legislating to allow trade unions lawfully to engage in industrial action, the Liberal governments of the beginning of the twentieth century had agreed, apparently, that industrial disputes ought to be kept out of the courts insofar as was possible; hence the use of statutory immunities, and not positive rights, to create a freedom to strike.[118]

A review of the historical sources suggests that this account is misleading in a number of respects.[119] There may be some truth to the suggestion that at the turn of the century some trade unionists sought a legal settlement which would keep industrial disputes out of *the courts*.[120] Pelling, for example, charts the plentiful experience of trade unions of judicial bias in the decades to the end of the nineteenth century, culminating in the case of Taff Vale, and their consequent

---

[114] Howell, chapter 3. [115] Kahn-Freund, 'Legal Framework', 65–6.
[116] Kahn-Freund, 'War Legislation', 143. See also 'Intergroup Conflicts', 44; *Labour Law*, 224; Davies and Freedland, *Labour and the Law*, 52–3.
[117] Davies and Freedland, *Labour and the Law* 53.
[118] *Labour Law*, 232 citing Winston Churchill speaking in 1911 as a member of the Liberal Party and President of the Board of Trade: 'It is not good for trade unions that they should be brought in contact with the courts, and it is not good for the courts.'
[119] I rely here mainly on Howell, Pelling, and Ewing.
[120] 'We are immediately on surer ground when we interpret the tradition [of voluntarism] as implying not so much a distrust of legislation as a distrust of courts of law': A Flanders, 'The Tradition of Voluntarism' (1974) *British Journal of Industrial Relations* 352–70, 354. See also S and B Webb, *The History of Trade Unionism* (2nd ed) (London 1911), 320.

inclination to steer clear of the courts insofar as possible.[121] He also notes the readiness of sufficient numbers of Liberal MPs to back the union drafted Trade Disputes Bill, though he suggests that their support was strategically motivated and not truly reflective of Liberal Party policy.[122] At the same time, however, he records the disagreement within the union movement on precisely the question of legal intervention—the arguments made by a significant section of the movement in favour of the introduction of a legally defined system of compulsory arbitration along the lines of those in force in New Zealand and Australia.[123] Howell describes, moreover, the resurfacing of such disagreement in the 1960s with industrially weaker trade unions again proposing the introduction of a legislative mechanism for recognition and wider legal frameworks.[124] In 1906, of course, it was the stronger trade unions' wishes for a broad 'freedom from the law' that came to be reflected in the terms of the Trade Disputes Act. But it is interesting to note that doubts were expressed at the time, echoing or foreshadowing Sinzheimer's work, regarding the potential of a system of collective liberalism, built upon statutory immunities, to facilitate furtherance of the common interest.[125] In a letter to Sidney Webb written in 1903, the prominent trade unionist George Barnes suggested that collective liberalism might be 'after all anti-social and but a glorified individualism, inasmuch as it seeks to get for groups of men anti-social rights'.[126] The assertion made by Kahn-Freund that trade unions preferred to rely on their own industrial strength rather than state-granted legal rights was therefore not true of all unionists, and not at all times. Some wished for greater legal rights as a prop to assist them in securing recognition, and others favoured greater state intervention as a matter of political principle.

A second weakness of Kahn-Freund's explanation of the emergence and persistence of the system of collective laissez-faire was its failure to give consideration to employer interests and motivations. The implication was that employers recognized trade unions because the unions were in a position to require them to do so, threatening and organizing strike action as necessary.[127] Allan Flanders famously disputed such accounts of what he called 'bootstrap voluntarism', arguing instead that it had often served the employers' own interests to recognize trade unions: to involve the unions in managerial control, and in the regulation of work and wages, in order to gain employee consent and cooperation; or to secure the unions' assistance in reducing wage competition.[128] Governments had also played

---

[121] H Pelling, 'Trade Unions, Workers and The Law' in Pelling *Popular Politics and Society in Late Victorian Britain: Essays* (London 1979); see also Flanders, 'The Tradition of Voluntarism', 354.
[122] Pelling, 72, 78.   [123] Pelling, 73–5.
[124] Howell, 127–30. See also Charles who describes the repeated requests made for the agreements reached by JICs to be given legally binding force: R Charles, *The Development of Industrial Relations in Britain 1911–1939* (London 1973), 205–10. And see Flanders, 'Tradition of Voluntarism', 356–7.
[125] H Sinzheimer, 'Die Reform des Schlichtungswesens' (1930) in H Sinzheimer, *Arbeitsrecht und Rechtssoziologie: gesammelte Aufsätze und Reden* (Frankfurt, Cologne 1976), 243.
[126] George Barnes was the secretary of the Amalgamated Society of Engineers, leader of the Labour Party 1910–11, and a member of the War Cabinet 1917–18: Pelling 80–1.
[127] See eg Kahn-Freund, 'War Legislation', 143.
[128] Flanders, 'Tradition of Voluntarism', 355.

an important role in promoting union growth, not least through the impact they had had on employer attitudes and organization.[129] Flanders wrote:

All this is not to say that trade unions get their members without making any effort to organise them, or regardless of their achievements, or without sometimes being involved in strikes for recognition. That would be nonsense. It is also true that Governments have acted partly because they were particularly concerned to gain trade union goodwill in time of war. But the crude notion that British unions have dispensed with any external assistance in obtaining their growth is greatly at odds with the facts.[130]

In his explanation of the origins of what he describes as the first national system of industrial relations, Howell follows Flanders, identifying the employers' interests in the spread of collective bargaining as the most significant explanatory factor.[131] Because of the nature of industrial organization at the end of the nineteenth and at the beginning of the twentieth centuries—the long, slow decline of the old staple industries and accompanying economic restructuring, the existence of a large number of small firms, intense competition and low profitability—sectoral collective bargaining was suited to the needs of the majority of employers. It removed wages from competition, provided means of resolving disputes peacefully, and at the same time allowed for the growth of managerial prerogative at workplace level and thus a wide measure of employer control of jobs. From the point of view of public policy, sectoral bargaining was thought to further two key economic goals, sometimes explicitly articulated, sometimes not: the minimization of class conflict and easing of economic restructuring, and the reduction of inter-firm competition. The state was not monolithic and different objectives were pursued at times by different organs of government, most obviously by the judiciary. Taking the period 1890 to the 1950s as a whole, however, and examining the recommendations of royal commissions and the policies, legislation, and administrative actions of government, it is reasonably clear that these *economic* goals of reducing class conflict and inter-firm competition informed, to a very significant extent, the creation of 'a new set of assumptions [in government] about the benefits of trade union organization and collective regulation of class conflict'.[132]

It seems then that Kahn-Freund's explanation of the emergence and persistence of the system of collective laissez-faire was not wholly borne out by the facts. It was focused too narrowly on a postulated union preference for freedoms above rights that only ever accorded with the preferences of *some* trade unions in respect of *some* types of state intervention (notably state intervention in the regulation of industrial disputes). Whereas Kahn-Freund's explanation suggested that trade union recognition resulted almost wholly from the industrial strength of the trade unions, the reality was that trade unions were often recognized by virtue of the preference of many employers and of government for industry-level collective bargaining.

---

[129] Flanders, 'Tradition of Voluntarism', 355.
[130] Flanders, 'Tradition of Voluntarism', 356.
[131] Howell, chapter 3, esp 46–9.
[132] Howell, 61.

Conclusion

In any system of industrial relations, state support for the construction or maintenance of particular institutions is likely to bring with it the possibility of state management or state control of those institutions. In conferring authority upon a trade union to bargain collectively, for example, or in guaranteeing freedom of association, a legislature or a judiciary is likely to be presented with the opportunity to define the limits of such authority and such freedom. It follows that the question of the autonomy of industrial actors from the state may generally be assumed to be more or less intimately connected to the question of state support.

In Sinzheimer's conception of the labour constitution, the state figured prominently as the architect and the enforcer of the encompassing legal framework. The state did not create trade unions and it was not responsible for the early development of collective bargaining arrangements between trade unions and employers.[133] But it lent its support to the unions in a variety of ways—guaranteeing them legal rights and capacities, and protecting those rights and capacities from infringement by third parties—so that ultimately the collective power of trade unions was 'not only a real existing power but also a legally recognised power'.[134] While it respected the importance of autonomy in industrial relations, the state also exercised a measure of control over the unions, and over the employers' associations and the collective regulation of the economy by them both. For Sinzheimer, as we have seen, state control was a matter of democratic principle: the economic constitution should be subsidiary to the political constitution and subject, ultimately, to the control of the people as represented by the state.[135] For some of his contemporaries, the surrender of significant elements of trade union autonomy was simply a fair price for the guardianship of the new 'social democratic' state. 'Today's state is no longer the trade union-hostile state of the pre-war era,' stated Clemens Nörpel, leader of the federation of socialist unions, in 1929. 'The trade unions participate in this state, they wield significant influence within its institutions, they can reconfigure those institutions, have reconfigured them to a great extent. This new state must have the right, within certain limits, to place restrictions on the freedom of action of the trade unions and the employers' associations.'[136]

Judged in comparison with the labour constitution of the Weimar Republic, the British case is remarkable, arguably, for the extent to which it combined strong state support for the creation and maintenance of collective-bargaining and dispute-resolution machinery with respect for a broad measure of union and employer autonomy. The state took steps to persuade or induce employers to recognize unions and to bargain with them, but it did not attempt to control or influence the outcomes of the bargaining process. Comparatively speaking, and

---

[133] Sinzheimer, *Grundzüge*, 67–9.   [134] Sinzheimer, *Grundzüge*, 67.
[135] Chapter 2.   [136] Cited Kittner, 470.

certainly with some measure of oversimplification, we might say that in the period between the 1890s and the 1950s the British state supported collective industrial relations while at the same time respecting the collective parties' freedom of action. The recommendations of the Whitley Committee in 1918 were indicative of this approach: 'We do not . . . regard government assistance as an alternative to the organization of employers and employed. On the contrary, we regard it as a means of furthering the growth and development of such organization.'[137]

From the detailed discussion of collective labour legislation contained in the 1950s trilogy, it is clear that Kahn-Freund was in no doubt that the legislation—and by implication, state intervention—was supportive of collective industrial relations. However, in his eagerness to emphasize the second part of the equation, ie state respect for union autonomy, and in the light of his knowledge and personal experience of the fate of the labour constitution of the Weimar Republic, he was apt to underemphasize and at times even to appear to deny the importance of state support to the emergence and persistence of the British system. 'What the State has not given', he wrote in 1959, 'the State cannot take away.'[138] 'The determination of the trade unions not to rely on the sanctions of the law has given to the autonomous forces of industry a position of strength in the British Constitution which is hardly paralleled elsewhere.'[139]

As descriptive of the system of industrial relations in place in the UK in the first half of the twentieth century, the real strength of collective laissez-faire lay with the way in which it lent coherence to a particular body of '(collective) labour law'. As illustrated by Kahn-Freund in his 1950s trilogy, the Trade Disputes Act of 1906, the Conciliation Act of 1896, the trade boards and wages councils legislation of 1909, 1918, and 1945, and the fair wages resolutions could all be classified, understood, and analysed quite satisfactorily with reference to the single unifying principle of collective laissez-fare. By developing that principle, Kahn-Freund contributed very significantly to the recognition in the UK of labour law as a distinctive, coherent field of study, and provided generations of scholars, practitioners, teachers, and students with a useful way of thinking about it—with a useful 'analytical edifice', as Lord Wedderburn put it.[140] As an explanation of the specific nature of the law, however, collective laissez-faire could be criticized for implying that it was a union preference for reliance on industrial strength that was the most significant influence on government policy and legislation. It could be criticized, in other words, for underemphasizing the importance for government of the economic goals of reducing class conflict and inter-firm competition. And it could be criticized, in places, for seeming to understate the importance of government policy and action in the construction and maintenance of the collectivist system. Understood, contrary to Kahn-Freund's intentions, to imply something

---

[137] Ministry of Reconstruction, Committee on Relations between Employers and Employed (Whitley), *Second Report on Joint Standing Industrial Councils*, Cd. 9002, Parliamentary Papers (1918) X.659, at para 22. [138] Kahn-Freund, 'Labour Law', 244.
[139] Kahn-Freund, 'Labour Law', 244.
[140] Lord Wedderburn (1971) *Bulletin of Industrial Law Society*, cited Lord Wedderburn, 'Otto Kahn-Freund and British Labour Law', 39.

universal about industrial relations, beyond the UK of the earlier twentieth century, collective laissez-faire bears the considerable disadvantage of appearing to deny or underplay the significance of state support for trade unions and collective bargaining, and to suggest that autonomy in industrial relations, understood very widely, is everywhere and always paramount.

5

From Collective Laissez-Faire to the Law of the Labour Market

The End of Consensus

In their influential history of labour legislation and public policy in the post-war decades, Paul Davies and Mark Freedland identified the 1950s as the heyday of collective laissez-faire: throughout that decade, governments of both political parties had given their support to what could broadly be termed 'abstentionism' in the field of collective labour relations.[1] After the 'easy decade' of the 1950s, however, the following years witnessed great upheaval in industrial relations and collective labour law.[2] From the beginning of the 1960s, the perception began to grow among politicians and members of the public that British industrial relations were in crisis.[3] One aspect of the problem, emphasized by Kahn-Freund and prominent in the public consciousness and popular media, was the perceived need to bring greater order to industrial relations. Since the end of the Second World War, there had been a rapid development in shop steward organization and shop-floor bargaining to the point where they had become a feature of the vast majority of workplaces, especially in engineering.[4] The result, according to the diagnosis of the Donovan Commission, was the co-existence of 'two systems of industrial relations': one formal, embodied in the trade unions and employers' associations, and in industry-wide collective bargaining; and one informal, involving bargaining between shop stewards and management representatives on the shopfloor.[5] As the practices of the informal system had come to exert ever greater influence on the

---

[1] P Davies and M Freedland, *Labour Legislation and Public Policy* (Oxford 1993), 101–6.
[2] Davies and Freedland contrast 'the easy decade' (ch 3) of the 1950s with 'the end of agreement' (ch 6) in the 1960s.
[3] R Taylor, *The Trade Union Question in British Politics: Government and Unions Since 1945* (Oxford 1993), 116–18; D Barnes and E Reid, *Governments and Trade Unions: The British Experience 1964–79* (London 1980), 41–2.
[4] WEJ McCarthy, *Shop Stewards and Workshop Relations: The Results of a Study Undertaken by the Government Social Survey for the Royal Commission on Trade Unions and Employers' Associations* (London 1968), 36. See also J Tomlinson, 'Productivity, Joint Consultation and Human Relations in Post-War Britain: The Attlee Government and the Workplace', in J Melling and A McKinlay (eds) *Management, Labour and Industrial Politics in Modern Europe: The Quest for Productivity Growth During the Twentieth Century* (Cheltenham 1996).
[5] Royal Commission on Trade Unions and Employers' Associations, *Report* (HMSO 1968). paras 46–52 and 143–54.

conduct of industrial relations, those of the formal system had become increasingly empty. While both sides of industry continued to act as if the industry-wide agreements set fixed standards, the truth of the matter was that those ostensibly 'in charge' of industrial relations were no longer in a position to temper the ever increasing wage demands from the shopfloor, or to address the associated frequency of shopfloor strike action.

In its recommendations, the Donovan Commission prescribed the introduction of greater order by way of the routine use of factory or company-wide collective agreements.[6] These could be used to regulate matters that were not easily dealt with at industry level: hours, work practices, facilities for shop stewards, and discipline.[7] They could be used to formalize the role of shop stewards within trade unions, putting an end to the duality of the formal and informal systems. And they could be used to link wage increases to advances in productivity, addressing the problem of wage-push inflation.[8] In asserting the potential of free collective bargaining to restore order to industrial relations, the Donovan Commission rejected proposals made elsewhere for more radical reforms, including the introduction of some kind of legally imposed corporatism, or stricter legal controls of industrial action.[9] The Report recommended elements of state intervention and legal regulation, but it also stated a clear preference for the avoidance of legal sanctions and for methods of legal intervention which would keep industrial disputes out of the courts.[10] In this way, it promoted the continuation of the system of collective laissez-faire, albeit with a marked change of focus from industry- to enterprise-level collective bargaining.

In the decade following publication of the Donovan Report, three attempts were made by three different governments to formulate plans for reform. In the 1969 White Paper, *In Place of Strife*, the first Wilson government proposed a set of measures that followed the Donovan recommendations to a significant extent, while also introducing stricter controls on industrial action.[11] In 1971, the incoming Heath government passed an Industrial Relations Act intended to create a comprehensive legal framework for the regulation of industrial relations, involving new institutions, a web of new procedural rules, and new legal rights for trade unions and individual workers.[12] In 1974, the second Wilson government repealed the 1971 Act and replaced it with the restoration of a widely-circumscribed freedom to take industrial action, and legislation aimed at promoting trade union organization and collective bargaining. At the same time it agreed a broader programme of economic and social reforms with the TUC: the so-called 'Social

---

[6] *Report*, paras 162–5.   [7] *Report*, para 166.
[8] *Report*, paras 157–8, 181–3; Howell, 104.
[9] Davies and Freedland, *Labour Legislation and Public Policy*, 248 ff.
[10] See eg *Report*, chapter 8, appendix 6.
[11] *In Place of Strife: A Policy for Industrial Relations*. Cmnd. 3888. For discussion see Davies and Freedland, *Labour Legislation and Public Policy*, chapter 6.
[12] The Act was preceded by a statement of policy, *Fair Deal at Work* (London 1968), and accompanied by a Code of Practice (London 1972). Davies and Freedland, *Labour Legislation and Public Policy*, chapter 7.

Contract'.[13] At the time, these three sets of reforms were understood to represent very different solutions to the crisis in industrial relations. In retrospect, it is easier to recognize significant areas of continuity across the three. Notwithstanding the differences between them, it is possible to characterize all three as attempts visibly to impose greater order on industrial relations, while at the same time still promoting collective bargaining as the principal regulatory mechanism.[14] It is possible, too, to identify in all three an ending of the era of collective laissez-faire.[15] From the late 1960s, a prioritization by both political parties of the need to combat rising inflation rates meant an end to government 'abstention' when it came to influencing the outcomes of collective bargaining and the negotiation of wages. The legal controls on the freedom to take industrial action contained in *In Place of Strife* and the Industrial Relations Act were aimed as much at limiting the ability of trade unions to demand ever higher wages as they were at imposing greater order on industrial relations.[16] Outside the sphere of labour law, these measures were flanked by the introduction of incomes policies.[17] The legislation of 1974 and 1975 restored the formal autonomy of the collective parties, but did so within the context of an extra-legal agreement between the government and the TUC intended to allow for governmental influence on the results of the collective bargaining process.[18] Such involvement by government in wage setting was quite clearly inimical to the principle of collective laissez-faire; as Kahn-Freund put it, 'the deepest inroad ever made into . . . the freedom of collective bargaining in Britain'.[19]

Kahn-Freund passed away in August 1979. For other scholars of labour law in the UK, the legal and political developments of the 1970s posed something of a challenge. While the world outside them changed, they continued to be housed in the 'analytical edifice' of collective laissez-fare.[20] Increasingly, it became clear to some that collective laissez-faire could no longer serve satisfactorily as a framework for the analysis of new government policies and legislation in the field. From the early 1980s, attempts were made to develop new approaches, widening the scope of study beyond collective laissez-faire. In the late 1990s, Hugh Collins was able to describe what he understood to be the 'productive disintegration' of labour law: over the course of the preceding ten or 20 years, different scholars had looked to different theories and methodologies from the social sciences to inform their own approaches so that a multiplicity of scholarly discourses had developed

---

[13] Davies and Freedland, *Labour Legislation and Public Policy*, 354–66.
[14] Davies and Freedland, *Labour Legislation and Public Policy*, 657.
[15] The era, in other words, in which collective laissez-faire provided a reasonably accurate description of the type of state intervention in industrial relations and the type of collective labour legislation typical of the UK.
[16] Davies and Freedland, *Labour Legislation and Public Policy*, 8–9.
[17] Davies and Freedland, *Labour Legislation and Public Policy*, 164–81, 328–33.
[18] Davies and Freedland, *Labour Legislation and Public Policy*, 657.
[19] Referring specifically to the incomes policy contained in the Prices and Incomes Acts of 1966 to 1968: O Kahn-Freund, *Labour Law: Old Traditions and New Developments* (Oxford 1968), 19.
[20] Lord Wedderburn (1971) *Bulletin of Industrial Law Society*, cited Wedderburn, 'Otto Kahn-Freund and British Labour Law', 39.

side by side.[21] For Collins, this was 'productive' because discussions henceforth proceeded 'by engaging with the insights supplied by diverse interpretations of context'.[22] By the end of the following decade, it would perhaps have been easier to make the case for the emerging dominance of one particular approach to the study of labour law—for an emerging consensus, among scholars in the UK and elsewhere, that labour law was now better understood as 'the law of the labour market'.[23]

Towards a Law of the Labour Market

A new conceptual framework?

The argument that labour law scholarship ought to be re-orientated to take greater account of questions of labour market regulation was first advanced in the UK by Paul Davies and Mark Freedland at the beginning of the 1980s.[24] As was made quite explicit by them, their suggestion was born out of a growing frustration with the then established ways of thinking about the subject. Their aim was to develop a new conceptual framework better suited to the explanation of current developments in labour legislation and government policy. '[W]e would be concerned with defining the agenda of labour law', they explained, 'and with operating from within it.'[25]

The matter was first addressed at length by Davies and Freedland in their editors' introduction to the 1983 edition of *Kahn-Freund's Labour and the Law*.[26] In updating that work six years after its second edition and four years after Kahn-Freund's death, the authors faced the challenge of rendering current a work which they judged to have become, in its very fundamentals, quite out of date. In its first and second editions, *Labour and the Law* had been written to reflect Kahn-Freund's belief that the guiding principle of labour law in the UK was the

---

[21] H Collins, 'The Productive Disintegration of Labour Law' (1997) 26 *Industrial Law Journal* 295–309. See also P Davies and M Freedland, 'National Styles in Labor Law Scholarship: The United Kingdom' (2002) 23 *Comparative Labor Law and Policy Journal* 765–87.
[22] Collins, 'Productive Disintegration', 308.
[23] P Davies and M Freedland, 'National Styles in Labor Law Scholarship', 781–5; J Fudge, 'Labour as a "Fictive Commodity": Radically Reconceptualizing Labour Law' in G Davidov and B Langille, *The Idea of Labour Law* (Oxford 2011). This chapter will focus solely on British scholars. For discussion of debates outside the UK and for references to further reading see, Fudge, 'Labour as a "Fictive Commodity"'; AD Frazer, 'Reconceiving Labour Law: The Labour Market Regulation Project' (2008) 8 *Macquarie Law Journal* 21–44; M Freedland, 'Labour Law Beyond the Horizon' (1998) 28 *Industrial law Journal* 197–200; H Arthurs, 'Charting the Boundaries of Labour Law: Innis Christie and the Search for an Integrated Law of Labour Market Regulation' (2011) 34 *Dalhousie Law Journal* 1–17.
[24] Davies and Freedland, *Kahn-Freund's Labour and the Law*; P Davies and M Freedland, *Labour Law Text and Materials* (2nd ed) (London 1984); see also their *Labour Legislation and Public Policy*.
[25] Davies and Freedland, *Labour Legislation and Public Policy*, 4.
[26] A version of the introduction was published in 1982 as: P Davies and M Freedland, 'Labour Law and the Public Interest: Collective Bargaining and Economic Policy' in KW Wedderburn and T Murphy (eds) *Labour Law and the Community: Perspectives for the 1980s* (London 1982).

principle of collective laissez-faire. 'The central purpose of labour law is seen as that of maintaining an equilibrium between employers and workers by ensuring the effective operation of a voluntary system of collective bargaining.'[27] It followed from this definition that the central focus of the book, in terms of its subject matter, should lie with collective bargaining and the legal regulation of collective employment relations. The problem with this conception of labour law, according to Davies and Freedland, was that it no longer offered an accurate description of the legislation and policies of British governments. In the six years since the publication of the second edition, there had been 'momentous developments for labour law, developments both legal, social and concerned with government policy' brought about by the election of the first Thatcher government in 1979.[28] Even before that time, however, analysis informed by the principle of collective laissez-faire had failed satisfactorily to describe and explain what Davies and Freeland argued was *the central concern* of a succession of governments in the postwar era: the control of inflation and the maintenance, at the same time, of high levels of employment.[29] Since the late 1950s and early 1960s, governments had sought, in particular, to combat *wage* inflation with recourse to a number of different strategies: incomes policy, the social contract, legal restriction of freedom of association, and control of industrial relations by the market.[30] An analysis focused around the principle of collective laissez-faire could do little to make sense of these strategies. If labour law, as an academic discipline, was to 'maintain its credentials as offering an explanatory framework of the legal regime within which the employment relation operates', scholars of the subject would have to re-orientate their studies and their writing to reflect more accurately the policy priorities and strategies of the governments of the day.[31] In particular, scholars should broaden the focus of their studies beyond collective bargaining to include legislation and government activity aimed at the control of inflation and the maintenance of high levels of employment. And they should adopt a new conceptual framework, one that was no longer constructed around the benefits and the promotion of collective laissez-faire.

[I]f we are talking about decisions by governments to exercise greater control by law over the collective bargaining process because of the latter's inflationary consequences, then we are dealing with a revolutionary change in the nature of labour law . . . Those who formulated the aims and directions of labour law early in the post-war period both at a governmental and an academic level . . . tended to conceive of it as having mainly *social* functions, above all those of redressing the inequality of bargaining power between individual employee and employer and providing machinery for resolving the inevitable conflicts of interest between employers and trade unions. To attempt to harness this system to

---

[27] Davies and Freedland, *Labour and the Law*, 2.
[28] Davies and Freedland, *Labour and the Law*, 1. And see B Simpson, 'British Labour Relations in the 1980s: Learning to Live with the Law' (1986) 49 *Modern Law Review* 796–818, 797–8.
[29] Davies and Freedland, *Labour and the Law*, 3–4.
[30] Davies and Freedland, *Labour and the Law*, 6–10.
[31] Davies and Freedland, *Labour and the Law*, 1.

the economic function of controlling the inflationary consequences of collective bargaining would necessarily be to effect revolutionary changes in it.[32]

In the second edition of their *Text and Materials* book (1984), Davies and Freedland asserted again the outdated nature of the established conception of labour law, with its narrow focus on collective bargaining and collective laissez-faire. Their prescription for a re-orientation of the subject referred here, however, not only to aspects of economic policy, including inflation control, but explicitly to the *functioning of the labour market*.[33] Their book would begin, they explained, with a treatment of the law that regulated aspects of the formation of the employment relationship. This would better reflect the importance ascribed by successive governments to the question of employment levels.[34] And it would allow for a more coherent conception of labour law as a whole, since 'questions of levels and patterns of employment have an impact or an interaction with all the different aspects of the employment relationship with which we shall be concerned in the course of this book'.[35] Not only did Davies and Freedland recommend a widening of the scope of labour law to include laws aimed at regulating the formation of the employment relationship—laws, for example, that regulated job creation and training—they also recommended a corresponding change in perspective. Instead of looking at the formation of the employment relationship as a transaction between a particular employee and particular employer, scholars should view each individual transaction as one component of a larger entity, the functioning of the labour market. Such a perspective might 'more clearly reveal the larger social and economic consequences of legal controls over the constituting of the employment relationship'.[36] It might reveal, in particular, the effect of legal controls on questions of supply and demand, of labour market segmentation, and of unemployment and social exclusion.

In 1989, the arguments of Davies and Freedland were criticized by Hugh Collins in his well-known article 'Labour Law as a Vocation'.[37] The article sought to compare what it termed the 'traditional' conception of labour law, as articulated in the work of Kahn-Freund and Lord Wedderburn, with the notion of labour law as the law of the labour market proposed by Davies and Freedland. The central strand of Collins' criticism of the latter involved the assertion that it lacked the measure of coherence necessary to mark out labour law as a discrete legal discipline. Whereas a small number of legal disciplines such as contract and criminal law could claim coherence with reference to a particular set of principles and concepts, disciplines such as labour law and family law found their coherence in a sense of vocation.

---

[32] Davies and Freedland, *Labour and the Law*, 5, emphasis in the original.
[33] Davies and Freedland, *Labour Law Text and Materials*, 4 and 11.
[34] Davies and Freedland, *Labour Law Text and Materials*, 1.
[35] Davies and Freedland, *Labour Law Text and Materials*, 2.
[36] Davies and Freedland, *Labour Law Text and Materials*, 11.
[37] H Collins, 'Labour Law as a Vocation' (1989) 105 *Law Quarterly Review* 468–84.

This vocation springs from a conviction that urgent social problems need to be addressed, and blossoms into a vision of justice in this sphere of social life in which law plays its appropriate role. The sense of vocation marks out a field of inquiry, establishes criteria of relevance of legal materials, and finally constructs a critical vantage-point from which to assess the substance and techniques of current law.[38]

Davies and Freedland had argued for a redefinition of the scope of labour law, Collins suggested, but they had *not* proposed a new vocation. 'Labour law, conceived as the regulation of the labour market, demonstrates a shifting balance of purposes rather than a single vocation.'[39]

As Freedland himself confirmed in later years, Collins was quite right to suggest that a labour market approach to conceiving of labour law resulted in a subject with 'a more diffuse and ultimately less self-contained set of concerns' than the established conception, tied closely to collective laissez-faire and collective bargaining.[40] To suggest that Davies and Freedland had failed to propose *any* new purpose for labour law, however, would be to overstate the point. Davies and Freedland's argument, from the very outset, was that scholars should orientate themselves more readily to the policy aims of the government of the day. Their concern was to promote an understanding of labour law as a field of study that was capable of offering an accurate description and a useful analysis of *actual* policies and legislation. And their logic was quite straightforward: if the government implemented policies, and the legislature passed statutes, aimed at achieving x, y, and z then, as a matter of fact, labour law as a field of study had to be understood to include policies and legislation with x, y, and z as their aim. The development of labour law was first and foremost a political process; 'a product of the formulation and application of governmental economic and social policies in the sphere of industrial society'.[41] Any attempt to describe or analyse labour law had necessarily to take account of such policies and of their formulation and application by means of legislation, among other things.

In their long and detailed contemporary history of postwar *Labour Legislation and Public Policy*, published in 1993, Davies and Freedland embarked upon the task suggested in their introduction to *Labour and the Law* of positing inflation control as the central concern of postwar governments and of analysing all legal and policy developments systematically from a corresponding point of view.[42] Regarding the period 1945 to 1990 as a whole, they confirmed and expanded the narrative suggested in 1983: that there had been a shift in policy discourses away from a conception of labour law as part of social law, and towards an understanding of labour law as comprising a set of tools which could be used to achieve particular economic objectives.[43] During the years of the Thatcher administrations the trend had continued, they now added, as labour law was subsumed

---

[38] Collins, 'Labour Law as a Vocation'.   [39] Collins, 'Labour Law as a Vocation'.
[40] Freedland, 'Labour Law Beyond the Horizon'.
[41] Davies and Freedland, *Labour Legislation and Public* Policy, 'Introduction', 7.
[42] Davies and Freedland, *Labour and the Law*, 5.
[43] Davies and Freedland, *Labour Legislation and Public Policy*, chapters 9 and 10.

under a wider vision of 'labour market regulation in the interests of a free market economy'.[44] In the opinion of Davies and Freedland, recognition of these shifts in policy discourses was critical to an accurate assessment of specific legislative provisions and policy objectives pursued by government in the field of employment relations. Legislative measures of the 1980s aimed on the face of them at reducing trade union power, for example, had in fact to be understood as one element of a wider set of measures intended to effect a restructuring of the labour market—'a restructuring which gradually focused upon the notion of a market economy as the ideal for industrial society'.[45]

A third way in labour law?

With the election of the Labour government in 1997, arguments similar to Davies and Freedland's were developed by several authors in the context of efforts to characterize and critique that government's 'third way' approach to regulating employment relations. While it is possible to trace a line from this later work to Davies and Freedland's original and more modest proposals for the adaptation of approaches to analysing labour law, it is also the case that the scholarship of the 2000s was shaped quite markedly by the changed legal and political context of that era. The election of 1997 marked the end of a period of 18 years of Conservative government. During that time, trade union organization and collective bargaining had been dramatically weakened: the coverage of collective bargaining had contracted very substantially, the scope of bargaining—in terms of subject matter—had narrowed, and the depth of union involvement had diminished.[46] As a general rule, the Conservatives in office had tended to favour deregulatory policies in the field of employment relations, adhering to a rhetoric that extolled the benefits of free markets, flexibility, and the absence of 'red tape'.[47] The case that scholars felt it necessary to make, under these changed circumstances, was not the case against a body of labour law scholarship focused around collective bargaining and collective laissez-faire, but rather the case for the very existence of labour law—the case for some measure of legal regulation of labour markets, as they might have put it, as more desirable than minimal regulation or no regulation at all. As the 'third way' came to be articulated by the Labour government in its legislation and policies of the late 1990s and early 2000s, the opportunity presented itself to make that case in a way that broadly followed, rather than challenged, the new government's objectives.[48]

As early as in 2000, Hugh Collins published a paper on the 'Third Way in Labour Law', which, by his own admission, followed the policy pronouncements

---

[44] P Davies and M Freedland, *Towards a Flexible Labour Market* (Oxford 2007), 5.
[45] Davies and Freedland, *Labour Legislation and Public Policy*, 527.
[46] W Brown 'The Contraction of Collective Bargaining in Britain' (1993) 31 *British Journal of Industrial Relations* 189–200; N Millward, A Bryson, J Forth, *All Change at Work? British Employment Relations 1980–98, Portrayed by the Workplace Industrial Relations Survey Series* (New York 2000).
[47] Howell, 141–64.
[48] Cf Davies and Freedland, *Towards a Flexible Labour Market*, 248.

of government very closely indeed.[49] His aim in the paper was to assemble a putative statement of a third way conception of labour law out of material gleaned from three sources: the articulation of the broader policy goals of the third way by politicians and academics; the statement of the government's policy goals in the field of employment relations contained in the 1998 white paper, *Fairness at Work*; and the terms of the legislation that followed the white paper, the Employment Rights Act 1999. In line with that aim, Collins' paper was largely expository rather than critical in tone, employing the government's chosen language of 'competitiveness' and 'flexibility' to articulate the central policy aims of labour law as it was now to be conceived. 'From the perspective of the Third Way, the number one problem is to improve the competitiveness of businesses . . . A key ingredient of competitiveness is to use the workforce efficiently and effectively. For this purpose the workforce has to be properly trained and prepared to work flexibly and to cooperate with all innovations.'[50]

In work published the following year, Collins expanded upon the notion of flexible employment relationships as key to the maximization of competitiveness, addressing the question of which kinds of legislative or regulatory intervention would best promote the achievement of flexible employment relations.[51] Again, the intention was decidedly not to engage critically with the stated policy priorities of the government. Indeed, the article was notable for the extent to which it appeared to endorse those priorities—particularly the goal of flexibility in employment relations—as holding the potential to benefit businesses and employees alike; as Collins put it, to achieve 'a stable compromise of interests between capital and labour'.[52]

Though he was not directly concerned in these papers to advocate a re-orientation of labour law scholarship towards the labour market, Collins did emphasize the importance of markets to third way and Labour government thinking. Fundamental to the third way conception of social justice, he explained, was the rejection of equality of distributive outcomes as a realistic policy objective, and its replacement with the goal of creating the conditions necessary for the eradication of social exclusion.[53] A second task for labour law, then, in addition to the improvement of competitiveness, was the maximization of labour market participation.[54] Policy and legislation should be directed at removing barriers to such participation (for example, by prohibiting discrimination in employment or increasing access to childcare); 'enhancing the employability' of would-be labour market participants; and strengthening incentives to work.

In 2007, Davies and Freedland published a sequel to their history of postwar *Labour Legislation and Public Policy*. The aim was to bring the narrative up

---

[49] H Collins, 'Is There a Third Way in Labour Law?' in J Conaghan, RM Fischl, K Klare (eds) *Labour Law in an Era of Globalization: Transformative Practices and Possibilities* (Oxford 2000), 449–69. [50] Collins, 'Third Way', 450–1.
[51] H Collins, 'Regulating the Employment Relation for Competitiveness' (2001) 31 *Industrial Law Journal* 17–48. [52] Collins, 'Regulating', 18–19.
[53] Collins, 'Third Way', 451–5, referring to T Blair, *The Third Way: New Politics for the New Century* (London 1998). [54] Collins, 'Third Way', 453–5.

to date, focusing for the most part on the Blair governments of 1997 to 2007, and through a comparison of the legislation and policy of the Blair governments with the Thatcher and Major governments, to assess the veracity of New Labour's claim to have found a new or 'third' way of regulating employment relations.[55] In the course of their description and analysis, Davies and Freedland identified important differences in the policy priorities and regulatory interventions of the Conservatives and Labour across the period 1979 to 2007, but they also highlighted what they understood to be a deep vein of continuity between the two: 'it is as accurate and appropriate to regard the Blair administration as it was to regard the Thatcher administration as having subsumed labour legislation and its associated body of social policy into a larger activity or pursuit of labour market regulation in the interests of a free and competitive market economy.'[56] That being the case, it was highly significant for the development of labour law after 1997 that the Blair administration had had a rather more nuanced vision of the labour market and labour market flexibility than its predecessors. Instead of deregulation and liberalization across the board, New Labour had used a variety of methods—including deregulation, re-regulation, and 'light' regulation—to achieve the goal of greater labour market flexibility.[57] Moreover, it had understood flexibility to offer a route not only to a more competitive economy, but also to the 'amelioration of social problems in the areas of social exclusion and child poverty'.[58] It had valued jobs as 'the most effective route out of poverty and the most effective way of promoting self-respect and improving social welfare'.[59]

When it came to identifying and describing the policy priorities of the Blair governments, Davies and Freedland, like Collins, relied for the most part on the governments' own statements of policy and legislation as evidence of its priorities.[60] In seeking to explain the nature of government policy, the authors gave particular weight to the electoral strategizing of the Labour Party, its prioritization of the need to win and stay in power. This went some way to explaining the importance accorded to the 'politically crucial' objectives of keeping employment levels up, and wage inflation and the number of days lost to industrial action down.[61] Where criticisms were made by the authors, these tended to be framed with reference to the government's own stated policy objectives. Legislation might be criticized, for example, because it did not achieve what the government had intended it to achieve.[62] In particular, policy decisions might be criticized for their

---

[55] Davies and Freedland, *Towards a Flexible Labour Market*, 7.
[56] Davies and Freedland, *Towards a Flexible Labour Market*, 7.
[57] Davies and Freedland, *Towards a Flexible Labour Market*, 246.
[58] Davies and Freedland, *Towards a Flexible Labour Market*, 234.
[59] Davies and Freedland, *Towards a Flexible Labour Market*, 234.
[60] Davies and Freedland, *Towards a Flexible Labour Market*, 9.
[61] Davies and Freedland, *Towards a Flexible Labour Market*, 105–10, 248.
[62] So for example, 'Welfare to work', is judged primarily in terms of its success in increasing the employment rate. The authors do also question whether enough has been done to ensure that there are opportunities for people to climb the 'jobs ladder' having secured a place on its lowest rungs, but this does not then form part of a broader critique of the whole 'jobs' strategy: Davies and Freedland, *Towards a Flexible Labour Market*, 234–5. Cf K Rittich, 'What "Makes" Markets?' (2014) *Northern Ireland Legal Quarterly* forthcoming.

lack of fit with the higher-order objectives of competitiveness and social inclusion.[63] In the concluding chapter of the book, the authors appeared to confirm that this was their preferred approach to labour law scholarship. 'It is perhaps appropriate for academic analysis of the labour legislation of the past decade to develop in new directions which follow the Government's objectives—without of course any automatic deference to them.'[64] They came closer here too than they had done in their earlier work to endorsing the government's policies, and to finding in them the suggestion of a single unifying aim—or set of aims—for labour law. Both the expansion of the productive economy and the promotion of social inclusion were, wrote Davies and Freedland, 'profoundly important social objectives', which scholars would do well to engage with.[65]

In 2004, Deakin and Wilkinson published *The Law of the Labour Market*. While it was not—for the most part or anywhere primarily—a commentary on the legislation and policy of the Labour governments, nonetheless it reads today as a book of its time.[66] The 'New Labour' context was invoked by the authors when they referred to their aim of developing a neo-Fabian agenda of labour market reform.[67] It was apparent in their choice of how to develop such an agenda *against* the type of arguments that had prevailed in the 1980s and 1990s in favour of free markets.[68] And it was apparent too in the optimism of their assertion that there were, at the time of writing, 'many signs of renewal and innovation in the forms of labour market regulation', suggestive of the emergence of a viable alternative to the neoliberal prescription of deregulation.[69]

The Law of the Labour Market is an incredibly rich book, and, taken as a whole, probably best characterized as a history of labour market regulation in the UK. The principal focus of study is the contract of employment and the main body of the book consists of a lengthy study of its historical development in the UK, supplemented by two further studies of the evolution of bodies of law concerned with aspects of the labour market; the 'duty to work' and the 'core labour market institution of collective bargaining'.[70] For our purposes, what is most significant about the book is the authors' suggestion, first stated in the introductory chapter, that the very idea of labour law had by the time of writing become outdated, having represented but one episode in a longer history of the law of the labour market.[71] Though the suggestion was undoubtedly controversial, it was not argued

---

[63] Eg the authors point out that 'employers were left in almost unfettered control of their training policies, despite general acceptance of the proposition that the skill levels of the workforce in the UK were lower than those of comparable countries': Davies and Freedland, *Towards a Flexible Labour Market*, 234.   [64] Davies and Freedland, *Towards a Flexible Labour Market*, 248.
[65] Davies and Freedland, *Towards a Flexible Labour Market*, 249.
[66] That said, however, parts of the book were in fact written before the election of New Labour: see Deakin and Wilkinson, *Law of the Labour Market*, 'Preface', viii.
[67] Deakin and Wilkinson, *Law of the Labour Market*, 274–7, 353.
[68] Deakin and Wilkinson, *Law of the Labour Market*, 2.
[69] Deakin and Wilkinson, *Law of the Labour Market*, 342, 277. See also their assessment of the EU as giving concrete expression to the idea that 'economic integration and social regulation are mutually complementary aspects of a process of market construction', 345.
[70] Deakin and Wilkinson, *Law of the Labour Market*, 39.
[71] Deakin and Wilkinson, *Law of the Labour Market*, 1–3.

at any length by the authors, nor did they attempt to define in detail the contours of their posited subject of study, the law of the labour market.[72] Insofar as they sought to make the case for a re-orientation of labour law scholarship towards the labour market, they did so primarily by explaining and employing their preferred approach, and not by arguing directly for the outdatedness of the old ways. The nature of the 'law of the labour market', at the time of writing and in the future, was not addressed directly until the final chapter.

As set out in the introduction to the final chapter, the authors' intention therein was to provide a rationalization of the law of the labour market, which could serve as descriptive of existing laws and as a normative basis for discussion of future policy and regulation.[73] The question to be addressed was expressed as follows: 'what kind of normative or regulatory framework is needed in order for labour markets to function in the interests of a range of societal goals, of which efficiency is one?'[74] In seeking to answer the question, the authors engaged at length with the writings of Friedrich Hayek, and of those who argued with Hayek that markets would function most efficiently without legal intervention, or with only a minimum of legal intervention to enforce property and contract rights.[75] As a starting point, Deakin and Wilkinson accepted the basic premise that the labour market, like other markets, was a spontaneous order that rested on a set of mutually reinforcing conventions, themselves the outcome of an evolutionary process.[76] They disputed, however, that it followed necessarily that the role of law should be limited to the enforcement of contract and property rights: working from the notion of the market as a spontaneous order, it could still be argued that a greater degree of regulation of the labour market was desirable.[77] Building on the work of Amartya Sen, it could be argued, more specifically, that the legal enforcement of *social rights* was desirable.[78] Social rights were not inimical to the effective functioning of the labour market: on the contrary, they were at the core of a labour market order in which the resources available to society were fully realized. In order for those resources to be fully realized, individuals should be provided with the means of achieving economic self-sufficiency. They should be provided with those social rights that would empower them with the means to realize their potential in a sustainable way, thereby enhancing the wealth or well-being of society as a whole.

In the second half of the chapter, the authors discussed a number of polices and instances of regulation introduced by the Labour government after 1997. These were presented as illustrative of the 'ways in which labour law is perhaps already

---

[72] Deakin and Wilkinson, *Law of the Labour Market*, 2.
[73] Deakin and Wilkinson, *Law of the Labour Market*, 275.
[74] Deakin and Wilkinson, *Law of the Labour Market*, 277.
[75] Deakin and Wilkinson, *Law of the Labour Market*, 278–303; See also S Deakin, 'Capacitas: Contract Law, Capabilities and the Legal Foundations of the Market' in S Deakin and A Supiot (eds) *Capacitas: Contract Law and the Institutional Preconditions of a Market Economy* (Oxford 2009). [76] Deakin and Wilkinson, *Law of the Labour Market*, 278–1.
[77] Deakin and Wilkinson, *Law of the Labour Market*, 281–90.
[78] Deakin and Wilkinson, *Law of the Labour Market*, 290–4.

in the process of reorientating its conceptual language and processes towards the goal of coordinating labour market relations'.[79] Through reference again to Sen and to the discussion of capabilities theory contained in the Supiot Report, the authors then sought to identify a unifying rationale for these policies and labour laws, and to extrapolate from them a 'framework for analysis and evaluation of the existing law and of proposals for legal change'.[80] They concluded by arguing that labour law should be conceptualized primarily as a means of improving the functioning of labour markets, arguing, in their own words, for a 'particular conception of "labour market law"' in which social rights played 'a central, constitutive role in the formation of labour market relations'.[81]

A new methodology?

In a review article published in 2007, Simon Deakin suggested that the proposal to reframe labour law as the law of the labour market had four dimensions or elements.[82] It was proposed, first, that the scope of the subject should be extended beyond the core institutions of the employment contract and collective bargaining to include aspects of social security law, tax law, family law, and other types of law potentially relevant to the task of understanding work relations. It was proposed that the conception of the 'aims' of the subject be widened in recognition of the fact that labour laws could be directed at the achievement of a multiplicity of policy objectives, of which protection of the employee was only one. It was proposed, third, that scholars of the subject should be committed legal pluralists, incorporating into their analyses consideration of forms of regulation other than formal law. And it was proposed, finally, that there was a need for 'a different methodology . . . —one which is explicitly interdisciplinary, and which is influenced by a long-term historical perspective'.[83]

In *The Law of the Labour Market*, Deakin and Wilkinson employed just such a methodology and explained it at some length.[84] Of itself, the choice of the labour market as the primary object of study was taken to imply the need to engage in legal and economic analysis, since the market was as much a juridical institution as it was an economic institution. Drawing on comparative institutional analysis and on critical legal studies, the authors characterized the relationship

---

[79] Deakin and Wilkinson, *Law of the Labour Market*, 303
[80] Deakin and Wilkinson, *Law of the Labour Market*, 275. The Supiot Report was published in English as Supiot, *Beyond Employment*.
[81] Deakin and Wilkinson, *Law of the Labour Market*, 277.
[82] S Deakin: 'A New Paradigm for Labour Law? Review of C Arup, P Gahan, J Howe, R Johnstone, R Mitchell, A O'Donnell (eds) *Labour Law and Labour Market Regulation: Essays on the Construction, Constitution and Regulation of Labour Markets and Work Relationships* (Sydney: The Federation Press, 2006)' (2007) 31 *Melbourne University Law Review* 1161–73.
[83] Deakin, 'Paradigm', 1162.
[84] Deakin and Wilkinson, *Law of the Labour Market*, esp. 5–18, 26–35. See also S Deakin, 'Conceptions of the Market in Labour Law' in A Numhauser-Henning and Mia Rönnmar (eds) *Normative Patterns and Legal Developments in the Social Dimension of the EU* (Oxford), discussed in chapter 8 of this volume.

between law and economics as 'co-evolutionary', emphasizing the fact that each could exercise reciprocal influence on the other.[85] This was highly significant for the study of the labour market and of particular institutions such as the contract of employment. Labour market institutions were the products of their time and if they were in crisis now—as the contract of employment surely was—then an analysis of their evolution might shed light on the nature of the crisis and on possible routes to its resolution.[86] A methodology was needed which could combine elements of doctrinal legal analysis with comparative institutional analysis, and which was directed at studying the historical evolution of institutions within the framework of the co-evolution of the social systems, law, and economics.[87]

Inherent in Deakin and Wilkinson's proposals for a new methodology was the suggestion that the old ways of studying labour law were no longer appropriate or no longer adequate. In the 2007 review article, Deakin contrasted the approach thought suited to the law of the labour market with the methods employed by Kahn-Freund and Sinzheimer.[88] Of course, these were also interdisciplinary and historical, as was related by Kahn-Freund in his discussion of Sinzheimer's work.[89] What marked the change from the old to the proposed new approach, then, was not the move to interdisciplinarity but the choice of *which* disciplines, other than law, to draw upon. Kahn-Freund and Sinzheimer had looked mainly to sociology and anthropology to inform their studies of labour law, using these 'to provide a critique of existing legal methods and to advance the case for social reform'.[90] 'Today' wrote Deakin, 'economics is more prevalent.'[91] For that reason, it was important that labour lawyers should engage with economic theories and analysis—not as experts, but 'with a degree of familiarity with the precepts and methods' of the field.[92] In contrast to Deakin, Collins showed a greater readiness to identify specific shortcomings of the traditional 'sociological' approach. In Collins' view, the traditional approach had caused 'other external analyses such as those provided by economics and liberal political theory [to be] largely ignored, so that the analysis offered by labour law was deaf to their rival interpretations of practice'.[93] Davies and Freeland appeared to confirm that economics was of increased relevance for scholars of labour law in the 1990s and 2000s when they highlighted the manifest shift in policy discourses away from the understanding that labour law was social law, towards the subsumption of labour legislation and social policy into the larger activity of labour market regulation in the interests of a free and competitive market economy.[94] If the government's policy objectives in the field were primarily economic, then their description and analysis of

---

[85] Deakin and Wilkinson, *Law of the Labour Market*, 10–11, 32.
[86] Deakin and Wilkinson, *Law of the Labour Market*, 3, 35.
[87] Deakin and Wilkinson, *Law of the Labour Market*, 29.
[88] Deakin, 'Paradigm', 1169–72.
[89] Kahn-Freund, 'Hugo Sinzheimer', 96–104; Ramm, 'Otto Kahn-Freund und Deutschland', xxii–xxiii.   [90] Deakin, 'Paradigm', 1170.   [91] Deakin, 'Paradigm', 1170.
[92] Deakin, 'Paradigm', 1171.   [93] Collins, 'Productive Disintegration', 297.
[94] Davies and Freeland, *Labour and the Law*, 5; Davies and Freeland, *Towards a Flexible Labour Market*, 7.

them, and of any associated legislation, would require engagement with economics among other things and in particular with labour market economics.[95]

In discussing different approaches to the study and academic analysis of labour law, it is of course important to distinguish between labour law as an academic discipline and labour law as a legal discipline.[96] Because labour law has always been regarded in the UK as a 'contextual field of study' and not a doctrinal category, scholars of the subject have felt it necessary to make the case for the existence of labour law as a distinct field of scholarship and practice, defining its scope and its aims in such a way as to lend it coherence.[97] In so doing, they have necessarily departed to some greater or lesser extent from the precise terms of the legislation and policy, overlooking, or at least underemphasizing, those terms which did not fit with the proposed scheme, and emphasizing those which did. While the academic discipline and the legal discipline are intimately related, insofar as the former involves the study of the latter, they are nonetheless distinct phenomena capable of differing in significant respects.

For Kahn-Freund and for Sinzheimer, labour law was social law. But it is rather less clear that this was ever so for government—even for the governments of the late 1940s and 1950s.[98] At the time of the Second World War, as Samuel Beer recounted, there was a readiness among the richer classes in the UK to share the country's wealth more evenly so as to avoid a return to the deprivations of the interwar years.[99] In 1940, the Labour Party came to power as part of Churchill's coalition, and in 1945 it won a landslide majority on a manifesto that promised to increase the working classes' share of wealth and political power.[100] There was nonetheless a strong sense in which labour laws were understood, even then, to be a means of achieving economic objectives, especially increased production.[101] When Ernest Bevin, as wartime Minister of Labour, took steps to promote trade union influence within industry and government, he did so in the firm belief that this would help to improve production: 'if you wanted people to co-operate it was common sense to discuss in advance what you proposed to do and get the views of those who would be most affected'.[102] When efforts were made in the first years of the Attlee government to use manpower policy as a central plank in a programme of economic planning, collective bargaining was understood in terms of its bearing on the choice of how to achieve the desired mobility of labour. 'If collective bargaining was to be retained as the means by which wages and conditions were determined, then labor direction would be necessary to get workers in

---

[95] Davies and Freedland, *Labour Legislation and Public Policy*, 3.
[96] Deakin, 'Paradigm', 1166–9; Davies and Freedland, 'National Styles in Labour Law Scholarship', 784.
[97] Collins, 'Productive Disintegration', 295; 'Labour Law as a Vocation'.
[98] 'Labour law has always been subordinate to prevailing economic orthodoxy': KD Ewing, 'Foreword' in C Fenwick and T Novitz (eds) *Human Rights at Work* (Oxford 2010), vii.
[99] S Beer, *Modern British Politics* (London 1969), 212–13.
[100] *Let us Face the Future: A Declaration of Labour Policy for the Consideration of the Nation* (London 1945).
[101] See chapter 4 this volume, *Labour Law and the British State: 1890s to 1950s*.
[102] A Bullock, *The Life and Times of Ernest Bevin, Volume 2* (London 1967), 96.

the right jobs. On the other hand, if collective bargaining could be eliminated, state wage-fixing would serve to attract workers voluntarily to where the plan showed they were needed.'[103]

Rather than ascribing to government a conception of labour law as, quite straightforwardly, social law, it is more accurate to recognize that labour legislation has always been shaped by a variety of policy objectives, some social, some economic.[104] As Beer commented in respect of the government's policy of nationalization: 'Public ownership was advocated on various grounds: to equalize wealth, to eliminate the political power of private wealth, to promote democracy in industrial life. But the principal case for it was the need for public control of the economy'.[105]

If it is possible to read in the proposals for a new methodology for the law of the labour market the suggestion that scholars of the past opted for a sociological or anthropological analysis *because* such analysis fitted well with some pre-existing notion on the part of the legislature of labour law as social law, then that suggestion ought to be rejected.[106] The method of the sociology of law revealed the need for (labour law as) social law by uncovering the iniquities of private law as applied to the field of employment relations, and the limits of the formal equality and formal freedom that it promised. Sociology of law, or specifically 'critical' sociology of law, established 'the social effect of the norm, . . . the way in which it appears in society and . . . its social function'.[107] By looking to sociology and to the sociology of law and by framing their analysis accordingly, Sinzheimer and Kahn-Freund made very political arguments establishing the need for labour laws that were protective—or rather, emancipatory—of labour.[108] 'The ultimate purpose of jurisprudence is legal policy,' wrote Sinzheimer. 'It is only in legal policy that the meaning of jurisprudence is fulfilled.'[109] 'The sociological method' added Kahn-Freund, 'is indispensable for the achievement of this purpose'.[110] 'At the very moment when jurisprudential thought advances beyond existing law and wishes to develop new forms of law, it becomes dependent on the sociological method. For only the latter provides the foundations for the tasks of legal policy.'[111]

---

[103] Beer, *Modern Politics*, 202.

[104] 'A congeries of objectives was served by labour market policy during the postwar "golden age"': Rittich. [105] Beer, *Modern Politics*, 190.

[106] 'industrial sociology offered an analysis of social relations, which was complementary to the aims of protective labour legislation': Deakin, 'Paradigm', 1171; 'The new subject of labour law that began to flourish in the 1960s discovered that this sociological discipline of industrial relations could be translated into a distinctive style of legal analysis': Collins, 'Productive Disintegration', 298. [107] Kahn-Freund, 'Hugo Sinzheimer', 98.

[108] Though see Sinzheimer's clarification of the scholar's role: 'Scholars cannot establish a "universally valid" ideal for legislation. . . Nothing has done more harm to the idea of legislative jurisprudence than the belief that its task is to tell the legislator which decisions to make in individual cases. . . It cannot take decisions out of the hands of the legislators, but it can provide them with those elements of knowledge which they need in order to make decisions'. H Sinzheimer, 'On Formalism in the Philosophy of Law' (1949), cited Kahn-Freund 'Hugo Sinzheimer', 100.

[109] H Sinzheimer, 'The Sociological and Positivistic Method in the Discipline of Labour Law' (1922), cited Kahn-Freund, 'Hugo Sinzheimer', 100.

[110] Kahn-Freund, 'Hugo Sinzheimer', 100.

[111] Sinzheimer, 'Sociological and Positivistic Method', cited Kahn-Freund, 'Hugo Sinzheimer', 100.

In the course of their labour law scholarship, Kahn-Freund and Sinzheimer each offered a framework for analysis of labour legislation and the decision-making of the judiciary which was closely tied to the terms of the law—did not ignore or dismiss them—but which read those terms in a particular light.[112] In so doing, they aimed to make a single coherent scheme of the collection of laws which was to be described as labour law.[113] At the same time, they aimed to accord a particular normative vision to that scheme. They engaged quite consciously, it might be said, in the politics of definition.

Today, labour law continues to be shaped by a variety of policy objectives, some of which could comfortably be termed social. Together with competitiveness and social inclusion, fairness to workers was an often stated policy objective of the Labour governments of 1997 to 2010.[114] The principle of equal treatment of workers and job applicants informed the enactment of a body of legislation during the same period, not only in the interests of social inclusion but also in recognition of the dignity of the individual.[115] In recent years, statements have been made by the judiciary and the legislature (albeit the Second Chamber) identifying the imbalance of bargaining power between the employer and the employee as an important policy consideration.[116] What has changed since the 1940s or 1970s is not so much the categorization of labour law by government as either social law or economic law, but rather the way in which all policy objectives have tended to become secondary to the perceived need to ensure that labour markets function well—to ensure, above all, that labour markets are *flexible*. Since the advent of the third way, flexibility has come to be understood, across the party political board, to be necessary to the achievement of high employment levels and a competitive economy. As a consequence, policies and legislation in the field of employment have tended to be judged—primarily—in terms of their propensity to increase or hinder labour market flexibility. Indeed, such is the ubiquity of the flexibility imperative in policy discourse and decision-making, that the case can be made quite convincingly that labour market flexibility is now the 'single organizing rationale' in the field, 'permeating and structuring debates about optimal labour and employment laws, the path of labour law reform, and forms and functions of social policy'.[117]

In the work reviewed in this chapter, Deakin and Wilkinson, Davies and Freedland, and Collins each attempted in their own way to rationalize the labour legislation and policy of the Blair governments, to make a coherent scheme of the whole, and to develop a framework for the analysis of constituent elements. In line with government policy, they each adopted the labour market as a primary

---

[112] They each worked their way 'through the black-letter analysis of the law' as Kahn-Freund memorably put it: they neither 'went round it nor got stuck in it'. 'Hugo Sinzheimer', 77.
[113] Deakin and Wilkinson describe collective laissez-faire as a 'rationalization' of the law: Deakin and Wilkinson, 200.   [114] See, for example, *Fairness at Work*, Cm 3968 (London 1998).
[115] See, eg, Department of Trade and Industry, *Towards Equality and Diversity* (London 2001).
[116] Lord Clarke in *Autoclenz Limited v Belcher* [2011] UKSC 41, at para 35. Lord Pannick (Liberal Democrats) in the House of Lords, 20 March 2013, debating the Growth and Infrastructure Bill.
[117] Rittich.

object of regulation and thus of analysis. Over and above that, they each displayed a degree of willingness to accept the government's definition of the overall aims of legislation and regulation in the field, and to evaluate specific proposals and laws with reference to those aims. Davies and Freedland, as we have seen, were quite explicit in suggesting that scholarship ought to develop in line with the policy objectives of government; the promotion of social inclusion and the expansion of the productive economy.[118] The task for scholars was then to pursue 'rigorous investigation into the question of what part the law of employment has played so far and might play in the future in achieving these profoundly important social objectives'.[119] For Collins, the task was to identify the regulatory techniques that would best facilitate and stabilize flexible employment relations.[120] For Deakin, the question 'at the core of an interdisciplinary research agenda for "labour market regulation"' was whether the impact of labour laws on unemployment, employment, and inequality could be examined empirically.[121] Of course, there was to be no assumption here that labour markets would function better *without* labour legislation. The question to be addressed by scholars was whether particular instances of legislative or regulatory intervention made it more or less likely that that the market would function so as to produce the desired outcomes: more jobs, greater productivity.

It is the acceptance of the objectives of social inclusion and competitiveness, and the consequent adoption of market functioning or market efficiency as the rationalizing or organizing principle of the field, I would suggest, which marks the change from the 'old' ways of studying labour law to the proposed new ways of studying the law of the labour market. Of itself, the widening of the *scope* of scholarship beyond the contract of employment and collective bargaining to include the functioning of the labour market does not imply, necessarily, either the increased appropriateness of economic methods of analysis or the obsolescence of sociological methods.[122] Employment relations, after all, are as much economic phenomena as they are legal or social, and the market is as much a social construction as it is an economic or legal one.[123] To define the *aims* of the field of law with reference to market functioning, however, is to send labour law scholarship down a different path indeed from the one followed since the 1950s. The suggestion, then, is that scholars should turn to economic methods not only to assist with the description and analysis of the law, but as a means of constructing normative or evaluative arguments. The case for labour law—for regulatory intervention in the labour market—should be supported by empirical evidence as to its propensity to improve, and not hinder, the capacity of the market to function so as to

---

[118] Davies and Freedland, *Towards a Flexible Labour Market*, 249.
[119] Davies and Freedland, *Towards a Flexible Labour Market*, 249.
[120] Collins, 'Regulating the Employment Relation'.   [121] Deakin, 'Paradigm', 1172.
[122] Lord Wedderburn, 'Labour Law 2008: 40 Years on' (2007) 36 *Industrial Law Journal* 397–424, 402–3.
[123] Deakin and Wilkinson, chapter 1; K Polanyi, *The Great Transformation: The Political and Ecnomic Origins of our Time* (Boston 2001); W Streeck, 'The Sociology of Labor Markets and Trade Unions' in NJ Smelser and R Swedberg (eds) *The Handbook of Economic Sociology* (Princeton 2005).

produce a particular set of outcomes. Description and analysis should be shaped accordingly.

The adoption by Deakin and Wilkinson, Davies and Freeland of a market-focused framework of analysis was apparent throughout their work, but most obviously perhaps in their discussion of collective labour relations. Here, as elsewhere, legislative proposals (or the lack thereof) were described and assessed primarily in terms of their propensity to improve or hinder the functioning of labour markets specifically, or the market economy more generally. In discussing the restriction by the Conservative governments of the 1980s and 1990s of the right to strike, and the decision of the Blair governments not to restore the right to its earlier, wider form, for example, Davies and Freedland explained that, 'legislating to control the externalities generated by industrial action [had been] given priority over the untrammelled operation of the principle of self-regulation or private ordering by employers and trade unions'.[124] While British governments had been subject to continuing criticism from legal scholars, the labour movement, and the ILO in respect of the limitation of the right to strike, 'the impact of these comments on the government was not such as to cause it to change its policy'.[125] In considering the Blair government's policy with respect to collective bargaining and corporatism, they pointed to the fact that the 'decentralisation of collective bargaining and the decline in the coverage of collective agreements were not unwelcome . . . [T]he government, or parts of it, took the view that an unreformed collective bargaining system already promoted wage flexibility, in the negative sense that it provided no obstacle to the process.'[126]

When it came to an assessment of the statutory recognition procedure that formed the centrepiece of the Government's innovations in the field, Davies and Freedland, like Deakin and Wilkinson, framed their comments, for the most part, with reference to the government's stated aim of encouraging 'partnership' or cooperative relations between labour and management.[127] 'The economic advantages which flow from cooperation . . . are now generally accepted and understood,' wrote Deakin and Wilkinson.[128]

For those who have long walked the path of 'old' labour law scholarship, commentary informed by the market-focused framework can be discomfiting. As viewed from the perspective of the law of the labour market, arguments that do not speak directly to the efficiency-enhancing or efficiency-obstructing potential of the legislation or policy in question are, bluntly put, not immediately relevant or persuasive. When compared with old or alternative approaches to the study of labour law, the exposition offered by Davies and Freedland, Deakin and Wilkinson. and Collins is remarkable for the way in which non-market considerations—such as the question of whether more, or more centralized, collective

---

[124] Davies and Freedland, *Towards a Flexible Labour Market*, 112.
[125] Davies and Freedland, *Towards a Flexible Labour Market*, 112.
[126] Davies and Freedland, *Towards a Flexible Labour Market*, 239.
[127] Davies and Freedland, *Towards a Flexible Labour Market*, 118–29; Deakin and Wilkinson, 326–39. [128] Deakin and Wilkinson, 338.

bargaining might improve working lives, securing more dignity for workers, or more democracy at work—seem to lose their force.[129] 'In their analyses of the history and functions of trade unions', Deakin and Wilkinson wrote, 'Sidney and Beatrice Webb identified *labour market regulation* as the central purpose of trade union organization.'[130] One cannot help but wonder what the Webbs might have made of that.[131]

The Labour Market and the State

There is no alternative

In scholarly and political expositions of the third way, globalization was identified as prominent among the factors which rendered 'old' social democracy ineffective and in need of updating.[132] In particular, globalization was said to make it necessary for social democrats to reconsider what they understood to be the appropriate role of the state. The old left had been 'preoccupied with state control', almost fetishizing state intervention and, in the UK, nationalization as ends in themselves.[133] Free market capitalism had been understood to produce undesirable outcomes, which had to be remedied by the state. The state had been regarded as responsible, ultimately, for the provision of those public goods which markets could not deliver, including greater substantive equality between citizens and a welfare system which protected individuals from the cradle to the grave. Globalization weakened the capacity of states to perform these functions. At the same time, it rendered more urgent the need for states to be competitive on the global stage. Each of these developments implied the need for a different kind of relationship between states and markets: instead of subordinating markets to government, states should direct their resources at promoting competitive and well-functioning markets. Contrary to the dogma of neoliberalism, markets did not necessarily function optimally when unregulated. Government could take positive steps to improve the functioning of markets, utilizing their 'dynamism . . . with the public interest in mind'.[134]

Though it was emphasized by proponents of the third way that globalization had been planned and facilitated by nation states, the suggestion was nonetheless clear that the choice now facing them, of how to respond to globalization,

---

[129] Cf T Novitz and P Skidmore, *Fairness at Work* (Oxford 2001); Bogg.
[130] Deakin and Wilkinson, 201, citing S and B Webb, *The History of Trade Unionism* (London 1894) and *Industrial Democracy* (London 1897). My emphasis.
[131] In *Industrial Democracy*, the Webbs advocated the replacement of the market as the means of organizing the economy with public administration under democratic control. Trade unions were understood to be economic and political actors, and collective bargaining the means of securing industrial democracy and thus the emancipation of the working class.'Trade Unions and Democracy', *Industrial Democracy*, esp. 840-2; S Webb, *Labour and the New Social Order* (1918), cited Beer, 190.
[132] See generally A Giddens, *The Third Way: The Renewal of Social Democracy* (1998); Blair.
[133] Blair, 1.   [134] Giddens, 100.

was severely limited.[135] The predicament of 'old social democracy' was universal. Welfare systems were everywhere in crisis, and the solution was everywhere the same.[136] Welfare spending should be directed primarily at 'investment in human capital' and, through a variety of demand and supply side measures, at job creation and high levels of employment.[137] Labour market rigidities such as 'protective' employment legislation were not the cause of unemployment, and deregulation was not the answer. But getting people into work surely was, and national governments could take a variety of steps in furtherance of that objective: encouraging entrepreneurship, investing in 'life-long' education and training, and ensuring the creation of family-friendly working practices.[138]

The matter of the desired role of the state in the economy was addressed at length by Deakin and Wilkinson in the final chapter of their book. In seeking to identify an 'effective rationale' for the present state of labour market regulation, and for future reform, the authors posited the idea of the well-functioning labour market as central to their deliberations: 'The question which we wish to address is: *what kind of normative or regulatory framework is needed in order for labour markets to function in the interests of a range of societal goals, of which efficiency is one?*'[139]

Their discussion began with a definition of the labour market, and other markets, as a 'spontaneous order' or 'self-organizing system'. The labour market was organized or ordered, in other words, by a set of mutually reinforcing conventions, themselves the outcome of an evolutionary process. The authors then identified the limits of self-ordering markets. Of particular significance to the discussion of labour markets were the ways in which markets could result in, or exacerbate, inequalities between market actors. Demand and supply were each structured by mutually reinforcing conventions (and by other norms and laws). Cumulatively, these conventions could result in 'dynamic processes which lead to the segmentation of the labour market and, as a result, to mismatches (or imperfections) in the process of pricing of labour power'.[140] As a consequence, inequality could become endogenous to the market in question. Using the language of resource endowments (eg labour power, family wealth), economic functionings (eg nourishment, healthcare), and capabilities (ie the substantive freedom to achieve various economic functionings), the authors explained this further:[141] 'A virtuous cycle is in operation through which ample resource endowment leads to labour market advantage which enhances capability and economic functioning, which in turn enables increase in resource endowment. By contrast, paucity of resource endowment interacts with reduced capabilities in reinforcing poor economic functioning, leading to a vicious cycle of disadvantage.'[142]

Through participation in the labour market, in other words, the rich might get richer while the poor got poorer. The rich, and the children of the rich, might get the better jobs, earning more money, and being positioned as a result to take

---

[135] Giddens, 28–33. [136] Giddens, 114–17. [137] Giddens, 117–28.
[138] Giddens, 124–6. [139] Deakin and Wilkinson, 277.
[140] Deakin and Wilkinson, 285. [141] Deakin and Wilkinson, 288–90.
[142] Deakin and Wilkinson, 288.

advantage of further labour market opportunities. The poor, and the children of the poor, might get stuck in low-end, low-paid jobs, lacking the resources to pay for all that was necessary—education, training, childcare, and other domestic help—to climb the jobs ladder, and increase their wealth, their capabilities.

In the scheme of Deakin and Wilkinson's argument, it was the identification of the limits of self-ordering which allowed for normative arguments to be made in favour of state intervention or regulation.[143] The state had a role to play in dealing with externalities.[144] Because a well-functioning market was a market in which everyone was able to participate (in which all of society's resources were utilized), the state also had a role to play in ensuring that everyone was in possession of *endowments*, in the sense of items of value that could be traded.[145] Without endowments, an individual would be unable to participate, to the detriment of that individual and of society as a whole. The state should intervene to redistribute wealth, not as a means of correcting the market, but as a means of ensuring the preconditions for a well-functioning market. That said, it was certainly not the case that the identification of ways in which regulation might be useful should be translated into uncritical support for all types of labour law.[146] The authors' intention was to advocate only those forms of regulation that were 'compatible with the preservation of a market order'.[147]

For Deakin and Wilkinson, the characterization of redistribution as market creating suggested a normative basis for social rights. Sen's observations regarding *conversion factors* were highly significant here, ie his identification of capabilities as a consequence not only of endowments, but also of an individual's ability to exploit those endowments.[148] It followed that in seeking to ensure the *preconditions* for a well-functioning market, the state might take steps not only to redistribute endowments themselves, but also to ensure access to the 'processes of socialization, education and training' which would enable individuals to exploit their endowments. It might take steps, in other words, to promote or guarantee particular social rights—to healthcare, education, equal treatment. The example of the right of a woman not to be dismissed by reason of her pregnancy could help to illustrate this point.[149] Understood with reference to Sen's capabilities approach, such a right could be seen to address the potential injustice done to individual pregnant women and at the same time to improve the overall well-being of society. Without laws aimed at protecting the right of pregnant women not to be dismissed, women generally would not expect to continue in work after becoming pregnant. A norm would emerge as a result of which there would be no investment in the skills and training of women of a certain age, and less investment of effort by such women in their jobs. As a result, society would be less well off. Pregnancy protection laws—and other social rights—could be understood as a form of

---

[143] Deakin and Wilkinson, 290.
[144] Deakin and Wilkinson, 283.
[145] Deakin and Wilkinson, 283–4.
[146] Deakin and Wilkinson, 294.
[147] Deakin and Wilkinson, 294.
[148] Deakin and Wilkinson, 290–4.
[149] Deakin and Wilkinson, 290–3.

institutionalized conversion factor. Such laws provided the conditions under which the formal freedom to enter the labour market became a substantive freedom.

As with other forms of market regulation, arguments in favour of social rights were made by Deakin and Wilkinson subject to the condition that such rights had to be compatible with the *preservation of a market order*. Viewed in this light, old ways of thinking about social rights became problematic. In his classic exposition of *Citizenship and Social Class*, TH Marshall had categorized social rights in opposition to the market: 'social rights imply . . . the subordination of market price to social justice'.[150] Today, there was a need for a new form of social rights which worked with and not against the market, guaranteeing 'the effective conditions for [its] functioning'.[151] There was a need, in particular, for social rights which functioned as institutionalized forms of capabilities, providing individuals with the means to realize the potential of their resource endowments.[152] Such rights would not interfere with the spontaneous order of the market, but rather would perform a market-creating function, widening the scope of the market and allowing economic agents, through market participation, to benefit themselves and others.[153]

As was clear from the terms of their argument, and from the choice of Hayek as an interlocutor, Deakin and Wilkinson were at pains, here, to construct a case for social rights which addressed the neoliberal objection that social rights or labour laws upset the 'spontaneous order' of the market, to the disadvantage of individuals and society alike. This explained the decision to tie their argument very closely to the question of labour market functioning, to emphasize the potential of social rights as market constituting. Even in times of globalization, even if the state felt itself under pressure to become more competitive, it did not make sense, so the argument went, to deregulate labour markets, dismantling existing social rights and labour protections. Social rights could contribute to efficiency *and* to other social goods.[154] To base the normative case for social rights—and labour law—on their potential to improve the functioning of labour markets, however, was to raise a number of questions. How extensive was the range of rights for which such a case could be made? Did it exclude labour laws that sought straightforwardly to improve workers' terms and conditions? As Deakin himself put it: 'If, for example, "enhancing labour market opportunity" replaces "job security" or "income protection", does this mean downgrading existing levels of regulation on the basis that they impede, not simply the efficient operation of market forces and competitiveness, but also market access to "outsiders" and the unemployed—perhaps even deny them "the right to work"?'[155] Could a convincing 'market-constituting' case be made for rights to collective representation, collective bargaining?

---

[150] TH Marshall, 'Citizenship and Social Class' reprinted in TH Marshall and T Bottomore, *Citizenship and Social Class* (London 1992), 40, cited Deakin and Wilkinson, 344.
[151] Deakin and Wilkinson, 345.   [152] Deakin and Wilkinson, 347.
[153] Deakin and Wilkinson, 348.   [154] Deakin and Wilkinson, 277.
[155] Deakin, 'Paradigm', 1172.

With reference to Sen and to the importance not only of endowments but also of conversion factors, Deakin and Wilkinson attempted to stretch the market-based case for social rights to encompass a wide range of rights. Like pregnancy protection laws, minimum wage laws, for example, were argued to represent a form of 'institutional conversion factor', since they 'require firms to adopt strategies based on enhancing the quality of labour inputs' and therefore have 'a positive impact on incentives and training'.[156] More generally, protective labour laws were characterized as a means of combating social exclusion arising by reason of discrimination and the undervaluation of labour.[157] With respect to collective labour rights, Deakin and Wilkinson acknowledged the existence of a conflict of interest between managers and workers concerning the distribution of profits, but argued nonetheless that social rights could benefit management and the workforce alike: social rights created a balance of power in the workplace, in organizations, in the wider society, which in turn improved 'the creation, development and use of productive resources, and [prevented] their dissipation in unemployment and poverty'.[158] Of course the condition that all state interventions should be compatible with the 'preservation of a market order' applied here too, and elsewhere the authors observed that 'sectionally-based trade unions . . . exercise control over entry to particular labour market segments . . . [restricting] access to and use of human capital'.[159] How the different statements were to be reconciled was nowhere fully explained.

'Little Red Riding Hood without any mention of the wolf'

In one of his last published works, Paul O'Higgins referred memorably to the story of Little Red Riding Hood without the wolf, drawing attention to the way in which globalization is often described, in academic writing, as politically neutral.[160] Little or no account is taken of the way in which the processes integral to globalization—trade liberalization, currency market liberalization, the relaxation of rules governing foreign investment and cross-border capital flows—have been politically driven, and have served greatly to weaken labour relative to capital around the globe, increasing inequalities of wealth within and between nation states.[161] A similar criticism could be made of third way discourse and its tendency to depict the economy and markets in abstract, apolitical terms, the labour market understood simply as a site where willing buyers of labour meet with willing sellers. Conflicts of interest between buyers and sellers are thereby greatly underemphasized—confined, on the face of it, to the matter of price—and the scope of common interests overstated.[162] Partnerships at work are said to be mutually

---

[156] Deakin and Wilkinson, 293. [157] Deakin and Wilkinson, 293–4.
[158] Deakin and Wilkinson, 348–9, 348.   [159] Deakin and Wilkinson, 287,
[160] P O'Higgins, 'The End of Labour Law as We Have Known It?' in C Barnard, S Deakin, G Morris (eds) *The Future of Labour Law; Liber Amicorum Bob Hepple QC* (Oxford 2004), 289.
[161] O'Higgins, 'The End of Labour Law', 289; Klare, 5–6; Wedderburn, 'Labour Law 2008'.
[162] Deakin and Wilkinson, 348–9.

beneficial, and flexible employment relations are claimed to benefit the employer and the employee alike. What is missing from such accounts is proper recognition that the very purpose of (private-sector, but increasingly also public-sector) employers is to exploit resources and people in the pursuit of profit (or savings).[163] Capitalist economies are characterized not only by their organization around markets, but also by systems of private property which enable the few to own the means of production and force the many to sell their labour power in order to live. Distinct social classes with oppositional political interests are a necessary feature of such economies, and conflicts of interest extend far beyond the price of labour to include even the fundamental question whether or to what extent labour ought to be treated as something that is bought and sold: 'as an exploitable resource, or as human capital, [or] instead as an essential area for self-realisation'.[164]

For Eric Tucker, it was a failure to take account of the structural features of capitalism which constituted the central weakness of Deakin and Wilkinson's account of the law of the labour market.[165] Only by considering labour markets in quite abstract terms were the authors able to argue that social rights were market constituting in a way that transcended old notions of conflict between social interests and the market. In fact, the definition of social rights as either market constituting or market constraining was simply a matter of perspective.[166] For Deakin and Wilkinson, social rights might figure as constitutive of ('well-functioning') labour markets insofar as they prevented markets from developing 'pathologically', causing or exacerbating substantive inequalities between market actors. For others, they might be experienced simply as barriers to be overcome in the drive to maximize profit. Recognition of the realities of existing capitalist labour markets, 'built on definite social and property relations and a social logic of accumulation', revealed that social rights did indeed conflict with ('push back against') labour markets.[167] 'Although the content of the capabilities approach may vary, it surely contains elements whose effect is partially to decommodify labour.'[168] Failure to recognize these realities resulted, in Tucker's estimation, in an 'overly optimistic assessment of the prospects for advancing the capabilities agenda within a largely untransformed capitalist market economy'.[169] Deakin and Wilkinson's account 'depends on the existence of a happy coincidence of the normatively desirable and the efficient, and on an unnamed agent capable of its enactment'.[170]

Tucker's reference to an 'unnamed agent' brings to mind the suggestion made in much of third way writing that the state could no longer, or ought not to take steps to require employers to do things that they did not want to do. In the 1998 White Paper, *Fairness at Work*, the Blair government explained its reluctance to

---

[163] Glasbeek.
[164] A Supiot, 'Towards a European Policy on Work' in N Countouris and M Freedland (eds) *Resocializing Europe in a Time of Crisis* (Cambridge 2013).
[165] Tucker, 'Renorming Labour Law'.
[166] Tucker, 'Renorming Labour Law', 124.
[167] Tucker, 'Renorming Labour Law', 126.
[168] Tucker, 'Renorming Labour Law', 122.
[169] Tucker, 'Renorming Labour Law', 131.
[170] Tucker, 'Renorming Labour Law', 136.

impose new legal obligations on employers with reference to the inherent limits of the law: 'a change of culture cannot be brought about by a change in the framework of the law'; 'the new culture we want to nurture and spread is one of voluntary understanding and co-operation because it has been recognized that the prosperity of each is bound up in the prosperity of all'.[171] There were strong echoes here of arguments made by proponents of new governance theory regarding the self-defeating nature of old-style 'command and control' legislation: that the imposition of substantive standards creates rigidities both in law and in the social fields that regulation is attempting to control; that the targets of regulation in any case resist what regulation there is and oppose any new interventions.[172] At the same time as the state's capacity to regulate in ways contrary to the interests of capital was doubted or denied, trade unions had in fact become greatly weakened, and in the majority of workplaces were simply absent. Insofar as the state couldn't or wouldn't take steps to require that workers be treated fairly, and because organized labour was only exceptionally in the position to do so, some were drawn to the conclusion that the *employers* must be relied upon to choose to act 'responsibly'.[173] Governments should attempt nothing more than to 'nudge' businesses in the right direction,[174] to 'encourage' or 'facilitate' the desired behaviour,[175] to help them to understand that treating workers fairly served their own interests too.[176] Bringing capitalism back into the picture was argued by others to cast doubt on the likely success of such a project.[177]

Given the corporation's recent historical role in the jettisoning of such job and income security as had been won and in the dismantling of a whole raft of welfare provisions in various countries, as well as the strategies it employs to play workers from poorer countries off against workers in richer ones, why should anyone believe that there will be a corporate drive to give back some of these gains? There is a limit to the extent that managers can indulge their personal sense of altruism and/or worker-friendliness and still be true to their real task.[178]

Today, ten years after the publication of *The Law of the Labour Market*, Tucker's characterization of Deakin and Wilkinson's account as 'overly optimistic' has added force. In the aftermath of the financial crisis of 2007–8, capitalism has

---

[171] *Fairness at Work*, Foreword by the Prime Minister. See also Department of Trade and Industry, White Paper, *Our Competitive Future: Building the Knowledge Driven Economy* (London 1998), chapter 3, para 5.4.
[172] E Tucker, 'Old Lessons for New Governance: Safety or Profit and the New Conventional Wisdom' (2012) 38 *Osgoode CLPE Research Paper* 14–15.   [173] Glasbeek 302–3.
[174] R Thaler and C Sunstein, *Nudge: Improving Decisions about Health, Wealth and Happiness* (New Haven, CT 2008). Shortly after becoming Prime Minister, David Cameron established a 'nudge unit' to assist with the development of policy in a variety of fields.
[175] See eg the terms of the statutory recognition procedure introduced by the Labour Government in 1999 and contained in the Trade Union and Labour Relations (Consolidation) Act 1992, schedule A1; discussed R Dukes, 'The Statutory Recognition Procedure 1999: No Bias in Favour of Recognition' (2008) 37 *Industrial Law Journal* 236–67.
[176] See generally, *Fairness at Work*; Collins, 'Regulating. . . for Competitiveness', esp 34.
[177] Streeck refers to the need to 'bring capitalism back in' Streeck, *Re-Forming Capitalism*, 25.
[178] Glasbeek, 303.

reared its ugly head again with renewed vigour, casting fresh light on the win–win promises of the third way.[179] Across national borders, the real losers from the crisis and the ensuing economic recession have been workers, who have suffered unemployment, cuts to real wages, and cuts to social welfare entitlements.[180] Income inequalities, augmented already under the watch of third way governments, have been stretched to new extremes.[181] In Colin Crouch's terms, the 'embedded' neoliberalism of the 2000s (largely congruous with third way thinking) has very quickly and very easily given way to a more 'simple-minded' neoliberalism, familiar to us from the 1980s and 1990s:[182] 'European and many national policy makers have driven a more uncompromising marketization policy that no longer accepts the logic of a need to balance the extension of markets with countering their negative externalities. Citizens' rights at work and social policy are again being seen in solely negative terms as a constraint on corporations' freedoms.'[183]

In the UK, the election of the Conservative Party in 2010, in coalition with the Liberal Democrats, marked a significant shift in policy in the field of employment relations.[184] In the years since, the third way rhetoric of flexibility and fairness has been employed by Conservatives and Liberal Democrats to explain a raft of measures aimed at deregulation and the 'removal of red tape'.[185] When judging the purported burdensomeness of particular laws and provisions, moreover, the government has shown a marked willingness to accord weight to *employer perceptions* of employment law.[186] For a provision to be at risk of being thrown onto the government's 'bonfire' of red tape, it has not been necessary to show that it limits flexibility and growth as a *matter of fact*, but only to show, or to assert, that it does so in the minds of employers.[187] By basing their policy decisions upon employer perceptions, and not upon empirical evidence as to the impact of labour standards on labour markets, employment levels, and efficiency, the government has been able to reassert the old idea that a 'well-functioning' labour market is simply one

---

[179] Supiot, 'Towards a European Policy on Work'.
[180] R Freeman, 'New Roles for Unions and Collective Bargaining Post the Implosion of Wall Street Capitalism' in S Hayter (ed) *The Role of Collective Bargaining in the Global Economy* (Cheltenham 2011), 264–7.
[181] Freeman, 'New Roles for Unions and Collective Bargaining', 264–7.
[182] C Crouch, 'Entrenching Neo-Liberalism: The Current Agenda of European Social Policy' in N Countouris and M Freedland (eds) *Resocialising Europe in a Time of Crisis* (Cambridge 2013).
[183] Crouch, 'Entrenching Neo-Liberalism'.
[184] B Hepple, 'Back to the Future: Employment Law under the Coalition Government' (2013) 42 *Industrial Law Journal* 203–23.
[185] See generally D Renton and A Macey, *Justice Deferred: A Critical Guide to the Coalition's Employment Tribunal Reforms* (Liverpool 2013).
[186] Or at least to what it claimed to be 'employers' perceptions': see eg Department of Business, Innovation and Skills (BIS), *Consultation on Implementing Employee Owner Status* (London 2012), 4. Research carried out on behalf of BIS and published in March 2013 suggested that employers generally considered that employment regulation was both necessary and fair: E Jordan, AP Thomas, JW Kitching, RA Blackburn, 'Employment Regulation Part A: Employer Perceptions and the Impact of Employment Regulation' (London 2013).
[187] The government has repeatedly promised a bonfire of red tape. See eg statements of Business Minister Michael on 14 December 2012: <http://news.bis.gov.uk/Press-Releases/Government-tackles-red-tape-head-on-with-package-of-measures–684dd.aspx> For extended comment on the government's use of evidence see Hepple, 'Back to the Future', 213–21.

in which employer freedom to allocate labour resources is maximized. According to that logic, of course, the scope for making normative arguments in favour of social rights as market constitutive or market compatible is narrowed very considerably.[188] The argument that social rights or labour rights are desirable *because* they help markets function better is quickly defeated by the claim that the latter premise is untrue (or is perceived by employers to be untrue).[189]

Conclusion

Over the past 20 years or so, the idea that labour markets ought to be highly flexible has achieved the status of a new global orthodoxy or common sense.[190] In substance, the idea is the expression, in the field of employment relations, of a particular strand of economic rationality or logic derived from a version of neo-classical economics.[191] Its essence or central premise, as applied to labour relations, is that labour market institutions—statutory rights, trade unions, collective bargaining practices—constitute barriers to the optimal functioning of labour markets; unless responding to a defined set of market failures, labour market institutions produce a series of labour market inefficiencies likely to generate both higher unemployment and depressed rates of economic growth. Both the nature of this rationale and the quite remarkable extent to which it has become accepted across the globe pose significant challenges for scholars of labour law. How can we construct arguments *against* the blanket deregulation or deconstruction of labour market institutions and at the same time defend ourselves against the charge of irrelevance or futility? The assumption, as Richard Freeman put it, is all too often that 'only some Rip Van Winkle unaware of modern thinking about the virtues of markets could possibly think that collective bargaining was essential and that minimum wage and hours regulation were useful'.[192]

In making the argument that labour law ought to be reconceived as the law of the labour market, British scholars have been motivated in large part by a wish to remain relevant and to be in a position to make the kinds of arguments that might have an impact on current government policy. This was expressed quite unambiguously by Davies and Freedland in the closing passages of *Towards a Flexible Labour Market*. Criticisms had been made of New Labour, they wrote, regarding 'the growth of precarious employment and of insecurity of income for large sections of the workforce or of the expansion of extreme inequalities of income between sections of the workforce' and regarding 'the very significant

---

[188] Commenting more generally on the 'flexibility' paradigm in labour law discourse, Rittich highlights the 'conundrum' of the resilience of the idea that labour market institutions constitute barriers to economic growth in the face of equivocal or even contradictory evidence and the 'naivety' of imagining that policy makers will be persuaded by the establishment of 'the facts': Rittich.
[189] Hepple makes a similar point when he suggests that 'Opponents of [labour market] regulation have managed to turn the business case on its head in times of economic recession': Hepple, 'Back to the Future', 220.   [190] Rittich.
[191] J Stiglitz, *Globalization and its Discontents* (London 2002).   [192] Freeman, 255.

omission... to construct or to reconstruct a strong institutional voice for trade unions'.[193] Because the 'political impact' of such criticisms had been limited, however, it might be concluded that scholars should better devote their energies to assessing the contribution of employment law to the achievement of the government's own (market-related) goals.[194] For Deakin and Wilkinson, the hegemonic nature of the flexibility imperative and neoclassical economic reasoning implied the need to engage specifically with economic arguments and methodologies so as to address head-on the claim that labour laws or social rights constituted barriers to economic growth.[195] This explained their choice of Hayek as an interlocutor, and Deakin's suggestion that labour lawyers ought to learn to engage with *economic* theories and *economic* lines of analysis.[196]

As has been argued in this chapter, it is one thing to acknowledge the importance of the labour market as an object of study, and quite another to adopt 'the market', or the objective of orchestrating a 'well-functioning market', as the rationalizing or organizing principle of the field of scholarship—the frame of reference for the formulation of normative claims and evaluative commentary. When scholars argue that the scope of labour law as an academic discipline ought to be extended to include the labour market in addition to employment relations, they readily convince. The questions raised by consideration of labour markets—questions of market access, of market segmentation, of the impact of labour standards on employment levels—are undoubtedly of great importance, both to policy debates and to the lives of working people. As Davies and Freedland first argued with characteristic insight in the 1980s, studying labour markets in addition to employment relations as such can allow for a very useful combination of micro and macro perspectives.[197] The traditional focus on employment relations and the rights and obligations of the individual worker can be supplemented with a market perspective that more clearly reveals the larger social and economic consequences of particular labour laws.[198] Moreover, giving consideration to labour markets turns the spotlight squarely on important forms of legislative and policy intervention that are often overlooked or underemphasized by traditional approaches to labour law: for example, aspects of family law and social security law which impact directly on questions of labour supply.[199] And it reflects the experience of a growing numbers of workers, who instead of enjoying long-term employment in

---

[193] Davies and Freedland, *Towards a Flexible Labour Market*, 248.
[194] Davies and Freedland, *Towards a Flexible Labour Market*, 248–9.
[195] Deakin and Wilkinson were quite explicit about this when writing together with Jude Browne: 'A capability approach could be highly useful in rebutting some of the criticisms offered of social rights from a neoliberal perspective, namely that they interfere with the workings of supply and demand and compromise the contractual autonomy of economic agents': J Browne, S Deakin, F Wilkinson, 'Capabilities, Social Rights and European Market Integration' in R Salais and R Villeneuve (eds) *Europe and the Politics of Capabilities* (Cambridge 2005).
[196] Deakin, 'Paradigm', 1171.
[197] Davies and Freedland, *Labour Law Text and Materials*, 11.
[198] Davies and Freedland, *Labour Law Text and Materials*, 11.
[199] Deakin and Wilkinson, chapter 3; Fudge, 'Labour as a "Fictive Commodity"'.

the form of a 'job for life', find themselves participating in external labour markets several or many times in the course of their working lives.

In the work of the 2000s reviewed in this chapter, the authors each moved beyond recommendation of an expansion of the scope of labour law as a field of study, to advocacy of a new unifying rationale for the field—as Deakin and Wilkinson put it, a new 'framework for analysis and evaluation of the existing law and of proposals for legal change'.[200] Without wishing to obscure significant differences between the authors, it is fair to suggest, I think, that they each proposed a rationale or framework that was tied quite closely to the idea of well-functioning labour markets and to the outcomes which such markets could deliver: social inclusion and greater competitiveness or productivity. In common with Kahn-Freund and Sinzheimer, the authors intended thereby to identify a framework for analysis which was closely informed by the terms of the law, but which, by reading those terms in a particular light, lent a degree of coherence to the relevant legislation and policy as a unified field of study. They also intended to ascribe to that field a particular normative vision, one that would allow for the construction of persuasive normative arguments in favour of certain types of labour market regulation.

In the 2007 book review article, Deakin himself raised the question whether, by seeking to base arguments regarding the desirability of labour rights or legislation on claims or evidence regarding the propensity of those rights to further market-related goals, scholars did not limit the kinds of right or regulation for which a case could be made.[201] If laws were judged against their capacity to 'enhance labour market opportunity', for example, could the case still be made for provisions that aimed to guarantee workers a measure of job or income security?[202] Could the case be made for rights to collective representation and collective bargaining? As was highlighted above, it is when applied to the field of collective labour rights that the limitations of the labour market approach are most strikingly revealed. In the course of their discussion of collective labour law, Deakin and Wilkinson referred in passing to the benefits of rights which created 'a balance of power in the workplace, in organizations, and in the wider society', and to the existence of conflicts of interests between managers and workers regarding the distribution of profits.[203] Davies and Freedland made mention of international law and human rights arguments in favour of reform of the domestic law of industrial action, emphasizing that the government had not found these persuasive.[204] For the most part, however, both sets of authors judged the government policies and legislation in the field of collective labour rights against the government's own objectives of encouraging partnership (in the interests of improved economic efficiency and competitiveness) and ensuring flexible labour markets. No arguments were made by the authors in favour of strengthening or widening the legal

---

[200] Deakin and Wilkinson, 275.   [201] Deakin, 'Paradigm', 1172.
[202] Deakin, 'Paradigm', 1172.   [203] Deakin and Wilkinson, 348.
[204] Davies and Freedland, *Towards a Flexible Labour Market*, 112.

protection of the right to strike, or of increased government support for unionization and for the spread or centralization of collective bargaining.[205]

In the final part of this chapter, the question was raised whether the decision to refer primarily to market-related goals such as social inclusion and competitiveness as providing a framework for analysis might have resulted in the underemphasis or failure adequately to take account of conflicts of interest. Where analysis and commentary followed the policy pronouncements of the Blair government quite closely, this was almost to be expected. It is a feature of third way discourse that it tends to depict the economy and markets in abstract, apolitical terms, overstating the scope of common interests between workers and employers: everyone stands to gain from the expansion of competitive markets, from the encouragement of entrepreneurism and enterprise. So, for example, Hugh Collins, following the rationale of New Labour very closely, in 2001 presented the model of 'flexible employment relations' as beneficial to businesses and employees alike: 'We cannot separate sharply between legal regulation designed to enhance competitiveness by encouraging flexible employment relations and legal regulation designed to ensure fairness at work.'[206] Though Deakin and Wilkinson's reasoning was developed at a greater remove from government policy, it too could be criticized for offering a win–win vision of social rights that was 'overly optimistic',[207] one that defined social rights as constitutive of well-functioning markets, and well-functioning markets as those which increased the wealth and well-being of all.[208] To argue in this way was to overlook or underemphasize the fact that rights to minimum wages or paid maternity leave or collective bargaining might well be perceived by employers as limiting or obstructive of their efforts to maximize profit (in the short term). For them, a 'well-functioning' labour market might indeed be one with few or only weak labour laws.

---

[205] Other than the argument that enterprise-level collective bargaining, and the 1999 statutory recognition procedure, might contribute to the creation of partnerships at work: Deakin and Wilkinson, 334–9.
[206] Collins, 'Regulating. . . for Competitiveness', 46. Cf *Fairness at Work*, eg para 1.8.
[207] Tucker, 'Renorming Labour Law', 131.   [208] Deakin and Wilkinson, 277.

6

The Labour Constitution of the European Union

The Social Dialogue

Introduction

As used in application to the European Union, the notion of the 'economic constitution' that is most familiar is that developed by the ordoliberal school of economists.[1] From the time of the birth of that school, in the 1930s, the ordoliberals used the term *Wirtschaftsverfassung* as Sinzheimer did, to describe the economic order of a particular nation state: the body of legal rules—'constitutional', in the strict sense, or otherwise—which facilitated or constrained the conduct of actors in the economy. Normatively, the ordoliberals insisted, contrary to Sinzheimer, that the economy ought to be insulated to a significant extent from political or democratic control.[2] Real world phenomena, such as the economy, had an inherent order that should not be disturbed by concepts originating from other orders. For that reason, the desired role of the state in the economy was limited: it should guarantee a legal framework for undisturbed competition and it should provide a regime of property rights to support private initiative. Social policy should function separately from 'the economy', 'correcting' or redistributing the outcomes of market functioning only after the event. As originally constituted in the Treaty of Rome of 1957, the economic order of the European Economic Community could be interpreted as fitting well with these prescripts.[3] The Treaty created 'an economic constitution for a market system'; the Community existed to establish a common market understood as self-organizing; and member states were obliged, as a matter of law, to respect the new order, removing restrictions of inter-state trade and fair competition.[4] In the Single European Act, however, and more so the

---

[1] See generally, A Peacock and H Willgerodt (eds) *Germany's Social Market Economy* (London 1989). For a useful short summary of the ordoliberal school see Schiek, 'Europe's Socio-Economic Constitution', 172–4.

[2] A Peacock and H Willgerodt, 'German Liberalism and Economic Revival' in Peacock and Willgerodt, 1–14.

[3] Joerges, 'What is Left of the European Economic Constitution?'. As Joerges notes, such interpretation entailed the dismissal of those parts of the constitution which didn't fit with the ordoliberal picture as aberrations or errors, including, notably, the CAP.

[4] Streit and Mussler, 5–30.

Treaty of Maastricht, 'non-market elements' were introduced into the economic constitution, so that it came to resemble more closely the economic constitution of a welfare state—a development which the second-generation ordoliberals found deeply regrettable.[5]

Viewed through the lens of Sinzheimer's notion of the economic, or labour, constitution, the history of the EU can be read quite differently. What takes centre stage, in that case, is the question of the status of collective labour in the EU constitution, and EU economic order, and the terms of the legal framework which define that status. What seems to demand attention is the markedly limited nature of the formal mechanisms that existed for the involvement of labour in the administration of the EEC, and the nascent 'European' economy, in the first decades of their existence. In the period after Maastricht, it is the shortcomings of the formalized 'social dialogue' that seem to require explanation: what were the intentions that informed its constitutionalization, and why did it never live up to the claims made for it by its architects and champions? In applying the idea of the labour constitution to the EU, of course, care must be taken to avoid the trap of treating the Union as a nation state, or state in the making.[6] Given the particular, supranational, nature of the EU, the projection onto it of the idea of the labour constitution raises additional questions regarding the 'state' capacity of the Union and its governing institutions; their capacity to fulfil the supporting and supervisory role assigned to 'the state' by Sinzheimer. Questions arise too regarding the organization of labour and capital at the European level: who are the 'trade unions' and 'employers' associations' in the Union; who are the 'social partners'?

In contradistinction to nation states, one of the key features of the European economic order is its split-level configuration. The European economy is constituted by a plurality of legal orders, one supranational and several national. In considering the question of the economic or labour constitution of the EU, then, attention is owed not only to the supranational economic and legal order, constituted originally by the Treaty of Rome, but also to the relations and interactions between that order and the pre-existing economic and legal orders of the member states. The plurality of economic orders, and specifically labour constitutions, within the Union forms the focus of the next chapter, chapter 7. In terms of subject matter, chapter 7 examines the only body of EU legislation to deal specifically with questions of collective labour law, namely, the several directives providing for employee rights to information and consultation. In addition, it examines the status of labour rights as 'fundamental' within the EU legal order. Discussion of these matters is intended to address the wider question of the viability of a plurality of divergent labour constitutions in the long term, and the alternative: harmonization in either an upwards or downwards direction.

---

[5] Streit and Mussler.
[6] Streeck, 'Neo-Voluntarism: a New European Social Policy Regime?' (1995) *European Law Journal* 31–59; G Majone, 'The European Community between Social Policy and Social Regulation' (1993) 31 *Journal of Common Market Studies* 153–70.

The subject matter of this chapter is the social dialogue: the formalized processes of negotiation between organized labour and management within the EU and, in particular, at the European, cross-sectoral level. Analysing the social dialogue through the lens of the labour constitution, the chapter raises the question of the potential of the dialogue to function in a way comparable with the collective bargaining and corporatist arrangements of the (old) member states: to democratize the EU economic order, and to deliver improved substantive outcomes for European workers. In an effort to answer this question, the chapter places the Treaty of Maastricht and the social policy agreement which first constitutionalized the social dialogue in historical context. Drawing on the work of historians and industrial relations scholars, as well as labour lawyers, it assesses the social dialogue as it is embedded in the constitutional or institutional structure of the EU, and influenced by the nature and motivations of the parties to the dialogue: the 'state', the 'trade unions', and the 'employers'. In doing so, it aims to comment usefully on the European model of capitalism, and, at the same time, to begin to test the applicability of the idea of the labour constitution to the *supranational* EU.

Maastricht and the Constitutionalization of the Social Dialogue

In the EU, the term 'social dialogue' is used to refer to negotiations between the representatives of management and labour—the 'social partners'—in a variety of fora: supranational, national, subnational, cross-sectoral, sectoral.[7] It is also used in a narrower sense to refer specifically to bipartite negotiations undertaken at the cross-sectoral and European levels between the cross-sectoral European social partners, principally, the ETUC, BusinessEurope, and CEEP.[8] The cross-sectoral social dialogue, which forms the main focus of this chapter, was constitutionalized in 1992.[9] In the Treaty of Maastricht of that year, a new Protocol and Agreement on Social Policy proclaimed the right of management and labour acting 'at Community level' to negotiate contractually binding agreements, and to have these implemented either by way of collective agreements within member states, or by Directive adopted by the Council. In addition, it formalized the

---

[7] The English-language version of the TFEU refers variously to 'management and labour' and to 'social partners': Arts 152–4. Neither term is defined within the Treaty. The term 'social dialogue' is used—eg in Article 152 TFEU—but not in Arts 154–5, which refer instead to the 'consultation' of management and labour and 'the dialogue between them'.

[8] The ETUC (European Trade Union Confederation) is the representative of labour at the cross-sectoral level. Private sector employers are represented at that level by BusinessEurope, and public sector employers by CEEP: the European Centre of Employers and Enterprises Providing Public Services.

[9] Since 1987, the Treaty had required the Commission to 'endeavour to develop the dialogue between management and labour at the European level', but had not made any further provision regarding the nature of that dialogue.

involvement of the social partners in Community social policy and legislation by way of a new legal obligation on the Commission to consult the partners in a two-stage process: on legislative proposals and, if action was to be taken on those proposals, on the content of the consequent legislation.

In effect, these new provisions allowed for two different types of process: the bipartite negotiation of agreements by the representatives of management and labour on the one hand and, on the other, the consultation of those representatives by the Commission on questions of social policy and legislation. With respect to the bipartite negotiation of agreements, the provisions allowed again for different types of 'dialogue': including what might broadly be categorized as a 'guided' social dialogue, prompted and implemented by the Commission and Council, and an 'autonomous' social dialogue, initiated and implemented by the parties themselves.

Though spoken of as a unitary phenomenon, 'the social dialogue' (at the cross-sectoral, European level) is therefore better understood as comprising a number of different dialogues, varying in manner of initiation and implementation (see Table 6.1). Under the terms of the Social Policy Agreement, and now the Treaty on the Functioning of the European Union, social partner negotiations may be initiated following a Commission consultation.[10] Where such negotiations result in an agreement, that agreement may be implemented by way of Council Directive (SD 1), or 'autonomously' by collective agreements at member state level (SD 2).[11] In either case, the Commission reserves the right to assess the content of the agreement for compliance with a set of Commission-authored requirements: does any part of the agreement contravene provisions or principles of European law, including the principles of subsidiarity and proportionality; are the parties to the agreement sufficiently 'representative'; does the agreement respect the need for the development and competitiveness of small and medium enterprises; can the Commission endorse it as 'appropriate' with respect to Union policy and needs?[12] Where the social partners opt to implement the agreement autonomously (SD 2), the Commission will also monitor its implementation.[13] As is clear from the terms of the Agreement and the TFEU, negotiations may also be initiated by the social partners themselves in respect of any matter of their choosing.[14] Where an agreement is reached following autonomously initiated negotiations, it may be implemented autonomously (SD 4) or, insofar as it seeks to regulate a matter falling within the legislative competence of the Union, by Council Directive (SD 3).[15] Where an agreement is intended for implementation

---

[10] Art 154 TFEU.   [11] Art 155 para 2 TFEU.
[12] These requirements were set out by the Commission in an explanatory memorandum attached to the proposal for implementation of the Parental Leave Agreement, discussed S Smismans, 'The European Social Dialogue between Constitutional and Labour Law' (2007) 32 *European Law Review* 341–64, 347. See also COM (2004) 557, 4.4. On the question of the representativity of the social partners, see Case T-135/96 *UEAPME v Council of the European Union* and for commentary eg P Syrpis, 'Social Democracy and Judicial Review in the Community Order' in C Kilpatrick et al (eds) *The Future of Remedies in Europe* (Oxford 2000).   [13] COM (2004) 557, 4.4.
[14] Art 155 TFEU.   [15] Art 155 para 2 TFEU.

Table 6.1 Types of bipartite negotiation

	Initiation	Implementation
SD 1 (guided)	Commission	Directive
SD 2	Commission	Autonomous
SD 3	Autonomous	Directive
SD 4 (aut'mous)	Autonomous	Autonomous

by way of Council Directive, it will be directed to the institutions of the EU. Where it is intended for autonomous implementation, it will be directed to the social partners' own member organizations, recommending or requiring action at member state level in implementation of the agreement.[16]

On the face of it at least, the guided dialogue, initiated after consultation by the Commission and implemented by way of Council Directive, might be thought to resemble corporatist arrangements within nation states more closely than it does collective bargaining.[17] This is a process designed, it would seem, to involve the representatives of management and labour in the policy and legislative procedures of government—an 'institutional arrangement', as Phillipe Schmitter defined corporatism more generally, 'for linking the associatively organized interests of civil society with the decisional structures of the state'.[18] The autonomous social dialogue, on the other hand, might appear to be more readily understood as a form of transnational collective bargaining, since the social partners are free not only to decide the subject matter and the terms of the agreement, but also the method of its implementation.[19] These preliminary categorizations would seem to accord broadly with the meaning attached to the dialogue by the EU institutions. The dialogue has routinely been discussed as a feature of European 'industrial relations', together with collective bargaining within member states, European Works Councils, and information and consultation at enterprise level.[20] In the decade or so after Maastricht, it was described on more than one occasion as fundamental to the European social model, a means both of initiating and directing social reform, and of securing good governance and respect for the principle of subsidiarity.[21] With statements such as these, the Union institutions appeared to suggest that the social dialogue should be understood as comparable with the

---

[16] COM (2004) 557
[17] See eg T Novitz and P Syrpis, 'Assessing Legitimate Structures for the Making of Transnational Labour Law: The Durability of Corporatism' (2006) 35 *Industrial Law Journal* 367–94, and further references cited by Novitz and Syrpis, n 1.
[18] P Schmitter, 'Still the Century of Corporatism?' (1974) 36 *Review of Politics* 85–131, 86.
[19] For a discussion of the legal basis of the autonomous social dialogue that is based upon a comparison of the dialogue with collective bargaining within member states, see D Schiek, 'Autonomous Collective Agreements as a Regulatory Device in European Labour Law' (2005) 34 *Industrial Law Journal* 23–56.
[20] European Commission, *Industrial Relations in Europe 2010* (Luxembourg 2011).
[21] See eg Presidency Conclusions, Barcelona European Council 2002, para 22; *Commission Communication on the European Social Dialogue*, COM (2002) 341 final.

collective bargaining and corporatist arrangements characteristic of some of the (old) member states—as a means of bringing greater democracy to the Union by allowing for the participation of labour in policy-making and legislation.

The history of the social dialogue since Maastricht can be divided into two periods: 1992 to 2002, and 2002 to date.[22] In the first period, the guided social dialogue was prominent. Of the three agreements reached by the cross-sectoral social partners (dealing with parental leave (1995), part-time work (1997), and fixed-term work (1999)), all three were initiated by Commission consultation, and implemented by way of Council Directive. At sectoral level, too, any agreements reached were closely tied to EU policy and implemented by way of Council Directive.[23] In the second period, efforts were made to develop the social dialogue along more autonomous lines. At a Social Summit in Laeken in 2001, the ETUC, BusinessEurope, and CEEP emphasized the importance of autonomy in the social dialogue and, while recognizing the continued importance of the guided social dialogue, declared their intention to develop a work programme for the autonomous type.[24] From 2002, the social partners began to issue periodic 'joint work programmes' in which they took steps to set their own policy agenda. On the basis of these, four trans-sectoral agreements were reached (dealing with telework (2002), work-related stress (2004), harassment and violence at work (2007), and inclusive labour markets (2010)), each of which made provision for its 'autonomous' implementation by the social partners at member state level, rather than by Council Directive.[25] (A fifth cross-sectoral agreement revising the first agreement on parental leave was implemented by way of Council Directive in 2008.) At sectoral level, too, agreements were reached which were intended to be implemented autonomously in the member states.[26] And in transnational companies, autonomous 'joint texts' were adopted, in some cases through the efforts of European Works Councils.[27]

Reviewing the concrete outputs of the cross-sectoral social dialogue in 2011, a senior researcher at the ETUI,[28] Stefan Clauwaert, described them as impressive in terms of their quantity.[29] In addition to the eight agreements mentioned above, the social partners had issued two 'frameworks of action' since 1992, and over 70 joint texts, ranging from declarations, statements, and opinions to joint reports.[30] In terms of their quality, however, Clauwaert conceded that the texts were, at best, mixed. The Parental Rights, Part-Time Work and Fixed-Term Work

---

[22] S Clauwaert, '2011: 20 Years of European Interprofessional Social Dialogue: Achievements and Prospects' (2011) 17 *Transfer* 169–79.   [23] Smismans, 344.
[24] Joint Contribution by the Social Partners to the Laeken European Council (7 December 2001).   [25] <http://www.etuc.org/actions>.
[26] Smismans, 344; European Commission, *Industrial Relations in Europe 2012* (Luxembourg 2013), 7.2.1.
[27] In the years 2000–2010, over 200 texts were adopted in 100 companies: European Commission, *Industrial Relations in Europe 2010* (Luxembourg 2011), Box 6.3. A further 70 texts were adopted between 2010 and 2012: Industrial Relations in Europe 2012, Table 7.2.
[28] European Trade Union Institute, the research and training centre of the ETUC.
[29] Clauwaert, 172.
[30] Clauwaert, 171. A third 'framework of action' was concluded in 2013 on youth unemployment.

Directives were no doubt important symbolically as the first fruits of the constitutionalized social dialogue, but in terms of their content they were widely criticized as delivering far less than had originally been proposed. Within the ETUC, a number of affiliates had been so disappointed with the substantive provisions of the three agreements at the time of their negotiation that they had argued for the Confederation's support for them to be withdrawn.[31] Commenting on the legislation in 2006, Sandra Fredman concluded that the social objectives (of the trade unions) had indeed been undermined by the economic objectives (of the employers): the Parental Leave Directive guaranteed workers only rights to *unpaid* leave, for example, and the Part-Time Work and Fixed-Term Work Directives embodied a 'highly diluted notion of equality'.[32]

While there was certainly some dissatisfaction with the substantive terms of the Directives, then, they did undoubtedly serve to create new legal rights for workers, and to compel the adoption of new legislation in some of the member states.[33] The same cannot be said of the 'new generation' texts intended for autonomous implementation. Taking the agreement on work-related stress as an example, all that the agreement purported to do was to 'increase the awareness and understanding of employers, workers and their representatives of work-related stress', and to 'provide employers and workers with a framework to identify and prevent or manage problems of work-related stress'. In the three years allowed for its implementation, it was implemented by binding national collective agreement in six member states, and in a further nine states was said to have 'triggered or substantially accelerated social dialogue and policy development'. In some states it was not implemented at all, and in others the matter of its implementation was not even reported upon.[34] In light of this experience, the Commission concluded that there was 'room for improvement' with respect to the development of 'adequate responses'.[35] Attempting a positive appraisal of the work-related stress agreement and the autonomous agreements on telework, harassment, and inclusive labour markets, the most that Clauwaert could find to say was that they had served to 'put the issues high on the agenda at many negotiating tables'.[36]

A comprehensive assessment of the achievements of the social dialogue must also take account of the failures of the social partners to reach agreements when negotiations have been initiated, either by the Commission or by the partners themselves. Prominent among these are the examples of the European Works Councils and Information and Consultation of Employees Directives of 1994 and 2002, the former being the first ever proposal considered under the social dialogue procedures introduced by the Maastricht Treaty. In the case of each of the Directives, the social partners were consulted twice by the Commission—on the possible direction of legislative action, and on the content of the Commission's

---

[31] J Dolvik and J Visser, 'ETUC and European Social Partnership: A Third Turning-Point?' in H Compston and J Greenwood (eds) *Social Partnership in the European Union* (Basingstoke 2001), 27–9.
[32] S Fredman, 'Transformation or Dilution: Fundamental Rights in the EU Social Space' (2006) 12 *European Law Journal* 41–60, 47.   [33] Clauwaert, 172.
[34] Industrial Relations in Europe 2010, 186–7.
[35] Industrial Relations in Europe 2010, 187.   [36] Clauwaert, 173.

proposals. In the case of each, negotiations between the partners failed to result in any agreement because of the objections of one or more of BusinessEurope's member organizations.[37] And significantly, in the case of each, the consultation process resulted in weaker legislation than had originally been proposed by the Commission, in terms of the rights to be accorded to workers and their representatives.[38]

Judged as a form of corporatism or transnational collective bargaining, then, the outputs of the social dialogue to date could only be described as disappointing. An explanation would appear to be required as to why there have been so few cross-sectoral agreements over the years, of such little substance. Viewing the history of the Union as a whole, additional questions arise. Why did it take until 1992 for the position of the social partners to be formally recognized in this way? What was the role and status of organized labour in the European Community prior to that year? How is labour organized at the European level? Who are the 'social partners'? If the social dialogue is comparable to the corporatist arrangements of some of the member states, how do the European institutions fulfil the functions of the 'state' in those arrangements: recognizing or authorizing the participant interest groups, coordinating negotiations between them, giving force to resulting agreements?[39] Is the characterization of the social dialogue as a form of corporatism or collective bargaining borne out, even, by further consideration of its nature as practised since 1992, of its forerunners prior to that year, and of the intentions and aspirations of those involved in its development?

Paris and Rome

At the time of the foundation of the European Communities in 1951 and 1957, the question of labour participation in their administration was closely intertwined with the question of whether the Communities were essentially intergovernmental or federalist in nature and in aspiration. If the Communities were to any significant extent federalist, governed by supranational bodies that were in some respects at least independent of the member states, then it followed that trade unions and other interest groups should have rights of representation and participation at the supranational level, as they did within the member states. If, however, the Communities were more clearly intergovernmental in nature, the case for the integration of trade unions and other interest groups in decision-making procedures was not as easy to make. If decision-making power was to remain in the hands of the member states, then it was within the member states, primarily, that trade unions would be able to pursue their interests. If Community decisions

---

[37] In the case of the EWC Directive, agreement seemed possible until the British CBI withdrew from negotiations. See further: G Falkner, 'European Works Councils and the Maastricht Social Agreement: Towards a New Policy Style?' (1996) 3 *Journal of European Public Policy* 192–208. In the case of the ICE agreement, BusinessEurope was not granted a mandate by its members to agree to legislation of that type.   [38] Falkner, 196–7.   [39] Schmitter, 93–4.

were to be conditional on the agreement of an intergovernmental Council, then the unions would anyway be able to exert an influence on such decisions from within the member states, through established channels. Importantly, the question of the institutional configuration of the Communities would also tend to influence the unions' and union members' own perceptions of where their interests lay and in which fora those interests would most easily be furthered. And these perceptions would, in turn, inform both the readiness of the unions to devote time and resources to lobbying for supranational representation, and their ability to act as effective representatives at the supranational level.

When Robert Schuman declared his plans for a Coal and Steel Community (ECSC) in 1950, the labour movements of Western Europe were characterized by nothing so much as their heterogeneity.[40] Within the six member states, trade unions were split along political and/or religious lines. In France and Italy, communist-oriented trade unions were particularly dominant, while in Belgium, France, and the Netherlands, Christian trade unions had significant membership. In Germany and the Benelux countries, the labour movements were relatively strong, organizationally and financially, whereas in France and Italy, the unions had fewer members and much more limited financial resources. Differences between national movements were further accentuated by marked disparities in the legal rights which unions enjoyed to participate in board-level or workplace managerial decision-making or to bargain collectively with employers. By 1950, there were three international federations in existence, split again along religious and Cold War political lines. The International Confederation of Free Trade Unions (ICFTU) represented non-Communist unions, the International Federation of Christian Trade Unions (CISC) represented Christian unions, and the World Federation of Trade Unions (WFTU) represented communist-oriented unions, mainly in China and the USSR. Within Europe, the ICFTU was by far the most representative international federation, with 24.5 million members in 1957, compared to the 3 and 4.5 million of the CISC and WFTU respectively.[41] Notwithstanding its high levels of membership, however, ICFTU, like the other federations, suffered from a serious lack of resources.[42]

With the exception of the communist trade unions, which were strongly opposed to integration in Western Europe, both national unions and international federations were broadly supportive of the creation of the ECSC.[43] In Germany, the cooperation of an originally sceptical *Deutsche Gewerkschaftsbund* (DGB) was secured by Konrad Adenauer in exchange for his promise of domestic legislation

---

[40] H-V Schierwater, 'Der Arbeitnehmer und Europa-Integrationstendenzen und -Strukturen im Sozialbereich des Gemeinsamen Marktes' in C Friedrich (ed) *Politische Dimensionen der europäischen Gemeinschaftsbildung* (Opladen 1968), 295–302.
[41] RC Beever, *European Unity and the Trade Union Movements* (Leyden 1960), 21–2.
[42] In the period to 1960, it had a total annual income of only £164,000: Beever, 32.
[43] See generally: E Haas, *The Uniting of Europe: Political, Social and Economic Forces 1950–1957* (Stanford 1958, 1968), chapter 6; Schierwater, 299–302.

on codetermination rights.[44] In France, Italy, and the Benelux countries, governments regarded the ECSC as an opportunity to strengthen the socialist trade unions against the communist unions, integrating the former in the Community and excluding the latter.[45] Initially, national union federations remained quite firmly tied to what they regarded as their primary function of promoting national interests. Indeed, one of the principal reasons for supporting integration was the belief that the ECSC might provide a new platform for the achievement of national aims: more jobs for Italian/German/French workers, and better terms and conditions for those workers. The idea of supranational controlling bodies in whose decision-making trade unions would be able to participate was also attractive.[46] Having given their support to the broad idea of integration, trade unions did not feel restricted in criticizing individual elements of the project, if they understood these to pose a threat to national interests. Fearing that German jobs might be at stake, for example, the DGB was quick to make efforts to limit the number of 'ECSC visas' available to coal and steel workers. French free trade unions, meanwhile, echoed their government's fears regarding the deleterious consequences for the French economy of dismantling tax barriers.[47] By reason of these national priorities, the supranational federations, the ICFTU and CISC, encountered serious difficulties in attempting to coordinate common points of view among member unions.[48] They were able nonetheless to lobby on behalf of members for more union representation within and vis-à-vis Community institutions.[49]

According to the terms of the Schuman Plan and the wider policies of the French, as formulated by Schuman and Jean Monnet, the ECSC was envisaged as a supranational organization. The French intended that the ECSC should serve certain political ends: European federation and French security against German growth. Solutions were sought, in particular, for the problem areas of the Saar and the Ruhr. With these political aims in mind, Schuman and Monnet insisted that the Community should be formed according to a 'principle of supranationality'. 'We persist in thinking', wrote Schuman, 'that the simple coordination of governmental efforts is insufficient. We must create communities of interest on concrete foundations without the preponderance of certain countries, for the advantage of all.'[50] With the prior agreement of the Germans, participation in the negotiations to draft a Treaty was made conditional on acceptance of the supranational principle, and negotiations proceeded accordingly.[51] National delegations consisted not only of government representatives, but, in addition, of 'independent personalities who [had], besides technical capacity, a concern for the general interest': academics, industrialists, and trade union representatives.[52] Trade unionists were thus

---

[44] Adenauer was first Chancellor of the Federal Republic. See further, H. Thum, *Mitbestimmung in der Montanindustrie: der Mythos von Sieg der Gewerkschaften* (Stuttgart 1982); J. Gillingham, *Coal, Steel, and the Rebirth of Europe, 1945–1955* (Cambridge 1991), 284.
[45] B Barnourin, *The European Labour Movement and European Integration* (London 1986), 5.
[46] Haas, chapter 6; Thum.   [47] Schierwater, 299–302.   [48] Haas, 369 ff.
[49] Beever, 123–38.   [50] Haas, 244.   [51] Haas, 246.
[52] Memorandum of the French Planning Council, cited: S Quack and M-L Djelic, 'Adaptation, Recombination and Reinforcement: The Story of Antitrust and Competition Law in Germany and

directly involved in drafting the terms of the Treaty of Paris, particularly those that concerned wages and social questions, production, prices, and investment.[53]

In line with the French preference for supranational government, involving leaders independent of national governments advised by technical experts and interest groups, trade unions were accorded fairly extensive rights to participate in the decision-making processes of the ECSC institutions.[54] Formally, their most significant role was within the so-called Consultative Committee, representing workers alongside two further groups of equal size of producers, and consumers and dealers. In practice, the Consultative Committee proved to be a relatively ineffectual institution. Though the governing 'High Authority' was required to listen to the advice of the Committee in a large variety of situations, it was not obliged to heed it.[55] In time, the High Authority developed a practice of consulting the unions directly on matters of importance to workers. Contacts between the Authority and the unions were reinforced by a rule that at least one of the nine members of the High Authority ought to be a person 'enjoying the confidence of the trade unions'.[56] In fact there were three labour representatives among the first nine members of the Authority and one of them, Paul Finet, served as its president for a time.

The creation of the ECSC served as an important early impetus for the establishment of specifically European, or European Community, trade union bodies. In 1950, ICFTU formed a 'European Regional Organization' (ERO) to represent trade unions in Western Europe, including those from both signatory and non-signatory states to the Treaty of Paris.[57] In 1951, the coal and steel unions in Luxembourg took steps to create a body more specific to the ECSC, the 'Committee of 21', made up of 21 representatives of the free trade unions of the six member states and of the ERO.[58] The Christian unions acted at the same time to create representative committees of their own.[59] As the trade unions' experience of supranational organization and action within Europe grew, in the context of their interactions in the ECSC, attitudes to European integration remained positive. In a 1955 resolution, the ERO expressed the hope that European integration would be accomplished 'within the framework of a policy of full employment and social progress in general, including an upward adjustment of social conditions'.[60] In 1956, it reiterated its support for further integration and proposed that labour should have an important voice in the preparatory stages of the formation of the new Communities, as well as in (all) of their institutions.[61]

Europe', in W Streeck and K Thelen (eds) *Change and Continuity in Institutional Analysis* (Oxford 2005), 255–81, 263. Full list of members of delegations available at <http://www.cvce.eu>.

[53] R Roux, 'The Position of Labour under the Schuman Plan' (1952) 65 *International Labour Review* 289, 292–3; Haas, 362.

[54] K Featherstone, 'Jean Monnet and the "Democratic Deficit" in the EU' (1994) 32 *Journal of Common Market Studies* 149–70, 155.   [55] Schierwater, 314–15.   [56] Roux, 295.

[57] Schierwater, 297.

[58] Schierwater, 305; M Bouvard, *Labour Movements in the Common Market Countries* (New York 1972), 51–5, 66–70.   [59] Schierwater, 309–10; Bouvard, 78–91.

[60] Barnourin, 5–6.   [61] Barnourin, 6; Bouvard, 72.

When it came to the drafting of the Treaties of Rome and the constitution of the EEC and Euratom, however, trade unions had a rather less straightforward path to positions of influence. By the mid-1950s, Schuman and Monnet were no longer at the forefront of political decision-making. Without their leadership, France showed itself more ambivalent to the idea of a United Europe, blocking the creation of the European Defence Community in 1954 as contrary to French interests. In West Germany, opinion was divided. Konrad Adenauer, chancellor from 1949 to 1963, remained convinced of the benefits of federation, but the minister responsible for specific measures of economic cooperation, Ludwig Erhard, was vehemently opposed to further political integration, considering it inimical to the greater priority of global free trade. Without leadership from France and Germany, it fell to the Benelux countries to take the next steps towards integration. In 1955, the foreign ministers of the three states drafted the so-called Benelux Memorandum, setting out plans for the creation of new supranational institutions to manage atomic energy throughout the member states, and to administer a general common market.[62] France agreed to the proposals in essence, explicitly reserving the question of the need for supranational institutions for later study.[63] Under the influence of Erhard, Germany's response was reserved, signalling agreement, but placing a clear emphasis on the benefits of intergovernmental rather than supranational cooperation.[64]

In 1956, the stated reticence of France and Germany to embrace supranationalism found independent expert approval in the form of the Ohlin Report. This was a report commissioned by the member states from an ILO committee of experts on the 'social aspects of problems of European co-operation'.[65] Led by Bertil Ohlin, a Swedish politician and economist, the ILO experts were particularly expert in the field of economics, as was reflected in their approach to the task.[66] On the basis of a primarily economic analysis of the functioning and potential benefits of a general common market, the committee recommended that supranational institutions be assigned a rather narrow role, ensuring freedom of movement across borders for economic resources. In the view of the committee, market integration would neither require nor render desirable the equalization of social costs across borders. Differences in wages and other social costs between member states would not, in themselves, pose a serious obstacle to the realization of efficiency gains from market integration. Despite the divergent starting points of member states, in terms of living and working conditions, and

---

[62] Jean Monnet was working 'behind the scenes' in tandem with Benelux foreign ministers: R Mayne, 'The Role of Jean Monnet' (1967) 2 *Government and Opposition* 349–71; F. Duchêne, *Jean Monnet* (New York 1994), ch 9.   [63] Haas, 272.

[64] Haas, 278; See also the letter from August Pinay, French Foreign Minister, of 10 June 1955, in which he describes German attitudes as 'inflexible... reflecting the concerns of Mr Erhard': <http://www.cvce.eu>.

[65] Group of Experts, *Report on the Social Aspects of European Economic Co-operation*, Studies and Reports, New Series, No. 46 (Geneva, ILO, 1956). Summarized at (1956) 74 *International Labour Review* 99.   [66] ILO 74 *International Labour Review* 99.

social guarantees, freer trade would lead to economic growth, and economic growth, in turn, would lead to an improvement in standards across the board. It was quite appropriate, then, that the regulation of social policy should remain in the hands of member states and national institutions. The supranational institutions would see to it that trade became free, and the national government and institutions would ensure that the economic returns from free trade resulted in higher standards of living and working. It was here, in the context of member state regulation of social standards, that trade unions had an important role to play.[67] Economic growth required free trade across borders, but the realization of economic gains from freer trade was dependent on the preservation of strong labour standards *within* member states. The Spaak Report of 1955, which was essentially the White Paper for the Rome Treaties, followed the same line of reasoning.[68]

As ultimately agreed by the foreign ministers of the six states, the terms of the Treaties of Rome closely resembled the Ohlin and Spaak blueprint for an Economic Community focused narrowly on the task of market integration. Little provision was made in the Treaty for direct intervention in social policy matters by the Community institutions. A short 'social provisions' chapter proclaimed a number of principles, including the promotion of improved working conditions and standards of living, and equal pay for men and women for equal work. But very little was done to empower the institutions to take action in furtherance of these principles.[69] With the exception of the right to free movement for workers, which was understood to be integral to the goal of market integration, no enforceable rights were granted to citizens in the realm of social policy, and no specific legal competences were conferred upon the institutions. The possibility remained that social legislation might be adopted by exercise of the Community's general legislative competences, but was limited by the requirement, in that context, for unanimous agreement within the Council of Ministers.[70] With respect to the institutional set-up of the EEC, the balance of power favoured the intergovernmental Council over the supranational 'Commission'. The Commission was given powers to initiate policy and legislation, but implementation of its initiatives was made conditional on the agreement of the Council. Under early drafts of the Treaties, no provision at all was made for the representation of trade unions within the institutions. After much union lobbying, an 'Economic and Social Committee' was created, consisting of representatives of trade unions, industry, and other interest groups, with responsibility for advising the Commissions and Councils on specified matters. This was a relatively weak body, however, with no power to draw up its own budget or to create its own rules of procedure, no

---

[67] ILO 74 *International Labour Review* 99, 112.

[68] *Rapport des chefs de délégations aux Ministres des Affaires Etrangères* (Brussels 1956). Part I of the Report (dealing with the common market) was summarised in English translation in 'Political and Economic Planning' (1956) 22(405) *Planning* 222–43. Reference to trade unions at 235.

[69] Articles 118 and 120 TEEC placed the Commission under obligation to make studies of various social standards in the member states and to report annually to the European Parliament.

[70] For example, Articles 100, 101, or 103 TEEC.

power of initiative, and no right to offer advice unless called upon to do so by the Council or Commission.[71]

As a matter of principle, the trade unions did not accept the Ohlin Report prescription of a common market without a social dimension. From 1957, they developed a 'programme for Europe' which aimed to prevent just that—the development of a 'free' common market.[72] They spoke in favour of far-reaching institutional reforms intended to render decision-making in the EEC more democratic and transparent (including a directly elected European Parliament with legislative and budgetary powers), and to strengthen the voice of labour (a right of initiative for the Economic and Social Committee, and 'parity' industrial committees for all sectors of the economy). In the field of employment relations, they called for the harmonization of living and working conditions, an employment policy guaranteeing full employment, and the democratization of decision-making within the enterprise.[73] Given the limited nature of their formal legal rights to participate in the EEC, the unions focused their attentions in the early years on developing practices of lobbying—lobbying both Community institutions and member state governments, since decision-making power remained, for the most part, in the hands of the intergovernmental Council of Ministers. Finding, in particular, members of the Commission and officers of the Directorates General quite open to regular contact (the Directorate General 'Economy and Internal Market' was an exception in this respect), the unions commented positively on their lobbying experience.[74] From as early as the 1950s, it was a deliberate policy of the Commission to encourage the formation of European-level interest associations, so that it might consult with them and rely upon them for providing expert advice.[75] As the number of interest associations grew, the Commission set up a procedure for recognizing them formally, and for reimbursing the expenses incurred by representatives when participating in advisory committees.[76] Extensive though these various means of communication were, the fact remained that with few legal rights to participate in Community policy-making and legislative processes, trade unions were more or less wholly reliant on the goodwill of the Commission and the people working for it to listen and take notice of their views. Significantly, the unions had no authority to dictate the timing or manner of the consultation and were often consulted only after plans and projects had assumed something close to a finished form.[77] The Economic and Social Committee too was consulted, routinely, late in the day.[78] As a result, the opportunities available to trade unions to shape Community projects and decisions were quite limited.[79]

---

[71] Barnourin, 126–32,
[72] Barnourin, 72–8, referring to the programme of the 'free' trade unions.
[73] Barnourin, 72–8.   [74] Schierwater, 321, 322.
[75] See generally: JA Sargent, 'Corporatism and the European Community' in W Grant (ed) *The Political Economy of Corporatism* (London 1985).   [76] Sargent.
[77] Schierwater, 324.   [78] Schierwater, 318.   [79] Schierwater, 328–9.

Rome to Maastricht

Given the involvement of six nation states in the foundation of the European Communities—and within those states an assemblage of politicians, economists, industrialists, and trade unionists—it goes without saying that a variety of motivations and intentions were at play in the process of agreeing the constitutional frameworks. Of course, the six shared an interest in lasting peace; and they were united, too, as Alan Milward emphasized, in the belief that a common market would encourage the kind of growing prosperity on which their domestic legitimacy rested.[80] At the level of specifics, however, as we have seen, the priorities of the states, and of groupings within the states, diverged.[81] In the midst of differing conceptions of the aims of the Communities, there was, significantly, no lasting consensus that the project was ultimately federalist in its ambitions. Notwithstanding the inclusion of the goal of 'ever greater Union' in the Preamble of the Treaty of Rome, many continued to advocate the retention of political control by the individual member states.

In the decades following the formation of the EEC, the status and role of trade unions in the Community continued to be influenced by the outcomes of the struggle between those who favoured political integration, and those who opposed it. In the late 1960s and early 1970s, efforts to reinvigorate the European project went hand in hand with plans to construct a body of social policy and legislation at the supranational level. Then, as at other times in the history of the Union, supporters of European integration and social democrats found themselves in something of a strategic coalition, recognizing that state-building and social policy could be mutually facilitative.[82] The greater involvement of the Community in social policy was championed, above all, by trade unions and by the social democratic governments of a number of the member states, and coincided with a 'worldwide wave of labour militancy'.[83] In 1972, the UK, Denmark, and Ireland acceded to the Communities, and in 1974, the EEC adopted its first Social Action Programme. With the more or less explicit aim of furnishing the common market with a greater degree of legitimacy in the eyes of member state citizens,[84] the Programme promised full and better employment, improvement of living and working conditions, and greater participation of workers and employers in Community decision-making.[85] In pursuance of this third objective, steps were taken in the middle 1970s to construct a form of corporatism at the European

---

[80] 'Western Europe was constructed, not from the destructive consequences of the Second World War only, but from those of the catastrophic economic collapse of 1929–32': A Milward, *The Reconstruction of Western Europe 1945–51* (Berkeley 1984), 463.

[81] Haas, *The Uniting of Europe*, ch. 7.   [82] W Streeck, 'Neo-Voluntarism', 39, 42, n 18.

[83] W Streeck, 'The Crisis of Democratic Capitalism' (2011) 71 *New Left Review* 5–29, 11; Streeck, 'Neo-Voluntarism', 42.

[84] 'Unless the process of growth can be put more fully at the services of society, growth itself may become politically unacceptable': European Commission, *The Social Action Programme*, European Community Bulletin, no 10 (1974), para 3.

[85] European Commission, *Social Action Programme*, para 9.

level, involving the participation of the representatives of management and labour in a variety of bipartite and tripartite committees and discussions.[86] Little resulted from these efforts, and in 1978, the ETUC withdrew its support from the process, dispirited by the lack of progress.[87]

In the mid-1980s, a second renewal of efforts to deepen integration took the form of a project to 'complete the single market'. As an adjunct to the primarily economic goals of the project, the Commission under Jacques Delors emphasized the importance of creating a 'European Social Space' or *Espace Sociale Européen*.[88] In 1989, the Community Charter of Fundamental Social Rights was adopted, closely followed by a Commission Action Programme containing proposals intended to implement the otherwise non-binding provisions of the Charter.[89] Again, steps were taken to encourage the institution of bi- and tripartite negotiations at Community level, between the Commission, the unions and the representatives of management. The hope, on the part of Delors, was that a form of collective bargaining might be developed which could function as an alternative means of agreeing and adopting social policy legislation at Community level.[90] In November 1985, he initiated a series of talks between the unions and management—known as the Val Duchesse talks—dealing with macro-economic policy, and social aspects of new technology.[91] These, like their predecessors, ended without the negotiation of any agreement of substance.[92] In 1987, Delors announced, nonetheless, that with the exception of health and safety, there would henceforth be no legislation on social policy matters without the agreement of both social partners.[93] At the same time, he made efforts to ensure that an obligation to develop the social dialogue would be included in the Single European Act.[94]

European 'corporatism' and the European 'social partners'

In the early 1970s, the prospect both of enlargement and of the formation at EEC level of social policy and legislation served to encourage the reform and strengthening of the trade unions' European representative bodies.[95] At the same time, a gradual thawing of religious and political divides in the labour movement

---

[86] W Streeck and PC Schmitter, 'From National Corporatism to Transnational Pluralism: Organized Interests in the Single European Market' (1991) 19 *Politics and Society* 133–65, 138–9.
[87] Dolvik and Visser, 17.
[88] C Barnard, *EU Employment Law* 4th ed (Oxford 2012), 12.
[89] European Commission, *Communication Concerning its Action Programme*, COM (89) 568 final (Brussels 1989).
[90] G Ross, *Jacques Delors and European Integration* (Cambridge 1995), 45.
[91] H Northrup, D Campbell, and B Slowinski, 'Multinational Union-Management Consultation in Europe: Resurgence in the 1980s?' (1988) 127 *International Labour Review* 525–43, 538.
[92] Northrup et al.   [93] Northrup et al.
[94] A Martin and G Ross, 'In the Line of Fire: The Europeanization of Labour Representation' in A Martin and G Ross (eds) *The Brave New World of European Labor: European Trade Unions at the Millenium* (New York, Oxford 1999), 323–4.
[95] See generally, BC Roberts and B Liebhaberg, 'The European Trade Union Confederation: Influence of Regionalism, Détente and Multinationals' (1976) 14 *British Journal of Industrial Relations* 261–73.

raised the possibility of unifying the representation of labour at the European level. In 1973, the European Trade Union Confederation was created out of the amalgamation of existing umbrella organizations. In contrast to the earlier organizations, the new Confederation was open to the affiliation of all national trade union centres throughout the Communities and EFTA, including Christian and Communist-oriented unions, provided only that these were 'democratic'.[96] European industrial committees such as the European Metal Workers Federation were also allowed to join. At the first meeting of the ETUC in Brussels in 1973, its membership extended to 18 national trade union organizations with a total membership of 28 million workers. By the time of the second Congress, in London in 1976, it had 30 affiliated organizations with a total of 37 million members.[97]

Of course, the strength of the new ETUC could not be measured with reference to its membership alone. As the European level representative of labour, the organization suffered from a number of shortcomings. First and foremost, it was financially very weak. Membership dues brought in an annual income of only half a million US dollars, which was barely enough to rent an office in Brussels and pay the salaries of a small staff.[98] Arguably, this was reflective of the rather limited expectations which member unions had of the ETUC.[99] The tendency within national umbrella organizations was still to prioritize national interests, and to pursue these either at the national level or through intergovernmental channels.[100] Nor did this look set to change as a result of the Community's expansion; the British TUC, in particular, remained highly sceptical of encouraging too much activity and authority in Brussels, being unconvinced that there was much to be gained from supporting the growth of Community power.[101] A second weakness of the ETUC resulted from the difficulties associated with reaching agreement among its members on policy positions. The diversity between national labour movements—in terms of their history, traditions, roles, power, and objectives—meant that there was often little commonality of interest across national divides. With respect to the growth of multinational enterprises, for example, it might have been easy enough to reach agreement on the need to democratize the enterprises, but it was much more difficult to agree the desired method of democratization.[102] With respect to an improvement of working and living conditions, the challenge was to identify standards which would benefit workers in richer countries, without over-burdening the economies of poorer countries.[103] Voting practices within the ETUC served only to compound such difficulties: though formally, decisions could be reached with the agreement of a two-thirds majority, consensus decision-making remained the norm. Nothing at all could be decided without the agreement of the TUC and DGB, and these were often at odds with

---

[96] Agreement regarding the affiliation of Christian and communist-oriented trade unions had not been reached by the time of the formation of the ETUC in 1973 but was negotiated during the course of the following years: Roberts and Liebhaberg, 264–6.
[97] Roberts and Liebhaberg, 266.   [98] Martin and Ross, 322.
[99] Martin and Ross, 322.   [100] Streeck and Schmitter, 140.
[101] Roberts and Liebhaberg, 271.   [102] Roberts and Liebhaberg, 268–9.
[103] Streeck and Schmitter, 140.

one another.[104] Despite all efforts to reach agreement between member unions, then, any joint platforms adopted by the ETUC tended to be deliberately vague, declaring general aims only.[105]

The principal representative of business at the European level, BusinessEurope, was created in 1958.[106] Its members were the umbrella federations and confederations of business and employers in all member states of the Council of Europe, and as such it was representative, indirectly, of millions of large, medium, and small companies.[107] Though BusinessEurope itself was small in terms of size and budget, it was able to draw on the much greater technical, legal, linguistic, and financial resources of its members.[108] Until 1987, it was regarded, in any case, as merely 'the eyes and ears' of business in Brussels, since by reason of the requirement for unanimity in the Council, companies and federations tended to concentrate their lobbying efforts at the national level, hoping to convince their national minister to veto the measure at the next Council meeting.[109] Within the Community, it was privileged among lobbyists. Whereas the ETUC was consulted almost exclusively by DG V regarding questions of social policy, BusinessEurope as the representative of 'industry' tended to be consulted regularly by all DGs on a wide variety of matters.[110] With respect to the potential development of corporatist bargaining at European level, the most significant characteristic of BusinessEurope was its consistent opposition to social policy initiatives.[111] From the very outset, it identified its interests as lying with an unregulated—'free'—single market, and consequently with the obstruction, at European level, of all market-constraining social policy initiatives.

On the face of it, at least, the Social Action Programme of 1974 represented an attempt to create a European labour constitution understood in the Sinzheimerian sense as entailing the use of labour law to democratize the economy. In a section entitled, 'Participation and Industrial Democracy', the Programme declared the intention of the Commission to create 'effective structures' for the participation of the two sides of industry in Community decision-making, 'to develop such participation and to render it *as effective as possible*'.[112] The objective of creating effective structures for participation was included after extensive lobbying by the trade unions and was informed, in part, by a widespread recognition that the Economic and Social Committee had failed to make much of an impact on Community policy and legislation.[113] In the years since 1957, it had failed both as a mechanism for involving the representatives of labour and management in decision-making, and as a means of constructing a 'social dimension' to the common market, as

---

[104] Martin and Ross, 323.   [105] Streeck and Schmitter, 140.
[106] Initially, it was called the *Union of Industrial and Employers' Confederations of Europe*: UNICE.
[107] Z Tyszkiewicz, 'UNICE: The Voice of European Business and Industry in Brussels', in D Sadowski and O Jacobi (eds) *Employers' Associations in Europe: Policy and Organization* (Baden-Baden 1991).   [108] Martin and Ross, 324.   [109] Tyszkiewicz, 94.
[110] R Hyman, 'Trade Unions and the Politics of the European Social Model' (2005) 26 *Economic and Industrial Democracy* 9–40.   [111] Bouvard, 116; Streeck and Schmitter, 141-2.
[112] Commission of the European Community, *The Social Action Programme*, para 12.
[113] Streeck and Schmitter, 138.

demanded consistently by the unions.[114] Notwithstanding the ambitious terms of the Programme, however, a corporatism involving one extremely reluctant participant, and another without the capacity to force its opponent's hand, was never very likely to succeed. In the 1970s, the employers resisted all efforts of the ETUC and the Commission to construct a social dimension to the EEC, participating in tripartite meetings without any intention of making any real concessions in that direction.[115] Prior to the Val Duchesse talks of the mid-1980s, BusinessEurope went so far as to insist, as a condition of its participation, that the Commission guarantee that it would not produce proposals for legislation from any agreement that might emerge.[116] As a result, the parties were restricted from the outset to producing non-binding, informal opinions.

Towards the end of the 1980s, and following the cessation of the Val Duchesse talks, the Commission once again urged the renewal of social partner efforts to engage in bipartite negotiations at Community level. Recognizing the difficulties that had been encountered during previous rounds of talks, it developed a strategy of bolstering the ETUC, on the one hand, and, on the other, creating an incentive for the representatives of management to engage more whole-heartedly in negotiations.[117] In addition to taking time to convince reluctant trade union groups and individuals of the benefits of participation, the Commission began to provide the ETUC with financial support to the value of several million euros per year. With the Commission's prompting, constitutional reform of the Confederation was attempted and, in 1993, it was granted the authority to represent its members in the social dialogue, albeit only on the basis of specific mandates drawn up and awarded on a case-by-case basis.[118] The perennial problem of having to forge common opinions and decisions among a group of nationally based organizations persisted. In respect of BusinessEurope, the Commission adopted a stance of 'negotiate or we will legislate': if the federation refused to participate in negotiations with labour, the Commission would come forward with legislative proposals of its own.[119] In 1991, the Commission wielded this threat successfully to encourage BusinessEurope to participate in the negotiation of an agreement as to how the social dialogue should proceed in the future.[120] The resulting 'October agreement' was then used as a template for the relevant provisions of the Maastricht Social Policy Agreement. Under the terms of the SPA, as we have seen, the Commission was henceforth required to consult the social partners in a two stage process—on all legislative proposals in the field of social policy and, if action was to be taken on those proposals, on the content of the legislation. The social partners were explicitly authorized to reach contractually binding agreements, and to have these

---

[114] Streeck and Schmitter, 138. [115] Streek and Schmitter, 138–9.
[116] Tyszkiewicz, cited P Teague, 'Constitution or Regime? The Social Dimension to the 1992 Project' (1989) 27 *British Journal of Industrial Relations* 310–29, 318.
[117] Martin and Ross, 324–7.
[118] Martin and Ross 327–9, 338–40. For a brief explanation of the ETUC's constitution today, see: <http://www.etuc.org/composition-and-organisation> The constitution is available at <http://www.etuc.org/a/70>.   [119] Dolvik and Visser, 21–2.   [120] Dolvik and Visser, 21–2.

implemented either by way of collective agreements within the member states or by Directive adopted by the Council.

A hostile environment?

Taken together, the Commission's machinations in the late 1980s and early 1990s might have been understood to have created the conditions necessary for the development of a successful social dialogue. Where BusinessEurope and/or CEEP was unwilling to bargain with the strengthened ETUC, the Commission could make proposals of its own which might result in legislation adopted by the Council of Ministers. As a means of providing management with an incentive to participate in negotiations, however, the 'negotiate or we will legislate' threat left a lot to be desired. From the viewpoint of management, the incentive offered was the incentive to negotiate an agreement that was more attractive, or less burdensome, than any legislation that might be approved by the Council of Ministers. Rather than setting a floor of legislative standards, in other words, Community legislation had come to represent a potential ceiling of standards, above which agreement would not be reached. On the face of it, the social dialogue was skewed, for that reason, in favour of the representatives of management. Even recognizing that fact, however, it was nonetheless possible to imagine that the social dialogue might result in numerous, effective social policy agreements.[121] All would depend on the capacity and willingness of the Commission to bring forward proposals in the field of social policy, and to back these with a realistic threat of Council legislation.[122]

In the Treaty of Rome, as we have seen, the EEC institutions were granted only very limited authority to intervene in social policy matters. In the short 'social provisions' part of the Treaty, obligations and goals were conferred on the Community institutions in rather general terms, but without the creation of either enforceable rights for citizens, or specific legislative powers for the institutions. In principle, social legislation could have been adopted on the basis of the Community's general competences, including Articles 100, 101, or 103.[123] The likelihood of this was restricted, however, by a requirement for unanimous agreement within the intergovernmental Council of Ministers, and by the need to tie any proposals to the economic objectives covered by the general competences, such as the achievement of the internal market.[124] Though it contained a fairly ambitious set of proposals for legislative action in the field of social policy, the Action Programme of 1974 did not amend the Treaty, nor otherwise extend the legislative competence of the Community, nor relax the requirement for unanimity in the Council of Ministers for the adoption of legislation. Reflecting

---

[121] See eg B Bercusson, 'The Dynamic of European Labour Law after Maastricht' (1994) 23 *Industrial Law Journal* 1–31, 21–2.
[122] Bercusson, 'The Dynamic of European Labour Law', 21–2.
[123] Articles 100, 101, and 103 allowed for legislation variously 'for the approximation' of member state law affecting the establishment or function of the common market; for the elimination of member state laws that distort competition; and in respect of 'conjunctural policy'.
[124] Unanimity was required by the Luxembourg compromise of 1966.

the need to be politically acceptable to all, and to be justified with reference to market-creating objectives, the social law directives passed in the 1970s were thus quite restricted in terms of subject matter, dealing chiefly with health and safety and sex discrimination.[125] In 1987, the Single European Act amended the Treaty of Rome to extend qualified majority voting to measures intended to improve health and safety at work. All other matters 'relating to the rights of employed persons' were specified as still requiring the unanimous agreement of the Council.

At the beginning of the 1990s, then, the scope for adopting social law in the EEC remained quite limited.[126] This was reflected both in the 'meagreness' of the proposals contained in the Social Action Programme of 1989, in terms of substance, and in the failure of the Community to adopt legislation pursuant to several of the proposals.[127] In the 1992 Agreement on Social Policy, the legislative competence of the Community in the field of labour and social policy was strengthened quite considerably.[128] On the part of the Commission, this was intended specifically to improve the chances of Action Programme proposals being implemented by way of legislation and, with respect to the development of the social dialogue, to lend greater weight to the underlying threat of 'negotiate or we will legislate'.[129] If, of themselves, however, the terms of the Treaty appeared to represent something of a victory for those who favoured the expansion of European social policy, then appearances were deceptive. Maastricht did not herald the beginnings of a campaign of measures to harmonize social standards across the member states. On the contrary, the years after 1992 marked a progressive move away from policies of harmonization in the social and labour fields, and a move away, too, from the use of centrally issued legislation to achieve social policy goals.[130] Whereas the Social Action Programmes of 1974 and 1989 had included proposals for legally binding 'hard law' directives (albeit 'meagre' in content), the Action Programmes of the 1990s, and the Social Policy Agenda of 2000–2005 proposed measures that were largely persuasive rather than coercive in nature, with a heavy emphasis on soft law methods and the principle of subsidiarity.[131]

---

[125] Proposals for wide-ranging rights to worker representation on the supervisory boards of all public companies, and to institutionalized participation in management, failed to result in legislation.

[126] See generally M Freedland, 'Employment Policy' in P Davies et al *European Community Labour Law: Principles and Perspectives* (Oxford 1996).

[127] W Streeck, 'European Social Policy after Maastricht: The "Social Dialogue" and "Subsidiarity"' (1994) 15 *Economic and Industrial Democracy* 151–77, 161–2.

[128] The power of the Council to issue directives by way of qualified majority voting was extended beyond health and safety to cover a whole range of social policy related subject matter: working conditions, the integration of those excluded from the labour market, equality between men and women with regard to labour market opportunities and treatment at work, and the information and consultation of workers. A further category of social policy matters was specified as requiring unanimous decisions, including 'representation and collective defence of the interests of workers, including co-determination'. Pay, the right of association, the right to strike and the right to impose lockouts were explicitly excluded from both lists, as lying still outside the legislative competence of the Community. [129] Streeck, 'European Social Policy after Maastricht', 162.

[130] Streeck, 'Neo-Voluntarism'.

[131] COM (95) 134 final, COM (98) 259 final, COM (2000) 379 final.

Writing in 1995, Wolfgang Streeck described the European 'social policy regime' as characterized principally by its reliance on various types of 'neo-voluntarism'.[132] Compared with the social policy of welfare states, the key distinguishing feature of social policy within the European Community was its low capacity to impose binding obligations on market participants.[133] Instead of hard law enforceable status rights and obligations for citizens and organized collectivities, European social policy dealt in soft law, in member state opt-outs, and in a shift of social policy-making from the 'state' to civil society.[134] The European approach was lauded by some as innovative, flexible, decentralized, and democratic. In fact, it was necessitated by the weakness of the European 'state' and the lack of 'state capacity' of the Community institutions.[135] In the years to 1995, the member states had succeeded in defending their position as 'masters of the Community'.[136] In the field of social policy, as elsewhere, the allocation of jurisdiction and competence remained in the hands of the collectivity of member states. Those states, meanwhile, shared an interest in preserving as much of their national sovereignty as possible in respect of social law since, as 'highly developed welfare states', they derived 'much of their domestic political legitimacy from their social policies'.[137] Notwithstanding the extension of qualified majority voting effected by the Treaty of Maastricht, then, the development of market-constraining social policy at the European level remained highly unlikely. It simply wasn't in the interests of member states to agree to an upward harmonization of social rights and labour standards—except, in some cases, for protectionist reasons—and the decision still lay with them.[138] Even assuming a willingness, in principle, on the part of states to adopt a particular social policy measure at European level, the difficult task of brokering unanimous agreement would be much exacerbated by the existence of differences in traditions and institutions at national level: differences which acted as very significant barriers to the harmonization of labour law, or of social welfare, or health insurance.[139]

Viewed in this light, the real *weakness* of the 'negotiate or we will legislate' strategy became apparent. From 1992, there were fewer and fewer occasions when the Commission could convincingly wield the threat of Council legislation on social policy matters. When it did, the representatives of business understood negotiations with the ETUC as an opportunity to secure an agreement that was less burdensome for its members than whatever might have been agreed in the Council. Nor did the Commission possess either the financial or the regulatory resources necessary to 'persuade' business representatives to be readier to make concessions to the ETUC, in the way that a nation state government might have done: concessions on taxes and trade, for example, or assistance for research and

---

[132] Streeck, 'Neo-Voluntarism'.　　[133] Streeck, 'Neo-Voluntarism', 45.
[134] Streeck, 'Neo-Voluntarism', 52.　　[135] Streeck, 'Neo-Voluntarism', 45, 52.
[136] Streeck, 'Neo-Voluntarism', 33–4.　　[137] Streeck, 'Neo-voluntarism', 39.
[138] Streeck, 'Neo-Voluntarism', 40–1.
[139] F Scharpf, 'Negative Integration and Positive Integration in the Political Economy of European Welfare States' in G Marks et al (eds) *Governance in the European Union* (London 1996), 32.

development.[140] Without any incentive to engage productively in the process, business representatives remained intent on blocking proposals and insistent upon a narrow interpretation of the relevant provisions of the Treaty, ie the legislative competences of the Community and the proper scope of the dialogue.[141] As negotiations proceeded, they drew strength from the fact that agreement in the Council was always difficult; it was always much easier to block new legislation than it was to forge agreement in favour of it.[142] Taking all of this into account, it was difficult to resist the conclusion that if the social dialogue was a form of corporatism at all, it was a corporatism that had been transplanted from its natural welfare state habitat to a singularly hostile environment. The chances of it thriving were small.

The Question of Autonomy

Autonomy as a frame of reference

With the constitutionalization of the social dialogue in the Treaty of Maastricht, the matter of the involvement of the social partners in negotiations at European level came to the attention of a number of labour law scholars.[143] The tendency among such scholars was to begin analysis of the dialogue from the terms of the Treaty and, on that basis, to come quite readily to the conclusion that it was a form of transnational collective bargaining.[144] The commentary offered by the scholars was not uncritical, but criticism and description both tended to be framed according to a pre-existing notion of collective bargaining gleaned from the experience and legislation of one or other, or several, of the member states, with which the terms of the Treaty were then compared. With little investigation of the nature of the ETUC, BusinessEurope, or CEEP, or of their relations prior to 1992, the social partners were assumed to be functionally equivalent to national unions and employers' federations, capable of performing equivalent roles in the 'bargaining' process. As a result, any conclusions drawn regarding the prospects of the dialogue tended to be overly optimistic. 'The path is clear', wrote Blanpain and Engels in 1995: 'time to dream'.[145]

---

[140] Streeck, 'European Social Policy after Maastricht', 170; A Lo Faro, *Regulating Social Europe: Reality and Myth of Collective Bargaining in the EC Legal Order* (Oxford 2000), 126–7.
[141] Streeck, 'European Social Policy after Maastricht', 169.
[142] Streeck, 'Neo-Voluntarism', 36–7; Streeck, 'European Social Policy after Maastricht'; Hyman, 15–16.
[143] This section builds on: A Bogg and R Dukes, 'The European Social Dialogue: From Autonomy to Here' in N Countouris and M Freedland (eds) *Resocializing Europe in a Time of Crisis* (Cambridge 2013), 466–92.
[144] Eg Bercusson, 'Dynamics of European Labour Law'; R Blanpain and C Engels, *European Labour Law* 3rd ed (Alphen aan den Rijn 1995), 351; S Sciarra, 'Social Values and the Multiple Sources of European Social Law' (1995) 1 *European Law Journal* 60–83, 70–1.
[145] Blanpain and Engels, 351.

In work published during the 1990s, Brian Bercusson wrote about the social dialogue in a manner which suggested that he had in mind, as he wrote, a notion of collective bargaining closely informed by the work of Kahn-Freund and the principle of collective laissez-faire.[146] The social dialogue was 'transnational collective bargaining' and the Commission's threat 'negotiate or we will legislate'—referred to by Bercusson as causing the social partners to 'bargain in the shadow of the law'—was the functional equivalent of industrial action.[147] The possibility of Council legislation provided labour with a 'weapon'—a means of forcing capital to the table, and of forcing it to make concessions.[148] Viewed through the lens of collective laissez-faire, the key issue raised by the terms of the Treaty was the question of the autonomy of the social partners and the bargaining process from the 'state'—the Commission and the Council. For Bercusson, the involvement of the Commission in proposing legislative initiatives and in being prepared to bring their proposals to the Council did not constitute an invidious infringement of the autonomy of the social partners. The Commission's actions were understood, it seems, as the functional equivalent of the support which the British state offered to labour by legislating to make industrial action lawful. 'It is for the Commission to give a clear signal that the factor breaking any deadlock in bargaining will not be the classic weapons of class struggle as evident in national contexts, but the stimulus of [Commission] proposals for social legislation.'[149] Such action on the part of the Commission would be 'crucial' to the future development of the dialogue.[150] What was problematic, in Bercusson's view, was the assumption by the Commission of a right to assess the 'representativity' of the parties to the dialogue; to decide, in effect, which of the various business and industry bodies were 'sufficiently representative' of the affected employers to participate in the negotiation of particular agreements.[151] (In the cross-sectoral context, the ETUC was the only organization representative of labour.) When the Court of Justice confirmed in 1998 that it was for the Commission and ultimately the Court itself to rule on the question of representativity, Bercusson criticized the Court for failing to pay due respect to the fact that the conceptual roots of the social dialogue were to be found principally in *industrial relations*.[152] Analysing the social dialogue as a type of collective bargaining, the Court should have recognized that it was for the parties themselves to decide such matters since the question of representativeness and mandate went 'to the heart of the autonomy of the social partners'.[153]

---

[146] Bercusson, 'Dynamics of European Labour Law'; B Bercusson, 'Maastricht: A Fundamental Change in European Labour Law' (1992) *Industrial Relations Journal* 177–90; B Bercusson, *European Labour Law* (London 1996), ch 34; B Bercusson, 'Democratic Legitimacy and European Labour Law' (1999) 28 *Industrial Law Journal* 153–70.

[147] Eg Bercusson, 'Maastricht', 184–5.

[148] Bercusson, 'Dynamics of European Labour Law', 20–1.

[149] Bercusson, 'Dynamics of European Labour Law', 22.

[150] Bercusson, 'Dynamics of European Labour Law', 22.

[151] Bercusson, 'Democratic Legitimacy'.

[152] *UEAPME v Council of the European Union* Case T-135/96; discussed in B Bercusson, 'Democratic Legitimacy'.   [153] Bercusson, 'Democratic Legitimacy', 162.

The question of the autonomy—or 'collective autonomy'—of the social partners was also central to the extended analysis of the social dialogue provided by Antonio Lo Faro in 2000.[154] In explanation of his application of the notion of autonomy to the dialogue, Lo Faro referred explicitly to Kahn-Freund, whose 'thinking on collective bargaining' could 'justifiably be regarded as part of the common heritage of concepts whose progressive creation has shaped the very birth of labour law as a distinct legal discipline'.[155] In attempting to understand the nature of the social dialogue, it was appropriate, following Kahn-Freund and the common European understanding of collective bargaining, to ask the question whether and to what extent 'Community collective bargaining' could rightly be regarded as an expression of collective autonomy.[156] Did a quasi-normative status attach to the agreements which resulted from the social dialogue; were the parties free to defend themselves and to give expression to conflicts of interest between them; were they free to determine the aims and content of their bargaining, and to identify the employers and employees covered by it?[157]

For Lo Faro, it was of great significance that these questions could not be answered in the affirmative. According to the terms of the Treaty of Maastricht, the social partners were confronted with an 'unhappy alternative'.[158] They could choose to have their agreements implemented by way of Council Directive, in which case their choice of subject matter would be limited to fields in respect of which the Community had legislative competence. Any agreement reached would be assessed by the Commission for compliance with a set of Commission-authored requirements: did any part of the agreement contravene provisions or principles of EC law, including the principles of subsidiarity and proportionality; were the parties to the agreement sufficiently 'representative'; did the agreement respect the need for the development and competitiveness of small and medium enterprises; could the Commission endorse it as 'appropriate' with respect to Union policy and needs?[159] Provided it met with the Commission's approval, the social partners' agreement would then be implemented by a Directive drafted by the Community institutions and given force by the member state institutions, with no right of participation for the social partners and no priority given to the social partners' interpretation of the meaning of their own agreement.[160] Alternatively, the social partners could choose to implement any agreement reached autonomously, but in that case the process would be skewed by the fact that, at European level, there was no freedom of association and no right to strike.[161] Taking all this into account, Lo Faro concluded that the social dialogue was best understood not as a form of collective bargaining but as a tool of regulation, championed by the Commission as a means of circumventing difficulties otherwise associated with the Community's legislative process.[162]

---

[154] Lo Faro.   [155] Lo Faro, 53.   [156] Lo Faro, 83.   [157] Lo Faro, 75–6.
[158] Lo Faro, ch 5.   [159] Lo Faro, 107.   [160] Lo Faro, 117–20.
[161] Lo Faro, 92–103.
[162] Lo Faro, 108, citing S Sciarra, 'Collective Agreements in the Hierarchy of European Community Sources' in Davies et al (eds) *European Community Labour Law: Principles and Perspectives* (Oxford 1996); Lo Faro, ch 6.

The application by these authors of the notion of autonomy to the social dialogue is problematic in a number of respects.[163] Notwithstanding Lo Faro's suggestion of a 'common heritage' of labour law concepts, 'autonomy' as a principle is quite indeterminate.[164] It may be generally agreed that, as applied to the field of industrial relations, 'autonomy' implies the independence or freedom of the collective actors, and collective relations, from the state. Over and above that, however, there is and never has been a shared understanding of its precise definition, across or even within member states. Just how independent of the state should the collective actors be, and in what respects? Where is the line to be drawn between acceptable and unacceptable state intervention? How is state support to be distinguished from state control? For Bercusson, 'state' adjudication of the question of the representativity of the parties was invidious; 'state' circumscription of the subject matter of collective negotiations (by way of the threat of Council legislation) was not. For Lo Faro, both types of 'interference' were highly undesirable.

A second and greater difficulty with autonomy as a frame of reference arises by reason of the significant differences that exist between the supranational social dialogue and collective bargaining arrangements within member states. To transplant a concept developed in the context of the nation state to the European context is to transplant a whole range of assumptions regarding the nature of the state, the parties to the dialogue, and the relations between the three which simply do not hold true at the supranational level. It is assumed, for example, that, left to their own devices, the parties to the dialogue would each have something to gain from negotiating with one another. It is assumed that—the 'union' having been granted a right to strike—the parties would, together, have the capacity to negotiate and to implement agreements themselves, without further institutional support. And it is assumed, finally, that the Commission and the Council, having granted the parties their 'autonomy', could perform whatever residual supportive role might be necessary: guaranteeing freedom of association at the EU level; bringing forward legislative proposals so that the parties might 'bargain in the shadow of the law'.

From the guided to the autonomous social dialogue

From 2002, as we have seen, efforts were in fact made to develop the social dialogue along more autonomous lines. Notwithstanding the stated wishes of the social partners, who in 2001 agreed that cross-sectoral bargaining should be initiated, in future, independently of the Commission's legislative proposals, the move to greater autonomy in the social dialogue must be understood against the background of the change in the sphere of social policy away from hard law towards soft law methods of governance.[165] In 2002, the Commission emphasized the

---

[163] Bogg and Dukes.   [164] As Lo Faro elsewhere admits, 75.
[165] A Branch, 'The Evolution of the European Social Dialogue towards Greater Autonomy: Challenges and Potential Benefits' (2005) 21 *International Journal of Comparative Labour Law and Industrial Relations* 321–46.

compatibility of the social dialogue with soft law and the open method of coordination (OMC), discussing the potential of the dialogue in a language not of rights and regulations, but of 'helping to guide the adaptation process', 'offering avenues and strategic orientations', '[putting] forward principles of action'.[166] Apparently the move to greater autonomy was to go hand in hand, in the Commission's conception, with a welcome move away from negotiations aimed at the creation of universally applicable, legally enforceable rules. Of course it was also the case, though it went unsaid, that with the stalling of legislative initiatives on the part of the Community institutions from the mid-1990s, the social dialogue could develop autonomously or not at all.

Holding to the received wisdom that autonomy in collective bargaining was a good thing, some commentators were quick, at the time, to emphasize the potential advantages of the move to more autonomy in the social dialogue.[167] The implementation of agreements by the social partners themselves could provide a means of circumventing the difficulties involved in fostering agreement on social policy initiatives in the Council of Ministers and the European Parliament. It could allow the social partners to negotiate and implement agreements dealing with subject matter that was excluded from the legislative competence of the Union. It could remove the matter of implementation from the hands of member states, not all of which had a good track record when it came to the transposition of Council Directives. And lastly, it could serve to strengthen the position of the social partners within the member states, since they would be assigned the important task of implementing the agreements.

In reality, the move to autonomous implementation of social partner agreements presented a serious challenge in terms of its *effectiveness*. Throughout the EU, trade unions were losing members and the coverage of collective bargaining was contracting.[168] In a number of the new member states, where there was no tradition of collective bargaining, its coverage was low indeed (less than 20 per cent of workers in Lithuania).[169] As a result, it was quite clear that where implementation proceeded autonomously it would not extend to anything like *all* workers and *all* enterprises in the EU. (An interpretative declaration annexed to the Treaty of Amsterdam indicated that member states would bear no responsibility for ensuring that it did.[170]) Even those collective agreements that purported to achieve the task of implementation might not be effective since, for example, the authority of the national umbrella organization might not extend to affiliates active at (subnational) sectoral or company level.[171] In light of these difficulties, the Commission's emphasis of the compatibility of the social dialogue with soft

---

[166] European Commission (2002) *Proposal for a Council Decision establishing a Tripartite Social Summit for Growth and Employment* COM (2002) 341.   [167] Branch, 338–42.
[168] J Visser, 'More Holes in the Bucket: Twenty Years of European Integration and Organized Labor' (2004–5) 26 *Comparative Labor Law and Policy Journal* 477–521. Industrial Relations in Europe 2012, chapter 1.
[169] Industrial Relations in Europe 2012, 22.
[170] Declaration 27 on Article 118b(2) of the Treaty establishing the European Community, annexed to the Treaty of Amsterdam.   [171] Branch, 330–1.

law methods and the OMC was something of an understatement: since the social partners did not have the capacity, in some member states, to create binding and universally applicable agreements, autonomous 'implementation' *could only ever* proceed by way of flexible guidelines, recommendations, and voluntary undertakings. It would be wholly unsuited to any agreement that sought to secure rights for workers or to impose duties on employers. In a 2004 Communication, the Commission appeared to distance itself a little from its earlier enthusiasm for autonomous implementation, acknowledging that it would not be appropriate in cases where 'fundamental rights or important political options' were at stake.[172] It also reserved the right to assess any agreement initiated by way of a Commission consultation for compatibility with its own set of requirements and to monitor the autonomous implementation of the agreement.[173]

A second weakness of the autonomous social dialogue resulted from the inability of the ETUC to organize industrial action at the supranational level. As was emphasized by labour law scholars including Bercusson and Lo Faro, there was (and is) no right to strike at that level.[174] What was not always emphasized by scholars was that the Confederation in any case lacked the authority to call out workers.[175] Indeed, the majority of its members—not workers, not even unions, but national federations of trade unions and European industrial committees—had no such authority either. Even assuming such authority on the part of the ETUC, the possibilities for transnational strike action were further limited by the profound difficulties involved in forging and re-forging transnational solidarities between 'European' citizen-workers.[176] With no possible resort by the ETUC to the threat of industrial action, the removal of the alternative threat of a Commission proposal for legislation meant the removal of *any* concrete incentive for the employers' organizations to concede *anything* in the course of negotiations. Indeed, given BusinessEurope's track record of using the social dialogue to dilute the impact of social policy measures, the question arose whether the employers' support for the development of the autonomous social dialogue might not have been motivated by a wish to prevent the effective implementation of any new social policy measures whatsoever.[177] It is interesting to note a difference of opinion here regarding the meaning of the term 'voluntary', used in the first years of the social dialogue to refer to agreements that were not intended for implementation by way of Council Directive. While the ETUC maintained that a 'voluntary' agreement was simply one that was initiated and implemented independently of the Commission, BusinessEurope insisted that 'voluntary' meant 'non-binding'; a

---

[172] *Partnership for Change in an Enlarged Europe* COM (2004) 557 final, 4.4.
[173] *Partnership for Change in an Enlarged Europe* COM (2004) 557 final, 4.4.
[174] See also eg P Germanotta and T Novitz, 'Globalisation and the Right to Strike: The Case for European-Level Protection of Secondary Action' (2002) 18 *International Journal of Comparative Labour Law and Industrial Relations* 67–82, 78–82.
[175] Wedderburn noted that transnational industrial action to support collective bargaining at the European level was 'extremely difficult to organise': Lord Wedderburn, 'Consultation and Collective Bargaining in Europe: Success or Ideology?' (1997) 26 *Industrial Law Journal* 1–34, 29.
[176] JM Denis, 'Les mobilisations collectives européenes: de l'impuissance à law nécessité d'alliance' (2006) 6 *Droit Social* 671–8.   [177] Branch, 334–5.

voluntary agreement was a recommendation of good practice to member organizations only.[178]

Where now for the social dialogue?

In 2009, the commitment of the Union to a successful social dialogue was reiterated in a new provision added by the Treaty of Lisbon to the beginning of the social policy chapter of the TFEU.[179] The provision extended responsibility for the promotion of the role of the social partners and facilitation of the social dialogue from the Commission to the Union, and explicitly acknowledged the role of the Tripartite Social Summit in contributing to the dialogue.[180] In 2010, and with reference to the TFEU, the Report of the Commission on Industrial Relations repeated its claim that the social dialogue was 'fundamental' to the European Social Model and a 'vital component of the EU's governance structure in employment and social policy'.[181]

Notwithstanding these statements of support, there have been fairly unambiguous indications in recent years that the Union no longer accords the social dialogue as much importance as it once purported to do. It is notable, for example, that the social dialogue was only one method among several promoted by the Treaty of Lisbon of improving the democratic accountability of the Union.[182] Emphasis was given too, in the new Treaties, to transparency and openness, to the Ombudsman, and to dialogue not only with the social partners but with civil society, the churches, and philosophical and non-confessional organizations.[183] As is suggested by these latter Treaty provisions, the Commission has demonstrated a growing tendency, since 2005, to consult the social partners as merely one set of interested parties, as one 'policy stakeholder' among many.[184] The Commission's reference in 2010 to 'stakeholders—business, local authorities, social partners, foundations, NGOs' is typical of this inclusive approach and of the diminution of the role of the social partners that it appears to involve.[185] More damaging still, it has taken to consulting the 'social partners' as a single unitary advisory body, taking into account only pre-agreed common positions.[186] In stark contrast to pronouncements made in connection with the Lisbon Strategy,[187] recent policy documents dealing with the Europe 2020 Strategy are notable for their failure to

---

[178] Visser, 514–15; Branch, 332–3.   [179] Article 152 TFEU.
[180] The Tripartite Social Summit was instituted in 2003 as a means of formalizing tripartite concertation. The cross-sectoral social partners meet twice a year with the Council Presidency and the Commission in advance of the spring and autumn European Council meeting.
[181] Industrial Relations in Europe 2010, 173.
[182] P Syrpis, 'The Treaty of Lisbon: Much Ado. . . But About What?' (2008) *Industrial Law Journal* 219–36, 227.
[183] Articles 16(8) TEU and 15 TFEU; Art 228 TFEU; Arts 11(2) TEU and 17 TFEU.
[184] ETUI/ETUC, *Benchmarking Working Europe 2011* (Brussels 2011), 85
[185] Cited ETUI/ETUC, 85.
[186] C Vigneau, 'The Future of European Social Dialogue' in M-A Moreau (ed) *Before and After the Economic Crisis: What Implications for the European Social Model?* (Cheltenham 2011), 279.
[187] COM (2002) 341 final.

refer to the social dialogue at all.[188] The new strategy tends to reduce the matter of the social dimension of the Union to the single issue of poverty reduction, and to ignore the social dialogue more or less entirely, both as a potential resource for achieving the policy aims of the Union and as a value in itself. In a report on the 'Social Dimension' of the Strategy, for example, there is no mention whatsoever of the social dialogue and only one reference to the social partners; the success of the Strategy depends, it is said, on 'close cooperation between all levels of government, social partners and civil society'.[189]

The apparent downplaying of the importance of the social dialogue in some quarters has gone hand in hand with the almost complete exhaustion of legislative initiatives in the social policy field. As mentioned, the Action Programmes of the 1990s, and the Social Policy Agenda of 2000–5 proposed measures that were largely persuasive rather than coercive in nature, with a heavy emphasis on soft law methods and the principle of subsidiarity. The Social Policy Agenda of 2006–10 and the Commission Green Paper of 2006 on the modernization of labour law contained no new legislative initiatives whatsoever.[190] In 2010, the social partners were consulted only twice by the Commission in respect of legislative proposals (as provided for in Article 154 TFEU), and on each occasion, the proposals involved the amendment of existing legislation rather than the adoption of new.[191] Despite a plea by the European Parliament to the Commission in 2009 to act ambitiously in respect of social policy, the Commission did not adopt any social policy agenda for the period 2010–15.[192]

In principle, of course, the social dialogue is not reliant on new legislative initiatives from the Commission or statements of Commission support for its development, and can proceed autonomously without either—though not perhaps without the financial contributions of the Union.[193] In practice, as we have seen, the development of the social dialogue along autonomous lines is seriously impeded by the incapacity of the social partners in several of the member states to conclude agreements binding on all relevant workers and enterprises. Without any prospect of legally binding and universally applicable agreements at member state level, autonomous social partner agreements must necessarily limit themselves to soft law recommendations and definitions of best practice, etc. It is striking that the new generation agreements concluded to date have dealt with the relatively non-contentious issues of tele-work, work-related stress, etc and, for the most part, have not attempted to progress beyond quite general statements of principle and best practice.[194] And yet, as time progresses, the possibility raises its head that the period 2002–10 might

---

[188] ETUI/ETUC, *Benchmarking Working Europe*, ch 8.

[189] European Commission, *The Social Dimension of the Europe 2020 Strategy: A Report of the Social Protection Committee* (Brussels 2011), 8.

[190] COM (2005) 33 final; 'Modernizing Labour Law to Meet the Challenges of the 21st Century' COM (2006) 708 final.   [191] ETUI/ETUC, *Benchmarking Working Europe*, 100.

[192] In which MEPs called upon the Commission 'to develop an ambitious social policy agenda for the period 2010–2015', May 2009.

[193] Total EU funding available for 'industrial relations and social dialogue' in 2012 amounted to 16.5 million Euros: *Industrial Relations in Europe 2012*, Box 7.6.

[194] With its direction that 'telework is voluntary for the worker and employer concerned', the telework agreement came closest to purporting to create new rights for workers; however, it is clear

The Question of Autonomy 153

turn out to have represented the *highpoint* of the autonomous social dialogue. At the time of writing, and in the midst of the crisis in the Eurozone, efforts to initiate and negotiate new cross-sectoral agreements have stalled. Neither the 2009-10 or the most recent 2012-14 work programme included plans for new cross-sectoral agreements.[195] In March 2009, the serious difficulties involved in reaching agreement on matters of fundamental importance to the European economy and to the social partners were demonstrated when negotiations regarding a social partner response to the financial crisis broke down.[196] The social partners disagreed on both the causes of the crisis and the nature of the necessary response.[197] And they disagreed too, quite fundamentally, on the implications of the *economic freedoms vs social rights* jurisprudence of the CJEU, on the measures that ought to be taken to address those implications, and on the more specific question of the revision of the posted workers Directive.[198] In December 2012, efforts to negotiate on a review of the Working Time Directive ended without an agreement.[199]

In 2013, the Commission issued a Communication on 'Strengthening the Social Dimension of Economic and Monetary Union', which echoed earlier claims regarding the importance of the social dialogue to 'our social market economy', and proposed the involvement of the social partners in efforts to address the negative consequences of austerity through a system of monitoring 'social indicators' of inter alia unemployment, youth unemployment, inequality, and poverty.[200] In its Communication, the Commission made no mention of the trenchant disagreement between the social partners on the causes of, and desired response to, the crisis, nor of the various ways in which the Commission has itself required or encouraged the weakening and decentralization of existing collective bargaining and dialogue mechanisms within the member states as a means, purportedly, of improving the functioning of labour markets.[201] Without any acknowledgement of the weakened state of bipartite and tripartite institutions at national level in the years since the crisis, or of the stalling of the social dialogue at supranational level, and without proposing any measures to address these problems, the Commission simply stated that the social partners at both levels could usefully contribute (more) to policy debates and decision-making processes.[202] By suggesting that the negative consequences of austerity could in any case be addressed through an improved system of monitoring, the Commission has come under criticism for

---

from the report on the implementation of the agreement that it was not understood to require the creation of universally applicable, legally enforceable rights: European Social Partners, *Report on the Implementation of the European Framework Agreement on Telework* (Brussels 2006). In the UK, for example, the agreement was 'implemented' by way of jointly authored guidance intended to 'provide a useful checklist of issues to consider when implementing telework': *Department of Trade and Industry, Telework Guidance* (London 2003), 6.

[195] Clauwaert, 174. Industrial Relations in Europe 2012, 7.2.2.
[196] Industrial Relations in Europe 2010, 174.
[197] Industrial Relations in Europe 2010, 174.
[198] Industrial Relations in Europe 2010, 189. See chapter 7.
[199] Industrial Relations in Europe 2012, Box 7.4.
[200] European Commission (2013) *Communication on Strengthening the Social Dimension of the Economic and Monetary Union* COM (2013) 690 provisoire. [201] See chapter 7.
[202] COM (2013) 690 provisoire, 12.

prescribing nothing more than a 'Charge of the Light Brigade' in the face of the artillery onslaught of an economic governance strategy still focused on internal wage devaluation.[203]

The stark truth overlooked by the Commission in its 2013 Communication as elsewhere is that without the support of a Commission working to implement social policy initiatives of its own devising, and without the agreement of BusinessEurope to new autonomous initiatives, the ETUC is impotent to secure further advances in social policy and legislation. Weakened from the outset by its lack of financial resources, by the tendency of its affiliates to prioritize national interests and to regard European matters as of secondary importance only, today it faces new and additional challenges arising in the wake of European enlargement and monetary union. One of the principal consequences for transnational industrial relations of economic and monetary union has been the sharpening of conflicts of interest—or the perceptions of such conflicts—between the labour movements of different member states.[204] Suffering real hardships as a result of prolonged economic recession and rocketing unemployment levels, workers in the economically weak countries of the south may point to the countries of the north as partly or largely to blame for their situation, having 'imposed' unhelpful restrictions on the freedom of their governments to manage their national economies, first as a condition of membership of the Euro, and later as a condition of bail-out loans. They may feel aggrieved that the countries of the north are enjoying relative economic stability and even growth at a time of crisis, in no small part by reason of their export of goods to the south and the social pacts that they have used to depress wage growth relative to productivity to keep costs and prices down.[205] In the north, meanwhile, there may be resentment at the southern countries' perceived irresponsibility or profligacy in running up such unmanageable debts.[206] What chance is there in such circumstances, Streeck asks, of pan-European solidarity between the workers of the north and the south, the providers and recipients respectively of economic assistance during the time of crisis?[207] What chance is there, he might have added, that the ETUC could now act to push through an agenda of its own against the wishes of management; or to insist of the EU institutions that efforts be devoted to a new social action programme; or to figure, even, as a focal point for the coordination of a programme of resistance to financial capitalism, austerity, and the dismantling of core labour

---

[203] R Janssen, 'The EU Social Dimension: The Charge of the Light Brigade' (2013) *Social Europe Journal*, 1 October.

[204] W Streeck, 'Markets and Peoples: Democratic Capitalism and European Integration' (2012) 73 *New Left Review* 63–71. See also Martin and Ross, 344–6.

[205] K Armingeon and L Barraro, 'Political Economy of the Sovereign Debt Crisis: The Limits of Internal Devaluation' (2012) 41 *Industrial law Journal* 254–75, 272–4. Streeck notes the statements made by the German trade union, IG Metall, justifying its support for the bailout of Greece. '[T]he joint currency has enormously contributed to the competitiveness of German products. If the debtor countries are thrown out of the common currency, they will devalue their currencies to increase their competitiveness.' IG Metall, *Zehn Gründe für den Euro und die Währungsunion*, 19 August 20011, cited Streeck, 'Markets and Peoples', 69.

[206] Armingeon and Baccaro, 225 fn 1.   [207] Streeck, 'Markets and Peoples', 69.

rights and social protections in several of the member states?[208] What chance is there now of a meaningful social dialogue?

Conclusion

The ambition to create a form of supranational collective bargaining or corporatism in the EEC was evident in the statements and actions of the trade union movement from the 1950s. It was evident in the terms of the Social Action Programme of 1974, in the attempts made in the 1970s and 1980s to develop negotiations between the social partners, and in the promotional statements made by the European institutions at the end of the last and beginning of the current centuries, emphasizing the contribution of the social dialogue to the democratic accountability of the Union. It is evident still in the Constitution of the ETUC, which commits the Confederation in its Preamble to working for 'the democratisation of the economy'.[209]

In the years following the constitutionalization of the dialogue in the Treaty of Maastricht, academic commentary tended to focus on the question of the extent to which it could rightly be thought of as a kind of transnational collective bargaining. Criticism of the dialogue was informed by that question—the 'guided' dialogue restricted the autonomy of the social partners; the 'autonomous' dialogue was skewed by the absence of a right to strike—and prescriptions for reform written accordingly. To compare the social dialogue with collective bargaining in the old member states, however, was to misjudge the significance of certain of its characteristics—to focus unduly on the role of the Commission in assessing the representativity of the parties to the dialogue, for example, or on the absence of a formal legal right to freedom of association. In some cases, it also led scholars to be unrealistically optimistic about the prospects for successful negotiations and new social legislation.

As viewed in this chapter through the lens of the labour constitution, the social dialogue was assessed quite differently. Attention was focused on the questions: what was the role of the trade unions in the formation of the EEC; why did it take until 1992 for their role in the formation of social policy to be recognized as it was in Maastricht; why has the social dialogue been so disappointing since 1992 in terms of its concrete outputs? The conclusion was drawn that if the social dialogue was a form of corporatism or collective bargaining *at all*, then it was one which was transplanted—in large part due to the efforts of the Commission under Delors—into a singularly hostile environment. Looking back to the early days of the Communities, it was suggested that the possibility of a more organic evolution of collective negotiations between representatives of labour and management at the European level was always limited by the constitutional framework within

---

[208] <http://www.etuc.org/a/5838>.
[209] Constitution of the ETUC, available <http://www.etuc.org/a/70>.

which the organizations acted. With questions of social policy and legislation the responsibility of member states, and with Community decision-making power located ultimately in the hands of the inter-governmental Council of Ministers, union and employer efforts to wield influence were concentrated, quite rationally, at the national level. When the Community acted to create greater competences for itself in the field of social policy, the possibility of the development of an effective system of European collective bargaining was limited nonetheless by reason of the turn to subsidiarity and soft law, and the gradual drying up of legislative proposals from the Commission. Identifying their interests quite consistently as lying with the maintenance of a 'free' common market, the representatives of business had little reason to engage positively in negotiations aimed at the adoption of social legislation. The Community-level trade union, meanwhile, was never in a position to force concessions from the business lobby. From its formation in 1973, it was restricted in its operations by the refusal (and/or inability) of its members to devolve decision-making power upwards. Without sufficient independent financial resources, without the authority to take decisions on behalf of its members, and without the right—or authority—to call workers out on strike, the ETUC was unable, from the outset, to figure as a countervailing force to the interests and endeavours of European capital.[210]

In the final section of the chapter, it was argued that in the current context of economic and political crisis in the Union, the categorization of the social dialogue as a form of collective bargaining has been strained yet further. The Commission ceased some time ago to drive the social dialogue with new social policy initiatives and legislative proposals. After a period of a few years in which the autonomous social dialogue looked set to replace the guided version, social partner initiatives for new cross-sectoral agreements have now stalled too. Given the additional barriers that have arisen in the wake of enlargement and monetary union to the development of social legislation and policy, and to the fostering of a common agenda across the labour movements of the many member states, the conclusion of new agreements of any import must be regarded as extremely unlikely, at least in the short to medium term.

How exactly the social dialogue might develop in the longer term remains unclear. In a much improved financial climate, it is not *inconceivable* that the Commission might again bring forward proposals for new labour or social legislation, and that such proposals might stimulate the negotiation by the social partners of new agreements resulting in new Directives. It is not inconceivable that the social partners might again identify matters on which they could usefully negotiate and implement autonomous agreements. And it is not inconceivable that member state governments might become involved in the implementation

---

[210] Compare the ETUC's own ambitions as stated in 1995: 'The emergence of new economic and political power systems at European level calls for the establishment of countervailing force by the unions... As a Unitarian and pluralist organisation and the representative of the labour movement in all its breadth and diversity, the ETUC sees itself as the instrument which will serve that purpose.' ETUC, 'Jobs and Solidarity at the Heart of Europe', Eighth Statutory Congress, Brussels, May 1995, 27, 29, cited Martin and Ross, 337.

Conclusion

of autonomous agreements, improving their reach and force.[211] While the social partners remain as weak as they are in some member states, and the coverage of collective bargaining remains so low, while the bargaining position of the ETUC is compromised by divisions within the Confederation and by the impossibility of resort to industrial action, it remains very difficult to see how the social dialogue could *ever* perform the function that collective bargaining has performed in certain of the member states, ie enabling labour to participate effectively in the democratization of the economy, and in the improvement of labour and social standards. With the renewed support of the Commission and the Council, the guided social dialogue might function again as a tool of legislation, and a useful one at that, given its potential to harness the expertise of the social partners and to involve in the legislative process those who will eventually be subject to the legislation at issue. As a means of allowing for the meaningful participation of labour in policy-making and legislation, however, it is forever seriously limited by the context within which it operates of decisions already taken by the Commission, and a constitutional framework tipped heavily in favour of the employers' organizations and their desire for inaction. The autonomous social dialogue, on the other hand, appears fated to remain—at best—little more than a policy forum, a means of highlighting the importance of certain issues, and of suggesting possible solutions. However true it is that the conceptual roots of the social dialogue are to be found in the industrial relations traditions and labour constitutions of the member states, however much the dialogue continues to be spoken of in the language of industrial relations and, even, of economic democracy, the social dialogue cannot rightly be thought of as a means of rendering the Union more democratic. It is, in the words of Streeck, only 'a reminder of what should and indeed must exist for European society to defend itself against being devastated by the anarchy of an ungoverned international market'.[212]

---

[211] Article 155 TFEU refers to implementation by way of 'procedures and practices specific to management and labour and the Member States'.
[212] Streeck, 'European Social Policy after Maastricht', 172–3.

7

A Plurality of Labour Constitutions?

The Question of Harmonization

The labour constitution, as conceived of by Sinzheimer in the context of the nation state, was unitary in nature and pyramidic in form.[1] A comprehensive system of workplace and district workers' and industrial councils was to be coordinated at the national level by a national workers' council and a national industrial council; trade unions were to act at sectoral level, functionally separate from the labour constitution, bargaining with employers over terms and conditions of employment. As a matter of law, it was to be provided that sectoral collective agreements, negotiated by trade unions, should take precedence over workplace agreements, negotiated by the works councils.[2] In a democratized economy, according to Sinzheimer, the proper role of the works councils was to implement decisions taken, in the interests of *all*, at a higher level of organization.[3] Without any coordination of bipartite labour/capital negotiations—and, particularly, wage negotiations—above the level of the workplace, worker solidarity and the objective of universal improvements in terms and conditions would be threatened by *Betriebsegoismus* and capitalist competitiveness between workers.[4] The standard of living of any worker would come to depend on the particular workplace in which he found employment.

In a short publication from 1925, Sinzheimer commented briefly on the possible creation of a 'European community of nations' or *Völkergemeinschaft*.[5] His main point of emphasis was the great significance of the idea of economic democracy to such a project. The idea contained within it, he suggested, an aspiration to create an economic community of autonomous social powers or actors (*gesellschaftliche Kräfte*) which extended in its reach beyond national borders.[6] Within a European economic community, international capital would demand a corresponding

---

[1] See chapters 2 and 3.
[2] If there was conflict between the two, in other words, the provisions of the former would apply. See eg Sinzheimer, 'Das Rätesystem', and 'Die Rätebewegung und Gesellschaftsverfassung'.
[3] Sinzheimer, *Arbeitsrecht*, 333–4.
[4] Sinzheimer, *Arbeitsrecht*, 332, 358–60. See also Fraenkel, 'Zehn Jahre Betriebsrätegesetz', 103 ff. *Betriebsegoismus*: literally, 'works egoism'.
[5] Sinzheimer, 'Europa und die Idee der wirtschaftlichen Demokratie', 221–5.
[6] Sinzheimer, 'Europa', 224–5.

international union of labour to figure as a countervailing force.[7] The creation of such a union was thus a prerequisite to the achievement of economic democracy.[8]

When the creation of a common market was first debated in the 1950s, the orthodox opinion, as reflected in the Ohlin Report, was that a corresponding unitary labour constitution, spanning the territory of the six member states, would *not* be required. In the terms employed by the authors of the Report, 'objective, scientific analysis' revealed that differences—even substantial differences—in labour costs between member states should not, in the normal run of things, distort competition. As a general rule, labour costs reflected differences in productivity levels. If production costs in any particular country became *too* high in comparison with its neighbours, then that country could in any case restore its balance of payments in a variety of ways without having (directly) to lower labour costs; it could invest in export industries, for example, or revise the rate of exchange of its currency downwards.[9] That being the case, the Committee could see 'no economic reason why the establishment of freer markets should lead to a levelling down of standards' in the 'high-wage' member states.[10] Following the creation of the internal market, free trade would result in increased productivity and economic growth across the board, as industry was enabled to benefit from the economies of scale and specialization that would come hand in hand with a more efficient international division of labour.[11] Increased productivity and economic growth would result, in turn, in improved living and working standards in all of the member states because trade unions and governments *within those states* would act to ensure that the gains won from the cross-border liberalization of trade were shared fairly between the owners of capital and the workers.[12] European-level coordination of social policies and legislation would be unnecessary, as the Ohlin Committee put it, because of the 'strength of the trade union movement in European countries and the sympathy of European governments for social aspirations'.[13]

In place of a unitary labour constitution, then, the Ohlin Report envisaged a common market constituted at two levels—national and supranational—by a plurality of legal and institutional frameworks. At EEC level, the legal framework would ensure the removal of barriers to trade, guaranteeing the free movement of goods, capital, services and workers, and prohibiting corporations from abusing their market power. At member state level, national labour constitutions would continue in existence, unaffected in their architecture by the creation of the common market, and functioning now to ensure that any consequent increase in productivity resulted in proportionate (and therefore appropriate) improvements in workers' terms and conditions. Differences in labour standards—'labour costs'—between countries were characterized as generally unproblematic for low-cost and high-cost countries alike. The threat of negative harmonization—of 'freer trade

---

[7] Sinzheimer, 'Europa', 225.   [8] Sinzheimer, 'Europa', 225.
[9] Group of Experts, *Report on the Social Aspects of European Economic Co-operation* (henceforth Ohlin), 107.   [10] Ohlin, 111.   [11] Ohlin, 100–1.   [12] Ohlin, 110–13.
[13] Ohlin, 112.

exerting pressure towards a levelling down'—was dismissed as negligible, and the case for positive harmonization—for the deliberate coordination of labour standards at European level—was judged to be unpersuasive.[14]

At the time of the publication of the Ohlin Report, the European representative of the free trade unions criticized its vision of a single internal market embedded within six national welfare states as 'too exclusively based on an unjustified confidence in the efficiency of liberalism and the permanent goodwill of the national interests concerned'.[15] The unions' point of view was informed by their primary objective of securing increased social and economic benefits for all workers, equitably distributed. In line with that objective, they advocated the upwards harmonization of living and working conditions across the member states as a means of achieving both improved standards and greater equality between different groups of workers.[16] From the outset, the unions also advocated the creation of strong, democratic supranational institutions to govern the new Community. The free trade unions were the 'radical democrats' of the European Communities, calling for greater democracy both as an end in itself and as a means of securing better outcomes for workers.[17] European institutions should be more democratic and there should be much wider scope for the involvement of the unions—and employers—in decision-making within the Communities. In addition to the upward harmonization of living and working conditions, the key policy objectives of the free unions were the achievement of a supranational employment policy guaranteeing full employment, and the democratization of relations within the enterprise.[18] The development by the trade unions of European-level coordination of national collective bargaining objectives was planned as a means of achieving upward harmonization, complementary to the hoped-for construction of supranational social policies and legislation.[19]

In the years immediately prior to the conclusion of the Treaty of Rome, there was little appetite on the part of either the French or the Germans for the creation of strong supranational institutions of the type advocated by the free trade unions.[20] The Spaak Report of 1956, which served in effect as the White Paper for the Treaty, was quick to adopt the same reasoning as the Ohlin Committee that inter-state competition did not require the harmonization of labour costs.[21] In doing so, it sought to forestall arguments for (among other things) the development of common labour standards at European level and the creation of supranational institutions capable of undertaking such a task.[22] Though the Spaak

---

[14] Ohlin, 111.   [15] Bouvard, 72.
[16] *First Congress of the ECFTUC: Premier Congrès: Discours, decisions, resolutions* (Brussels, April 1969), cited Bouvard, 75.   [17] Bouvard, 73.
[18] *First Congress of the ECFTUC*, cited Bouvard, 75.
[19] *First Congress of the ECFTUC*, cited Bouvard, 75.   [20] Chapter 6.
[21] *Rapport des chefs de délégations aux Ministres des Affaires Etrangères* (henceforth Spaak Report). Part I of the Report was summarised in English translation in Political and Economic Planning, Planning, 1956, vol. 22 No. 405, 222-43, 233–4.
[22] C Barnard and S Deakin, 'European Labour Law after *Laval*', in M-A Moreau (ed), *Before and After the Economic Crisis: What Implications for the 'European Social Model'?* (Cheltenham 2011), 261.

Report, like the Ohlin Report, emphasized the importance of strong trade unions at member state level, it came much closer to suggesting that the upwards harmonization of workers' terms and conditions would result *automatically* from the liberalization of trade.[23] This was the logic which came to be embodied in the Treaty of Rome: Article 117 declared that improvements in working and living conditions would 'ensue from the functioning of the common market', and no specific legal authority was provided for legislation to achieve that aim. Nor was any attempt made to ensure that the strong trade unions, which the Ohlin Committee had identified as necessary to the fair distribution of the gains of trade liberalization, were a lasting feature of the new split-level economic order. It was simply assumed, perhaps, that they would be.

Today the European Union differs in important respects from the EEC which the authors of the Ohlin and Spaak Reports had in mind. It is a Union of 28 rather than six member states, economically and socially extremely diverse. It is a Union in which the majority of the member states lack the kind of strong trade unions capable of acting to ensure that profits and revenues are equitably distributed within national borders. It is a Union in which the Court of Justice has declared that national labour laws, and industrial action taken in accordance with such laws, can constitute unlawful barriers to the exercise of (supranational) free trade and free movement rights. And it is a Union in which 17 of the 28 national governments, bound by the terms of economic and monetary union, are greatly restricted in the steps that they might take to restore balances of payments or to stimulate growth and job creation without resorting to measures aimed *directly* at reducing labour costs. In this new and very different EU, the question addressed by Ohlin and Spaak requires to be revisited: is a Union of states with divergent economic and labour constitutions viable in the long term, or must those economic and labour constitutions eventually be harmonized in an upward or downward direction? In what follows, this question is addressed through a discussion of two bodies of law: the several Directives providing for employee rights to information and consultation which constitute the only body of EU legislation to deal specifically with questions of collective labour law; and the two European Charters of 1989 and 2000, which declare various labour rights, including freedom of association, to have 'fundamental' status within the EU legal order.[24] With respect to the information and consultation legislation, the intention is to explore how efforts to harmonize national labour constitutions *upwards* were made from the 1970s but with only very limited success. In the case of the Charters, discussion focuses on the capacity of fundamental labour rights to constitute a defence against the deregulation, or harmonization *downwards*, of national labour constitutions.

---

[23] Spaak Report at 233, reference to trade unions at 235; S Deakin, 'Labour Law as Market Regulation: The Economic Foundations of European Social Policy', in P Davies et al (eds) *European Community Labour Law: Principles and Perspectives* (Oxford 1996), 69.

[24] Community Charter of the Fundamental Social Rights of Workers (1989); Charter of Fundamental Rights of the European Union (2000).

Upward Harmonization of National Labour Constitutions?

In the late 1960s and 1970s, the labour constitutions of the member states differed significantly in terms of the rights afforded to trade unions and other representative bodies to collective bargaining; to workplace information, consultation, and codetermination; and to worker participation in corporate governance.[25] As originally conceived, in the Social Action Programme of 1974, Community legislation in the field of worker representation was inspired by the notion of industrial democracy, and aimed at the generalization of best national practice—at upward harmonization. By reason of the differences in national practices, institutions, and traditions, however, upward harmonization proved to be unpopular politically and difficult to achieve. In the late 1980s, a new approach to Community legislation was developed in the context of the project to complete the single market. While the objective of improving worker rights to involvement in managerial decision-making was still in evidence, emphasis was also given increasingly to market-related goals, and specifically to the improvement of efficiency and competitiveness. Accordingly, efforts were focused on the introduction of procedural rules, on the establishment of minimum standards, and on respect for the principle of subsidiarity. In the late 1990s and 2000s, the Commission made efforts to entrench employee information and consultation as a key component of the European social model, claiming for it the capacity to further simultaneously the two objectives of 'competitiveness' and 'solidarity'.[26] In 2000, the right to information and consultation was given the status of a 'fundamental right of the European Union', in the 'solidarity' chapter of the Charter of Fundamental Rights of that year.[27] At the same time, however, the expansion of the EU to include states with very divergent histories and practices of employment relations further complicated the task of legislating for the creation of even common *minimum* standards in the field of worker representation. As further legislation was adopted, conforming to the 'procedural rules only, no one-size-fits-all' model developed in the late 1980s and 1990s, the danger arose that the provisions might by now be so 'flexible' as to have lost any real force; that, as implemented by a reluctant or unenthusiastic member state government, the legislation might fail to achieve the—historically, at least—central objective of improving workers' rights to participate in managerial decision-making.

---

[25] European Commission (1975) Green Paper, 'Employee Participation and Company Structure' (Luxembourg 1975), 49–100. Throughout the chapter, I use the term 'participation' in connection with worker representation on the board, and 'involvement' as a general term covering collective bargaining, information and consultation, codetermination and board-level participation. By 'co-determination', I mean co-decision making by virtue of a statutory right.

[26] European Commission (1994) *European Social Policy—A Way Forward for the Union* COM (94) 333 final; B Bercusson, 'The European Social Model Comes to Britain' (2002) 31 *Industrial Law Journal* 209–44.

[27] Article 27 provides that 'workers or their representatives must, at the appropriate levels, be guaranteed information and consultation in good time in the cases and under the conditions provided for by Union law and national laws and practices'.

Legislating for industrial democracy

In January 1974, the Council stated its intention to legislate, for the first time, in the field of collective labour law.[28] Specifically, it intended to guarantee employee rights to participate in decision-making in the event of changes in the ownership of undertakings, and in the event of collective dismissals. Two Directives followed in 1975 and 1977 dealing, respectively, with the approximation of member state laws relating to collective redundancies, and the approximation of member state laws relating to the safeguarding of employee rights in the event of a transfer of the undertaking.[29] With the aim of 'approximating' or harmonizing national laws and practices,[30] rights were created to be informed and consulted, which in some cases obliged certain member states to amend existing legislation so as to strengthen or widen the scope of employee rights.[31] When judged against the Action Programme objective of improving industrial democracy, however, the terms of the Directives were nonetheless pretty meagre.[32] In the absence of a specific Treaty basis for legislation on worker representation, the Directives had been issued under the powers conferred by Article 100 of the Rome Treaty and as such had had to be acceptable to all member states. During the course of negotiations, original drafts were amended so that instead of conferring rights on employees to negotiation or codetermination, they provided only for information and consultation of the workforce.[33] Instead of declaring redundancies and transfers carried out in contravention of the specified procedures null and void, they left the matter of sanctions for failures to inform and consult to the discretion of the member states.[34]

In 1975, the Commission published a Green Paper which signalled its intention to propose legislation on employee involvement in multi-national, public limited, and 'European' companies, the latter being a new type of company incorporated under as-yet-to-be-adopted Community rules.[35] Again, the objectives of the Commission were presented with reference to the idea of industrial democracy: Community legislation would answer the '*democratic imperative* that those who will be substantially affected by decisions . . . must be involved in the making of those decisions'.[36] In the short to medium term at least, however, the requirement

---

[28] Council Resolution of 21 January 1974 Concerning a Social Action Programme.
[29] Directive on Collective Redundancies: Council Directive 75/129/EEC; Acquired Rights Directive: Council Directive 77/187/EEC.
[30] The Preambles to the Directives referred directly to Art 117 of the Rome Treaty and 'the approximation of laws. . . while maintaining the improvement. . . '.
[31] P Teague, 'Constitution or Regime? The Social Dimension to the 1992 Project' (1989) 27 *British Journal of Industrial Relations* 310–29, 314.
[32] See eg Wedderburn, 'Consultation and Collective Bargaining in Europe', 4–5.
[33] The original draft of the Acquired Rights Directive (77/187) granted employees a right to negotiate a 'social plan' and, in the case of failure to reach agreement, to have the matter arbitrated by a bi-partite authority: Green Paper, 'Employee Participation and Company Structure', 13.
[34] M Weiss, 'Workers' Participation in the European Union' in P Davies et al (eds) *European Community Labour Law: Principles and Perspectives* (Oxford 1996), 213–35, 219.
[35] Green Paper, 'Employee Participation and Company Structure', referring also to 'Multi-National Undertakings and the Community' (Bul. Suppl. 15/73).
[36] Green Paper, 'Employee Participation and Company Structure', 9, my emphasis. See also 'Multi-National Undertakings and the Community'.

for unanimity in the Council proved an insurmountable hurdle to the adoption of legislation. Throughout the late 1970s and 1980s, the Commission remained committed to its plans and continued to work on drafting legislation acceptable to the member states.[37] In the case of public limited and European companies, it recommended that employees should have a right to elect one-third of the members of supervisory boards, and in the case of European companies, it recommended, in addition, that 'European works councils' should be created: standing bodies with rights to information, consultation, and codetermination.[38] Proposals for worker representation in multi-national companies were published in 1980, in the form of the Vredeling Directive, providing for the annual disclosure of specified information to employees, and for a 30-day consultation over proposed decisions likely to have a substantial effect on employees' interests.[39] Though the draft legislation was amended on a number of occasions, agreement in the Council of Ministers was not forthcoming. Several member states objected because of the perceived incompatibility of the legislation with existing laws and practices.[40] (In respect of the public limited and European company proposals, it was of particular and understandable concern that the draft legislation only really made sense in application to the 'two-tier' corporate governance systems characteristic of Germany and the Netherlands.[41]) Others objected on broader political or ideological grounds, the UK arguing, by the 1980s, that legislation of this sort would damage the competitive position of industry in the Community and disrupt existing good industrial relations practices.[42] In respect of the Vredeling Directive, strong opposition was also voiced by BusinessEurope and other representatives of business from within and outside the EEC that the Directive, if implemented, would cause delays, difficulties in planning, and, as a result, reduced competitiveness.[43]

European Works Councils and the procedural turn

In 1994, the political stalemate of the late 1970s and 1980s was broken with the adoption of new legislation providing for worker representation in multinational companies: the Directive on the establishment of a European Works Council (the EWC Directive). Having been rejected by the Council of Ministers, and modified,

---

[37] See the Amended Proposal for a Council Regulation on a Statute for European Companies, the Amended Proposal for a Fifth Directive concerning the Structure of Public Limited Companies and the Powers and Obligations of their Organs, and the 'Vredeling' draft Directive 1980 and 1983, OJ C 297, 15.11.80, 3 and OJ C 217, 12.12.83, 3; all discussed in C Docksey, 'Information and Consultation of Employees: The UK and the Vredeling Directive' (1986) 49 *Modern Law Review* 281–313; M Hall, 'Behind the European Works Councils Directive: The European Commission's Legislative Strategy' (1992) 30 *British Journal of Industrial Relations* 547–66.
[38] Co-determination means that the works council can prevent specified courses of action being taken without its agreement.
[39] Vredeling proposal, 1980, OJ C 297 of 15.11.80, 3; OJ C 217 of 12.12.83, 3.
[40] M Hall, 'Beyond the EWC Directive: The Commission's Legislative Policy' (1992) 30 *British Journal of Industrial Relations* 547–66, 554–6.   [41] Weiss, 'Workers' Participation', 220.
[42] Department of Employment, 1983 Consultative Document: *Draft European Communities Directive on Procedures for Informing and Consulting Employees*, 1.
[43] Weiss, 'Workers' Participation', 224–6.

a number of times, the Directive was finally agreed under the terms of the Social Policy Agreement of Maastricht by 11 member states, the UK excluded.[44] By reason of its adoption alone—and not because it could yet be said to have fulfilled its stated objectives of preventing unequal treatment of employees across different member states or easing the functioning of the internal market[45]—the Directive was declared 'an undeniable success' by a Commission rather self-congratulatory in tone.[46] By the same token, the Directive represented a significant success for the ETUC, which had lobbied for legal support to be given to the establishment of European-level worker–management relations since its formation in 1973.[47]

In the late 1980s, and in the context of the project to complete the single market, the Commission had renewed its determination to secure the adoption of legislation on worker involvement in managerial decision-making. A new rationale had been developed with reference to the extensive 'transnationalization' of corporate structures which the project was likely to encourage.[48] As greater numbers of employees became subject to transnational corporate decision-making, the Commission argued, employees in different countries might be treated differently—'unequally'—according to domestic laws and practices. European legislation could ensure that all employees were kept informed and consulted about important decisions, irrespective of the country in which they worked. In the ETUC, meanwhile, internal divisions had been overcome, which had long prohibited the adoption of any detailed programme of desired legislation in the field of worker representation.[49] In 1989, demands were made by the Confederation for the creation of a European legal framework for group works councils in European transnational companies, which resonated strongly with the Commission's own plans and argumentation.[50] As drafted by the Commission in the early 1990s, the terms of the EWC Directive were influenced in a number of respects by the priorities of the ETUC, and by the 'prototype' works councils established voluntarily in a number of mainly French-based multinationals in the late 1980s.[51] Though small in number, the experience of these works councils was regarded as highly significant by the Commission, and was taken into account, in particular, when deciding the contents of the minimum requirements for the establishment of an EWC.[52]

---

[44] R Blanpain and P Windey, *European Works Councils* (Leuven 1994).
[45] EWC Directive, Preamble.
[46] European Commission (1995) *Communication on Worker Information and Consultation* COM (95) 547 final, 2.
[47] Hall, 'Beyond the EWC Directive', 550–1; K Abbott, 'The ETUC and its Role in Advancing the Cause of European Worker Participation Rights' (1998) 19 *Economic and Industrial Democracy* 605–31.
[48] European Commission, *The Social Dimension of the Internal Market* (Luxembourg 1988).
[49] Abbott, 614–5; Hall, 'Beyond the EWC Directive', 551.
[50] European Trade Union Confederation (ETUC), 'ETUC Proposals for the Action Programme' (Brussels 1989).
[51] Hall, 'Beyond the EWC Directive', 551; Abbott, 621–2. Abbott refers to 'the long established and particularly well-developed' channels of communication between the ETUC and the Commission, particularly DG 5: 616
[52] Hall, 'Beyond the EWC Directive', 551–2.

In other respects, the Directive was shaped very significantly by the prioritization by the Commission of the need to win the approval of the Council of Ministers and by lessons learned in that respect from the experiences of the 1980s.[53] In form, the EWC legislation was a framework Directive, which allowed member states significant room for manoeuvre when drafting their own implementing measures. In content, the Directive consisted mainly of procedural requirements, rather than substantive rights and duties. The representatives of management and the workforce within multinational—'Community-scale'—undertakings were directed to negotiate for themselves the establishment of an EWC or similar information and consultation mechanism, deciding together on matters such as the composition of the works council, the number of members, etc, the frequency of its meetings, and the functions and procedures for information and consultation.[54] Only where there was failure to reach agreement would the legislation impose a set of 'subsidiary requirements', to be laid down by each member state in accordance with provisions contained in an Annex to the Directive.[55] In contrast to the model preferred by the ETUC, the Directive referred only to the information and consultation of employees, and made no provision for codetermination rights.[56] Importantly, it made no provision either for the involvement of 'external' trade unions, whether national or European, in the EWC procedure.[57]

While the emphasis on procedure over substance certainly eased the course of the Directive's adoption by the Council of Ministers, it also resulted in the introduction of a scheme which was arguably largely 'voluntarist' rather than mandatory in nature.[58] Under the terms of the Directive, no action whatsoever was required of a 'Community-scale' undertaking until the legislation was triggered by the submission of a written request of at least 100 employees or their representatives, in at least two undertakings or establishments, in at least two different member states.[59] If an EWC or equivalent procedure could not be agreed subsequent to such a trigger, or following the voluntary initiation of negotiations by management, the general rule was that 'subsidiary requirements' should apply, providing for the creation of an EWC with rights to be informed and consulted regarding specified subject matter, once

---

[53] European Commission, *Communication on Worker Information and Consultation* COM (95) 547 final (1995); Hall, 'Beyond the EWC Directive'.

[54] EWC Directive, Arts 4–6. 'Community-scale' undertakings were defined as: undertakings with at least 1000 employees within the member states and with at least 150 employees in each of at least two member states: Art 2.   [55] EWC Directive, Art 7 and Annex.

[56] Abbott, 619, citing: ETUC, 'Executive Committee Declaration on Proposed European Works Council Directive' (Brussels 1991).

[57] As is the case in all of the 'information and consultation' legislation, 'employees' representatives' were defined in the EWC Directive as 'the employees' representatives provided for by national law and/or practice' (Art 2). With respect to the constitution of the special negotiating body, it was provided that, 'the Member States shall determine the method to be used for the election or appointment of the members of the [SNB] who are to be elected or appointed in their territories' (Art 5, para 2). For discussion, see Hall, 'Beyond the EWC Directive', 553–4.

[58] Streeck, 'Neo-Voluntarism', 49.

[59] Article 5. A 'community-scale' undertaking is one with at least 1000 employees in the member states.

a year.⁶⁰ Special provision was made in the case of 'Article 13' agreements—agreements on information and consultation already in force on the date when the Directive became effective—rendering an undertaking immune from the obligation to negotiate a new EWC or equivalent procedure and from the obligation to respect the principles and minimum requirements contained in the Directive.⁶¹ All that was required of Article 13 agreements was that they should 'cover the entire workforce' and provide 'for the transnational information and consultation of employees'. 'Information' was not defined in the Directive and the definition of 'consultation' was imprecise, referring only to 'the exchange of views and establishment of dialogue'.⁶²

Read together with the failure of the Directive to provide for the involvement of trade unions in the negotiation of an EWC or Article 13 agreement, the terms of Article 13 caused Lord Wedderburn to question whether the Directive might function more often than not as a mechanism for union avoidance.⁶³ In principle, the focus of the Directive on procedural rather than substantive rules was a positive step, which properly executed might have allowed the collective parties freedom to negotiate the institution of an arrangement suited to them, and to coordinate with existing arrangements for employee representation in the relevant member states. Without the guaranteed involvement of an independent trade union, however, 'the balance of bargaining power' was likely to be 'hugely weighted in management's hands'.⁶⁴ 'A management which has offered small advantages to its workforce for an agreement before [the date upon which the Directive comes into force] need rarely be bothered by the Directive; and that in itself may encourage others to be less than welcoming towards trade unions.'⁶⁵ Comparing the EWC Directive with German works councils legislation, Streeck made a similar point. 'By leaving the institutionalization of information and consultation procedures to "free" negotiations, without enabling the weaker party, labour, to make the stronger party, management, negotiate in good faith, the new European-style subsidiarity leaves social relations in the integrated market to the mercy of market conditions and economic power relations.'⁶⁶

These objections notwithstanding, the principal strength of the EWC Directive was that it created, for the first time, a truly *transnational* mechanism for the representation of employees' interests. In their study of European works councils in the second half of the 1990s, Lecher et al painted a very positive picture of the kind of role that EWCs might play in the single market.⁶⁷ As the first distinctly 'European' worker representative bodies, EWCs could serve as a focal point for the 'Europeanization' of industrial relations by: providing European and national representatives with an opportunity to share information and resources; allowing

---

⁶⁰ Articles 6 and 7 and Annex.   ⁶¹ Article 13.   ⁶² Article 2.
⁶³ Wedderburn, 'Consultation and Collective Bargaining'.
⁶⁴ Wedderburn, 'Consultation and Collective Bargaining', 22.
⁶⁵ Wedderburn, 'Consultation and Collective Bargaining', 22.
⁶⁶ Streeck, 'Neo-Voluntarism', 49. See also W Streeck, 'Neither European nor Works Councils' (1997) 18 *Economic and Industrial Democracy* 325–37.
⁶⁷ W Lecher, H-W Platzer, S Rüb, K-P Weiner, *Europäische Betriebsräte—Perspektiven ihrer Entwicklung und Vernetzung* (Baden-Baden 1999).

for regular contact between representatives across whole sectors, and thereby for the coordination of common points of view and programmes of action vis-à-vis management; gathering and passing on information to trade unions; and developing collective bargaining relationships within the multinational undertaking coordinated with national unions and with their existing bargaining arrangements. In their extended discussion of the potential of EWCs, the authors envisaged a field of industrial relations organized not in pyramid form, but as a series of *networks* between European-level and national representatives, and European, national, and local 'sites' of negotiation: workplaces, undertakings, sectors. In 2004, the Commission suggested, along similar lines, that links (synergies) might usefully be constructed between the sectoral social dialogue and EWCs.[68]

Experience of EWCs to date could be argued to have vindicated more fully the scepticism of Wedderburn and Streeck than the greater optimism of Lecher et al.[69] By 2008, a total of 820 EWCs had been set up, representing 36 per cent of all undertakings falling within the scope of the Directive and around 60 per cent of relevant employees.[70] These figures fall well short of anything approaching comprehensive coverage, and compare unfavourably with figures taken from Germany, indicating the prevalence of works councils established in large workplaces according to national works constitution law: in 2012, works councils existed in 86 per cent of German workplaces with more than 500 employees, representing around 88 per cent of the relevant workforce.[71] In terms of the *quality* of representation afforded by EWCs, recent research confirms that they have developed, for the most part, into mechanisms for receiving and communicating information only.[72] Notwithstanding the terms of the constituting agreements—which in some cases purport to confer wider rights on EWCs than contained in the Directive's 'subsidiary requirements'—consultation has remained, in practice, a 'minority phenomenon'.[73] As for the quality of information—the subjects covered, the level of detail imparted, the timing of the information—this has varied from undertaking to undertaking.[74] Where resources have allowed, unions—and particularly ETUFs—have been successful in improving the functioning of EWCs as well as crucially the levels of communication and coordination between EWCs and existing worker representatives at national and supranational levels.[75] In a small number of cases, EWCs have participated in transnational collective bargaining arrangements, as either instigators of the bargaining, negotiators, or co-signatories.[76] At the other end of the scale, however, a significant minority of

---

[68] COM 2004 (557) final, para 3.2.3.
[69] J Waddington, 'European Works Councils: The Challenge for Labour' (2011) 42 *Industrial Relations Journal* 508–29. [70] COM 2008 (419) final.
[71] Note, however, that for all workplaces falling within the scope of the German legislation, including small and medium-sized workplaces, the figure was very much lower: 9 per cent of such workplaces had a works council, covering around 40 per cent of employees: P Ellguth and S Kohaut, 'Tarifbindung und betriebliche Interessenvertretung' (2013) 4 *WSI-Mitteilungen*.
[72] Waddington, 513–16.   [73] Waddington, 515, 526   [74] Waddington, 513–16.
[75] Waddington, 516–26.
[76] Ales et al identify 'around 35' international framework agreements in place at the time of writing: E Ales, S Engblom, T Jaspers, S Laulom, S Sciarra, A Sobczak, F Valdes Dal-Re, 'Transnational

EWCs have remained ineffective, meeting with management only once a year, and failing to communicate between meetings, either among themselves, or with other worker representatives, national or supranational.[77] Whether an EWC functions effectively or ineffectively depends of course on a number of factors, including the attitudes of management, the composition of the EWC, and the competences of the national representatives. Of particular importance has been the level of trade union (and especially ETUF) involvement in the identification of 'suitable' multinational corportations, the initial trigger, the negotiation of the constituting agreement, the coordination of the EWC with existing worker representative bodies, and the training of EWC members.[78] ETUFs and national unions have devoted much effort to supporting EWCs, but have been significantly limited in their efforts due to a lack of resources.[79]

Information and consultation in the interests of employability and economic growth

In the same breath as it in 1995 declared the EWC Directive 'an undeniable success' the Commission raised the prospect of further legislation on 'information and consultation' within smaller national corporations.[80] The aim behind the new legislation would be to coordinate existing mechanisms for information and consultation in the event of imminent collective redundancies or business transfers. Where such mechanisms existed 'in isolation' from standing representative arrangements, as was often the case in Ireland and the UK, they didn't always function as intended to protect the interests of employees. New legislation would address this problem by requiring the creation of standing workplace representative bodies, which could act on behalf of the workforce whenever the threat of collective redundancies or a transfer of ownership arose.[81] In March 1997, a decision taken by Renault to close its plant in Vilvoorde, Belgium, was communicated by management to the workforce at the last minute, leaving workers ill-prepared to deal with the consequences. Treating the incident as a prompt, the Commission acted quickly to invite the social partners, at European level, to agree on legislation implementing a binding obligation to inform employees about important company decisions.[82] BusinessEurope was unwilling to contemplate such

---

Collective Bargaining: Past, Present and Future' (Brussels 2006), 21–7. Papadakis calculates that of the just over 80 International Framework Agreements signed by MNCs and Global Union Federations by 2010, EWCs were involved, one way or another, in the negotiation and conclusion of approximately one-third: K Papadakis, 'Globalizing Industrial Relations: What Role for International Framework Agreements?' in S Hayter (ed), *The Role of Collective Bargaining in the Global Economy* (Cheltenham 2011).

[77] According to Waddington's research, around 20 per cent of EWC members did not communicate with representatives from other countries between annual meetings; nor did they 'report' back to local works councils or trade unions: 516–22.   [78] Waddington, 526–7.
[79] Waddington, 526–7.
[80] Commission Communication 1995. References were focused on 'information and consultation' from the outset.   [81] Commission Communication 1995.
[82] Under Art. 139(2) EC Treaty.

legislation and for that reason the Commission drafted its own Directive, presented 17 November 1998.[83] Agreement was reached on a final version of the text between the Parliament and the Council in December 2001, and the Directive establishing a general framework for informing and consulting employees (the ICE Directive) was adopted in March 2002.[84]

In making the case for the ICE Directive, it seems that the Commission was motivated, then, by its longstanding objective of improving employee rights to participate in company decision-making. As stated in the Preamble to the Directive, that objective was formulated in terms that aligned with the political priorities of the time and, in particular, the Lisbon Strategy goals of a strengthened 'knowledge economy' and employment creation.[85] A general framework setting out minimum requirements for the right to information and consultation was said to be necessary, because existing national legislation had not always prevented serious decisions affecting employees being taken and made public without adequate information and consultation.[86] The promotion of the social dialogue and the development of information, consultation, and participation for workers along appropriate lines, were identified as particular objectives of the Community.[87] And it was claimed that legislation directed at the strengthening of dialogue and the promotion of mutual trust would bring benefits both to employees and to undertakings by improving risk anticipation, flexibility, and employee access to training, making employees aware of adaptation needs, increasing employees' availability to take action to increase their employability, promoting employee involvement in the operation and future of the undertaking, and increasing its competitiveness.[88] At the time of its adoption, Anna Diamantopoulou, the EU Social Affairs Commissioner, presented the Directive as a 'modern business tool. Enlightened self-interest is already driving companies to anticipate and manage change ... All businesses should provide a baseline level of involvement.'[89]

With an eye to ensuring the agreement of the member states to its adoption, the Commission drafted the new Directive to consist almost entirely of procedural rules.[90] Given the variety of arrangements in place already in member states, and the need to respect the principle of subsidiarity, the resultant ICE Directive was markedly less prescriptive even than its predecessor, the EWC Directive.[91] Having set out what appeared to be some generally applicable rules—'information and consultation

---

[83] OJ C 2, 05.01.1999, 3 ff.
[84] [2002] OJ L 80/29.
[85] The Lisbon Strategy aimed to make the EU 'the most competitive and dynamic knowledge-based economy in the world capable of sustainable economic growth with more and better jobs and greater social cohesion' by 2010. [86] Preamble to the ICE Directive, Recital 6.
[87] Recitals 1 and 2.   [88] Preamble to the ICE Directive, Recitals 7–11.
[89] Cited M Gold, 'Employee Participation in the EU: The Long and Winding Road to Legislation' (2010) 31 *Economic and Industrial Democracy* 9–23, 19.
[90] For discussion of the terms of EC Directive 2001/86, see M Weiss, 'Workers' Involvement in the European Company' in M Biagi (ed), *Quality of Work and Employee Involvement in Europe* (The Hague 2002); P Davies, 'Workers on the Board of the European Company' (2003) 32 *Industrial Law Journal* 75-96.
[91] The principle of subsidiarity is referred to in Recital 17, together with the assertion that the Directive does not go beyond what is necessary to achieve its objectives.

shall cover [the following]'; 'information shall be given at such time, in such fashion and with such content as are appropriate to enable, in particular, employees' representatives to conduct an adequate study and, where necessary, to prepare for consultation'—the ICE Directive went on to provide that member states could empower 'management and labour' to define, by agreement, an alternative arrangement for informing and consulting employees. Moreover, any such alternative arrangement need *not* respect the general rules specified in the preceding Article.[92]

On at least one interpretation of these provisions, very little indeed was required of the member states and the 'social partners' at company level when implementing the Directive.[93] Employing a strategy, apparently, of allowing employers as much flexibility as possible while remaining within the terms of the Directive,[94] the UK government drafted implementing legislation which was remarkable for the scope that it created for doing nothing at all.[95] No obligations were conferred upon employers until the legislation was triggered by a request made in writing by at least 10 per cent of the relevant employees, or in the case of smaller undertakings by as many as 30 per cent of employees.[96] Following a trigger, representatives of management and the representatives of the employees were allowed almost total freedom in negotiating an 'I&C' agreement of their choice.[97] Since no provision was made for the involvement of trade unions in the procedures, there was a significant risk that freedom of choice would mean here simply unilateral control by management.[98] And where management was in a position to dictate the terms of an agreement, there was a further risk that it would avail itself of the option contained in the Regulations to commit only to informing and consulting employees *directly* and not through an elected or appointed representative.[99]

---

[92] Article 5 provided that negotiated agreements did have to respect the principles contained in Art 1 and Art 1 included the direction that 'the practical arrangements for information and consultation shall be defined and implemented... in such a way as to ensure their effectiveness'.

[93] Article 5 of the Directive refers to 'management and labour at the appropriate level, including at undertaking or establishment level', and in other language versions to the 'social partners...'.

[94] For evidence of UK government opposition to the Directive, see M Hall and J Purcell, *Consultation at Work: Regulation and Practice* (Oxford 2012), 58–60.

[95] The Information and Consultation of Employees (ICE) Regulations 2004, SI 2004/3426. For a discussion of the Directive and its implementation in the UK see K Ewing and G Truter, 'The Information and Consultation of Employees Regulations: Voluntarism's Bitter Legacy' (2005) 68 *Modern Law Review* 626–41. For a discussion of the effect of its implementation on information and consultation practice in the UK see Hall and Purcell.

[96] Regulation 7 provides that 'A valid employee request' is a single request or, a number of separate requests, made, in writing, by at least 10 per cent of the employees in the undertaking, subject to a minimum of 15 and a maximum of 2,500 employees. In establishments of 50 employees, the minimum of 15 employees amounts to 30 per cent of the workforce.

[97] In addition to a number of technical requirements—the agreement must be in writing, dated and signed by both parties—it is provided only that a negotiated agreement must cover all the employees in the undertaking, set out the circumstances in which the employer must inform and consult its employees, and regulate the matter of whom it must inform: regulation 16.

[98] Under Art 2 of the Directive, 'employees' representatives' were defined with reference to national laws and practices. In the ICE Regulations, no provision was made for trade union involvement in the negotiation of an ICE agreement, even in respect of undertakings in which trade unions were recognized for the purposes of collective bargaining.

[99] Regulation 16.

In the years since the legislation came into force in the UK, there has been little evidence of an overall increase in the number of workplaces with an I&C procedure.[100] Where new procedures have been introduced, evidence suggests that they have been shaped for the most part by management, without trade union involvement.[101]

Form over substance?

Notwithstanding concerns about its efficacy, the 'procedural rules only, no one-size-fits-all' approach of the EWC Directive has since become the template for all legislation in the field of worker involvement in managerial decision-making. More than three decades after it was first proposed, a European Companies Statute was adopted in 2001, together with an accompanying Directive containing provision for 'employee involvement' in such companies.[102] Premised on the assertion that a 'single European model' would be 'inadvisable',[103] the Directive allowed for the negotiation of an agreement on employee involvement within each European company, subject to a number of rules intended to prevent, insofar as was possible, both the use of the company as a means of escaping national provisions on employee participation and the imposition of employee participation mechanisms on management or employees contrary to their wishes.[104] In 2004, the Takeover Bids Directive created employee rights to information and consultation in the event of company takeovers, and in 2005 the Cross-Border Mergers Directive provided for employee 'involvement' in the event of cross-border mergers in much the same way as the Directive accompanying the European Company Statute.[105] In 2009, the EWC Directive was amended, or 'recast', with the aim of strengthening and clarifying a number of its provisions, but without any changes to the original basic framework.[106] It remained the case, then, that all of the legislation adopted since 1994 was flexible in a similar kind of way: allowing member states significant scope to shape the terms of the implementing legislation, and—subject to the terms of that legislation—giving 'social partners' the opportunity to negotiate company-specific

---

[100] The legislation came into effect in the UK in April 2005. WERS data from 2011 suggests that only 7 per cent of all workplaces have a 'joint consultative committee' (defined as 'any committee of managers and employees that is primarily concerned with consultation rather than negotiation'), with no change evident in that overall percentage since 2004: B van Wanrooy, H Bewley, A Bryson, J Forth, S Freeth, L Stokes, S Wood (eds), *The 2011 Workplace Employment Relations Study: First Findings* (2013), 14–15.

[101] Hall and Purcell concluded in 2012 that there had been 'extensive scope for management unilateralism': Hall and Purcell, 97–8.

[102] EC Directive 2001/86. 'Involvement' is the catch-all term used in the Directive to refer to both information and consultation and 'participation', the latter referring to employee participation in the election, or appointment, or selection of members of the board of the European Company.

[103] Preamble, recital 5.

[104] Davies, 'Workers on the Board of the European Company'.

[105] Directive 2004/25 on takeover bids and Directive 2005/56 on cross-border mergers of limited liability companies.

[106] Directive 2009/38. For discussion see S Laulom, 'The Flawed Revision of the European Works Council Directive' (2010) 39 *Industrial Law Journal* 202–8.

agreements. In light of the rather weak nature of the implementing legislation passed in several member states, and of empirical evidence speaking both to the less than comprehensive coverage of information and consultation mechanisms, as well as the, at times, poor quality of the representation and communication involved, it seems fair to conclude that the 'success' of the Commission's strategy has been rather more ambiguous than it is likely ever to admit.[107]

Labour Rights as Fundamental Rights: A Defence against Negative Harmonization?

By the mid to late 1980s, it was more or less clear to all that there was little prospect of further upward harmonization of the various labour constitutions of the member states by way of Community legislation. In 1992, as we have seen, legislative competence was bestowed upon the Council, acting by qualified majority, to adopt Directives in the field of 'the information and consultation of workers'.[108] It was specified quite unambiguously, however, that any Directive so adopted should consist only of 'minimum requirements for gradual implementation, having regard to the conditions and technical rules obtaining in each of the Member States'. In respect of 'representation and collective defence of the interests of workers and employers including codetermination', the Council was directed to act, if at all, unanimously rather than by qualified majority voting. In respect of 'pay, the right of association, the right to strike or the right to impose lock-outs', it was provided that the foregoing provisions did not apply; in other words, there was no specific legislative competence for the Community in respect of those matters.[109]

At the same time as the Community appeared to confirm the relatively modest nature of its legislative ambitions in the field of worker representation, the threat of *negative* harmonization of national laws was argued by some to have increased. In 1981 and 1986, Greece, Spain, and Portugal had acceded to the Communities, all low-wage countries in comparison to West Germany and other northern European states. In debates about the 1992 project to complete the single market, the risk of 'social-dumping' was frequently invoked—the possibility that the low-wage countries might attempt artificially to restrain the future growth of wages and other social benefits, either to increase exports or to reduce import penetration of their home market.[110] By following such policies, the low-wage states would, in effect, export potential domestic unemployment to other member

---

[107] COM (2008) 146 final; Commission, *Industrial Relations in Europe 2010* (Brussels 2010), 42–6; ETUI/ETUC, *Benchmarking Working Europe 2011* (Brussels 2011), 98–9.

[108] Social Policy Agreement annexed to the Treaty of Maastricht 1992.

[109] For discussion see ACL Davies, 'Should the EU have the Power to Set Minimum Standards for Collective Labour Rights in the Member States?' in P Alston, *Labour Rights as Human Rights* (Oxford 2005).

[110] Teague, 321–3. For an alternative, wider definition of social dumping, see D Vaughan-Whitehead, *EU Enlargement versus Social Europe* (Cheltenham 2013), 325: 'any practice pursued by an enterprise that deliberately violates or circumvents legislation in the social field or

states. This might trigger a race to the bottom—competition on the basis of cost and price reduction and, potentially, rising unemployment throughout.

Unforeseen by the Ohlin and Spaak Committees, the possibility had also arisen that negative harmonization might actually be *required*, as a matter of law, by the terms of the EC Treaty as interpreted by the Court of Justice. In the decades since 1957, the Court had developed two legal doctrines—the doctrine of direct effect and the doctrine of the supremacy of Community law—which had increased the likelihood of this occurring. According to the first of these, the Treaty commitments of member states to create a common market amounted to legal duties conferring corresponding rights upon individuals and firms.[111] According to the second, Community law figured as a form of higher law within the member states, ie as a set of norms which national institutions were powerless to amend or overrule, but obliged to enforce.[112] Taken together, these doctrines amounted to a conferral of authority upon the Court to review national laws, including labour laws, for compliance with Community law, including competition law and the laws protecting the free movement of goods, workers, services and capital.[113] If a firm believed that its right to freedom of establishment or freedom to provide services had been impeded by reason of a particular national law, it could seek redress before the courts.[114] Whether its claim would be successful would depend ultimately on the Court of Justice's interpretation of Community law: its interpretation of what it understood to constitute a barrier to the free movement of goods, services and capital, and its interpretation of the circumstances in which such barriers could be justified, as well as its answer to the question, whether Community competition law applied to (national) labour laws and, in particular, to collective agreements on wages and conditions. By reason of these doctrines, however, the danger existed that, as a result of the enforcement of European law, the autonomy of member states in respect of national labour constitutions and social welfare systems might be significantly restricted.

Fundamental rights in European policy discourse

The creation of a charter of fundamental social rights for the European Community was first proposed in 1987 by a Belgian presidency concerned by the prospect of deregulation and negative harmonization raised by the project to complete the single market.[115] The 1980s had been a decade characterized by conflict in

---

takes advantage of differentials in practice and/or legislation in the social field in order to gain an economic advantage, notably in terms of competitiveness, the state also playing a determinant role in this process'.

[111] *Van Gend en Loos v Nederlandse Administratie der Belastingen* Case C-26/62, 05.02.1963.

[112] JHH Weiler, 'A Quiet Revolution: "The European Court and its Interlocutors"' (1994) 26 *Comparative Political Studies* 510–34.

[113] P Davies, 'Market Integration and Social Policy in the Court of Justice' (1995) 24 *Industrial Law Journal* 49–77; Scharpf.

[114] In the national courts, but with the interpretation of EU law remaining a matter, ultimately, for the CJEU.

[115] Teague, 320–1.

the Community between those who favoured the improvement of social standards by means of Community policy and legislation, and those who did not.[116] In 1986, the UK government under Margaret Thatcher had published its *Action Programme for Employment Growth*, aimed at directing policy discourse within the Community towards an acceptance of the neoliberal conception of labour rights and social rights as barriers to economic growth and job creation.[117] As an alternative to this vision, the Belgian presidency proposed a 'plinth' of social rights similar in content to the European Social Charter. While recognizing the need for greater adaptability in the European labour market, the Belgians argued, the Community ought also to commit itself to ensuring that the completion of the single market did *not* undermine established statutory guarantees for workers.

In the face of potentially deep and enduring political divisions over the question of new social rights, the Economic and Social Committee produced a Report at the end of 1987 which proposed a compromise solution: a Charter of Social 'Rights' that were 'exemplary' rather than legally binding in nature.[118] The solution was welcomed by the Commission which worked throughout 1988 and 1989 to produce a draft Charter along just those lines, together with an accompanying Social Action Programme. In December 1989, the *Charter of Fundamental Social Rights of Workers* was solemnly declared by the European Council, the UK dissenting. Care was taken in the Preamble to the Charter and elsewhere in the text to emphasize that it was declaratory of existing rights only, and not intended to create new rights or to provide workers with new legal claims.[119] Insofar as collective labour rights were concerned, the Charter referred in a section entitled 'Freedom of association and collective bargaining' to the right of association, the right to negotiate and conclude collective agreements, and the right to take collective action, but qualified these with reference to 'conditions laid down by national legislation and practice'. In a further section entitled 'Information, consultation and participation for workers', reference was made to the need to develop such practices 'along appropriate lines', taking into account existing practices in member states. In places, the text of the Preamble appeared to confirm that the overarching aim of the Charter was chiefly defensive, that the proclamation of social rights was intended to serve as a defence against negative harmonization occurring in the context of completion of the single market.[120] Elsewhere there were suggestions of a more positive role

---

[116] B Hepple, 'The Crisis in EEC Labour Law' (1987) 16 *Industrial Law Journal* 77–87.
[117] Teague, 318–19.
[118] Economic and Social Committee, *Social Aspects of the Internal Market* [The 'Beretta' Report] (Brussels 1987).
[119] The aim of the Charter was declared in the Preamble to be 'to consolidate the progress made in the social field'. For discussion, see B Bercusson, 'The European Community's Charter of Fundamental Social Rights of Workers' (1990) 53 *Modern Law Review* 624–42.
[120] It was declared variously that: 'in the context of the establishment of the single European market, the same importance must be attached to the social aspects as to the economic aspects and whereas, therefore, they must be developed in a balanced manner'; 'the completion of the internal market must offer improvements in the social field for workers of the European Community, especially in terms of freedom of movement, living and working conditions, health and safety at work, social protection, education and training'; and that the aim of the Charter was 'to declare solemnly

for social rights within the Community legal order, serving not only as a defence against deregulation, but also as a means of increasing the competitiveness of the European economy, and of creating employment: 'the social consensus contributes to the strengthening of the competitiveness of undertakings and of the economy as a whole and to the creation of employment; . . . in this respect it is an essential condition for ensuring sustained economic development'.[121]

The vision of social rights or social policy as a means of achieving economic objectives was expanded on in the Commission's Green Paper of 1993 and its White Paper of 1994.[122] Social rights and a 'high level of social protection' were proclaimed to be a 'key element' of economic competitiveness in Europe and categorically *not* a cost to be borne by the economy.[123] Social progress and competitiveness were 'two sides of the same coin'.[124] That said, it was not the intention of the EU to seek to create new social rights or social standards at the supranational level.[125] 'Total harmonization' was not an objective of the Union.[126] Instead there was to be a continued emphasis on minimum standards acceptable to all, and on the free and harmonious coexistence of the different national systems through the convergence of social policies, especially in the field of employment. Employment was the number one priority of the Union; labour law, as such, was much further down the list.[127] There was not thought to be any need for a new programme of legislative proposals in the field of labour law, and it was emphasized that any further legislation adopted in pursuance of the 1989 Social Action Programme would take the form of Directives on minimum standards whose primary purpose would be to prevent unfair competition.[128]

After the political divisions of the 1980s, the 'win–win' vision of high social standards and a competitive economy as mutually facilitative—as two sides of the same coin—held the promise of being attractive to many, and of creating a wide stretch of common ground between those who were concerned about labour market rigidities and high unemployment levels, and those who were concerned to secure the maintenance or improvement of social standards throughout the Union. In substance, it echoed, or foreshadowed, the 'third way' policy statements of centre left governments of the time, including, prominently, those in Germany and the UK.[129] The concern was to carve out a role for Europe in a

---

that the implementation of the Single European Act must take full account of the social dimension of the Community and that it is necessary in this context to ensure at appropriate levels the development of the social rights of workers of the European Community, especially employed workers and self-employed persons'. [121] Preamble.

[122] European Commission, *European Social Policy—Options for the Union* COM (93) 551 final; COM (94) 333 final. For discussion see M Rodriguez-Piñero and E Casas, 'In Support of a European Social Constitution' in P Davies et al (eds) *European Community Labour Law: Principles and Perspectives* (Oxford 1996).

[123] White Paper COM (94) 333, 4; Deakin, 'Labour Law', 84.
[124] White Paper COM (94) 333, 6.   [125] White Paper COM (94) 333, 13.
[126] White Paper COM (94) 333, 7.
[127] See European Commission, *Growth Competitiveness and Employment* COM (93) 700 final
[128] White Paper COM (94) 333, 21–5.
[129] The German government was led by the SPD and Gerhard Schröder from 1998 to 2005; the UK government by New Labour and Tony Blair from 1997 until 2007. Together the two authored

'globalized economy', to ensure that Europe could 'compete' in the global market place, and to retain a commitment to high social standards and solidarity, while at the same time recognizing that old welfare states were in need of 'modernization' and 'flexibilization'.[130] In the decade or so after the publication of the Commission's White Paper, the win–win narrative came to dominate policy discourse, finding expression in a variety of attempts to offer workers 'flexicurity', in the Employment Title of the Treaty of Amsterdam and, above all perhaps, in the Lisbon Strategy's ambition that the Union should become 'the most competitive and dynamic knowledge-based economy in the world'; in its rallying cry of 'more and better jobs'.[131]

In the course of the late 1990s and 2000s, academics such as Simon Deakin and Bob Hepple articulated their own versions of a win–win social policy for the European Union, which emphasized the importance of the role of fundamental social rights. In a notable contribution from 1996, Deakin argued persuasively that the best course of action at European level would be to legislate to create a transnational floor of rights.[132] Such a floor of rights could serve as a defence against social dumping and a race to the bottom, but it could also serve to improve the competitiveness of the European economy and to further the goal of social inclusion. With an eye to these latter goals it was important that labour and other social rights should be complementary, universal in their coverage, and adaptable to particular industries, corporations, and changing economic circumstances.[133] In his 2007 book, *Labour Laws and Global Trade*, Hepple held the EU up as an example of a largely successful attempt to link economic and employment growth with rising social and labour standards at a supranational regional level.[134] Describing the move in the years after Maastricht away from centrally issued substantive legislation in the field of social policy to decentralized, flexible and soft-law methods, such as the social dialogue and the OMC, Hepple suggested that 'fundamental social rights expressing common values' had, as a consequence, become 'indispensible'.[135] EU judges and institutions, member state courts, and tribunals should all have reference to fundamental social rights when interpreting EU legislation or domestic legislation implementing EU obligations, using those rights to imply a hard core or minimum into otherwise soft laws and regulations.[136]

In making such arguments, authors were able to look not only to the 1989 Charter of Fundamental Social Rights of Workers, but also to the European

---

a manifesto for Europe which emphasized the need for reform of existing social welfare systems and 'flexibilization', rather more than it did the potential of social standards to contribute positively to economic growth: T Blair and G Schroeder, *Europe: The Third Way/Die Neue Mitte* (London 1999). Discussed Vaughan-Whitehead, 499–501. [130] White Paper COM (94) 333.

[131] Lisbon Strategy, my emphasis. For discussion see D Ashiagbor, *The European Employment Strategy* (Oxford 2005). [132] Deakin, 'Labour Law'.
[133] Deakin, 'Labour Law', 88–92.
[134] B Hepple, *Labour Laws and Global Trade* (Oxford 2007), 193.
[135] Hepple, *Labour Laws and Global Trade*, 245.
[136] Hepple, *Labour Laws and Global Trade*, 245.

Union Charter of Fundamental Rights adopted in 2000. This second Charter had been conceived as part of the move to create a Constitution for Europe and, as such, had been aimed, primarily, at securing a greater degree of popular legitimacy for the Union.[137] Like the 1989 Charter before it, it was drafted so as to clarify that it did not create new rights, but served rather to list existing rights and to confirm their status as 'fundamental'.[138] Nonetheless, Hepple was able to state that the Charter was important as a 'benchmark of the common values which bind together the Member States . . . an inspiration for action by the Commission, Council and Parliament, and . . . an aid to the ECJ and national courts when interpreting EU legislation'.[139] Writing together with Frank Wilkinson in 2004, Deakin described the social rights contained in the Charter as a 'concrete expression of the idea that economic integration and social regulation are mutually complementary aspects of a process of market construction'.[140]

Too much diversity?

In 2004, the EU was enlarged on an unprecedented scale.[141] A total of ten new countries joined the Union, increasing its population by 28 per cent and its surface area by 35 per cent.[142] Of the ten, eight had formerly been part of the Eastern Bloc. By the time of their accession to the Union, they had undergone a process of transition, closely directed by the international monetary institutions, and intended to turn them from planned economies into free-market-oriented capitalist economies. While their economies had grown significantly, however, they still lagged far behind existing member states, so that their accession caused GDP per head across the Union to fall by 18 per cent.[143] Treating the accession states as a whole, it was also the case that wages and working conditions there had *not* risen in line with economic growth.[144] In comparison with the EU-15, average wages in the EU-10 were very low;[145] minimum wages, where they existed, were set below subsistence levels; working hours were long; high numbers of workers were employed in the extensive informal economies; and health and safety standards were extremely poor, and worsening rather than improving.[146] Trade union membership levels were low, as was the coverage of collective bargaining, especially in the nascent private sector.[147] 'Social dialogue'-type tripartite arrangements at the

---

[137] G de Burca, 'The Drafting of the European Union Charter of Fundamental Rights' (2001) 26 *European Law Review* 126–38, 128–9.
[138] Hepple, *Labour Laws and Global Trade*, 241–3.
[139] Hepple, *Labour Laws and Global Trade*, 241.   [140] Deakin and Wilkinson, 345.
[141] Czech Republic, Estonia, Cyprus, Latvia, Lithuania, Hungary, Malta, Poland, Slovakia, and Slovenia joined the EU in 2004. In 2007, Romania and Bulgaria also joined.
[142] Vaughan-Whitehead, 31.   [143] Vaughn-Whitehead, 31.
[144] Vaughan-Whitehead, 46–56.
[145] Average income in the ten new member states was around 46 per cent of the average income in the EU-15. Average monthly gross wage levels in the 10 were around 41 per cent of the EU-15 average: European Commission, *Report of the High Level Group on the Future of Social Policy in an Enlarged European Union* (Brussels 2004), 13.
[146] Vaughan-Whitehead, ch 2.
[147] Vaughan-Whitehead, ch 6; Visser, 'More Holes in the Bucket'.

national level were over-formalized and dominated by the state.[148] In countries where employee information and consultation had been promoted, it tended to be concentrated in large state-owned enterprises, and was mostly absent in the private sector.[149]

As a condition of accession, the EU-10 were required to adopt the entire EU legal *acquis*, including social and employment standards. As we have seen, however, the labour law of the EU, insofar as it was deserving of that name, was limited in scope and in ambition, having only ever been intended to supplement existing national laws and practices in particular discrete respects.[150] As such, it fell well short of creating a floor of minimum standards or rights. Even where extensive legislative provisions existed, as, for example, in the field of health and safety, the improvement of standards in the new member states was hampered by reason of the absence of mechanisms for ensuring or monitoring compliance at enterprise level.[151] In the field of collective labour law, the European *acquis* amounted only to the social dialogue provisions of the Treaty and the set of Directives providing for employee information and consultation. In countries with weak trade unions and no culture among new entrepreneurs and managers of participation, dialogue, and social standards, the likelihood of *effective* transposition of these provisions appeared low.[152]

Given the obvious and significant differences in wage costs and social conditions in the old and the new member states, the threat of social dumping loomed large in public debates about enlargement. Capital flight to the East might threaten jobs at home, as would the likely massive influx of migrant workers drawn by the promise of high wages and high standards of living; competition from low-wage, low-cost enterprises in the new member states might be too much for companies in the old member states to bear, leading to bankruptcies and yet more job losses. In institutional and academic depictions of high-wage, high-productivity Social Europe, in contrast, the threat of social dumping and downward harmonization tended still to be downplayed.[153] The Commission showed a marked reluctance to engage with the issue, characterizing it as an insignificant or marginal phenomenon.[154] In institutional negotiations leading up to accession, social policy and divergences in social standards were only very cursorily addressed, the assumption apparently being that accession would lead to economic growth and to a consequent improvement of social standards in the new member states.[155] Such was the failure to address the implications of the massively increased disparities in wages

---

[148] Vaughan-Whitehead, ch 5.   [149] Vaughan-Whitehead, 318.
[150] Chapter 6. See also: Freedland, 'Employment Policy'.
[151] Vaughan-Whitehead, 107; *Report of the High Level Group on the Future of Social Policy in an Enlarged European Union*, 16–17.   [152] Vaughan-Whitehead, 318.
[153] Eg Hepple, *Labour Laws and Global Trade*, 211–18. In the 2004 *Report of the High Level Group on the Future of Social Policy in an Enlarged EU*, fears regarding social dumping and other adverse economic consequences were argued to be largely unfounded: 11–14.
[154] Vaughan-Whitehead, xiv, 358. See eg the very scant attention paid to enlargement and possible challenges/problems resulting therefrom in the Commission's Social Policy Agendas for 2000–2005 and 2006–2010.
[155] *Report of the High Level Group on the Future of Social Policy in an Enlarged EU*, 9, 15.

and social standards that would result from enlargement that Brian Bercusson referred to the issue memorably as the 'elephant lurking in the European social model'.[156]

In optimistic accounts of how enlargement should or would function, fundamental social rights again played an important role.[157] It was suggested, for example, that the 2000 Charter of Fundamental Rights might serve to fill—or at least to highlight—the many gaps in the existing labour law *acquis*, proclaiming as 'fundamental' rights to a minimum income, to freedom of association, and to collective bargaining.[158] The capacity of the Charter to function in this way would of course be improved if it were made legally binding by incorporation into the Treaties.[159] It was suggested that the existence of a floor of minimum standards would help to ensure that the economic growth resulting from enlargement would go hand in hand with an improvement in working and living conditions.[160] Together with the social dialogue, the identification of shared minimum standards or fundamental rights could serve as a means of encouraging or ensuring the maintenance and improvement of social standards while taking into account the significant differences between the EU-25 states.[161] It was suggested, finally, that fundamental rights might act as means of defence for an actor charged with having restricted another's right to free movement as protected by the Treaty: the actor could seek to justify her actions on the grounds that she had been exercising her fundamental rights or respecting those of a third party.[162]

In 2007, the Court of Justice had occasion in the landmark decisions of *Laval* and *Viking* to give its opinion on the status of fundamental rights and on the question, in particular, of whether such rights could constitute a defence to a charge of having infringed another's market freedom.[163] In both cases, the Court was asked in effect to judge the matter of the constitutional 'ranking' of free movement rights as against labour rights, the latter being protected by national legislation and declared fundamental under the 1989 and 2000 Charters. If there was conflict between the two, which should prevail? In the context of an enlarged EU of 27 states, the question assumed an augmented significance: would the Court interpret the Treaty so as to require old member states to dismantle or weaken existing labour rights as incompatible with a single market that extended now to include states with much weaker rights and poorer terms and conditions?

As is by now well known, the Court began its reasoning, in both *Laval* and *Viking*, by confirming that freedom of association was a fundamental right within the EU. It then went on, however, to state that action taken in exercise of that right

---

[156] B Bercusson, 'The Trade Union Movement and the European Union: Judgement Day' (2007) 13 *European Law Journal* 279–308, 305.   [157] Vaughan-Whitehead, 33.
[158] Vaughan-Whitehead, 108.   [159] Vaughan-Whitehead, 108.
[160] *Report of the High Level Group on the Future of Social Policy in an Enlarged EU*, 10.
[161] *Report of the High Level Group on the Future of Social Policy in an Enlarged EU*, 8.
[162] Hepple, *Labour Laws and Global Trade*, 212–13.
[163] Case C-341/05 *Laval v Svenska Byggnadsarbetareförbundet* 2007 ECR I-11767; Case C-438/05 *International Transport Workers' Union v Viking* 2007 ECR I-10779. See also Case-346/06 *Rüffert v Land Niedersachsen* 2008 ECR I-01989; Case C-319/06 *Commission v Luxemburg* 2008 ECR I-04323.

might nonetheless constitute an unlawful barrier to freedom of establishment and freedom to provide services. As had been 'reaffirmed' in the 2000 Charter, it explained, the exercise of freedom of association had only to be protected 'in accordance with Community law and national law and practices'.[164] 'Community law' included, of course, the Treaty provisions on free movement, which also figured as constitutionally protected fundamental rights in the EU legal order. In the Court's opinion, moreover, the free movement provisions could apply horizontally to the actions of trade unions. Accordingly, it was not the member state legislation, but the industrial action *itself* which was regarded as constituting a barrier to free movement.[165] When the Court came to address the possibility that the barriers might be justified, and therefore lawful, it was thus with reference to the industrial action that the questions of aims and proportionality were assessed. The Court took a very strict view of these matters and made no reference to any margin of appreciation. In *Laval*, it tied the question of the legitimacy of the union's aims directly to its interpretation of the Posted Workers' Directive.[166] Since the terms of the collective agreement which the union wished the employer to sign went beyond the minimum necessary to protect posted workers, as defined by the Directive, the union's actions could not be justified.[167] In *Viking*, the decision turned on the fact that the employer had given an assurance that the terms and conditions of *current* employees would not be affected by the re-flagging of a ship in Estonia. The right to take action for the protection of workers was a legitimate interest, the Court affirmed. Since current workers would not be affected, however, the union could not be said to be pursuing that interest in this case. The Court also objected to the fact that the union's action had been successful. '[T]o the extent that [the union's] policy results in shipowners being *prevented* from registering their vessels in a State . . . the restrictions on freedom of establishment resulting from such action *cannot* be objectively justified' (emphasis added).[168] The more successful the industrial action, it seems, the more difficult it will be to establish proportionality.[169]

As the extensive and ever-growing literature on these cases suggests, there is very much that could be said about the Court's reasoning and its implications for the legal systems of the Union and the member states.[170] For present purposes, the most significant aspect of the decisions is their apparent contradiction of the logic subscribed to by the authors of the Ohlin and Spaak Reports—and, more recently, by the various authors, institutional and academic, of win–win narratives of European integration—that economic integration through the creation of

---

[164] *Laval*, para 91; *Viking* para 44.
[165] Compare Case-112/00 *Schmidberger v Austria* (2003) ECR I-05659.
[166] EC Dir 96/71. For discussion see P Davies, 'The Posted Workers Directive and the EC Treaty' (2002) 31 *Industrial Law Journal* 298–306. [167] *Laval*, paras 106–11.
[168] *Viking*, para 88.
[169] ACL Davies, 'One Step Forward, Two Steps Back? The Viking and Laval Cases in the ECJ' (2008) 37 *Industrial Law Journal* 126–48.
[170] For an excellent overview of the jurisprudence and the most important lines of academic enquiry see C Barnard, 'Labour Law and the Internal Market' in *EU Employment Law* 4th ed (Oxford 2012).

a single market does *not* require the harmonization of social standards throughout the Union.[171] In *Laval* and *Viking*, and in the subsequent case of *Rüffert*, the Court reasoned contrary to Ohlin and Spaak that differences in labour standards between member states can give rise, in and of themselves, to restrictions of free movement.[172] Where that is the case, such differences ought to be removed. And if they are not to be removed by means of upward harmonization—which is highly unlikely given the political and practical difficulties involved in drafting and agreeing common labour standards, all the greater in an EU of 27 member states—then the Court is quite prepared to oversee the dismantling or weakening of established national standards. The fact that the national standards in question have the status of fundamental rights in the EU legal order will not prevent them figuring as unlawful restrictions of free movement, since fundamental rights have only to be protected 'in accordance with Community law'.[173]

With the *Laval* and *Viking* decisions and subsequent jurisprudence, the Court of Justice has thus opened the door to 'greater regulatory competition and ... the destabilization of national labour law regimes'.[174] Whether negative harmonization of national labour laws and labour constitutions will in fact result remains to be seen and is likely to depend both on the legislative responses of member states to the Court's judgments, and on the continued willingness of the Court to find in favour of those who raise claims of breaches of their fundamental market freedoms.[175] Who exactly stands to win and who to lose from any resulting deregulation is also a matter of some debate. It is sometimes assumed that a weakening of standards in the old 'high-wage' member states will benefit the accession states and their enterprises and workers, since it will facilitate access to markets in the wealthier parts of the Union.[176] One person's social dumping is another's market access;[177] one's undercutting of collectively agreed terms is another's utilization of comparative advantage.[178] Authors such as Novitz and Vaughan-Whitehead have highlighted the possibility, however, that it is often firms and shareholders in the *old* member states that are best placed to exploit the dismantling of barriers to trade in a situation of unequal wages and costs.[179] In the course of the current

---

[171] Barnard and Deakin, 261.

[172] Barnard and Deakin, 261. Case C-346/06 *Dirk Rüffert v Land Niedersachsen* [2008] ECR I-1989.

[173] For discussion see T Novitz, 'The Right to Strike as a Human Right' (2007–2008) 10 *Cambridge Yearbook of European Law* 357. [174] Barnard and Deakin, 262

[175] Barnard, 'Labour Law and the Internal Market', 238–9; T van Peijpe, 'Collective Labour Law after Viking, Laval, Rüffert, and Commission v. Luxembourg' (2009) 25 *International Journal of Comparative Labour Law and Industrial Relations* 81–107; D Sack, 'Europeanization through Law, Compliance and Party Differences' (2012) 34 *Journal of European Integration* 241–60.

[176] Barnard, 'Labour Law and the Internal Market', 207–8.

[177] Barnard, 'Labour Law and the Internal Market', 207, cites D Kukovec, 'Myths of Social Europe: The Laval Judgment and the Prosperity Gap', talk delivered to the Harvard Law School, 16 April 2010. Kukovec argues that the debate could 'just as well be framed in terms of social rights of [Estonian or Latvian] workers against the [Finnish or Swedish] interpretation of the freedom of movement provisions which ignores their realisation'.

[178] See *Rüffert v Land Niedersachsen*, opinion of Bot AG, at para 41.

[179] T Novitz, 'From Trade in Goods to Trade in Services—Implications for Transnational Labour Law', paper delivered at the 2013 Labour Law Research Network Conference, 27–8;

recession, writes Novitz, service providers from the EU-15 have established subsidiaries in accession states which they have used to hire a cheaper 'posted' workforce in order to be in a position to bid more competitively for service contracts at home.[180] (In *Laval*, for example, the majority shareholder of the Swedish building contractor and the 'Latvian' service-provider were one and the same.[181]) Rather than exercising their right to free movement, workers from the accession states who work in the EU-15 have tended to be hired through agencies as posted workers.[182] As such, they do not have the right to equal treatment with host state workers that workers exercising the right to free movement would enjoy. Instead they are guaranteed only such minimum wages and terms and conditions that have been set in the host state in accordance with the Posted Workers Directive, even if those minima are significantly lower than the going rate.[183] Without easy access to collective representation, moreover, they may also be more vulnerable to (unlawful) ill-treatment at the hands of employers.[184]

With reference to the jurisprudence of the Court prior to *Laval* and *Viking* and in the years since, it is possible to argue that there was nothing inevitable about the two decisions.[185] Following the rationale of the *Albany* ruling, the Court might have declared that collective bargaining and industrial action—as fundamental rights in EU law—were quite simply excluded from the scope of the free movement rules.[186] Following *Schmidberger*, it might have treated the national law sanctioning the industrial action, rather than the industrial action itself, as the potential barrier to free movement, and judged the questions of justification and proportionality with reference to a wide margin of appreciation.[187] In line with the opinion of the Advocate General in the more recent case of *Commission v Germany (occupational pensions)*, it might have taken a more symmetrical approach to the exercise of balancing fundamental rights and fundamental freedoms, asking not only whether exercise of the fundamental right constituted a barrier to the exercise of free movement, but also whether the exercise of free movement unreasonably restricted the exercise of the fundamental right.[188]

Emphasizing the importance of the institutional structure of the EU in influencing the choices of particular actors, Fritz Scharpf has argued, to the contrary,

---

Vaughan-Whitehead, 325; and more generally, part II of the same book ' Social Dumping: Myth or Reality?'   [180] Novitz, 'From Trade in Goods to Trade in Services', 25.

[181] Novitz, 'From Trade in Goods to Trade in Services', 22. For further examples see Vaughan-Whitehead, 344–9.

[182] Novitz, 'From Trade in Goods to Trade in Services', 25–7.

[183] Directive 96/71 on the posting of workers in the framework of the provision of services. For discussion see Barnard, 'Labour Law and the Internal Market', 218–39.

[184] Novitz, 'From Trade in Goods to Trade in Services', 26–7.

[185] Barnard and Deakin, 264, citing B Bercusson, *European Labour Law*, 2nd ed (Cambridge 2009), 698; Barnard, 'Labour Law and the Internal Market', 193–200.

[186] Case C–67/96 Albany [1999] ECR I–5751. Discussed in *Viking*, para 51–2; *Laval* 89–95.

[187] Case C–112/00 *Eugen Schmidberger, Internationale Transporte und Planzüge v Austria* [2003] ECR I-5659. For discussion see Davies, 'One Step Forward, Two Steps Back?', 141–2.

[188] Opinion of Advocate General Trstenjak in Case C–271/08 [2010] ECR I–-7087. Discussed Barnard, 'Labour Law and the Internal Market', 212–13.

that the *Laval* and *Viking* decisions were indeed inevitable, coming from a Court impelled by a 'liberalizing' dynamic of its own making.[189] In addition to the creation of the doctrines of supremacy and direct effect, the Court took a further step in the 1960s and 1970s which set it squarely down the path to becoming a key actor in the extension of the reach of negative integration, at the expense of democratic self-determination in the national polity.[190] In *Dassonville* and *Cassis de Dijon*, it widened its interpretation of the free movement provisions very considerably so that even *non-discriminatory* national measures could be judged unlawful barriers to the exercise of free movement of goods, freedom of establishment, and freedom to provide services.[191] As a result, the Court was able to exercise a 'quasi-discretionary' control over both the substance of member state policies (did they aim to satisfy a 'mandatory requirement'?), and the question of their proportionality.[192] The doctrine of direct effect, meanwhile, meant that the questions and cases which came before the Court tended always to 'reflect the interest of parties who have a major economic or personal stake in increased factor or personal mobility as well as the financial and organizational resources to pursue this interest'.[193] Parties with an interest in the maintenance of existing national laws and regulations were not heard. Moreover, the only remedy that the Court could offer private litigants was to disallow those national regulations that were found to hinder free movement. 'What the Court cannot do is to establish a common European regime that would respond to some of the values and policy purposes, which, as a consequence of its decisions, can no longer be realized at the national level.'[194]

The inability of the Court to rule in a way that would create common labour standards at the supranational level is compounded, Scharpf argues, by the fact that political action to reverse any decision of the Court is likely to be extremely difficult, as was apparent in the aftermath of *Laval* and *Viking*.[195] Where the Court's decision has been based on primary European law, it can only be reversed by a Treaty amendment, requiring ratification by all member states. Where it has been based on secondary law, a reversal will require a legislative initiative from the Commission, itself requiring at least qualified majority support in the Council, and usually an absolute majority in the European Parliament. Given the ever-increasing diversity of national interests and preferences in an enlarged EU, political agreement of this type is likely to be 'nearly impossible' to achieve.[196] The result, writes

---

[189] Scharpf, 222. In Barnard's opinion, the adoption by the Court of the 'market access' approach made it inevitable that collective action should be judged a restriction on freedom of establishment and the freedom to provide services: Barnard, 'Labour Law and the Internal Market', 207.

[190] Scharpf, 221, 223.   [191] Cases C-8/74, 11.07.1974; C-120/78, 20.02.1979
[192] Scharpf, 217–21.   [193] Scharpf, 221.   [194] Scharpf, 223.
[195] Scharpf, 217. For discussion of the attempts to clarify or minimize the effects of the *Laval* and *Viking* jurisprudence by means of legislation (the Monti II Regulation and 'enforcement' Directive), see Barnard, 'Labour Law and the Internal Market', 209–13, 237–8; P Syrpis and T Novitz, 'Economic and Social Rights in Conflict: Political and Judicial Approaches to their Reconciliation' (2008) 33 *European Law Review* 411–26.
[196] Scharpf, 217.

Scharpf, is a stark 'institutional asymmetry' in the Union, grossly favouring negative integration through law over positive integration by way of concerted political action.[197] For as long as that is the case, he concludes, a 'European social market economy' simply cannot be.[198]

Too little autonomy?

In the *Laval* and *Viking* jurisprudence, the CJEU confirmed that member states' autonomy to shape their own labour constitutions is significantly limited by the obligation when doing so to respect the Treaty-based market freedoms of individuals and firms.[199] (As a direct result of the *Laval* decision, for example, the right to strike in Sweden would have to be restricted so as to comply with the terms of the Treaty-based freedom to provide services, and the Posted Workers' Directive, as interpreted by the Court.[200]) At the same time, it interpreted those market freedoms in a way that also limited the autonomy of trade unions acting within member states to protect or further the interests of their members. Any union considering industrial action in a context which involves some element of free movement within the EU will henceforth face the possibility that the industrial action might be found unlawful, leaving it vulnerable to claims for potentially crippling damages.[201] As was acknowledged by the ILO Committee of Experts on the Application of Conventions and Recommendations, this is likely to have a 'significant restrictive effect on the exercise of the right to strike'.[202]

In fact, it is not necessarily even the case, any more, that a labour right such as freedom of association need be exercised in a context involving an attempt to exercise free movement within the EU, in order for the laws or actions in question to be categorized as unlawful barriers to such movement. As a consequence of the Court's embrace of the 'market access' or 'restrictions' approach to the question of barriers to trade or movement, in place of the discrimination approach, national labour laws and the actions of trade unions acting in accordance with those laws have become liable to challenge as barriers to free movement wherever they are judged liable to discourage or deter even hypothetical cross-border transactions.[203] In the *Volkswagen* case, for example, a German law providing for a blocking minority of 20 per cent (rather than the more usual 25 per cent) in the shareholder assembly in Volkswagen was regarded as a *potential* deterrent to foreign direct investment, and hence to the free movement of capital.[204] As such, the rule had to be repealed, as it

---

[197] Scharpf, 211–14.
[198] Scharpf, 211–14, referring to the commitment in Art 3(3) of the Lisbon Treaty to create a European social market economy. [199] Scharpf, 228–39.
[200] M Rönnmar, 'Laval Returns to Sweden' (2010) 39 *Industrial Law Journal* 280–7.
[201] K Apps, 'Damages Claims against Trade Unions after Viking and Laval' (2009) 34 *European Law Review* 141–54. In the aftermath of *Laval*, the Swedish trade union was ordered by the Swedish labour court to pay 55,000 Euros in damages: Rönnmar, 282.
[202] ILO Conference, *Report of the Committee of Experts on the Application of Conventions and Recommendations* (Geneva 2010), 236–7.
[203] Barnard, 'Labour Law and the Internal Market', 201–2.
[204] *Commission v Germany* C-112/05, 23.10.2007.

applied to German investors and (potential) foreign investors alike.[205] Such being the reasoning of the Court, the question arises whether it would not also regard the German legislation providing for codetermination on company boards as a potential deterrent to foreign direct investment and, therefore, as an unlawful barrier to the free movement of capital, were it asked to consider the matter.[206] More generally, the question arises: what level of homogeneity of systems of labour law and corporate governance rules does the Court regard as necessary to allow for an integrated single market? With reference to what, other than the lowest standards currently applied within the Union, will it fix its notions of proportionate and justifiable barriers to free trade and free movement? If the fact that a right is declared fundamental under the terms of the EU Charter is not sufficient, in the eyes of the Court, to prevent legislation protecting it, or action taken in exercise of it, figuring as an unlawful restriction of free movement, what weight will the Court accord to a decision of the European Court of Human Rights, or the Committee of Experts of the ILO, that the right to freedom of association is thereby breached?[207]

It is with respect to the question of member state autonomy that Scharpf concludes his argument regarding the inevitability of the Court's decisions in *Laval* and *Viking* and associated cases. By reason of the doctrine of supremacy, Scharpf explains, the court assumes the role of a constitutional court in such cases, judging questions of the appropriate relationship between supranational and national laws.[208] In doing so, however, it does not aim, as a federal constitutional court would, to strike an appropriate and stable balance between the 'mandates, legitimacy bases and functional requirements' of the two levels of government.[209] In the case law of the Court, there is no place for discussions of the relative importance of European and national concerns, and no concepts that could identify, define, and evaluate legitimate concerns of member states that should be beyond the reach of European law.[210] The Court understands itself as an instrument for promoting a dynamic process of ever increasing European integration, and the logic that it applies to such cases is 'unipolar', maximizing Europeanization at the expense of national autonomy.[211] Moreover, reasons Scharpf, even if the Court were to attempt to define 'effective hard-law' limits of European law, and corresponding 'protected spheres' of member state autonomy, its task would be an impossible one because of the diverse histories, traditions, cultures, institutions, and legal systems of the member states.[212] Any legitimate judge-made rule of this type would need to be of general application, capable of defining the relationship between the EU and all of the member states.[213] And what is an appropriate sphere

---

[205] Scharpf, 14. SME stands for social market economy.   [206] Scharpf, 236.
[207] For discussion of the likely impact of the EU's planned accession to the European Convention on Human Rights see Syrpis, 'The Treaty of Lisbon'. For the observations of the ILO Committee of Experts finding that Swedish legislation enacted as a response to *Laval* (limiting the right of Swedish trade unions to take industrial action in order to convince a foreign service provider posting workers to Sweden to sign a collective agreement) is in violation of ILO Convention 87 on the freedom of association and the right to organize; see ILO, *Report of the Committee of Experts on the Application of Conventions and Recommendations* (Geneva 2013), 176.   [208] Scharpf, 228.
[209] Scharpf, 228.   [210] Scharpf, 229–30   [211] Scharpf 228, 231.
[212] Scharpf, 240–1.   [213] Scharpf, 240.

of autonomy for one member state is simply not appropriate for all. 'A general rule that would respect politically salient concerns in the most highly regulated member state ... would obviously define European economic competences far too narrowly, but an equally general rule that would merely protect the practices of the most liberal member state might massively interfere with the political identity and legitimacy of SME member states.'[214] No general Court-made rule could establish a fair vertical balance appropriate to all of the member states.

Economic and monetary union and member state autonomy

Quite independently of the Court of Justice, the freedom of member states to shape their labour constitutions and employment laws has been restricted since 1992 by reason of the adoption of the programme for economic and monetary union, incorporated into the Treaty of Maastricht. As was explained by commentators at the time, the terms of the programme tied member states into a macroeconomic policy framework, dictated from above, which drastically limited their autonomy to manage their economies.[215] In particular, the framework obliged member states to keep budget deficits and public debt low, to restrict public borrowing and fiscal adjustments, and to adopt interest rates set by the European Central Bank (ECB), in line with its obligation to prioritize price stability *over* other objectives, including full employment. As a result, the framework served to rule out many of the instruments traditionally employed by countries seeking to stimulate growth and job creation. In particular, of course, the very idea of economic and monetary union ruled out the option of devaluing a national currency as a means of improving competitiveness and stimulating growth. That being the case, the most obvious alternative left open to countries seeking to improve their competitiveness relative to other member states was to adjust welfare state provisions and labour rights and standards *downwards* in order to compete on the basis of low labour costs.[216]

Prior to 2009, the impact of economic and monetary union on the labour laws of member states appears to have been limited.[217] On the face of it, at least, national labour laws remained mostly stable throughout the 2000s, albeit within a context of trade union decline and growing inequality between lower and higher earners.[218] Beginning in late 2009, however, the sovereign debt crisis which followed the public bailouts of the 'too big to fail' banks has resulted in quite radical changes to national labour laws.[219] In response to the crisis, the EU has pursued

---

[214] Scharpf, 241.
[215] Streeck, 'Neo-Voluntarism', 56.
[216] Streeck, 'Neo-Voluntarism', 56. For an explanation of the workings of internal devaluation and possible alternatives to it, see Armingeon and Baccaro, 'Political Economy of the Sovereign Debt Crisis: the Limits of Internal Devaluation', 254–75.
[217] S Deakin and A Koukiadaki, 'The Sovereign Debt Crisis and Evolution of Labour Law in Europe' in N Countouris and M Freedland (eds), *Re-Socializing Europe in a Time of Crisis* (Cambridge 2013), 164–72.
[218] Deakin and Koukiadaki, 164–72.
[219] For an excellent overview see S Clauwaert and I Schömann, 'The Crisis and National Labour Law Reforms: A Mapping Exercise', ETUI Working Paper 2012.04 (Brussels 2012),

policies of 'internal devaluation', imposing these more or less directly on member states. In the case of Portugal, Ireland, and most dramatically Greece, the 'Troika' of the ECB, the Commission, and the IMF has required, as a condition of loans, that existing labour laws, terms and conditions of employment, and social benefits be cut. In respect of the countries that are not in receipt of loans, Spain and Italy, it has otherwise exerted significant pressure in favour of similar drastic measures.[220] Even in non-Eurozone countries, such as the UK, its blueprint of deregulation as the best means of addressing budget deficits and public debt has been influential in shaping proposed reforms of labour laws.[221] The logic behind these policies has been a straightforward extension of the logic embodied in the original programme for economic and monetary union: with the aim of restoring the competitiveness of national economies and ensuring economic growth, states should undergo a process of internal devaluation so that they can compete with wealthier states on the basis of low labour costs.

As directed by the Troika, or by national governments apparently persuaded by the Troika- and Commission-endorsed characterization of labour rights and decent wages as obstacles to economic growth, wide-ranging changes have been introduced to national systems of labour law in the years since 2009.[222] In the field of individual employment rights, reforms have targeted rules relating to, among other things, dismissal compensation, collective redundancies, working time, flexible forms of employment, and contracts for young workers. In respect of dismissals and redundancies, notice periods and compensation rates have been reduced; in respect of flexible employment, rules have been changed to allow for much greater flexibility, to the benefit of employers. In the field of collective labour law, the aim has been to amend key features of national systems so as to ensure both lower wages, judged commensurate with productivity levels, and the decentralization and dismantling of existing collective wage-setting mechanisms.[223] In furtherance of that aim, legislation has been passed which interferes very significantly with the autonomy of the unions and employers' associations and their rights to freedom of association. In Greece, for example, young workers and the previously long-term unemployed have been excluded from the scope of the national collective agreement and from generally binding collectively agreed terms relating to minimum wages and conditions of work.[224] The national minimum wage as agreed in the national collective agreement has been set aside and replaced by a state-imposed minimum, 22 per cent lower for 'standard' employees

---

and associated national reports available: <http://www.etui.org/Publications2/Working-Papers/The-crisis-and-national-labour-law-reforms-a-mapping-exercise>.

[220] Deakin and Koukiadaki, 176.

[221] C Barnard, 'The Financial Crisis and the Euro Plus Pact: A Labour Lawyer's Perspective' (2012) 41 *Industrial Law Journal* 98–114.

[222] Clauwaert and Schömann; Deakin and Koukiadaki, 177–85; Barnard, 'Financial Crisis'; A Koukiadaki and L Kretsos, 'Opening Pandora's Box: The Sovereign Debt Crisis and Labour Market Regulation in Greece (2012) 41 *Industrial Law Journal*, 276–304.

[223] Koukiadaki and Kretsos, 301.

[224] Deakin and Koukiadaki, 180–5; Koukiadaki and Kretsos, 286.

and lower still for young workers and apprentices. A freeze in minimum wages has been imposed until 2015.[225] With the aim of undermining the existing system of national collective bargaining, so as to move wage setting closer to company level, legislation has given firms the right to conclude firm-level collective agreements that derogate *in pejus* from sectoral-level agreements.[226] In addition, legislation has destroyed the unions' monopoly position as the representative of workers for the purposes of collective bargaining, creating a right for 'associations of persons' to conclude enterprise-level collective agreements that again can derogate *in pejus*.[227]

In a paper published in 2013, Colin Crouch emphasized the ways in which the response to the crisis has been at odds with the by now outdated win–win narrative of the European Social Model.[228] In the early 2000s, writes Crouch, there was widespread agreement that the EU ought to take a 'high road' to global competitiveness, upgrading skills, research and innovative capacity, and infrastructure, to enable the economy to compete in mainly up-market, high-value-added sectors. While this might have required some reform of existing welfare systems and labour legislation, it would also have allowed for their continued existence.[229] Since 2009, the Troika and some national policy-makers have 'treated all sophisticated discussion of how to achieve competitiveness through the high-road of upgrading as so much baggage'.[230] Little or no heed has been paid to the ways in which the well-developed labour constitutions of the northern member states have contributed positively to the superior economic competitiveness of those states.[231] Struggling states have been required to compete on low prices alone, with no time or effort to be 'wasted' on any up-skilling or improvement of the quality of the labour force. There has been resort, in short, to a 'crude, unreconstructed neoliberalism.'[232] As for the consequences of these policies, there is growing evidence that they have led, in the short term, to the deterioration of working and living conditions while failing to deliver economic growth.[233] In the medium to long term, the turn to deregulation and the underlying logic of labour standards and welfare provision as barriers to growth risk a Union-wide race to the bottom.[234]

To a Troika apparently convinced that its policy prescriptions reflect what is necessary to ensure the recovery of national economies and the repayments of their loans, the fundamental rights of workers in Greece, Ireland, and Portugal have been of as little import, apparently, as the wishes of the citizens of those countries. Neither the terms of the European Union's Charter of Fundamental Rights—legally binding as incorporated into the Treaty since 2007—or additional Treaty commitments to respect the values of 'human dignity, freedom,

---

[225] Koukiadaki and Kretsos, 299. [226] Koukiadaki and Kretsos, 290–1.
[227] Koukiadaki and Kretsos, 292–3. [228] Crouch, 'Entrenching Neo-Liberalism'.
[229] Crouch, 'Entrenching Neo-Liberalism', 39–40.
[230] Crouch, 'Entrenching Neo-Liberalism', 41. [231] Deakin and Koukiadaki, 175.
[232] Crouch, 'Entrenching Neo-Liberalism', 41.
[233] Deakin and Koukiadaki, 163, 185; Clauwaert and Schömann, 17. For Greece see Koukiadaki and Kretsos, 302–3. For a first acknowledgement from the Commission that internal devaluation has entailed significant social costs, see European Commission, *Communication Regarding the Strengthening the Social Dimension of the Economic and Monetary Union* COM (2013) 690
[234] Barnard, 'Financial Crisis', 98; Deakin and Koukiadaki, 163; Koukiadaki and Kretsos, 303.

democracy, equality, the rule of law and . . . human rights' have acted as any kind of brake on those intent on pursuing deregulatory reforms. As the Troika has dictated policies and national governments have set about implementing them, there has been only limited evidence of either political or social dialogue at the national level.[235] Where trade unions—and employers' associations—have been invited to discuss particular policies, it has been clear that discussion would proceed within a context that allowed them little choice but to agree with what was proposed, using any room for manoeuvre only to attempt to limit the damage inflicted upon members.[236] If they dared to disagree with proposed cuts, they were simply overruled.[237] Confirmation, if any was needed, that the reforms enacted in response to the crisis breach the fundamental rights of workers has come, after the event, from the ILO, the European Committee of Social Rights, and the Greek Council of State.[238] Action by the EU Commission in the face of national measures implemented in violation of fundamental rights has been notable by its absence.[239]

Conclusion

The idea of the labour constitution implies a single bounded 'space'—a workplace, company, industry, or nation—within which the respective roles of organized labour and management are governed by a single set of norms. Central to Sinzheimer's conception of the labour constitution of the Weimar Republic was recognition of a variety of subnational spaces as sites of organization and rule-making, coupled with an insistence upon the importance of centralized (national-level) circumscription and coordination of the lower-level activities. Only peak-level representatives, reasoned Sinzheimer, could have the breadth of knowledge, the overview necessary to ensure that production was managed in furtherance of the good of *all*. Without such coordination, the danger existed that workers would identify too closely with their own particular workplace; that they would act only in the interests of themselves and their immediate co-workers; and that the wages and conditions of each worker would come to depend, quite directly, on the matter of where he worked. In his brief discussion of the possible creation of a European Community of Nations, Sinzheimer followed the same line of reasoning to conclude that the achievement of economic democracy within such a Community would require the creation of a supranational economic constitution, and an international or European trade union capable of figuring as a countervailing force to international capital.

---

[235] Deakin and Koukiadaki, 176–7; Koukiadaki and Kretsos, 283–4; Armingeon and Baccaro, 267.
[236] Armingeon and Baccaro, 267.
[237] Armingeon and Baccaro, 267; Koukiadaki and Kretsos, 295–7.
[238] ILO, *Report of the Committee of Experts on the Application of Conventions and Recommendations* (Geneva 2012): Greece, 159–64; Decision of the European Committee of Social Rights on Collective Complaints no. 65/2011 and 66/2011; Decision of the Greek Council of State Regarding the Constitutionality of Law 4046/2012. [239] Clauwaert and Schömann, 16.

Conclusion

In fact, the economy of the European Union was—and still is—constituted by a plurality of legal and institutional frameworks, supranational and national. Separate and significantly different labour constitutions exist within each member state, and the vision which the European representative of the free trade unions had in the early years of the EEC, of European-level coordination of those constitutions, has never been realized.[240] In the mid-1970s, political pressure applied by trade unions, and by the social democratic governments of a number of the member states, resulted in the first wave of European legislation in the field of social policy and, specifically, collective labour law. In line with the European trade union's 'radical democratic' objective of more democracy in the Community through more union involvement, Directives were drafted by the Commission which aimed to harmonize upwards worker rights to participate in the management of workplaces and companies. In the 1970s and 1980s, these Directives met with resistance on the part of several member state governments, objecting to the 'Germanification' of their systems of industrial relations or, for ideological reasons, to the very idea of industrial democracy. Some of the Directives drafted by the Commission were never adopted; others were amended to the point where the goal of upward harmonization was barely recognizable in their terms. In this the fate of the information and consultation Directives illustrated well the more general point made by Fritz Scharpf about the difficulties involved in brokering agreement in the Council to legislation in the field of social welfare: that differences in the traditions and institutions of each member state constitute very significant barriers to the achievement of upward harmonization.[241] With each round of enlargement of the Communities, such barriers have been strengthened by the accession of states with their own particular traditions and institutions, to the point where the brokering of political agreement in favour of raising labour or social standards has been judged by Scharpf 'nearly impossible'.[242]

By 1992, when the European Community acted to extend its powers to adopt legislation in the field of social policy in the Maastricht Treaty, it was more or less clear to all that those powers would not be used to attempt the further upward harmonization of national labour laws. Instead, efforts would be concentrated on the creation of certain common minimum standards as a means of defence against the negative harmonization of labour laws or, more positively presented, as a means of improving the competitiveness of the European economy and of encouraging the creation of employment. Throughout the 1990s and early 2000s, fundamental social rights were increasingly advocated by the EU institutions, and by several academic commentators, as capable of facilitating the achievement of economic goals—as indicative of the Union's intention to take a 'high road' to global competitiveness, combining economic growth with policies designed to achieve social justice and respect for human rights, and as a means of ensuring that it did. In 2009, the Charter of Fundamental Rights became legally binding as part of the Treaty of Lisbon. At the same time, however, the capacity

---

[240] Bouvard, 72–5.   [241] Scharpf, 19, 32.   [242] Scharpf, 217.

of fundamental rights to figure as any kind of break upon trends or pressures towards downward harmonization was shown to be extremely limited. In *Laval* and *Viking*, the Court of Justice ruled that action taken in exercise of a fundamental right (freedom of association) could constitute an unlawful barrier to a company's freedom of establishment or freedom to provide services. As a result of these decisions, national laws protecting freedom of association needed to be weakened. In the context of the sovereign debt crisis of recent years, the Commission and the Central Bank acted together with the IMF to require or encourage member states to weaken labour rights, and to dismantle and decentralize existing collective bargaining arrangements. In the course of these developments, the fundamental rights of workers as declared by the 2000 Charter, and as protected in international and national law, have apparently been of as little import to the Court as to the Commission or the Central Bank.

At the time of writing, it would be no exaggeration to suggest that the survival of a plurality of national labour constitutions within the EU appears threatened by a variety of pressures to deregulate labour standards and to decentralize—or to borrow Streeck's term, to *disorganize*—collective representation and collective bargaining practices and institutions.[243] In the short space of the past six or seven years, the downward harmonization of national labour constitutions has assumed a bleak inevitability; the rights and capacities of trade unions to bargain collectively, and to participate effectively in the governance of workplaces or companies, will everywhere be weakened, just as collective bargaining coverage contracts and wage disparities and income inequalities between and within member states will continue to grow.[244] Without any or with only a muted voice at work, workers will become ever more vulnerable to unfair or harsh treatment, to abuses of their remaining rights and of health and safety standards.[245] And this will be so in part *because* of the European Union, its constitution, and institutions, and not in spite of them. The Court of Justice will require the dismantling or weakening of an ever wider variety of labour rights and standards as unlawful barriers to the economic freedoms of companies.[246] Increasingly, it will interpret the common standards set in EU Directives as maxima rather than minima—as a ceiling rather than a floor of labour standards—curtailing the capacity of member states to guarantee workers anything better.[247] While the Commission aids the Court in its endeavours, bringing actions against member states that have enacted such 'unlawful barriers',

---

[243] Streeck describes the 'disorganization' of the German economy in *Re-Forming Capitalism* (2009), discussed in chapter 3 this volume.
[244] For a discussion of existing evidence relating to collective bargaining and wage inequality see S Hayter and B Weinberg, 'Mind the Gap: Collective Bargaining and Wage Inequality' in S Hayter (ed), *The Role of Collective Bargaining in the Global Economy* (Cheltenham 2011).
[245] See the description of the tragic collapse of a supermarket in Riga in 2013 in C Woolfson and A Juska, 'A Very Baltic Tragedy' in J Sommers and C Woolfson, *The Contradictions of Austerity: The Socio-Economic Costs of the Neoliberal Baltic Model* (London 2014).
[246] See eg discussion of *Commission v Germany* C-112/05, 23.10.2007 above.
[247] See eg the Court's interpretation of the Posted Workers' Directive in *Laval* and of the Acquired Rights Directive in Case-C 426/11 *Alemo-Herron v Parkwood Leisure Ltd* discussed by J Prassl, 'Case-C 426/11 Alemo-Herron v Parkwood Leisure Ltd' (2013) 42 *Industrial Law Journal* 434–46.

it will be notably less conscientious in its pursuit of states which act in violation of workers' fundamental rights.[248] Alone or together with the ECB and the IMF, it will continue to require or persuade states that the best route to greater competitiveness lies with lowering labour costs, and therefore labour standards.[249] Any attempts to address trends towards deregulation and disorganization through the adoption of new common standards at European level (if such are made) will falter, meanwhile, by reason of the almost insurmountable difficulties involved in brokering agreement in the Council of Ministers. Dismal as it is, this vision of the future functioning of the EU is much too firmly rooted in current practices to be easily dismissed as dystopian. The conclusion that the European Social Model and the promises it once seemed to embody are things of the past is difficult to avoid.[250]

---

[248] Clauwaert and Schömann, 16.
[249] See eg European Commission (2009) *Economic Crisis in Europe: Causes, Consequences and Responses* <http://ec.europa.eu/economy_finance/publications/publication15887_en.pdf>, 35–40.
[250] Mario Draghi, President of the ECB, stated in an interview with the *Wall Street Journal*, February 2012, that the European Social Model 'has already gone'. Cf Lazlo Andor, Commissioner responsible for Employment Social Affairs and Inclusion, on the 'long term reconstruction of the European Social Model' in a speech from September 2013: <http://europa.eu/rapid/press-release_SPEECH-13-752_en.htm>.

8

Labour Law or the Law of the Labour Market?

Introduction

In this concluding chapter, the intention is to make the case for the usefulness of the idea of the labour constitution as a framework for the scholarly analysis of labour law today. Drawing on the work presented in previous chapters, consideration is given to the question of what it would mean to use the idea as a framework for analysis now, under conditions of advanced globalization. In particular, how might the idea be abstracted sufficiently from the particularities of the context in which it was developed so as to render it applicable to current conditions, while holding on still to the normative principles at its core? What would the framework of the labour constitution assume, and what would it focus attention upon as matters to be investigated? Given the importance of the 'state' to Sinzheimer's original conception, how would the framework take account of the changed nature of nation states today—of the narrowing of their capacity to set and enforce labour standards autonomously, and of the increased significance of supranational and transnational entities as sites or sources of regulation?

Consideration of the potential benefits of the labour constitution as a framework for analysis proceeds in the first instance from a comparison of the scholarship of Sinzheimer and Kahn-Freund with the approach adopted by the 'law of the labour market' scholars. Building on the discussion contained in chapter 5, it is suggested again that the central weakness of the labour market approach is its tendency to underemphasize conflicts of interest. In their well-developed account of the normative principles informing law of the labour market scholarship, Deakin and Wilkinson choose Hayek as their interlocutor, intending thereby to construct arguments which defeat neoclassical or neoliberal claims, or assumptions, regarding the market-constraining nature of labour rights and institutions. But the conception of markets they advance relies on the same basic premise as Hayek that some kinds of market intervention are desirable (for all) because they help markets function better, and some kinds are bad (for all) because they interfere with or prohibit optimal market functioning. Their analysis can tend therefore towards the suggestion, or implication, that good economic policy—and good labour law (good labour market regulation)—is non-political by definition.[1] Following

---

[1] Streeck, 'Crisis of Democratic Capitalism', 10.

Wolfgang Streeck, it is argued that there is a need to bring capitalism back into the study of labour law and labour markets.[2] Markets must be understood not in abstract terms, but as institutions of *capitalist* political economy, the configuration of which can impact very differently on different sections of society.[3] Capitalism can usefully be understood with Karl Polanyi as driven by a conflictual interplay—or 'double movement'—between (individual) efforts to expand the reach of markets in pursuit of economic gain on the one hand, and (collective political) efforts at protecting society on the other.[4] On the basis of these understandings, it becomes much more difficult to make the claim that certain labour rights and institutions can be characterized *objectively* as desirable or undesirable in accordance with their propensity to make markets function 'better'.[5] What falls to be investigated is precisely the question of *who* benefits and *who* suffers disadvantage when the economy—comprising markets and non-market institutions and modes of interaction—is configured in a particular way. Recognition that the regulation of the economy, and labour law in particular, are inherently political matters serves, moreover, to reveal the compelling nature of the case for collective worker voice as a question of democracy. If the definition of well-functioning markets and even the prior question of the inherent desirability of markets as a means of organizing social interactions are matters of perspective, then workers ought to be in a position to argue for the type of *economic order*, for those laws and institutions, which will better protect their interests.

Against the critique of the law of the labour market paradigm, the primary claim made for the usefulness of the idea of the labour constitution is that it offers a framework for considering and analysing the regulation of work and working relationships as a matter of political, as well as economic, significance. Like Polanyi's 'double movement', the labour constitution assumes the existence of conflicts of interest between those who seek to maximize profits through participation in free markets and those who stand to gain through the subordination of the economy to democratic control.[6] Viewed through the framework of the labour constitution, trade unions are understood to be political as well as economic actors, and labour law is understood as a mechanism for introducing democratic rights and modes of action into the economy, transforming subordinated workers into economic or industrial citizens.[7] Politics is given full recognition as a force which can—in principle at least—be harnessed by those who wish to resist the expansion of markets into ever greater spheres of social life, to see institutions and laws retained or reconfigured so that markets function in line with their interests,

---

[2] Streeck, *Re-Forming Capitalism*; Tucker, 'Renorming Labour Law'.
[3] Streeck, 'Sociology of Labour Markets'.   [4] Streeck, *Re-Forming Capitalism*, 4.
[5] Streeck, *Re-Forming Capitalism*, 232.
[6] In the *Great Transformation*, Polanyi defines socialism as 'the tendency inherent in an industrial civilization to transcend the self-regulating market by consciously subordinating it to a democratic society': Polanyi, 242.
[7] Marshall, 'Citizenship and Social Class'; C Crouch, 'The Globalized Economy: An End to the Age of Industrial Citizenship?' in T Wilthagen (ed) *Advancing Theory in Labour Law and Industrial Relations in a Global Context* (Amsterdam 1998).

with what they understand (quite *independently of markets* and the rules or logic of market-functioning) to be right. Instead of limiting scholars sympathetic to the interests of labour to instrumentalist arguments that labour rights might improve labour market efficiency or flexibility, the framework of the labour constitution allows for arguments to be made on the basis of the legitimacy *in themselves* of workers' claims to human dignity, liberty, and equality (these values understood quite independently of markets and market logic). Instead of dismissing those labour rights which cannot convincingly be said to improve efficiency or flexibility as impossibly idealistic or anachronistic, it assumes that everything is to play for: economic freedoms and social rights; trade liberalization and state intervention in the interests of social justice or environmental protection; deregulation and reregulation of the financial sector. As such, the advantage of the labour constitution as a framework for analysis is that it turns the spotlight squarely on questions of power and influence—economic power, political power, social power—and on the myriad ways in which laws and legal frameworks constitute, reinforce, and limit such power.

Given the very significant changes that have occurred since Sinzheimer's time in the organization of production and in the political landscape, the argument that his work remains useful to the study of labour law today can of course be met with significant objections: that globalization to date has insulated global trade and global finance from political and democratic control; that an asymmetry has developed between global capital and weakened trade unions and other democratic, representative institutions still tied to the national level; that there is no global 'state', no global trade union, capable of performing the role of constitutionalizing the global economy in the way prescribed by Sinzheimer with respect to the national economy.[8] In the final section of the chapter, and with reference to the analysis of the European Union in chapters 6 and 7, the idea of the labour constitution is shown to bear the advantage of allowing for the recognition of the existence of a plurality of economic constitutions or orders: state, non-state, supranational, subnational. What appeared in Sinzheimer's work as an emphasis on the importance of the 'state' is interpreted more broadly as an emphasis on the critical nature of the link between democracy and labour law. Analysis undertaken using the framework of the labour constitution is argued, on that basis, to point to the urgency of further research aimed at the reassertion of the importance of democratic deliberation within (the 'democratization of') a variety of sites of decision-making: nation states and national economic orders, but also supranational regulatory bodies, trade organizations, transnational corporations, financial institutions. The question as to how worker organization might be strengthened or re-imagined so that trade unions could figure again as primary sites for the formulation and expression of demands for the protection of workers' interests is identified as central to such research.

---

[8] H Arthurs, 'The Constitutionalisation of Employment Relations: Multiple Models, Pernicious Problems' (2010) 19 *Social and Legal Studies* 403–22; E Tucker, 'Labor's Many Constitutions (and Capital's too)' (2012) 33 *Comparative Labor Law and Policy Journal* 355–78.

Approaches to Labour Law Scholarship

In seeking to understand and to contribute to scholarly debates regarding the idea of labour law, it is important to recognize that answers to the question 'what is labour law?' are likely to be influenced in important ways by, among other things, individual understandings of the purpose of labour law scholarship. To put it another way, the project of ascribing to labour law a particular scope and objective, or set of objectives, is likely to be closely informed by the answer given to the necessarily prior question of the purpose of engaging in that project: the project of attempting to define the field of labour law. Whom do we wish to convince with our definition of the field, or with our corresponding assessment of a particular legislative provision or judicial ruling: policy-makers, judges and other legal practitioners, the business community, workers and trade unionists, fellow academics, students? Why and in what capacity do we wish to convince: as those with expert knowledge or practical experience, as teachers, as advocates of a particular political programme or of the interests of a particular section of society? Though our answers to such questions may often be left unsaid, they will likely lead us to take quite different views of essential preliminary matters, such as whether the definition we seek to build should be primarily descriptive, of the law as it is, or normative, of the law as it ought to be. If the definition is to be normative, if an 'idea' of labour law is to be constructed to some extent independently of the stated policy aims of the government of the day, with reference to some alternative vision of social or economic or procedural justice, then our answers to the prior questions—whom, why, and in what capacity do we wish to convince—are likely to inform our view of the appropriate source or rationale of such an alternative vision. Made explicit, our different conceptions of the purpose of labour law scholarship might go some way to explaining why we answer the question 'what is labour law?' in different ways.[9]

Scholars of labour law

In the opening chapters of this book, it was suggested that the approaches to labour law scholarship adopted by Hugo Sinzheimer and Otto Kahn-Freund were broadly similar. This was, perhaps, an unsurprising conclusion to draw, given that Kahn-Freund had learned the craft directly from Sinzheimer, that both combined scholarship with legal practice, that both brought to their work a fully formed and deeply held set of political convictions regarding the rightful status of the worker in society and the role that the law might play in securing that status.[10] In the work of Kahn-Freund, as in the work of Sinzheimer, legal analysis and political

---

[9] For very useful accounts of national traditions in labour law scholarship see contributions to the special issue: (2002) 23(3) *Comparative Labor Law and Policy Journal*.

[10] 'Sinzheimer's whole approach to the teaching and study of labour law. . . resonated most profoundly with Kahn-Freund's own emergent intellectual and political ideas and aspirations': Freedland, 'Otto Kahn-Freund', 303.

argument were closely combined. As each author described a piece of legislation or court ruling, he had reference to a particular normative framework which he used variously to make sense of the law, to argue for law reform, and to analyse and critique judicial decision-making. Neither author was concerned that his analysis should be politically neutral. At the same time, however, neither ignored nor rejected the terms of the law in force at the time. Each constructed his normative framework with reference to that law, seeking to identify the underlying principles that could be read or abstracted from it and used subsequently as a basis for analysis and commentary. Significantly, each succeeded (in Weimar Germany and in postwar Britain) in identifying a set of principles in the legislation that aligned closely with his own political convictions.

For Sinzheimer, as for Kahn-Freund, the ultimate purpose of legal scholarship was to influence policy- and law-making.[11] The role of the scholar was not that of the politician, or the electorate, or the legislator; it was categorically not for scholars to 'tell the legislator which decisions to make in individual cases'.[12] Instead, however, the scholar should provide the legislators 'with those elements of knowledge which they need in order to make decisions'.[13] The 'elements of knowledge' in question, according to Sinzheimer, were partly of a descriptive or positivistic ('black-letter') nature, and partly historical and comparative. Certainly, it was an important part of the work of the scholar to analyse the law as it then was. It was also the case, however, that positivist analysis could only ever be fully adequate 'in calm periods of history when a certain degree of equilibrium is achieved in the relations between the social forces . . . [I]n times of sudden change, where the old disappears and the new craves recognition, a purely *technical* insight into the existing legal order is not sufficient.'[14] In addition, it was absolutely necessary that the scholar should engage in the construction of normative arguments, offering the legislator guidance more directly on the question of what the law should be.

To what evidence or philosophy should scholars look, in the opinion of Sinzheimer and Kahn-Freund, when constructing normative arguments? I have suggested, following Kahn-Freund, that Sinzheimer's work was shaped throughout his life by a concern for human freedom.[15] Freedom was understood by him in decidedly socialist terms with reference to the goal of the emancipation of workers from their subordination to capital: workers should be both free from abuses of power at the hands of others and free to participate in the exercise of power. Since the individual worker was powerless under capitalist conditions of production, under bourgeois law, this notion of freedom necessarily invoked the idea of

---

[11] 'The ultimate purpose of jurisprudence is legal policy': Sinzheimer, 'Sociological and Positivistic Method', 100. See further, Kahn-Freund, 'Hugo Sinzheimer', 100–4. Kahn-Freund aimed to play 'a significant role in the practical development of labour law... according to his social ideals': Freedland, 'Kahn-Freund', 304.

[12] Sinzheimer, 'On Formalism in the Philosophy of Law', cited Kahn-Freund, 'Hugo Sinzheimer', 100.

[13] Sinzheimer, 'On Formalism in the Philosophy of Law', cited Kahn-Freund, 'Hugo Sinzheimer', 100.

[14] Sinzheimer, 'On Formalism in the Philosophy of Law', cited Kahn-Freund, 'Hugo Sinzheimer', 101, my emphasis.   [15] Chapter 2.

workers acting collectively to effect an improvement of their *collective* working and living conditions. The situation of the individual could only be improved through an improvement in the situation of the collective. Sinzheimer's 'call to the emancipation of man', then, was also a call for greater substantive equality between the social classes.[16] In his work on English labour law, Kahn-Freund combined a deeply held personal commitment to a similar socialist notion of human freedom with elements of liberal and pluralist thinking.[17] He insisted much less strongly than Sinzheimer did on the public nature of the economy, coming closer at times to suggesting that the common good would be served through different groups pursuing the furtherance of their own (private) interests.[18] But he was no less insistent on the importance of trade unions and collective action to the achievement of just and equitable outcomes; to the emancipation of the worker, though, he may not always have expressed himself in precisely those terms.[19]

Following Kahn-Freund again, I have described the methodology adopted by the two scholars as primarily sociological or socio-legal.[20] This label is not intended, of course, to suggest that either scholar engaged extensively in empirical research, but rather that their normative arguments were closely informed by the work of sociologists and political economists, including Marx, who sought to identify and explain the injustices inherent in bourgeois society and 'bourgeois' private law.[21] On the face of it, bourgeois law guaranteed the equality of all legal actors; behind the façade of formal equality, vast inequalities persisted. Sociological analysis was the primary method chosen to make the case for labour law—to explain why the application of private law rules to working relationships was unjust, and to identify the kinds of laws which might deliver just and equitable outcomes. The sociology of law, wrote Kahn-Freund, established 'the social effect of the norm, . . . the way in which it appears in society and . . . its social function'.[22] As such it was 'indispensable' to the task of formulating legal policy.[23]

Though it is certainly fair to say then that neither author was directly concerned in his scholarship with economic theories or methodologies, it is also the case that the normative arguments that they made were broadly supported by the orthodox or mainstream economics of the time. At the end of the First World War, it was quite widely assumed in Germany that nineteenth-century 'free market' capitalism would be replaced by a new form of twentieth-century planned economy: 'that the correlate of the modern world was an organized economy in which rational deliberation would replace profit and the market as the mechanism for the allocation of resources'.[24] Sinzheimer's 1919 blueprint for a councils system or economic constitution was intended precisely as a proposed means of organizing

---

[16] Kahn-Freund, 'Hugo Sinzheimer', 103.   [17] Chapter 4.   [18] Bogg, ch 1.
[19] For an explicit reference to the role of labour law in enlarging the range of the worker's freedom, see Davies and Freedland, *Kahn-Freund's Labour and the Law*, 18.   [20] Chapter 5.
[21] Both scholars devoted time to the study of the terms of collective agreements and practical and legal their significance.   [22] Kahn-Freund, 'Hugo Sinzheimer', 98.
[23] Kahn-Freund, 'Hugo Sinzheimer', 100.
[24] K Tribe, *Strategies of Economic Order: German Economic Discourse 1750–1950* (Cambridge 1995), 140.

a planned economy and of ensuring that production proceeded efficiently in the interests of all. Following the war and the revolution, Sinzheimer wrote, we can no longer afford the *luxury* of a liberal market economy.[25] Under the terms of a new economic constitution, all economic actors—workers and owners—should work together in furtherance of the common interest: the increase of productivity, the minimization of the costs of production, and the *direction of production to meet the needs of all*. In the UK at the end of the Second World War, governments of all political persuasions adhered broadly to the teaching of Keynes and his school that trade unions and collective bargaining were essentially a welcome feature of the economy, since they contributed to making wages downwardly rigid, stabilizing demand in periods of recession.[26] 'The economic role of unions appeared clearly defined and securely established in a Fordist economy generating continuing growth based on economies of scale and steadily expanding mass consumption fuelled by yearly increases in real wages.'[27] When governments gave their support to the spread of union organization and collective bargaining, they did so in the belief that this would bring economic as well as social benefits.[28]

Scholars of the law of the labour market

The approach adopted by those British scholars who have advocated a realignment of the study of labour law more closely with the labour market is similar, in several respects, to that of Kahn-Freund and Sinzheimer.[29] In common with the older generation, the 'law of the labour market' scholars appear to have been motivated, in large part, by a wish to contribute to policy as well as to scholarly debates. In Davies and Freedland's characterization of their own work, as we have seen, emphasis was given above all to the aim of providing a useful description and analysis of current policy and legislation. Rather than making openly political criticisms of the current law, the authors preferred to provide a description and analysis that was, on the face of it, politically neutral.[30] In their study of the legislation and policy of the Blair governments of 1997–2007, they based their evaluation for the most part on the question of whether the government had achieved its own stated policy objectives. External frames of reference, including those provided by international and human rights law, were not employed to any great extent. That said, the authors were quite clear that at least part of the motivation for employing such an approach—politically neutral on the surface—was the

---

[25] Sinzheimer, 'Über die Formen und Bedeutung der Betriebsräte' (1919), 322; and 'Rätebewegung und Gesellschaftsverfassung' (1920) in Sinzheimer, *Arbeitsrecht*, 357.
[26] Streeck, 'Sociology of Labor Markets', 257.
[27] Streeck's comments are made in respect of the USA, but the point applies equally to the UK of the time: Streeck, 'Sociology of Labor Markets', 273.   [28] Chapter 4.
[29] Again, there is a direct link between the generations in the figure of Mark Freedland, who studied for a PhD under Otto Kahn-Freund.
[30] '[T]he enterprise of writing about labour law and politics is made feasible if one realizes that political scientists can write in an acceptably detached way about politics, as their works (or, rather, the best of them) demonstrate.' Davies and Freedland, *Labour Legislation and Public Policy*, 3.

wish to provide a line of analysis and commentary that might have some 'political impact'.[31] The weakness of criticisms based more directly on human rights or worker protective perspectives was that they were unlikely to be heard.[32] In their study of the *Law of the Labour Market*, Deakin and Wilkinson described their own approach in terms of aiming to provide a rationalization of the law that could serve as descriptive of existing laws *and* as a normative basis for the discussion of future policy and regulation.[33] Like Davies and Freedland, and Kahn-Freund and Sinzheimer before them, they sought to abstract *from the terms of the current law* a set of principles which could be used to construct a frame of reference for the further analysis and evaluation of particular laws and institutions.[34] The idea was that the frame of reference should be closely informed by—capable of describing and explaining—the law as it then was, but should also be constructed so as to allow for the articulation of normative arguments, 'charting a path for reform'.[35]

In seeking to provide an analysis and evaluation of law and policy capable of influencing current policy debates and judicial decision-making, the 'law of the labour market' scholars faced a number of challenges which did not much trouble either Sinzheimer or Kahn-Freund.[36] Prominent amongst these was the emergence in the 1980s and 1990s of a new economic orthodoxy which taught that labour markets must be highly flexible, and that labour market institutions—individual employment rights, trade unions, collective bargaining practices—constitute barriers to flexibility and to optimal market functioning.[37] Unless responding to a defined set of market failures, so the reasoning went, labour market institutions produce a series of inefficiencies likely to generate both higher unemployment and depressed rates of economic growth. As was certainly recognized by the law of the labour market scholars, those who wish to argue today in favour of unionization and collective voice, or against deregulation and the persistent ratcheting down of standards, must either find a means of countering this very basic claim or assumption regarding the economic consequences of labour market regulation or risk the charge of irrelevance or futility. If they aim to influence policy-makers and decision-making within courts and legislatures, scholars risk having their arguments overlooked or ignored in favour of apparently more compelling claims regarding the (deregulatory) steps necessary to ensure job creation and growth. If their aim is, more modestly, to describe and analyse the law as it is, they face the rather different challenge of how to avoid appearing to endorse policies and legislative programmes based on the 'flexibilization' deregulatory logic; how to avoid

---

[31] P Davies and M Freedland, *Towards a Flexible Labour Market* (Oxford 2007), 248.
[32] Davies and Freedland, *Towards a Flexible Labour Market*, 248, 112.
[33] Deakin and Wilkinson, *Law of the Labour Market*, 275.
[34] Note that Deakin and Wilkinson describe collective laissez-faire as a 'rationalization' of the law: *Law of the Labour Market*, 200.
[35] Deakin and Wilkinson, *Law of the Labour Market*, 277.
[36] For an excellent discussion of the challenges facing labour law scholars today see Klare, 'Horizons of Transformative Labour Law'.
[37] A Supiot, 'Law and Labour: A World of Market Norms?' (2006) 39 *New Left Review* 109–21.

inching towards the conclusion that the very field of law which they seek to study is disintegrating or disappearing even as they write.[38]

A second and related challenge faced by scholars today arises due to changes in the organization of work and working relationships during the late twentieth and early twenty-first centuries. While it could have been assumed by scholars in the past that most workers were 'employees', hired under a contract of employment with a view to a long-term engagement, today the picture is rather more complicated.[39] Motivated by a desire to 'maximize flexibility', to be in a position to shrink and grow the workforce as circumstances demand, employers have made ever greater use of a variety of working relationships that do not fall within the category 'employment'. Throughout the developed world, there has been a massive rise in the number of workers hired through agencies, or as part-time or casual or zero-hours workers.[40] From the point of view of workers, this has been experienced first and foremost as a loss of security in employment, as the substitution of *precariousness* for security.[41] Instead of enjoying a 'job for life' with the same company or factory or hospital, workers have had to adjust to the new reality of short-term or fixed-term hires, weak or no legal protections against redundancy or dismissal, and the prospect of participating several or many times throughout their lives in external labour markets. From the point of view of scholars, the changes have resulted in a 'crisis of concepts':[42] 'employment' can no longer serve, it would seem, as either the peg upon which to hang (protective) labour rights and standards or as the foundation upon which to construct a defining paradigm of the subject of study.[43]

The arguments and approaches of the law of the labour market scholars were in part constructed in response to these challenges. Engagement with questions of labour supply and demand—social inclusion, job creation—was advocated by them as a means of focusing scholarly endeavours on the questions most relevant to policy- and law-makers, of allowing for a reframing of labour law as a subject of scholarship in a way that accurately reflected the terms of legislation and common law rules in force today. 'For labour lawyers only to see the employment relationship separated off from other aspects of the labour market', argued Mitchell and Arup, 'was to miss some very important issues, issues of increasing importance to labour law.'[44] It was advocated too as a means of constructing counter-arguments

---

[38] Cf A Hyde, 'The Idea of the Idea of Labour Law: A Parable' in G Davidov and B Langille (eds) *The Idea of Labour Law* (Oxford 2011).

[39] It may be recalled that for Sinzheimer the category 'Arbeitnehmer' extended beyond those workers employed under a contract of employment: chapter 2.

[40] KVW Stone, 'The Decline in the Standard Employment Contract: A Review of the Evidence' in KVW Stone and H Arthurs, *Rethinking Workplace Regulation: Beyond the Standard Contract of Employment* (London 2013).

[41] J Fudge, 'Blurring Legal Boundaries: Regulating for Decent Work', in J Fudge, S McCrystal, K Sankaran (eds) *Challenging the Legal Boundaries of Work Regulation* (Oxford 2012).

[42] Deakin and Wilkinson, *Law of the Labour Market*, 18.

[43] For discussion of the inadequacies today of the 'imbalance of bargaining power' paradigm, see eg M Freedland and N Kountouris, *The Legal Construction of Personal Work Relations* (Oxford 2011), 370–1.

[44] R Mitchell and C Arup, 'Labour Law and Labour Market Regulation' in C Arup, P Gahan, J Howe, R Johnstone, R Mitchell, A O'Donnell (eds) *Labour Law and Labour Market*

to the claim or assumption that labour rights and institutions come with an economic cost. 'The alternative to [that assumption] is to understand labour law as a mode of market governance which provides the basis for sustainable economic development.'[45] In the UK, during the period in office of the Blair and Brown governments, scholars succeeded in identifying in the terms of government policy and legislation a set of objectives which went some way towards offering an alternative to the 'flexibilization' or 'deregulation' orthodoxy, and which they could approve as setting an appropriate agenda for scholarly investigations. The 'law of the labour market' was defined accordingly with reference to the market-focused objectives of maximizing social inclusion and improving the competitiveness of the economy (Davies and Freedland), or, building on the work of Amartya Sen, of facilitating labour market access and optimal labour market functioning (Deakin and Wilkinson). The advocacy by the scholars of a move away from the old paradigmatic objectives of encouraging the collectivization of labour and the autonomous regulation of terms and conditions through processes of free collective bargaining did not follow, therefore, from a rejection of those objectives as no longer desirable *in principle*. It resulted rather from a belief that the old paradigms no longer accurately reflected the policy priorities of government or the terms of the legislation then in force, that the old normative arguments in favour of collectivization and collective bargaining were unlikely to be heard by policy- and law-makers.

In his discussion of the methodology appropriate to study of the 'law of the labour market', Deakin suggested that the new methodology should have much in common with the old.[46] As Sinzheimer and Kahn-Freund had done, scholars today should aim to analyse legal concepts in a comparative and historical context. They should have reference to a variety of forms of analysis, drawn from a variety of disciplines. Instead of sociology and anthropology, however, or in addition to those disciplines, scholars today should engage with approaches and methods taken from economics. This would allow them to address head-on the neoliberal or neoclassical objection that labour laws and institutions constitute barriers to economic growth, that they upset the 'spontaneous order' of the market to the disadvantage of individuals and society alike.[47] It would allow them, in other words, to construct normative arguments in favour of labour standards and labour market institutions which spoke to the *economic* benefits of labour laws and institutions and which stood a better chance, for that reason, of being heard by politicians, policy-makers, and legislatures, than arguments based solely upon sociological or anthropological data or reasoning. In the work of Deakin and Wilkinson, economic methodologies were combined with insights taken from Sen and capabilities theory. Drawing on Sen, and with reference to the terms of UK law under New Labour, the scholars argued that labour rights, and social

---

Regulation: Essays on the Construction, Constitution and Regulation of Labour Markets and Work Relationships (Sydney 2006), 12.   [45] Deakin, 'Conceptions', 159.

[46] Deakin: 'A New Paradigm for Labour Law?'.
[47] Deakin and Wilkinson, *Law of the Labour Market*, ch. 5; Deakin, 'Conceptions'.

rights more generally, should be conceptualized primarily as a means of ensuring the preconditions for well-functioning labour markets—as a means, more specifically, of providing people with endowments and with the ability to exploit those endowments through market participation, maximizing their capabilities.

In his most recent work on the subject of methodology, Deakin has described the contribution that scholars of labour law could make to the construction of models of the market that were useful beyond the study of labour markets and labour laws.[48] Whereas models used by economists (including Hayek) could be criticized for neglecting important features of 'real life' markets, he argued, 'conceptions of the market' developed from labour law scholarship might more accurately reflect reality, providing a sounder basis for policy- and law-making. In particular, conceptions of the market drawn from labour law might help to demonstrate that markets have a 'normative base'; that, contrary to the assumption central to neo-classical economics of market actors motivated by rational self-interest, the rationality displayed by market actors is in fact conditioned by shared understandings of reciprocal obligations, articulated in part at the level of the legal system.[49] Viewed in this light, norms of reciprocity and fairness would appear not as an 'interference with freedom of contract and a distortion of the operation of the market but rather a device permitting more effective coordination and thus more efficient contracting'.[50] Conceptions of the market drawn from labour law might also be used to demonstrate that markets are not self-equilibrating,[51] and that labour laws and regulations do not interfere with 'natural' market trends towards equilibrium, but rather compensate for the absence of a general self-equilibrating mechanism.[52] And they might be used to demonstrate that markets are institutionally bounded: 'interdependent' with societal institutions, including labour market institutions, that function according to an alternative ('non-market') logic.[53] They might be used to demonstrate, in other words, that the matter of whether particular labour market institutions prohibit or undermine or alternatively encourage and facilitate optimal market functioning is not to be assumed but rather *investigated*.[54]

Though his focus lies primarily with legal rather than sociological methods, Deakin's approach here is similar to that of scholars working in the field of economic sociology.[55] In common with economic sociologists, he aims to uncover certain truths about the functioning of markets, and labour markets in particular, that are routinely obscured in orthodox economic analysis. Like the economic sociologists, he insists upon the essential significance of social relations for the operation of markets, and of rules and institutions as indicative of the social understandings that guide and constrain market actors' 'rationalities'.

---

[48] Deakin, 'Conceptions'. [49] Deakin, 'Conceptions', 151.
[50] Deakin, 'Conceptions', 154. [51] Deakin, 'Conceptions', 154–6.
[52] Deakin, 'Conceptions', 155. [53] Deakin, 'Conceptions', 156–7.
[54] 'Conceptions'.
[55] J Beckert, 'The Great Transformation of Embeddedness: Karl Polanyi and the New Economic Sociology' in C Hann and K Hart (eds) *Market and Society, The Great Transformation Today* (Cambridge 2009); Streeck, 'Sociology of Labor'.

There is, of course, much to be said for attempts such as these to improve our understandings of markets as firmly embedded in social relations, of workers and employers as compelled by motivations other than those of 'rational self-interest' or wealth-maximization. A weakness of Deakin's analysis, however, and of some of the economic sociology scholarship, is that it can appear to assume or suggest that those rules and institutions which evolve and persist do so *because* they are 'efficient', *because* they are conducive to 'optimal' market functioning.[56]

[L]abour and social security law together commodify labour power, in the dual sense of indentifying the capacity to work subject to the coordinating power of the employer as the essential subject matter of the contract of employment, and in putting in place the mechanisms of protection and co-insurance which form the basis for the reproduction of labour capacity or the power to labour over time . . . Labour law rules should be thought of not as external interferences with the market, but as endogenous responses to market failures, triggered by self-regulatory mechanisms and, in turn, supporting their operation.[57]

With his characterization of labour laws in this way as devices for the commodification of labour and the correction of market failures, Deakin identifies and advocates a particular way of thinking about labour laws and markets. From a rather different perspective, such laws can be understood, together with other socioeconomic institutions, as the product of political conflicts and agreements regarding their design and their interpretation or functioning.[58] This alternative characterization, it might then be argued, explains why it is that while some labour laws or institutions do indeed *support* commodification, others may be found empirically to contain or prohibit it.[59] While some measure of containment or prohibition of total commodification may indeed be necessary to allow for the reproduction of labour, and for the continued functioning of labour markets, labour laws and institutions are not often designed or created with that purpose in mind.[60] 'Countermovements to capitalism may be needed for capitalism to survive, but the survival of capitalism will not usually be their objective.'[61]

In overlooking or underemphasizing the inherently political nature of labour laws and institutions, Deakin runs the risk of appearing to suggest that the *evaluation* of such laws and institutions as desirable or undesirable is also essentially non-political, an exercise simply in assessing, in a scientifically grounded manner, their capacity to facilitate (optimal) market functioning. For Deakin and Wilkinson, 'well-functioning' markets are those which maximize the resources available to society to the good of all; desirable forms of labour market regulation, labour rights, and labour market institutions, are those which improve the functioning of markets to the benefit of management and workers alike. For some market actors, however, labour rights and institutions might rather figure as little more than barriers to be dismantled or circumvented in the drive to maximize

---

[56] Streeck, *Re-Forming*, 4–11, 246–53.   [57] Deakin, 'Conceptions', 150, 155.
[58] Beckert, 51; Streeck, *Re-Forming*, 4–6, 15; B Hepple, 'Factors Influencing the Making and Transformation of Labour Law in Europe' in G Davidov and B Langille (eds) *The Idea of Labour Law* (Oxford 2011).   [59] Streek, *Re-Forming*, 6.   [60] Streek, *Re-Forming*, 6.
[61] Streeck, *Re-Forming*, 6.

profit.[62] From that perspective, a 'well-functioning' labour market might be one with few or only weak labour laws. Bringing capitalism back into the analysis, and recognizing the existence of such differences of perspective, we can recognize the fragility of win–win arguments such as those made by Deakin and Wilkinson:[63] claims that labour rights are desirable *because they help markets function better* might quickly and easily be rejected by the counter-claim (made from an alternative perspective) that the latter premise is untrue. Bringing capitalism back into the analysis, we can recognize too the compelling nature of the case for collective worker voice *as a question of democracy*. If the definition of well-functioning markets and even the prior question of the inherent desirability of markets as a means of organizing social interactions are essentially matters of perspective, then workers ought to be in a position to argue for those laws and institutions which will better protect their interests.

In chapter 5, I raised the question as to whether approaches such as Deakin's which sought to construct normative arguments in favour of labour rights and institutions with reference to their propensity to improve the functioning of markets might bring with them the disadvantage of appearing to undermine the significance of arguments based on non-market considerations. If that were the case, if arguments which did not speak to the efficiency-enhancing or efficiency-obstructing potential of the legislation or policy in question did not register in the law of the labour market paradigm as directly relevant or persuasive, then how extensive was the range of rights for which a normative case could be made? Could a convincing 'market-constituting' case be made for laws that sought straightforwardly to improve workers' terms and conditions—to redistribute wealth from shareholders to the workforce with the aim of reducing substantive inequalities? Could such a case be made for rights to collective representation and collective bargaining? How might trade unions figure, according to the labour market paradigm, other than as a means by which members negotiate a higher price for their labour—a higher price which may *or may not*, in any given set of circumstances, be judged to facilitate or encourage optimal market functioning in the interests of all? How much would be lost in such a picture of the history and tradition of trade unions as a primary means of giving voice to working people *as a good in itself* ?

In his recent discussion of 'conceptions of the market', Deakin explicitly acknowledges the 'intensely political' nature of labour law and of the hard-fought struggles, historic and current, over its adoption, amendment, and repeal.[64] Labour law rules have 'distributional consequences', he writes, and it is not surprising, therefore, that 'employers lobby against labour law rules and describe them as an "imposition" or "burden", any more than trade unions can be expected to stand quietly when laws limiting strike action or restricting the scope of freedom of association are enacted and applied'.[65] Though this acknowledgement is

---

[62] Tucker, 'Renorming Labour Law'; Glasbeek, 'Book Review'.
[63] Streeck argues for the importance of 'bringing capitalism back in' in ch 17, *Re-Forming*.
[64] Deakin, 'Conceptions', 151.   [65] Deakin, 'Conceptions', 151.

tidily bracketed by Deakin within a much more developed and extended discussion of labour law 'as a form of economic governance', it serves nonetheless to raise the following question in the mind of the reader: why should we be content with an approach to the study of labour law which characterizes it solely or primarily as a mode of market governance, a means of commodifying (and *not* decommodifying) labour power, to the benefit of workers and employers alike?[66] Why should we be content with an approach which casts trade unions solely or primarily as economic, and not also political, actors? Accepting much of what the 'law of the labour market' scholars aim to teach us, learning from their arguments and their methodologies, is it not possible to develop an approach which recognizes the importance of labour markets as an object of study, recognizes the role of labour law in constituting markets, but also takes into account the 'intensely political' nature of the question *how* markets are constituted, how markets are combined with or constrained by non-market institutions and modes of interaction? Cannot an approach be found which allows us to ask the question 'who stands to win and who to lose if the economy is constituted in a particular way?', and which judges the question of winning and losing not only in terms of market access and market functioning, but also with reference to non-market values such as democracy, freedom, and human dignity?

Reassessing the Old Approaches

The original motivation for the writing of this book was a suspicion on the part of the author that the case made by a number of scholars for the obsolescence of 'old' or 'traditional' approaches to the study of labour law might not be wholly convincing. It is true, of course, that the organization of production and of working relations has changed quite dramatically since the 1910s or 1920s or 1950s. Any discussion of labour law in times of globalization must begin with an iteration of the many ways in which current conditions differ from the 'traditional' model of stable, full-time employment relationships, male breadwinners and female care-givers, high levels of union membership, managerial hierarchies within firms and vertical hierarchies within production chains, nationally based and confined employer-producers and worker-consumers, and nationally based and confined markets. But the question arises nonetheless, whether the outdatedness of the old approaches has at times been overstated. In the course of efforts to emphasize change and to adapt analysis accordingly, have important continuities been obscured? However much the economy and society have changed in the past 50 or 100 years, what has remained the same is their fundamental nature as capitalist. Any attempt to rethink the idea of labour law for the twenty-first century—to articulate the scope and the essential aims of the subject in a way that lends it both

---

[66] Deakin, 'Conceptions', 150.

coherence and fit with the realities of working relations today—ought to keep this essential point within its sights.[67]

In the course of his discussion of current scholarship in the fields of institutional theory and comparative political economy, Streeck has advocated an analytical model which builds on the work of Karl Polanyi, emphasizing the dynamic nature of capitalism as a 'double movement' of market expansion and social protection.[68] 'The market [expands] continuously but this movement [is] met by a countermovement checking the expansion in definite directions.'[69] The advantage of the model, according to Streeck, is that it 'makes visible the enduring presence of conflicts, not just between classes in different market positions battling over the distribution of economic benefits, but also over the extent to which social life should be controlled by competitive markets and by imperatives of economic efficiency'.[70] It allows, for that reason, for a consideration of politics as an 'independent autonomous force', and decisively not as a mechanism for the improvement of market efficiency or the advancement of national competitiveness.[71] 'Where markets expand, politics, according to Polanyi, is always liable to be put at the service of interests in the self-protection of society from the destructive potential of self-regulating relative prices.'[72] It is always possible, in principle at least, that politics could be used by progressive 'movements for social protection' to further their efforts to subordinate the market to society.[73] The question then stands to be addressed, whose interests are being protected and furthered by governments within national and supranational arenas? Who is in a position to influence government or otherwise to wield political power? How are relations of influence and power constituted, reinforced, or limited by laws and legal frameworks?

Like Polanyi's notion of the double movement, traditional approaches to the study of labour law took as fundamental the existence of conflicts of interest between social classes, workers, and employers. Sinzheimer did not use the language of markets and he understood 'the economy' to extend beyond market activity to include the organization of production in furtherance of the common good. Democracy was understood by him to entail democratic control of the economy, implying the involvement of *all* (collective) economic actors and not only the most economically powerful. In substance, the labour constitution was a body of procedural rules intended to allow for the resolution of conflicts of interests within the economic sphere—to allow for the registering of interests other than those of the owners of capital. In Kahn-Freund's Weimar writings, the 'establishment of a collectivist system of labour law' was described in terms of class conflict between the 'bourgeoisie' and the 'working class', of the struggle of the latter to 'create for itself a series of legal norms'.[74] In the Germany of the time, he recalled in old age, 'the conflictual element was . . . palpable, . . . visible

---

[67] Tucker, 'Renorming Labour Law'.
[68] Streek, *Re-Forming*, ch 17, esp. 246–53. See also Streeck, 'Crisis of Democratic Capitalism'.
[69] Polanyi, 136.   [70] Streeck, *Re-Forming*, 233.   [71] Streeck, *Re-Forming*, 251.
[72] Streeck, *Re-Forming*, 251.   [73] Polanyi, 136–40.
[74] Kahn-Freund, 'The Changing Function of Labour Law', 166–7.

to the eye'.⁷⁵ In work written in the more peaceable England of later years, he insisted still upon the universality of conflicts of interest, but circumscribed these as arising between 'management' and 'labour' over questions of the division of profits, and the desired measure of flexibility—or stability and security—in working arrangements.⁷⁶

Notwithstanding the many changes to production, distribution, finance, and work implied by the umbrella term *globalization*, an approach to the study of labour law is needed which begins, as the old ways did, from an appreciation of the nature of capitalism, and of the historical development of capitalism and capitalist institutions as a 'conflictual interplay between the individual pursuit of economic advantage and collective political efforts at restoring and protecting social stability'.⁷⁷ An approach is needed which recognizes the existence of conflicts of interest: conflicts arising between social classes regarding the distribution of wealth, or the question of the extension of markets into ever greater areas of social life; conflicts between workers, or groups of workers, regarding the distribution of labour market opportunities; or new conflicts characteristic of late capitalism, such as those between workers seeking protection from the progressive intensification of work and the growing flexibility of employment, and consumers (often also workers) concerned with efficient production and service provision.⁷⁸ As scholars, we must seek to frame our subject in a way which allows questions to be asked regarding the effects of the organization of the economy, and working relationships in particular, on society at large, and on certain sections of society.⁷⁹ At the same time, we must take care to frame it such that questions can be asked too regarding the implications of labour laws and institutions for citizenship and democracy: especially, how can democratic participation be re-envisioned and institutions for worker participation reconstituted under conditions of globalization, and what is lost if they are not?⁸⁰

Collective laissez-faire

In scholarly discussions of the idea of labour law, collective laissez-faire is often quite quickly dismissed as inappropriate to the study of labour law today—sometimes on the basis of an equation of the principle with state abstentionism in industrial relations, sometimes because it is thought to accord a prominence to collective bargaining which no longer reflects the policy priorities of government

---

⁷⁵ Kahn-Freund continues: 'The concluding words of the Communist Manifesto—. . . ("Nothing to lose but your chains, and a world to win")—really made sense in Germany in 1930': 'Postscript', 195.   ⁷⁶ Davies and Freedland, *Labour and the Law*, 66.
⁷⁷ Streeck, *Re-Forming*, 4.
⁷⁸ Streek, *Re-Forming*, 265. On conflicts of interest arising between workers, or groups of workers, see G Mundlak, 'The Third Function of Labour Law: Distributing Labour Market Opportunities among Workers' in G Davidov and B Langille, *The Idea of Labour Law* (Oxford 2011).
⁷⁹ Beckert, 51.
⁸⁰ C Estlund and B Bercusson, 'Regulating Labour in the Wake of Globalisation: New Challenges, New Institutions' in B Bercusson and C Estlund (eds) *Regulating Labour in the Wake of Globalisation* (Oxford 2008), 1–18, 14–18; Freeman.

or the lived experience of the majority of workers. If we can quickly reject the notion that Kahn-Freund meant collective laissez-faire to imply a complete absence of the law or of the state in the regulation of working relationships, it is undoubtedly the case that he intended it to highlight the wide measure of autonomy that trade unions and collective labour-management relations enjoyed in the UK in comparison to other jurisdictions. A belief in the importance of trade union independence from the state lay at the heart of Kahn-Freund's criticisms of Weimar labour law, and in the 1940s and 1950s, it was a mistrust of too much state intervention which informed his initial admiration for the British system.[81] With the notion of collective laissez-faire he sought to give expression, above all, to the English pluralist 'tradition' and preference for small government as it had shaped, in his understanding, the development and practice of collective industrial relations.[82]

As was illustrated in chapter 6, it is the implication of the importance of a wide measure of trade union autonomy, so central to the meaning of collective laissez-faire, which most obviously limits the potential usefulness of the principle today.[83] In its identification of the role of trade unions and employers as extending to the interpretation, application, and enforcement of collective agreements, for example, collective laissez-faire assumes the existence of strong trade unions with the capacity to organize effective campaigns of industrial action and of union recruitment. It assumes that, left to their own devices, trade unions and employers, or employers' organizations, each have something to gain from negotiating with one another—that employers are sufficiently invested in the particular locality, that capital is sufficiently fixed, for employers faced with worker unrest to choose loyalty (concessions) over exit (shutting down and relocating). And it assumes, lastly, the existence of a 'state' willing and able to perform residual supportive roles, while remaining always neutral as to the outcomes of collective negotiations: guaranteeing workers' freedom of association, encouraging or inducing employers to recognize trade unions, or extending collective agreements to unorganized sectors of the workforce. Under conditions of globalization or late capitalism, none of these assumptions is safely made. Used nonetheless as a framework for analysis, collective laissez-faire brings with it the danger of encouraging a misleading appraisal of current labour laws and institutions, and a misguided set of recommendations for reform.[84]

In addition to its advocacy of a wide measure of autonomy for trade unions and employers' associations, collective laissez-faire also implies a strong normative commitment to the collectivization of labour as a matter of democratic principle. While most scholars of labour law would still approve a commitment to collectivization, some have taken issue with the underlying justification that Kahn-Freund provided for it. Such criticism often begins from an assertion that in Kahn-Freund's writing collective bargaining and individual labour rights alike were advocated on the basis that they could *counteract the inequality of bargaining power inherent in the employment relationship.*[85] In time, and as successive

---

[81] Chapter 4.   [82] Kahn-Freund, 'Labour Law'.   [83] Chapter 6.
[84] Chapter 6.
[85] Reference is usually made to the very famous sentence in Davies and Freedland, *Labour and the Law*, 18.

generations of labour law scholars learned their trade, this conception of the purpose of labour law achieved the status of a defining paradigm. Today, it is 'out of date'.[86] As Brian Langille has put it:

> This idea of labour law coming to the aid of employees who do 'and must' lack bargaining power is the moral foundation of the constituting narrative of labour law . . . Both the logic of collective bargaining as a procedural device structuring a countervailing power in the process of bargaining, and the logic of employment legislation as simply removing certain issues from the bargaining process, are driven by [this narrative].[87]

The narrative is out of date, according to Langille, because it is normatively 'thin': 'There is no normativity here other than the idea of equality in bargaining . . . To the obvious question—"why are we interested in that?" we have no response.[88]

While essentially agreeing with Langille about both the status of the idea of 'counteracting an imbalance of bargaining power' as a defining paradigm of labour law and its current obsolescence, other scholars have explained that obsolescence with reference to the failure of the paradigm adequately to explain government policy and legislation in the field of employment and employment relations. It is simply no longer the case that governments and legislatures are primarily concerned with worker protection, as they once were.[89] Some have approved 'the basic normative idea' contained within the paradigm,[90] but have highlighted the difficulties arising from its over- and under-inclusiveness: not all employees are disadvantaged or vulnerable and in need of the protection of the law; many who are in need of such protection do not work under contracts of employment.[91]

It is true, of course, that Kahn-Freund referred in his work to the 'inequality of bargaining power which is inherent and must be inherent in the employment relationship'.[92] In one of his most-often quoted passages he suggested that 'the main object of labour law has always been, and we venture to say will always be, to be a countervailing force to counteract [such] inequality'.[93] As is readily ascertained by reading just beyond the precise terms of the famous quotation, however, Kahn-Freund understood inequality of bargaining power in the individual employment relationship as but one particular expression or manifestation of the deeper-seated problem of the subordination of the worker to the employer, labour to management. His concern was not only with contractual bargaining power, in other words, but with 'social power' more broadly conceived.

> Labour law is chiefly concerned with this elementary phenomenon of social power . . . As a social phenomenon the power to command and the subjection to the power are the same

---

[86] Langille, 'Theory of Justice', 105. [87] Langille, 'Theory of Justice', 105–6.
[88] Langille, 'Theory of Justice', 110.
[89] See eg Davies and Freedland, *Towards a Flexible Labour Market*, 5.
[90] Freedland and Kountouris, 370.
[91] Freedland and Kountouris, 20, 370–1, 438–9; Arthurs, 'Constitutionalizing Employment Relations', 403–4.   [92] Davies and Freedland, *Labour and the Law*, 18.
[93] Davies and Freedland, *Labour and the Law*, 18.

no matter whether the power is exercised by a person clothed with a 'public' function, such as an officer of the Crown or a local authority, or by a 'private' person, an employer . . . [94]
. . .

The relation between an employer and an isolated employee *or worker* is typically a relation between a bearer of power and one who is not a bearer of power. In its inception it is an act of submission, in its operation it is a condition of subordination.[95]

For Kahn-Freund, as for Sinzheimer, it was the identification of this power relation which explained the need for labour law: 'the law may restrict the managerial power', he wrote, limiting 'the range of the worker's duty of obedience and [enlarging] *the range of his freedom*'.[96] To acknowledge that Kahn-Freund's advocacy of the collectivization of labour, and of labour law in general, was tied not only to the existence of an imbalance of *bargaining* power in the *employment* relationship, but also more broadly to questions of power relations and human freedom, makes it rather harder to dismiss as outdated. The objection that governments today are not any more motivated by the desire to protect the worker is weakened if we acknowledge, furthermore, that Kahn-Freund intended in these passages to make a political, normative argument, and not only to describe the labour laws of the time, if we acknowledge that labour laws then, as today, were shaped by a variety of policy objectives of which protection of the worker was but one.[97] The strength of collective laissez-faire was that it framed all of labour law—to some extent irrespective of the policy objectives that had informed its adoption—so as to emphasize the normative principles that Kahn-Freund believed to be important.

Labour constitution

Though it cannot perhaps be known for certain, it seems likely that Sinzheimer took the term 'economic constitution' originally from the Webbs' *Industrial Democracy*.[98] Like them, he used the notion of a *constitution* to draw an analogy between the exercise of public (political) and private (economic) power, and to make the case, on that basis, for the democratization of the economy. In terms used by the Webbs, the idea encapsulated in the notion of an economic or industrial constitution was that the legal recognition of collective bargaining and the elaboration of a labour code would signify the concession to the working class of a 'Magna Carta'—the extension of the values of liberty and equality from the political to the industrial sphere.[99] As used by Sinzheimer, the term economic or labour constitution also drew attention to the role that law (and especially labour law) played in constituting, or ordering, the economy,[100] configuring, in particular,

---

[94] Davies and Freedland, *Labour and the Law*, 14.
[95] Davies and Freedland, *Labour and the Law*, 18, my emphasis.
[96] Davies and Freedland, *Labour and the Law*, 18.   [97] Chapter 5.
[98] Chapter 2. The German *Wirtschaft* can be translated as either 'economy' or 'industry'.
[99] S and B Webb, *Industrial Democracy*, vol 2 (London 1897), 840–2.
[100] On the enduring significance of the idea of order in German economic thinking see Tribe.

the institution of property and configuring thereby the legal status of economic actors, ie the owners of property and those (workers) who were dependent upon it for their means of subsistence.[101] Though it is true, then, that Sinzheimer conceived of labour law, and social law, essentially as a corrective to 'bourgeois' private law, it would not be fair to accuse him of the error of understanding labour law as regulating a 'naturally' pre-existing set of private law relationships—as Klare has put it, of 'viewing labour law as a contingent, political artefact superimposed on an immutable private law background'.[102] For Sinzheimer, labour law was the body of law that would constitute the economy anew along democratic lines. In a social democracy, private law institutions, especially property, would be reconfigured by the labour rights and institutions declared in the constitution. The worker, who had appeared in bourgeois law only as a legal person, would be constituted anew as a human being.

In chapter 3, a comparison of the *economic constitution* as conceived of in the immediate aftermath of revolution, and the *labour constitution* as invoked in the 1920s as descriptive of the terms of Weimar labour law, helped to shed further light on the essential tenets or principles underlying the idea. In contrast to the economic constitution, based upon a proposed 'councils system', the labour constitution of the 1920s 'took effect' through worker organization (workplace organization and trade, or sector, organization), industrial action, and arbitration. In common with the economic constitution, it was in substance a body of procedural rules—'state law'—which allowed for the participation of collectivized labour in economic decision-making and norm creation, and which set limits to such participation. In 1927, as in 1919, use of the term constitution was intended by Sinzheimer first and foremost to emphasize the role that labour legislation should play in democratizing the economy and emancipating workers, in reordering economic institutions and relations so that the economy could be governed by all in the interests of all. In 1927, as in 1919, the idea of the constitution also implied a particular role for the state in the economic sphere, as the architect, overseer, and guardian of the relevant framework of rules. And it implied, at the same time, that the economic actors must be, to a significant extent, autonomous of the state.

In chapter 3, it was further suggested that, understood with reference to these core principles, the idea of the labour constitution could equally be applied to the labour legislation and industrial relations of the postwar Federal Republic. In the 1950s, as in the 1920s, the legislation in force could convincingly be read as creating a framework for the autonomous regulation by workers and employers of workers' terms and conditions, and the organization of work and production. If, on the face of it, the terms of the legislation appeared to suggest that the trade unions and employers' associations were more autonomous of the state than they had been in the Weimar Republic—that the system of industrial relations was closer in nature to the Anglo-American model of interest representation in

---

[101] See esp. Sinzheimer, 'Demokratisierung', discussed in chapter 2.
[102] Klare, 14. Klare suggests that this was a regrettable feature of 'labour law's fundamental approaches', 14.

a liberal market economy than to the Weimar model of economic democracy—then those terms were misleading. The Federal Republic was not simply a liberal market economy, but a social market economy with very significant corporatist features. In the 1950s and 1960s, as in the 1920s, trade union and employer association involvement in public functions, and in particular in the administration of social welfare, resulted in relations of mutual dependence with the state. As a result, the German state was in a position to wield rather more influence on industrial relations than was suggested by the legal framework. Again, it was apt to characterize the state as the architect, overseer, and guardian of the postwar labour constitution. Again, it could convincingly be said that with the aim of emancipating workers from relations of subordination, the state had taken steps to order the economy and the process of its regulation by employers' associations and trade unions, while at the same time respecting the autonomy of those actors.

The strength of the idea of the labour constitution lay then, like that of collective laissez-faire, with the way in which it framed a whole body of law so as to give emphasis to particular normative principles. Applied in chapter 3 to the changing legislation and institutions of the immediate postwar era and the later twentieth century, the labour constitution as a framework for analysis suggested both a particular field of enquiry and a particular set of questions to be asked about that field. Attention was drawn in particular to the question of the capacity of labour laws and labour market institutions to introduce elements of democratic participation to the economy, furnishing workers with a voice and with a means to secure improved terms and conditions. The question of the role of the state in industrial relations, and the nature of the relationship more broadly between the state, the trade unions, and the employers' associations was also considered. The framework of the labour constitution thus suggested a widening of the field of enquiry beyond collective labour law and codetermination, which allowed for the conclusion to be drawn that the postwar German 'model' of industrial relations more closely resembled a form of corporatism than one of interest representation. It allowed too for an explanation to be found as to the ways in which and reasons why the collectivist model has been weakened over the past 20 years or so, notwithstanding the fact that the terms of collective labour law have remained essentially unchanged. In contrast to collective laissez-faire, the idea of the labour constitution remained appropriate to the study of labour law and industrial relations today for the reason that it could be taken to imply the importance of state support and guardianship, and of trade union autonomy, while leaving open the question of the precise nature and extent of the relationship between the two. Viewed through the framework of the labour constitution, the withdrawal since the 1990s of direct and indirect state support for the collectivist system of industrial relations figured as highly significant, but did not serve to render the framework itself inappropriate or misleading.

Globalization, constitution, and state

Today, any approach to the study of labour law which focused exclusively on the nation state as the source or site of such law would be inadequate. Under conditions of advanced globalization, the capacity of nation states to decide autonomously questions of policy in the field of working relationships and work organization, to legislate in implementation of policy decisions, and to enforce legislation effectively is constrained in a variety of ways. As has long been recognized, the increased mobility of capital and the intensification of global competition that result from the liberalization of trade each threaten the ability of nation states to maintain and enforce labour standards. Capital is free to threaten or choose relocation, thereby resisting or circumventing the strictures of national laws and institutions. As a result, states may feel under pressure to lower labour standards and corporate taxes as a means of retaining or attracting capital investment. The liberalization and integration of finance, meanwhile, create a new source of discipline for national governments, which must now either toe the orthodox economic line or face the—potentially devastating—prospect of capital flight or an increase in the rate of interest charged on government bonds. As the example of the European Union illustrates, governments might choose to enter into multilateral or bilateral trade agreements which place further limits on their capacity to retain or enact labour rights and standards, as such rights and standards come to figure as prohibited breaches of the contract or property or free trade rights enjoyed by private actors under the terms of the trade agreements.[103] States in need of financial aid from international organizations such as the World Bank or IMF, meanwhile, may quite routinely be required to agree to programmes of deregulation or 'flexibilization' of their labour markets as conditions of loan agreements.

For scholars of labour law, such developments imply a need to re-orientate fields of enquiry so as to take account of new sites of decision-making, and new centres of power and influence, with the capacity to impact significantly on labour laws and labour market institutions such as supranational regulatory bodies, trade organizations, transnational corporations, financial institutions. Whether seeking to describe and analyse domestic or international labour law, it is important to recognize and to take account of the ways in which the legislative and policy-making capacities of nation states have been limited and constrained as economic policy decisions have come, increasingly, to be taken elsewhere. At the same time, however, it is equally important that the significance of pressures on states to order national economies in particular ways—to remain 'competitive on the global stage' or to offer financial markets stable and profitable opportunities for investment—should not be *over*emphasized.[104] However weakened or constrained, nation states are still best characterized as sites of political struggle, sites where pressures for capitalist progress compete for the attention of government with—potentially conflicting but in principle no less urgent—demands for social stability and social justice.[105] In light, especially, of the striking dearth

---

[103] Other examples abound: see eg Tucker's discussion of Canada's 'free trade federalism' and membership of NAFTA: Tucker, 'Labor's Many Constitutions', 362–7.
[104] Streeck, *Re-Forming*, 5–7.
[105] Streeck, *Re-Forming*, 5.

of democratic institutions at the supranational level, the remaining democratic potential of nation states should not be overlooked.[106] Nation states ought still to be regarded as sites, or potential sites, of 'constitutionalization', the term understood here to imply a search for more legitimate and more democratic forms of governance.[107] The question ought to be asked, moreover, what role states play, or could play, as democratic sources of law in the constitutionalization of non-state 'spaces', bounded either territorially or organizationally, such as regional trading blocks, individual workplaces or corporations, cities or localities.[108]

A significant advantage of the idea of the labour constitution as a framework for analysis is that it allows—notwithstanding the 'unitary bias of the very term constitution'—for the recognition of the existence of a *plurality* of economic orders, or economic constitutions: national, supranational, and subnational.[109] It encourages the analysis of labour legislation and the broader normative frameworks that regulate representation and voice (comprising constitutional laws, human rights instruments, trade agreements, corporate codes) as integral elements of those orders[110] (highlighting, for example, that the constitutional entrenchment of labour and social rights may be of little consequence in a country that is directed by its supranational financiers to dismantle existing collective bargaining arrangements in the interests of greater labour market flexibility[111]). And it raises questions regarding the interaction of different economic constitutions or orders with one another, and the implications of the uneven development of such constitutions in different countries, regions, or places of work[112]—questions of inequalities between workers and conflicts of interest between insiders and outsiders, of the manipulation of such inequalities by TNCs and other investors, and of threats of competitive deregulation.[113]

In chapters 6 and 7, the idea of the labour constitution was used as a framework for the examination of the historical development of the constitution, or economic order, of the European Union. In recognition of the very significant respects in which the Union differed from Weimar or Federal Germany, the intention was decidedly not to transplant the idea straightforwardly from the latter to the former context. It was intended rather that the notion of the labour constitution

---

[106] C Joerges, 'The Idea of a 3-Dimensional Conflicts Law as Constitutional Form' RECON Online Working Paper 2010/05, 12–14; C Joerges and F Rödl, 'Reconceptualizing the Constitution of Europe's Post-National Constellation—By Dint of Conflict of Laws' in I Liannos and O Odudu (eds) *Regulating Trade in Services in the EU and the WTO: Trust, Distrust and Economic Integration* (Cambridge 2011).   [107] Joerges, 'Idea of a 3-Dimensional Conflicts Law'.
[108] K Stone, 'Flexibilization, Globalization, and Privatization: Three Challenges to Labour Rights in Our Time' in B Bercusson and C Estlund, *Regulating Labour in the Wake of Globalisation* (Oxford 2008).
[109] G Teubner, *Constitutional Fragments: Societal Constitutionalism and Globalization* (Oxford 2012), 13.
[110] This point is argued forcefully by Harry Arthurs and Eric Tucker: Arthurs, 'Labour and the "Real" Constitution'; Tucker, 'Labor's Many Constitutions'.
[111] Koukiadaki and Kretsos; E Christodoulidis, 'Europe's Donors and its Supplicants: Reflections on the Greek Crisis', in J van der Walt and J Ellsworth (eds) *Constitutionalism, Sovereignty and Social Solidarity in Europe* (Baden-Baden 2014), forthcoming.
[112] Tucker, 'Renorming Labour Law', 122.   [113] Mundlak; Hayter and Weinberg.

should be taken to suggest particular areas of focus to be examined, a set of questions to be asked, and a methodology to be adopted. While the framework of the labour constitution might suggest the importance of the question of state support and state control of collective institutions and procedures, then, it wouldn't be taken to imply any particular answer to that question: to imply, for example, that a certain measure of state support or influence was necessarily desirable or undesirable. While it might suggest that attention should be paid to the relations and interactions between different organizations or geographical locations as sites, or potential sites, of constitutionalization, it would not be taken to imply that those relations should necessarily conform to any particular pattern.

That said, it was certainly not intended that, used in this way as a framework or paradigm, the idea of the labour constitution should be stripped of its normative content. Like Polanyi's notion of the 'double movement', the labour constitution implied a normative concern above all with the introduction of democratic principles and modes of action to the economic sphere. In this respect, it differed quite fundamentally from the idea of the economic constitution developed by the ordoliberal school of economists and more commonly applied to analysis of the European Union, with its insistence upon the need to insulate the economy to a significant extent from political or democratic control. From the perspective of the *labour* constitution, the constitutional moment to be celebrated in the history of the EU was not the ratification of the Treaty of Rome, or even the Treaty of Maastricht, but rather the adoption in 1974 of the Community's first Social Action Programme. Here, in the brief terms of that text, could be found a commitment to democratize the economy through the creation of worker rights to participate in decision-making. It followed that the story of the constitutional history of the Union, as told through the framework of the labour constitution, was, first and foremost, the story of why that moment came so late, and why its promise of industrial democracy was never fulfilled. Why did the social dialogue and its precursors in the ECSC and EEC, and the series of Directives granting rights to information and consultation fall so short in the end of the 'effective participation' in Community decision-making and corporate governance long lobbied for by the trade unions and promised in 1974 by the member states in Council?

In chapter 6, the main focus for discussion was the social dialogue and the question of union participation in Community decision-making. The primary question to be addressed was understood to lie with the potential of the dialogue to democratize the European economic order, and to deliver improved substantive outcomes for workers. Given the particular, supranational, nature of the EU, the projection onto it of the idea of the labour constitution raised additional questions regarding the 'state' capacity of the Union and its governing institutions: their capacity to fulfil the supporting and supervisory role assigned to the state by Sinzheimer. Questions arose too regarding the organization of labour and capital at the European level: who were the 'trade unions' and 'employers' associations' in the Union; who were the 'social partners'? Were the trade unions able to identify and represent the collective interests of so many workers, employed within so many jurisdictions? Was the EU 'state' able to guarantee to the unions rights to participate with employers in decision-making or law-making *on a parity basis*? Did the unions in fact figure as a countervailing force to the power of European and international capital? How far did the authority of the social partners extend: how extensive was the sphere within which they were empowered and/or authorized to make decisions and to create legal norms? Was the dialogue otherwise constrained by the constitutional and institutional context within which it proceeded? Which decisions and norms had been made by the partners to date?

In chapter 7, the framework of the labour constitution was understood to suggest the need for an investigation of the interaction of the supranational economic order with the pre-existing national orders, or labour constitutions, of the member states. Did these exist in a hierarchical relation to one another: were the various national labour constitutions coordinated at the highest level, as works constitutions and company constitutions had been coordinated, within Germany, by the sectoral trade unions and employers' associations? If not, if it was more accurate to think in terms of a plurality of largely segregated labour constitutions, one supranational and several national, was such an arrangement viable in the long term? Alternatively, would the various national labour constitutions eventually be harmonized in an upward or downward direction? In the meantime, how had the creation of the EU and especially the single market and the currency union affected the capacity of nation states to legislate and to decide policy in the field of labour law and social welfare?

When it came to the matter of the methodology to be adopted in addressing these questions, the idea of the labour constitution—and Sinzheimer's approach to scholarship more generally—was taken to suggest the importance of examining laws and institutions in an historical context. In common with Sinzheimer, the development of laws and institutions was understood, first and foremost, as the outcome of political struggles: struggles between the social classes, as he might have expressed it, or, as we might otherwise put it today, between pressures for the expansion of markets and the increasing commodification of social relations on the one hand, and social demands for the political stabilization of relative prices and extant social structures on the other.[114] At the same time, it was recognized that institutions, including labour legislation, serve to configure the context within which economic activity and political struggles proceed, influencing the courses of action available or attractive to actors. More particularly, institutions can variously constrain actors, or provoke resistance, evasion, or reinterpretation; in turn, the actions and reactions of actors can cause or encourage further institutional change.[115] With reference to primary and secondary historical sources, an attempt was made in chapters 6 and 7 (as it had been in chapter 3) to give consideration to two questions: why had the law and institutions under examination taken the form that they had, and who had benefited and who had suffered disadvantage as a result of institutional and legal change? Though the focus of each chapter lay, in essence, with the question of the role of collectivized labour in the management

---

[114] Streeck, *Re-Forming*, 5.   [115] Streeck, *Re-Forming*, 246, 237–46.

of the economy (and the company and the workplace), the field of enquiry was understood to extend beyond collective labour law as such to include additional instances of trade union and employers' association involvement in government, and the wider constitutional context within which such involvement took place.

The primary benefit of the approach adopted was that it allowed for a realistic assessment of particular legal frameworks and provisions with respect to questions of workers' participation and terms and conditions. By focusing on instances of legal and institutional change as they had affected the status and interests of labour, and by extending the field of enquiry beyond collective labour law and the institutions of collective bargaining and codetermination, the analysis contained in chapter 6 uncovered the error involved in characterizing the social dialogue, with reference to the terms of the Treaty, simply as a form of transnational collective bargaining—of projecting onto it a constellation of actors and relationships familiar from the experience of national systems of collective bargaining and corporatism, and of diagnosing its weaknesses and identifying appropriate remedies accordingly. In chapter 7, a further extension of the field of enquiry to include consideration of a plurality of legal and economic orders and the interactions between them revealed in the starkest light that the characterization of certain labour rights as 'fundamental' constituted little by way of a defence against social dumping and the pressures towards negative harmonization arising by reason of the law of the single market and the single currency.

In line with Sinzheimer's teaching, the key finding of the analysis contained in chapters 6 and 7 was the continued importance of state support to the maintenance of collective industrial relations and effective mechanisms for the registering of worker voice. From the outset, the development of the social dialogue was greatly impeded by the fact that the employers had little incentive to participate productively in negotiations, shaping rather than simply blocking proposed legislation. In principle, of course, the employers were to have been marshalled by the Commission's threat: 'negotiate or we will legislate'. Given the difficulties involved in brokering agreement among member state governments to new initiatives in the social policy field, however, there were by 1992 fewer and fewer occasions when the Commission could convincingly wield the threat of Council legislation. Neither was the Commission in a position otherwise to persuade business representatives to be readier to make concessions to the ETUC in ways that a national government might have done: offering concessions on taxes and trade, for example, or assistance for research and development.[116] It simply lacked both the financial and the regulatory resources necessary. In chapter 7, the story of the Commission's longstanding efforts to improve worker rights to information and consultation illustrated, again, the difficulties faced by any actor seeking to promote the adoption at EU level of worker-protective social or labour legislation. The subsequent discussion of the Laval/Viking jurisprudence and the response of the Troika to crisis in the Eurozone highlighted, in addition, the narrowing of

---

[116] Streeck, 'European Social Policy after Maastricht', 170; Lo Faro, 126–7.

the capacity of member states, by reason of their membership of the EU, to retain existing (or adopt new) worker-protective legislation and institutions.

As was the case in chapter 3 and its discussion of the disorganization of the German model of industrial relations, the conclusions drawn in chapters 6 and 7 did not serve to imply the outdatedness or inappropriateness of the labour constitution as a framework for the analysis of labour law today. On the contrary, the framework of the labour constitution drew attention, in a way that other approaches did not, to the critical nature of the link between democracy and labour law in the constitutional order of the Union. Understood primarily as the outcome of political struggles between those who sought to expand the reach of markets in pursuit of economic gain, and those who stood to benefit from the introduction of elements of democratic decision-making and democratic control into the economic sphere, the development of labour rights and labour market institutions could be seen very clearly to depend on the assertion of such control by democratic organizations—trade unions, as representative of working people, and nation states as representative of all. The narrowing of the autonomy of national democratic legislatures and the weaknesses of the European trade union and the institution of the social dialogue could each be recognized as posing direct threats to the development of new, or the maintenance of existing, labour standards. The assumption by the CJEU and the Troika of the authority to strike down democratically agreed nationally labour legislation and labour rights could be seen to be thoroughly anti-democratic, a further step along the road to the creation of a market order insulated from democratic control.[117]

Analysis undertaken using the framework of the labour constitution pointed therefore to the urgency of further research aimed at the reassertion and re-thinking of the roles of member states and trade unions still as important sites of democratic deliberation and democratic control within the EU.[118] Instead of acknowledging the CJEU's jurisdiction to decide questions of the compatibility of national labour laws with supranational trade and competition law, could member states provide for processes of political deliberation of these matters, involving unions and other interested or expert parties?[119] Could trade unions— national, European—be accorded a greater role in the resolution of conflicts

---

[117] Joerges and F Rödl, at 388–9; E Christodoulidis, 'A Default Constitutionalism? A Disquieting Note on Europe's Many Constitutions' in K Tuori and S Sankari (eds) *The Many Constitutions of Europe* (Aldershot 2010).

[118] For a discussion of how analyses of transnational constitutionalism might be developed along these lines see R Dukes, 'A Global Labour Constitution?' (2014) 65 *Northern Ireland Legal Quarterly*, forthcoming. For an analysis of decision-making in the WTO and EU which places a similar emphasis on the link between democratic decision-making and workers' interests, see J Fudge and G Mundlak, 'Justice in a Globalizing World: Resolving Conflicts Involving Workers Rights beyond the Nation State', *European University Institute, Faculty of Law Working Papers*, 2013/06. Lastly, for an imagining of how nation states and trade unions might act together to accord migrant workers 'transnational labour citizenship', see J Gordon, 'Transnational Labor Citizenship' (2007) 80 *Southern California Law Review* 503–87.

[119] Joerges and Rödl, 388–9.

arising by reason of labour migration and cross-border service provision?[120] What role could nation states play in encouraging and supporting the constitutionalization of transnational corporations by means of corporate codes, international framework agreements, or the institution of European works councils?[121] Above all, how might worker organization be strengthened or re-imagined so that unions could figure again as primary sites for the formulation and expression of demands for the protection of social interests and social rights—as organizations capable of exerting pressure on states and supranational governance regimes to take steps to regulate or control economic actors or practices so as to protect social interests, or, where transnational corporations and other economic actors are capable of escaping state control, directly on those actors to 'self-limit'?[122]

Were it to be used in application to the *global* economy or economic order—global markets, international trade agreements, international law—the framework of the labour constitution would be understood, again, to emphasize the critical nature of the link between democracy and the protection of workers' interests; to imply, again, a concern with the introduction to that order, the 'uploading' from the national to the global level, of democratic principles and modes of action.[123] Given the current dearth of democratic institutions at the global level, the asymmetry between the emergence of *global* markets and forms of political organization still tied to the nation state, it would have to be readily admitted that the prospects for a constitutionalization project along the lines envisaged by Sinzheimer are bleak.[124] Even the task of imagining what a labour constitution might entail at the global level is not straightforward.[125] It is not suggested here, therefore, that the idea of the labour constitution provides easy answers to the challenges posed to the protection of workers' interests by the development of global capitalism. Rather, the much more modest claim is made that the idea of the labour constitution used as a framework for scholarly analysis continues to focus our attention on important questions and important fields of enquiry—on questions, not least, of the consequences for workers of the narrowing and disappearance of spaces for democratic deliberation and democratic decision-making as markets continue to expand.

---

[120] Gordon.
[121] G Teubner, 'Self-Constitutionalizing TNCs? On the Linkage of "Private" and "Public" Corporate Codes of Conduct' (2011) 18 *Indiana Journal of Global Legal Studies* 617–38; KD Ewing, 'International Regulation of the Global Economy—the Role of Trade Unions' in B Bercusson and C Estlund (eds) *Regulating Labour in the Wake of Globalisation* (Oxford 2007); Papadakis.
[122] Teubner, 'Self-Constitutionalizing TNCs?'.
[123] Christodoulidis uses the idea of 'uploading' in 'Politics of Societal Constitutionalism'. Ewing, 'International Regulation'.
[124] Christodoulidis, 'Politics of Societal Constitutionalism', 638–44.
[125] Dukes, 'A Global Labour Constitution?'.

Bibliography

K Abbott, 'The ETUC and its Role in Advancing the Cause of European Worker Participation Rights' (1998) 19 *Economic and Industrial Democracy* 605–31.

J Abel and P Bleses, 'Eine Variante unter vielen?—Zur Gegenwart der dualen Struktur der Interessenvertretung' *WSI-Mitteilungen* 5/2005.

E Ales, S Engblom, T Jaspers, S Laulom, S Sciarra, A Sobczak, F Valdes Dal-Re, 'Transnational Collective Bargaining: Past, Present and Future' (Brussels 2006).

K Armingeon and L Baccaro, 'Political Economy of the Sovereign Debt Crisis: The Limits of Internal Devaluation' (2012) 41 *Industrial law Journal* 254–75.

H Arthurs, 'Labour and the "Real" Constitution' (2007) 48 *Les Cahiers de Droit* 43–64.

H Arthurs, 'The Constitutionalization of Employment Relations: Multiple Models, Pernicious Problems' (2010) 19 *Social and Legal Studies* 403–22.

H Arthurs, 'Charting the Boundaries of Labour Law: Innis Christie and the Search for an Integrated Law of Labour Market Regulation' (2011) 34 *Dalhousie Law Journal* 1–17.

C Arup et al (eds) *Labour Law and Labour Market Regulation* (Sydney 2006).

K Apps, 'Damages Claims against Trade Unions after Viking and Laval' (2009) 34 *European Law Review* 141–54.

D Ashiagbor, *The European Employment Strategy* (Oxford 2005).

C Barnard, 'The Financial Crisis and the Euro Plus Pact: A Labour Lawyer's Perspective' (2012) 41 *Industrial Law Journal* 98–114.

C Barnard, *EU Employment Law*, 4th ed. (Oxford 2012).

C Barnard, 'Labour Law and the Internal Market' in *EU Employment Law*, 4th ed (Oxford 2012).

C Barnard and S Deakin, 'European Labour Law after Laval' in M-A Moreau (ed) *Before and After the Economic Crisis: What Implications for the 'European Social Model'?* (Cheltenham 2011).

D Barnes and E Reid, *Governments and Trade Unions: The British Experience 1964–79* (London 1980).

B Barnourin, *The European Labour Movement and European Integration* (London 1986).

M Becker, *Arbeitsvertrag und Arbeitsverhältnis während der Weimarer Republik und in der Zeit des Nationalsozialismus* (Frankfurt am Main 2005).

J Beckert, 'The Great Transformation of Embeddedness: Karl Polanyi and the New Economic Sociology' in C Hann and K Hart (eds) *Market and Society, The Great Transformation Today* (Cambridge 2009).

S Beer, *Modern British Politics* (London 1969).

RC Beever, *European Unity and the Trade Union Movements* (Leyden 1960).

M Behrens and W Jacoby, 'The Rise of Experimentalism in German Collective Bargaining' (2004) 42 *British Journal of Industrial Relations* 95–123.

B Bercusson, 'The European Community's Charter of Fundamental Social Rights of Workers' (1990) 53 *Modern Law Review* 624–42.

B Bercusson, 'Maastricht: A Fundamental Change in European Labour Law' (1992) 21 *Industrial Relations Journal* 177–90.

B Bercusson, 'The Dynamic of European Labour Law after Maastricht' (1994) 23 *Industrial Law Journal* 1–31.

B Bercusson, *European Labour Law* (London 1996).
B Bercusson, 'Democratic Legitimacy and European Labour Law' (1999) 28 *Industrial Law Journal* 153–70.
B Bercusson, 'The European Social Model Comes to Britain' (2002) 31 *Industrial Law Journal* 209–44.
B Bercusson, 'The Trade Union Movement and the European Union: Judgement Day' (2007) 13 *European Law Journal* 279–308.
B Bercusson, *European Labour Law*, 2nd ed (Cambridge 2009).
B Bercusson and C Estlund, *Regulating Labour in the Wake of Globalisation* (Oxford 2008).
R Bispinck, 'Kontrollierte Dezentralisierung der Tarifpolitik—Eine schwierige Balance' *WSI-Mitteilungen* 5/2004.
T Blair, *The Third Way: New Politics for the New Century* (London 1998).
T Blair and G Schroeder, *Europe: The Third Way/Die Neue* Mitte (London 1999).
R Blanpain and C Engels, *European Labour Law* 3rd ed (Alphen aan den Rijn 1995).
R Blanpain and P Windey, *European Works Councils* (Leuven 1994).
A Bogg, *Democratic Aspects of Trade Union Recognition* (Oxford 2009).
A Bogg and R Dukes, 'The European Social Dialogue: From Autonomy to Here' in N Countouris and M Freedland (eds) *Resocializing Europe in a Time of Crisis* (Cambridge 2013).
A Börsch, *Global Pressure, National System: How German Corporate Governance is Changing* (New York 2007).
B Bösche and H Grimberg, 'Die deutschen Gewerkschaftsgesetze' in T Klebe, P Wedde, and M Wolmerath (eds) *Recht und soziale Arbeitswelt: Festschrift für Wolfgang Däubler zum 60. Geburtstag* (Frankfurt am Main 1999).
M Bouvard, *Labour Movements in the Common Market Countries* (New York 1972).
A Branch, 'The Evolution of the European Social Dialogue Towards Greater Autonomy: Challenger and Potential Benefits' (2005) 21 *International Journal of Comparative Labour Law and Industrial Relations* 321–46.
S Braun, W Eberwein, J Tholen, *Belegschaften und Unternehmer: Zur Geschichte und Soziologie der deutschen Betriebsverfassung und Belegschaftsmitbestimmung* (Frankfurt, New York 1992).
G Braunthal, *Socialist Labor and Politics in Weimar Germany* (Connecticut: Hamden 1978).
K Brigl-Matthiaβ, *Das Betriebsräteproblem* (Berlin, Leipzig 1926).
W Brown 'The Contraction of Collective Bargaining in Britain' (1993) 31 *British Journal of Industrial Relations* 189–200.
J Browne, S Deakin, and F Wilkinson, 'Capabilities, Social Rights and European Market Integration' in R Salais and R Villeneuve (eds) *Europe and the Politics of Capabilities* (Cambridge 2005).
A Bullock, *The Life and Times of Ernest Bevin, Volume 2* (London 1967).
G de Burca, 'The Drafting of the European Union Charter of Fundamental Rights' (2001) 26 *European Law Review* 126–38.
M Castells, 'Informationalism, Networks, and the Network Society: A Theoretical Blueprint' in M Castells (ed) *The Network Society: A Cross-Cultural Perspective* (Cheltenham 2004).
R Charles, *The Development of Industrial Relations in Britain 1911–1939* (London 1973).
E Christodoulidis, 'A Default Constitutionalism? A Disquieting Note on Europe's Many Constitutions' in K Tuori and S Sankari (eds) *The Many Constitutions of Europe* (Aldershot 2010).

E Christodoulidis, 'On the Politics of Societal Constitutionalism' (2013) 20 *Indiana Journal of Global Legal Studies* 629–63.
E Christodoulidis, 'Europe's Donors and its Supplicants: Reflections on the Greek Crisis' in J van der Walt and J Ellsworth (eds) *Constitutionalism, Sovereignty and Social Solidarity in Europe* (Baden-Baden forthcoming).
J Clark, 'Towards a Sociology of Labour Law' in KW Wedderburn, R Lewis, and J Clark, *Labour Law and Industrial Relations: Building on Kahn-Freund* (Oxford 1983).
S Clauwaert, '2011: 20 Years of European Interprofessional Social Dialogue: Achievements and Prospects' (2011) 17 *Transfer* 169–79.
S Clauwaert and I Schömann, 'The Crisis and National Labour Law Reforms: a Mapping Exercise' *ETUI Working Paper* 2012.04.
H Clegg, 'Otto Kahn-Freund and British Industrial Relations' in Lord Wedderburn, R Lewis, and J Clark (eds) *Labour Law and Industrial Relations: Building on Kahn-Freund* (Oxford 1983).
H Collins, 'Against Abstentionism in Labour Law' in J Eekelaar and J Bell (eds) *Oxford Essays in Jurisprudence* (Oxford 1987).
H Collins, 'Labour Law as a Vocation' (1989) 105 *Law Quarterly Review* 468–84.
H Collins, 'The Productive Disintegration of Labour Law' (1997) 26 *Industrial Law Journal* 295–309.
H Collins, 'Is There a Third Way in Labour Law?' in J Conaghan, R M Fischl, K Klare (eds) *Labour Law in an Era of Globalization: Transformative Practices and Possibilities* (Oxford 2000).
H Collins, 'Regulating the Employment Relation for Competitiveness' (2001) 31 *Industrial Law Journal* 17–48.
Committee of Inquiry on Industrial Democracy, *Report* Cmnd. 6706 (London 1977).
Conservative Party, *Fair Deal At Work* (London 1968).
C Crouch, 'The Globalized Economy: An End to the Age of Industrial Citizenship?' in T Wilthagen (ed) *Advancing Theory in Labour Law and Industrial Relations in a Global Context* (Amsterdam 1998).
C Crouch, 'Entrenching Neo-Liberalism: The Current Agenda of European Social Policy' in N Countouris and M Freedland (eds) *Resocializing Europe in a Time of Crisis* (Cambridge 2013).
C Dartmann, *Re-distribution of Power, Joint Consultation or Productivity Coalitions? Labour and Postwar Reconstruction in Germany and Britain, 1945–1953* (Bochum 1996).
W Däubler, 'Co-Determination: the German Experience' (1975) 4 *Industrial Law Journal* 218–28.
G Davidov and B Langille (eds) *Boundaries and Frontiers of Labour Law* (Oxford 2006).
G Davidov and B Langille (eds) *The Idea of Labour Law* (Oxford 2011).
ACL Davies, 'Should the EU have the Power to Set Minimum Standards for Collective Labour Rights in the Member States?' in P Alston, *Labour Rights as Human Rights* (Oxford 2005).
ACL Davies, 'One Step Forward, Two Steps Back? The Viking and Laval Cases in the ECJ' (2008) 37 *Industrial Law Journal* 126–48.
P Davies, 'Market Integration and Social Policy in the Court of Justice' (1995) 24 *Industrial Law Journal* 49–77.
P Davies, 'The Posted Workers Directive and the EC Treaty' (2002) 31 *Industrial Law Journal* 298–306.
P Davies, 'Workers on the board of the European Company' (2003) 32 *Industrial Law Journal* 75–96.

P Davies and M Freedland, 'Labour Law and the Public Interest: Collective Bargaining and Economic Policy' in KW Wedderburn and T Murphy (eds) *Labour Law and the Community: Perspectives for the 1980s* (London 1982).

P Davies and M Freedland (eds) *Kahn-Freund's Labour and the Law*, 3rd ed (London 1983).

P Davies and M Freedland 'Editors' Introduction' to P Davies and M Freedland (eds) *Kahn-Freund's Labour and the Law*, 3rd ed (London, 1983).

P Davies and M Freedland, *Labour Law Text and Materials,* 2nd ed (London 1984).

P Davies and M Freedland, *Labour Legislation and Public Policy* (Oxford 1993).

P Davies and M Freedland, 'National Styles in Labor Law Scholarship: The United Kingdom' (2002) 23 *Comparative Labor Law and Policy Journal* 765–87.

P Davies and M Freedland, *Towards a Flexible Labour Market* (Oxford 2007).

P Davies and Lord Wedderburn, 'The Land of Industrial Democracy' (1977) 6 *Industrial Law Journal* 197–211.

S Deakin, 'Labour Law as Market Regulation: The Economic Foundations of European Social Policy' in P Davies et al (eds) *European Community Labour Law: Principles and Perspectives* (Oxford 1996).

S Deakin: 'A New Paradigm for Labour Law? Review of C Arup, P Gahan, J Howe, R Johnstone, R Mitchell, A O'Donnell (eds) *Labour Law and Labour Market Regulation: Essays on the Construction, Constitution and Regulation of Labour Markets and Work Relationships* (Sydney 2006)' (2007) 31 *Melbourne University Law Review* 1161–73.

S Deakin, 'Capacitas: Contract Law, Capabilities and the Legal Foundations of the Market' in S Deakin and A Supiot (eds) *Capacitas: Contract Law and the Institutional Preconditions of a Market Economy* (Oxford 2009).

S Deakin, 'Conceptions of the Market in Labour Law' in A Numhauser-Henning and Mia Rönnmar (eds) *Normative Patterns and Legal Developments in the Social Dimension of the EU* (Oxford 2014).

S Deakin and F Wilkinson, *The Law of the Labour Market: Industrialization, Employment and Legal Evolution* (Oxford 2004).

S Deakin and A Koukiadaki, 'The Sovereign Debt Crisis and Evolution of Labour Law in Europe' in N Countouris and M Freedland (eds) *Resocializing Europe in a Time of Crisis* (Cambridge 2013).

JM Denis, 'Les mobilisations collectives européenes: de l'impuissance à law nécessité d'alliance' (2006) 6 *Droit Social* 671–8.

Department of Business, Innovation and Skills, *Consultation on Implementing Employee Owner Status* (London 2012).

Department of Employment, *Industrial Relations Act: Code of Practice* (London 1972).

Department of Trade and Industry, White Paper, *Our Competitive Future: Building the Knowledge Driven Economy* (London 1998).

Department of Trade and Industry, *Towards Equality and Diversity* (London 2001).

Department of Trade and Industry, *Telework Guidance* (London 2003).

C Docksey, 'Information and Consultation of Employees: The UK and the Vredeling Directive' (1986) 49 *Modern Law Review* 281–313.

J Dolvik and J Visser, 'ETUC and European Social Partnership: A Third Turning-Point?' in H Compston and J Greenwood (eds) *Social Partnership in the European Union* (Basingstoke 2001).

F Duchêne, *Jean Monnet* (New York 1994).

R Dukes, 'The Origins of the German System of Worker Representation' (2005) 19 *Historical Studies in Industrial Relations* 31–62.

R Dukes, 'Constitutionalizing Employment Relations: Sinzheimer, Kahn-Freund and the Role of Labour Law' (2008) 35 *Journal of Law and Society* 341–63.

R Dukes, 'The Statutory Recognition Procedure 1999: No Bias in Favour of Recognition' (2008) 37 *Industrial Law Journal* 236–67.

R Dukes, 'Otto Kahn-Freund and Collective Laissez-Faire: An Edifice without a Keystone?' (2009) 72 *Modern Law Review* 220–46.

R Dukes, 'A Global Labour Constitution?' (2014) 65 *Northern Ireland Legal Quarterly* forthcoming.

P Ellguth, 'Tarifbindung und betriebliche Interessenvertretung: Ergebnisse aus dem IAB-Betriebspanel 2012' *WSI-Mitteilungen* 3/2013.

P Ellguth and S Kohaut, 'Tarifbindung und betriebliche Interessenvertretung' (2013) *WSI-Mitteilungen* 4/2013.

C Estlund, 'The Death of Labor Law?' (2006) 2 *Annual Review of Law and Social Sciences* 105–23.

C Estlund, 'The Ossification of American Labor Law' (2007) 102 *Columbia Law Review* 1527–2002.

C Estlund and B Bercusson, 'Regulating Labour in the Wake of Globalisation: New Challenges, New Institutions' in B Bercusson and C Estlund (eds) *Regulating Labour in the Wake of Globalisation* (Oxford 2008).

European Commission, 'Multi-National Undertakings and the Community', Bul. Suppl. 15/73 (Luxembourg 1973).

European Commission, *The Social Action Programme*, European Community Bulletin, no. 10 (Luxembourg 1974).

European Commission, Green Paper, 'Employee Participation and Company Structure' (Luxembourg 1975).

European Commission, 'The Social Dimension of the Internal Market' (Luxembourg 1988).

European Commission *Communication Concerning its Action Programme* COM (89) 568 final (1989).

European Commission, *European Social Policy—Options for the Union* COM (93) 551 final (1993).

European Commission, *Growth Competitiveness and Employment* COM (93) 700 final (1993).

European Commission, *European Social Policy—A Way Forward for the Union* COM (94) 333 final (1994).

European Commission, *Communication on Worker Information and Consultation* COM (95) 547 final (1995).

European Commission, *Medium-Term Social Action Programme* COM (95) 134 final (1995).

European Commission, *Social Action Programme 1998–2000* COM (98) 259 final (1998).

European Commission, *Agenda for Social Policy 2000–2005* COM (2000) 379 final.

European Commission, *Communication on the European Social Dialogue* COM (2002) 341 final.

European Commission, Proposal for a Council Decision Establishing a Tripartite Social Summit for Growth and Employment COM (2002) 341.

European Commission, Partnership for Change in an Enlarged Europe COM (2004) 557 final.

European Commission, *Report of the High Level Group on the Future of Social Policy in an Enlarged European Union* (Brussels 2004).

European Commission, Social Agenda 2005–2010 COM (2005) 33 final.

European Commission, Green Paper 'Modernizing Labour Law to Meet the Challenges of the 21st Century' COM (2006) 708 final.

European Commission, *Communication on the Review of the Application of Directive 2002/14* COM (2008) 146 final.
European Commission, *Proposal for a Directive on the Establishment of a European Works Council* COM (2008) 419 final.
European Commission, *Economic Crisis in Europe: Causes, Consequences and Responses* (Brussels 2009), <http://ec.europa.eu/economy_finance/publications/publication15887_en.pdf>.
European Commission, *Industrial Relations in Europe 2010* (Luxembourg 2011).
European Commission, *The Social Dimension of the Europe 2020 Strategy: A Report of the Social Protection Committee* (Brussels 2011).
European Commission, *Industrial Relations in Europe 2012* (Luxembourg 2013)
European Commission, *Communication Regarding the Strengthening the Social Dimension of the Economic and Monetary Union* COM (2013) 690.
European Commission, *Communication on Strengthening the Social Dimension of the Economic and Monetary Union* COM (2013) 690 provisoire.
European Committee of Social Rights, Decision on Collective Complaints no. 65/2011 and 66/2011 (2011).
European Confederation of Free Trade Unions in the Community, *First Congress: Premier Congrès: Discours, decisions, resolutions* (Brussels 1969).
European Council, Resolution of 21 January 1974 Concerning a Social Action Programme (1974).
European Economic and Social Committee, *Social Aspects of the Internal Market* [The 'Beretta' Report] (Brussels 1987).
European Social Partners, *Report on the Implementation of the European Framework Agreement on Telework* (Brussels 2006)
European Trade Union Confederation, 'ETUC Proposals for the Action Programme' (Brussels 1989).
European Trade Union Confederation, 'Executive Committee Declaration on Proposed European Works Council Directive' (Brussels 1991).
European Trade Union Confederation, 'Jobs and Solidarity at the Heart of Europe', Eighth Statutory Congress (Brussels 1995).
European Trade Union Confederation, *Economic and Social Crisis: ETUC Positions and Actions* (Brussels 2009), <http://www.etuc.org/a/5838>.
European Trade Union Confederation, *Constitution of the ETUC* (Brussels 2014) <http://www.etuc.org/a/70>.
European Trade Union Confederation, Union of Industrial and Employers' Confederations of Europe, European Centre of Enterprises with Public Participation and of Enterprises of General Economic Interest, *Joint Contribution by the Social Partners to the Laeken European Council* (2001).
European Trade Union Institute/ European Trade Union Confederation, *Benchmarking Working Europe 2011* (Brussels 2011).
KD Ewing, 'The Death of Labour Law?' (1988) 8 *Oxford Journal of Legal Studies* 293–300.
KD Ewing, 'The State and Industrial Relations: "Collective laissez-faire" Revisited' (1998) 5 *Historical Studies in Industrial Relations* 1–31.
KD Ewing, 'International Regulation of the Global Economy—the Role of Trade Unions' in B Bercusson and C Estlund (eds) *Regulating Labour in the Wake of Globalisation* (Oxford 2007).
KD Ewing, 'Foreword' in C Fenwick and T Novitz (eds) *Human Rights at Work* (Oxford 2010).

KD Ewing, and G Truter, 'The Information and Consultation of Employees Regulations: Voluntarism's Bitter Legacy' (2005) 68 *Modern Law Review* 626–41.

G Falkner, 'European Works Councils and the Maastricht Social Agreement: Towards a New Policy Style?' (1996) 3 *Journal of European Public Policy* 192–208.

K Featherstone, 'Jean Monnet and the "Democratic Deficit" in the EU' (1994) 32 *Journal of Common Market Studies* 149–70.

N Fishman, '"A Vital Element in British Industrial Relations": A Reassessment of Order 1305, 1940–51' (1999) 8 *Historical Studies in Industrial Relations* 43–86.

A Flanders, *Trade Unions* (London 1952).

A Flanders, 'The Tradition of Voluntarism' (1974) 12 *British Journal of Industrial Relations* 352–70.

G Flatow and O Kahn-Freund, *Betriebsrätegesetz vom 4. Februar 1920 nebst Wahlordnung, Ausführungsverordnungen und Ergänzungsgesetzen* (Berlin 1931).

E Fraenkel, 'Hugo Sinzheimer' (1958) 13 *Juristen-Zeitung* 457–61.

E Fraenkel, 'Kollektive Demokratie' in T Ramm (ed) *Arbeitsrecht und Politik: Quellentexte 1918–1933* (Neuwied 1966).

E Fraenkel, 'Zehn Jahre Betriebsrätegesetz' in T Ramm (ed) *Arbeitsrecht und Politik: Quellentexte 1918–1933* (Neuwied 1966).

E Fraenkel, 'Die politische Bedeutung des Arbeitsrechts' in T Ramm (ed) *Arbeitsrecht und Politik: Quellentexte 1918 – 1933* (Neuwied 1966).

AD Frazer, 'Reconceiving Labour Law: The Labour Market Regulation Project' (2008) 8 *Macquarie Law Journal* 21–44.

S Fredman, 'Transformation or Dilution: Fundamental Rights in the EU Social Space' (2006) 12 *European Law Journal* 41–60.

M Freedland, 'Employment policy' in P Davies et al (eds) *European Community Labour Law: Principles and Perspectives* (Oxford 1996).

M Freedland, 'Labour Law beyond the Horizon' (1998) 28 *Industrial Law Journal* 197–200.

M Freedland, 'Otto Kahn-Freund' in J Beatson and R Zimmerman (eds) *Jurists Uprooted: German-Speaking Émigré Lawyers in Twentieth-Century Britain* (Oxford 2004).

M Freedland and N Kountouris, *The Legal Construction of Personal Work Relations* (Oxford 2011).

R Freeman, 'New Roles for Unions and Collective Bargaining Post the Implosion of Wall Street Capitalism' in S Hayter (ed) *The Role of Collective Bargaining in the Global Economy* (Cheltenham 2011).

J Fudge, *Labour Law's Little Sister: The Employment Standards Act and the Feminization of Labour* (Ontario 1991).

J Fudge, 'Constitutionalizing Labour Rights in Europe' in T Campbell, KD Ewing, A Tomkins (eds) *The Legal Protection of Human Rights: Sceptical Essays* (Oxford 2011).

J Fudge, 'Labour as a "Fictive Commodity": Radically Reconceptualizing Labour Law' in G Davidov and B Langille, *The Idea of Labour Law* (Oxford 2011).

J Fudge, 'Blurring Legal Boundaries: Regulating for Decent Work', in J Fudge, S McCrystal, K Sankaran (eds) *Challenging the Legal Boundaries of Work Regulation* (Oxford 2012).

J Fudge and G Mundlak, 'Justice in a Globalizing World: Resolving Conflicts Involving Workers Rights Beyond the Nation State', *European University Institute, Faculty of Law Working Papers*, 2013/06 (Florence 2013).

J Fudge and R Owens (eds) *Precarious Work, Women, and the New Economy: The Challenge to Legal Norms* (Oxford 2006).

P Germanotta and T Novitz, 'Globalisation and the Right to Strike: The Case for European-Level Protection of Secondary Action' (2002) 18 *International Journal of Comparative Labour Law and Industrial Relations* 67–82.

H Gester, 'Zur Stellung der Gewerkschaften im Betrieb nach dem neuen Betriebsverfassungsgesetz' (1972) *Gewerkschaftliche Monatshefte* 19–24.

A Giddens, *The Third Way: the Renewal of Social Democracy* (Polity 1998).

O von Gierke, *Die soziale Aufgabe des Privatrechts* (Berlin 1889).

J Gillingham, *Coal, Steel, and the Rebirth of Europe, 1945–1955* (Cambridge 1991).

H Glasbeek, 'Book Review: S Marshall, R Michell, I Ramsay (eds) *Varieties of Capitalism, Corporate Governance and Employees* (Melbourne 2008)' (2008) 22 *Australian Journal of Corporate Law* 293–304.

M Gold, 'Employee Participation in the EU: The Long and Winding Road to Legislation' (2010) 31 *Economic and Industrial Democracy* 9–23.

J Gordon, 'Transnational Labor Citizenship' (2007) 80 *Southern California Law Review* 503–87.

Greek Council of State, Decision Regarding the Constitutionality of Law 4046/2012 (2012).

Group of Experts, *Report on the Social Aspects of European Economic Co-operation* [Ohlin Report] Studies and Reports, New Series, No. 46 (Geneva 1956).

T Haipeter, 'Erosion, Exhaustion or Renewal? New Forms of Collective Bargaining in Germany' paper presented at the LLRN Conference, Barcelona, 2013.

E Haas, *The Uniting of Europe: Political, Social and Economic Forces 1950–1057* (Stanford 1958, 1968).

M Hall, 'Behind the European Works Councils Directive: The European Commission's Legislative Strategy' (1992) 30 *British Journal of Industrial Relations* 547–66.

M Hall, 'Beyond the EWC Directive: The Commission's Legislative Policy' (1992) 30 *British Journal of Industrial Relations* 547–66.

M Hall and J Purcell, *Consultation at Work: Regulation and Practice* (Oxford 2012).

S Hayter and B Weinberg, 'Mind the Gap: Collective Bargaining and Wage Inequality' in S Hayter (ed) *The Role of Collective Bargaining in the Global Economy* (Cheltenham 2011).

B Hepple, 'The Crisis in EEC Labour Law' (1987) 16 *Industrial Law Journal* 77–87.

B Hepple, *Labour Laws and Global Trade* (Oxford 2007).

B Hepple, 'Factors Influencing the Making and Transformation of Labour Law in Europe' in G Davidov and B Langille (eds) *The Idea of Labour Law* (Oxford 2011).

B Hepple, 'Back to the Future: Employment Law under the Coalition Government' (2013) 42 *Industrial Law Journal* 203–23.

W Herschel, 'Der Betriebsrat—damals und heute' in F Gamillscheg (ed) *Im memoriam Sir Otto Kahn-Freund* (Munich 1980).

R Hoffman, 'Einleitung' in R Crusius, G Schiefelbein, M Wilke (eds) *Die Betriebsräte in der Weimarer Republik* (Berlin 1978).

C Howell, *Trade Unions and the State: The Construction of Industrial Relations Institutions in Britain, 1890–2000* (Princeton 2005).

A Hyde 'What is Labour Law For?' in G Davidov and B Langille (eds) *Boundaries and Frontiers of Labour Law* (2006).

A Hyde, 'The Idea of the Idea of Labour Law: A Parable' in G Davidov and B Langille (eds) *The Idea of Labour Law* (Oxford 2011).

R Hyman, 'Trade Unions and the Politics of the European Social Model' (2005) 26 *Economic and Industrial Democracy* 9–40.

ILO Conference, Report of the Committee of Experts on the Application of Conventions and Recommendations (Geneva 2010).

ILO, Report of the Committee of Experts on the Application of Conventions and Recommendations (Geneva 2012).

ILO, Report of the Committee of Experts on the Application of Conventions and Recommendations (Geneva 2013).

R Janssen, 'The EU Social Dimension: The Charge of the Light Brigade' (2013) *Social Europe Journal*, 1 October.

C Joerges, 'What is Left of the European Economic Constitution?' (2004) *EUI Working Paper Law* No. 2004/13.

C Joerges, 'The Idea of a 3-Dimensional Conflicts Law as Constitutional Form' RECON Online Working Paper 2010/05, 12–14.

C Joerges and F Rödl, 'Reconceptualizing the Constitution of Europe's Post-National Constellation—By Dint of Conflict of Laws' in I Liannos and O Odudu (eds) *Regulating Trade in Services in the EU and the WTO: Trust, Distrust and Economic Integration* (Cambridge 2011).

E Jordan, AP Thomas, JW Kitching, RA Blackburn, 'Employment Regulation Part A: Employer Perceptions and the Impact of Employment Regulation' (London 2013).

O Kahn-Freund, 'Collective Agreements under War Legislation' (1943) 6 *Modern Law Review* 112–43.

O Kahn-Freund, 'The Illegality of a Trade Union' (1944) 7 *Modern Law Review* 192–205.

O Kahn-Freund, 'Intergroup Conflicts and their Settlement' (1954) 5 *British Journal of Sociology* 193–227.

O Kahn-Freund, 'Legal Framework' in A Flanders and HA Clegg, *The System of Industrial Relations in Great Britain* (Oxford 1954).

O Kahn-Freund, 'Labour Law' in M Ginsberg (ed) *Law and Opinion in England in the 20th Century* (London 1959).

O Kahn-Freund, *Labour Law: Old Traditions and New Developments* (Oxford 1968).

O Kahn-Freund 'Industrial Relations and the Law—Retrospect and Prospect' (1969) 7 *British Journal of Industrial Relations* 301–16.

O Kahn-Freund, 'Trade Unions, the Law and Society' (1970) 33 *Modern Law Review* 241–67.

O Kahn-Freund, *Labour and the Law*, 1st ed (London 1972).

O Kahn-Freund, 'The Industrial Relations Act 1971—Some Retrospective Reflections' (1974) 3 *Industrial Law Journal* 186–200.

O Kahn-Freund, 'Introduction' to K Renner, *The Institutions of Private Law and their Social Functions* (London 1976).

O Kahn-Freund, 'Industrial Democracy' (1977) 6 *Industrial Law Journal* 65–84.

O Kahn-Freund, 'Preface' to O Kahn Freund, *Arbeit und Recht* (Cologne and Frankfurt: Bund-Verlag, 1979), published in translation as 'Labour Law and Industrial Relations in Great Britain and West Germany' in Lord Wedderburn, R Lewis, J Clark (eds) *Labour Law and Industrial Relations: Building on Kahn-Freund* (Oxford 1983).

O Kahn-Freund, *Labour Relations: Heritage and Adjustment* (Oxford 1979).

O Kahn-Freund, 'The Study of Labour Law—Some Recollections' (1979) 8 *Industrial Law Journal* 197–201.

O Kahn-Freund, 'The Social Ideal of the *Reich* Labour Court' in R Lewis and J Clark (eds) *Labour Law and Politics in the Weimar Republic* (Oxford 1981).

O Kahn-Freund, 'The Changing Function of Labour Law' in R Lewis and J Clark (eds) *Labour Law and Politics in the Weimar Republic* (Oxford 1981). O Kahn-Freund,

'Hugo Sinzheimer' in R Lewis and J Clark (eds) *Labour Law and Politics in the Weimar Republic* (Oxford 1981).

O Kahn-Freund, 'Postscript' in R Lewis and J Clark (eds), *Labour Law and Politics in the Weimar Republic* (Oxford 1981).

O Kahn-Freund, 'Labour Law and Industrial Relations in Great Britain and West Germany' in Lord Wedderburn, R Lewis, J Clark (eds) *Labour Law and Industrial Relations: Building on Kahn-Freund* (Oxford 1983).

P Katzenstein, *Politics and Policy in West Germany: The Growth of a Semi-Sovereign State* (Philadelphia 1987).

D Kettler and T Wheatland, *Learning from Franz Neumann: Theory, Law, and the Brute Facts of Life* (London 2014), forthcoming.

M Kittner, *Arbeitskampf. Geschichte, Recht, Gegenwart* (Munich 2005).

K Klare, 'Horizons of Transformative Labour Law' in J Conaghan, RM Fischl, K Klare (eds) *Labour Law in an Era of Globalization: Transformative Practices and Possibilities* (Oxford 2002).

S Knorre, *Soziale Selbstbestimmung und individuelle Verantwortung. Hugo Sinzheimer (1875–1945). Eine politische Biographie* (Frankfurt 1991).

A Koukiadaki and L Kretsos, 'Opening Pandora's Box: The Sovereign Debt Crisis and Labour Market Regulation in Greece' (2012) 41 *Industrial law Journal* 276–304.

K Kubo, *Hugo Sinzheimer—Vater des deutschen Arbeitsrechts* (Nördlingen 1985).

D Kukovec, 'Myths of Social Europe: The Laval Judgment and the Prosperity Gap', talk delivered to the Harvard Law School, 16 April 2010.

Labour Party, Let Us Face the Future: A Declaration of Labour Policy for the Consideration of the Nation (London 1945).

B Langille, 'What is International Labour Law For?' (2009) 3 *Law & Ethics of Human Rights* 47–82.

B Langille, 'Labour Law's Theory of Justice' in G Davidov and B Langille (eds) *The Idea of Labour Law* (Oxford 2011).

S Laulom, 'The Flawed Revision of the European Works Council Directive' (2010) 39 *Industrial Law Journal* 202–8.

W Lecher, H-W Platzer, S Rüb, K-P Weiner, *Europäische Betriebsräte—Perspektiven ihrer Entwicklung und Vernetzung* (Baden-Baden 1999).

R Lewis 'Collective Agreements: The Kahn-Freund Legacy' (1979) 42 *Modern Law Review* 613–22.

R Lewis, 'Kahn-Freund and Labour Law: An Outline Critique' (1979) 8 *Industrial Law Journal* 202–21.

R Lewis, 'Review: Labour Relations: Heritage and Adjustment. By Sir Otto Kahn-Freund' (1981) 44 *Modern Law Review* 239–42.

R Lewis and J Clark, 'Introduction' in R Lewis and J Clark (eds) *Labour Law and Politics in the Weimar Republic* (Oxford 1981).

R Lewis and J Clark (eds) *Labour Law and Politics in the Weimar Republic* (Oxford 1981).

A Lo Faro, *Regulating Social Europe: Reality and Myth of Collective Bargaining in the EC Legal Order* (Oxford 2000).

R Luxemburg, 'What does the Spartacus League Want?' first published in *Die Rote Fahne*, 14 December 1918. Reproduced in R Luxemburg, *Selected Political Writings of Rosa Luxemburg* (New York, London 1971).

WEJ McCarthy, *Shop Stewards and Workshop Relations: The Results of a Study Undertaken by the Government Social Survey for the Royal Commission on Trade Unions and Employers' Associations* (London 1968).

G Majone, 'The European Community Between Social Policy and Social Regulation' (1993) 31 *Journal of Common Market Studies* 153–70.
P Manow, 'Welfare State Building and Coordinated Capitalism in Japan and Germany' in W Streeck and K Yamamura (eds) *The Origins of Nonliberal Capitalism* (Ithaca, NY 2001).
A Markovits, *The Politics of West German Trade Unions* (Cambridge 1986).
TH Marshall, 'Citizenship and Social Class' reprinted in TH Marshall and T Bottomore, *Citizenship and Social Class* (London 1992).
A Martin and G Ross, 'In the Line of Fire: the Europeanization of Labour Representation' in A Martin and G Ross (eds) *The Brave New World of European Labor: European Trade Unions at the Millenium* (New York, Oxford 1999).
M Martiny, *Integration oder Konfrontation? Studien zur Geschichte der sozialdemokratischen Rechts- und Verfassungspolitik* (Bonn, Bad Godesberg 1976).
K Marx, *Capital: A Critique of Political Economy* Volume 1 (Moscow 1959 [1844]).
K Marx, 'Estranged Labour' in *Economic and Philosophical Manuscripts* (Moscow 1959 [1844]).
R Mayne, 'The Role of Jean Monnet' (1967) 2 *Government and Opposition* 349–71.
N Millward, A Bryson, J Forth, *All Change at Work? British Employment Relations 1980–98, Portrayed by the Workplace Industrial Relations Survey Series* (New York 2000).
W Milne-Bailey, *Trade Union Documents* (London 1929).
A Milward, *The Reconstruction of Western Europe 1945–51* (Berkeley 1984).
Ministry of Reconstruction, Committee on Relations between Employers and Employed (Whitley), *Second Report on Joint Standing Industrial Councils*, Cd. 9002, Parliamentary Papers (1918) X.659.
R Mitchell and C Arup, 'Labour Law and Labour Market Regulation' in C Arup, P Gahan, J Howe, R Johnstone, R Mitchell, A O'Donnell (eds) *Labour Law and Labour Market Regulation: Essays on the Construction, Constitution and Regulation of Labour Markets and Work Relationships* (Sydney 2006).
W Müller-Jentsch, 'Germany: From Collective Voice to Co-management' in J Rogers and W Streeck (eds) *Works Councils* (Chicago 1995).
G Mundlak, 'The Third Function of Labour Law: Distributing Labour Market Opportunities among Workers' in G Davidov and B Langille, *The Idea of Labour Law* (Oxford 2011).
F Naphtali, *Wirtschaftsdemokratie: ihr Wesen, Weg und Ziel* (Berlin 1928).
W-D Narr, *CDU-SPD: Programm and Praxis seit 1945* (Berlin 1966).
H Northrup, D Campbell, and B Slowinski, 'Multinational union-management consultation in Europe: Resurgence in the 1980s?' (1988) 127 *International Labour Review* 525–43.
T Novitz, 'The Right to Strike as a Human Right' (2007–2008) 10 *Cambridge Yearbook of European Law* 357.
T Novitz, 'From Trade in Goods to Trade in Services—Implications for Transnational Labour Law' paper delivered at the 2013 *LLRN Conference, Barcelona*.
T Novitz and P Skidmore, *Fairness at Work* (Oxford 2001).
T Novitz and P Syrpis, 'Assessing Legitimate Structures for the Making of Transnational Labour Law: The Durability of Corporatism' (2006) 35 *Industrial Law Journal* 367–94.
P O'Higgins, 'The End of Labour Law as We Have Known It?' in C Barnard, S Deakin, and G Morris (eds) *The Future of Labour Law; Liber Amicorum Bob Hepple QC* (Oxford 2004).
K Papadakis, 'Globalizing Industrial Relations: What Role for International Framework Agreements' in S Hayter (ed) *The Role of Collective Bargaining in the Global Economy* (Cheltenham 2011).

A Peacock and H Willgerodt (eds) *Germany's Social Market Economy* (London 1989).
A Peacock and H Willgerodt, 'German Liberalism and Economic Revival' in A Peacock and H Willgerodt (eds) *Germany's Social Market Economy* (London 1989).
T van Peijpe, 'Collective Labour Law after Viking, Laval, Rüffert, and Commission v. Luxembourg' (2009) 25 *International Journal of Comparative Labour Law and Industrial Relations* 81–107.
H Pelling, 'Trade Unions, Workers and The Law' in H Pelling, *Popular Politics and Society in Late Victorian Britain: Essays* (London 1979).
K Polanyi, *The Great Transformation: The Political and Economic Origins of our Time* (Boston 2001 [1944, 57]).
'Political and Economic Planning' (1956) 22(405) *Planning* 222–43
J Prassl 'Case-C 426/11 Alemo-Herron v Parkwood Leisure Ltd' (2013) 42 *Industrial Law Journal* 434–46.
S Quack and M-L Djelic, 'Adaptation, Recombination and Reinforcement: The Story of Antitrust and Competition Law in German and Europe', in W Streeck and K Thelen (eds) *Change and Continuity in Institutional Analysis* (Oxford 2005).
T Ramm, 'Nationalsozialismus und Arbeitsrecht' (1968) 1 *Kritische Justiz* 108–20.
T Ramm, 'Otto Kahn-Freund und Deutschland' in F Gamillscheg (ed) *In Memoriam Sir Otto Kahn-Freund* (Munich 1980).
Rapport des chefs de délégations aux Ministres des Affaires Etrangères [Spaak Report] (Brussels 1956).
D Renton and A Macey, *Justice Deferred: A Critical Guide to the Coalition's Employment Tribunal Reforms* (Liverpool 2013).
GA Ritter, 'Die Entstehung des Räteartikels 165 der Weimarer Reichsverfassung' (1994) 258 *Historische Zeitschrift* 73–111.
K Rittich, 'What "Makes" Markets?' (2014) *Northern Ireland Legal Quarterly*, forthcoming.
BC Roberts and B Liebhaberg, 'The European Trade Union Confederation: Influence of Regionalism, Détente and Multinationals' (1976) 14 *British Journal of Industrial Relations* 261–73.
F Rödl, 'Labour Constitution' in A von Bogdandy and J Bast (eds) *Principles of European Constitutional Law*, 2nd ed (Oxford 2011).
M Rodriguez-Piñero and E Casas, 'In Support of a European Social Constitution' in P Davies et al (eds) *European Community Labour Law: Principles and Perspectives* (Oxford 1996).
M Rönnmar, 'Laval Returns to Sweden' (2010) 39 *Industrial Law Journal* 280–7.
A Rosenberg, *A History of the German Republic* (London 1936).
G Ross, *Jacques Delors and European Integration* (Cambridge 1995).
R Roux, 'The Position of Labour under the Schuman Plan' (1952) LXV *International Labour Review* 289–320.
Royal Commission on Trade Unions and Employers' Associations, *Report* (London 1968).
D Sack, 'Europeanization through Law, Compliance and Party Differences' (2012) 34 *Journal of European Integration* 241–60.
J A Sargent, 'Corporatism and the European Community' in W Grant (ed) *The Political Economy of Corporatism* (London 1985).
F Scharpf, 'Negative Integration and Positive Integration in the Political Economy of European Welfare States' in G Marks et al (eds) *Governance in the European Union* (London 1996).
D Schiek, 'Autonomous Collective Agreements as a Regulatory Device in European Labour Law' (2005) 34 *Industrial Law Journal* 23–56.

D Schiek, 'Europe's Socio-Economic Constitution ("Verfasstheit") after the Treaty of Lisbon' in T Dieterich, M Le Friant, L Nogler, K Kezuka, H Pfarr (eds) *Individuelle und kollektive Freiheit im Arbeitsrecht—Gedächtnisschrift für Ulrich Zachert* (Baden-Baden 2010).

D Schiek, *Economic and Social Integration: The Challenge for EU Constitutional Law* (Cheltenham 2012).

H-V Schierwater, 'Der Arbeitnehmer und Europa-Integrationstendenzen und -Strukturen im Sozialbereich des Gemeinsamen Marktes' in C Friedrich (ed) *Politische Dimensionen der europäischen Gemeinschaftsbildung* (Opladen 1968).

E Schmidt, *Die verhinderte Neuordnung 1945–1952: zur Auseinandersetzung um die Demokratisierung der Wirtschaft in den westlichen Besatzungszonen und in der Bundesrepublik Deutschland* (Frankfurt am Main 1970).

K Schmierl, 'Wird das deutsche Modell der Arbeitsregulierung die Umschichtung in der Arbeitsgesellschaft überleben?' *WSI-Mitteilungen* 11/2003.

P Schmitter, 'Still the Century of Corporatism?' (1974) 36 *Review of Politics* 85–131.

M Schneider (ed), *Kleine Geschichte der Gewerkschaften* (Bonn 1989).

S Sciarra, 'Social Values and the Multiple Sources of European Social Law' (1995) 1 *European Law Journal* 60–83.

S Sciarra, 'Collective Agreements in the Hierarchy of European Community Sources' in P Davies et al (eds) *European Community Labour Law: Principles and Perspectives* (Oxford 1996).

A Seifert, '"Von der Person zum Menschen im Recht"—zum Begriff des sozialen Rechts bei Hugo Sinzheimer' (2011) 2 *Soziales Recht* 62–73.

B Simpson, 'British Labour Relations in the 1980s: Learning to Live with the Law' (1986) 49 *Modern Law Review* 796–818.

H Sinzheimer, 'Über die Formen und Bedeutung der Betriebsräte' (1919) in H Sinzheimer, *Arbeitsrecht und Rechtssoziologie: gesammelte Aufsätze und Reden* (Frankfurt, Cologne 1976).

H Sinzheimer, 'Das Rätesystem' (1919) in H Sinzheimer, *Arbeitsrecht und Rechtssoziologie: gesammelte Aufsätze und Reden* (Frankfurt, Cologne 1976).

H Sinzheimer, 'Die Zukunft der Arbeiterräte' (1919) in H Sinzheimer, *Arbeitsrecht und Rechtssoziologie: gesammelte Aufsätze und Reden* (Frankfurt, Cologne 1976).

H Sinzheimer, 'Rätebewegung und Gesellschaftsverfassung' (1920) in H Sinzheimer, *Arbeitsrecht und Rechtssoziologie: gesammelte Aufsätze und Reden* (Frankfurt, Cologne 1976).

H Sinzheimer, *Grundzüge des Arbeitsrechts* (Jena 1921).

H Sinzheimer, 'Die Fortbildung des Arbeitrechts' (1922) 9 *Arbeitsrecht* cols 178–80.

H Sinzheimer, 'Otto Gierke's Bedeutung für das Arbeitsrecht: Ein Nachruf' (1922) in H Sinzheimer, *Arbeitsrecht und Rechtssoziologie: gesammelte Aufsätze und Reden* (Frankfurt, Cologne 1976).

H Sinzheimer, 'The Sociological and Positivistic Method in the Discipline of Labour Law' (1922) 9 *Arbeitsrecht* cols 187–98.

H Sinzheimer, 'Europa und die Idee der wirtschaftlichen Demokratie' (1925) in H Sinzheimer, *Arbeitsrecht und Rechtssoziologie: gesammelte Aufsätze und Reden* (Frankfurt, Cologne 1976).

H Sinzheimer, *Grundzüge des Arbeitsrechts*, 2nd ed (Jena 1927).

H Sinzheimer, 'Demokratisierung des Arbeitsverhältnisses' (1928) in H Sinzheimer, *Arbeitsrecht und Rechtssoziologie: gesammelte Aufsätze und Reden* (Frankfurt, Cologne 1976).

H Sinzheimer 'Zur Frage der Reform des Schlichtungswesens' (1929) in H Sinzheimer, *Arbeitsrecht und Rechtssoziologie: gesammelte Aufsätze und Reden* (Frankfurt, Cologne 1976).

H Sinzheimer, 'Die Reform des Schlichtungswesens' (1930) in H Sinzheimer, *Arbeitsrecht und Rechtssoziologie: gesammelte Aufsätze und Reden* (Frankfurt, Cologne 1976).

H Sinzheimer, 'Eine Theorie des Sozialen Rechts' (1936) XVI *Zeitschrift für öffentliches Recht* 31–57; reproduced in H Sinzheimer, *Arbeitsrecht und Rechtssoziologie: gesammelte Aufsätze und Reden* (Frankfurt, Cologne 1976).

H Sinzheimer, 'On Formalism in the Philosophy of Law' (1939) 2 *Zeitschrift für freie deutsche Forschung* 30–40.

H Sinzheimer, *Arbeitsrecht und Rechtssoziologie: gesammelte Aufsätze und Reden* (Frankfurt, Cologne 1976).

S Smismans, 'The European Social Dialogue between Constitutional and Labour Law' (2007) 32 *European Law Review* 341–64.

G Steinmetz, 'Workers and the Welfare State in Imperial Germany' (1991) 40 *International Labor and Working Class History* 18–46.

G Steinmetz, *Regulating the Social: The Welfare State and Local Politics in Imperial Germany* (Princeton 1993).

J Stiglitz, *Globalization and its Discontents* (Penguin 2002).

KVW Stone, 'Flexibilization, Globalization, and Privatization: Three Challenges to Labour Rights in Our Time' in B Bercusson and C Estlund, *Regulating Labour in the Wake of Globalisation* (Oxford 2008).

KVW Stone, 'The Decline in the Standard Employment Contract: A Review of the Evidence' in KVW Stone and H Arthurs, R*ethinking Workplace Regulation: Beyond the Standard Contract of Employment* (London 2013).

W Streeck, *Social Institutions and Economic Performance* (London, Newbury Park, New Delhi 1992).

W Streeck, 'European Social Policy after Maastricht: The "Social Dialogue" and "Subsidiarity"' (1994) 15 *Economic and Industrial Democracy* 151–77.

W Streeck, 'Neo-Voluntarism: a New European Social Policy Regime?' (1995) 1 *European Law Journal* 31–59.

W Streeck, 'Neither European nor Works Councils' (1997) 18 *Economic and Industrial Democracy* 325–37.

W Streeck, 'German Capitalism. Does it Exist? Can it Survive?' (1997) 2 *New Political Economy* 237–56.

W Streeck, 'Industrial Relations: From State Weakness as Strength to State Weakness as Weakness. Welfare Corporatism and the Private Use of the Public Interest' in S Green and WE Paterson (eds) *Governance in Contemporary Germany: The Semi-Sovereign State Revisited* (Cambridge 2005).

W Streeck, 'The Sociology of Labor Markets and Trade Unions' in NJ Smelser and R Swedberg (eds) *The Handbook of Economic Sociology* (Princeton 2005).

W Streeck, *Re-Forming Capitalism: Institutional Change in the German Political Economy* (Oxford 2009).

W Streeck, 'The Crisis of Democratic Capitalism' (2011) 71 *New Left Review* 5–29.

W Streeck, 'Markets and Peoples: Democratic Capitalism and European Integration' (2012) 73 *New Left Review* 63–71.

W Streeck and P C Schmitter, 'From National Corporatism to Transnational Pluralism: Organized Interests in the Single European Market' (1991) 19 *Politics and Society* 133–65.

ME Streit and W Mussler, 'The Economic Constitution of the European Community: From "Rome" to "Maastricht"' (1995) 1 *European Law Journal* 5–30.

A Supiot, *Beyond Employment: Changes in Work and the Future of Labour Law in Europe* (Oxford 2001).

A Supiot, 'Law and Labour: a World of Market Norms?' (2006) 39 *New Left Review* 109–21.

A Supiot, 'Towards a European Policy on Work' in N Countouris and M Freedland (eds) *Resocializing Europe in a Time of Crisis* (Cambridge 2013).

P Sypris, 'Social Democracy and Judicial Review in the Community Order' in C Kilpatrick et al (eds) *The Future of Remedies in Europe* (Oxford 2000).

P Syrpis, 'The Treaty of Lisbon: Much Ado…But About What?' (2008) 37 *Industrial Law Journal* 219–36.

P Syrpis and T Novitz, 'Economic and Social Rights in Conflict: Political and Judicial Approaches to their Reconciliation' (2008) 33 *European Law Review* 411–26.

R Taylor, *The Trade Union Question in British Politics: Government and Unions since 1945* (Oxford 1993).

P Teague, 'Constitution or Regime? The Social Dimension to the 1992 Project' (1989) 27 *British Journal of Industrial Relations* 310–29.

G Teubner, *Constitutional Fragments: Societal Constitutionalism and Globalization* (Oxford 2012).

G Teubner, 'Self-Constitutionalizing TNCs? On the Linkage of "Private" and "Public" Corporate Codes of Conduct' (2011) 18 *Indiana Journal of Global Legal Studies* 617–38.

R Thaler and C Sunstein, *Nudge: Improving Decisions about Health, Wealth and Happiness* (New Haven, CT 2008).

K Thelen, *Union of Parts: Labor Politics in Postwar Germany* (New York 1991).

H Thum, *Mitbestimmung in der Montanindustrie: der Mythos von Sieg der Gewerkschaften* (Stuttgart 1982).

F Tillyard and WA Robson, 'The Enforcement of the Collective Bargain in the United Kingdom' (1938) 48 *Economic Journal* 15–25.

J Tomlinson, 'Productivity, joint consultation and human relations in post-war Britain: the Attlee Government and the workplace', in J Melling and A McKinlay (eds) *Management, Labour and Industrial Politics in Modern Europe: The Quest for Productivity Growth During the Twentieth Century* (Cheltenham 1996).

C Trampusch, 'From Interest Groups to Parties: The Change in the Career Patterns of the Legislative Elite in German Social Policy' (2005) 14 *German Politics* 14–32.

C Trampusch, 'Postkorporatismus in der Sozialpolitik: Folgen für die Gewerkschaften' *WSI-Mitteilungen* 6/2006.

K Tribe, *Strategies of Economic Order: German Economic Discourse 1750–1950* (Cambridge 1995).

E Tucker, 'Renorming Labour Law: Can We Escape Labour Law's Recurring Regulatory Dilemmas?' (2010) 39 *Industrial Law Journal* 99–138.

E Tucker, 'Labor's Many Constitutions (and Capital's too)' (2012) 33 *Comparative Labor Law and Policy Journal* 355–78.

E Tucker, 'Old Lessons for New Governance: Safety or Profit and the New Conventional Wisdom' (2012) 38 *Osgoode CLPE Research Paper* 14–15.

Z Tyszkiewicz, 'UNICE: The Voice of European Business and Industry in Brussels', in D Sadowski and O Jacobi (eds) *Employers' Associations in Europe: Policy and Organization* (Baden-Baden 1991).

UK Government (1969) White Paper, *In Place of Strife: A Policy for Industrial Relations*, Cmnd 3888.

UK Government, White Paper, *Fairness at Work*, Cm 3968 (London 1998).
UK Government, White Paper, *Our Competitive Future: Building the Knowledge Driven Economy*, Cm 4176 (London 1998).
D Vaughan-Whitehead, *EU Enlargement versus Social Europe?* (Cheltenham 2003).
C Vigneau, 'The Future of European Social Dialogue' in M-A Moreau (ed) *Before and After the Economic Crisis: What Implications for the European Social Model?* (Cheltenham 2011).
J Visser, 'More Holes in the Bucket: Twenty Years of European Integration and Organized Labor' (2004–5) 26 *Comparative Labor Law and Policy Journal* 477–521.
J Waddington, 'European Works Councils: The Challenge for Labour' (2011) 42 *Industrial Relations Journal* 508–29.
B van Wanrooy, H Bewley, A Bryson, J Forth, S Freeth, L Stokes, and S Wood (eds) *The 2011 Workplace Employment Relations Study: First Findings* (London 2013).
S and B Webb, *Industrial Democracy* (London 1897).
S and B Webb, *Theorie und Praxis der englischen Gewerkvereine* (Stuttgart 1898).
S and B Webb, *The History of Trade Unionism* (London 1894).
S and B Webb, *Die Geschichte des britischen Trade Unionism us* (Stuttgart 1895).
S and B Webb, *Industrial Democracy*, 2nd ed (London 1902).
S and B Webb, *The History of Trade Unionism*, 2nd ed (London 1911).
Lord Wedderburn, 'Otto Kahn-Freund and British Labour Law' in Lord Wedderburn, R Lewis, J Clark (eds) *Labour Law and Industrial Relations: Building on Kahn-Freund* (Oxford 1983).
Lord Wedderburn, 'Labour Law: From Here to Autonomy?' (1987) 16 *Industrial Law Journal* 1–29.
Lord Wedderburn, 'Consultation and Collective Bargaining in Europe: Success or Ideology?' (1997) 26 *Industrial Law Journal* 1–34.
Lord Wedderburn, 'Labour Law 2008: 40 Years on' (2007) 36 *Industrial Law Journal* 397–424.
JHH Weiler, 'A Quiet Revolution: "The European Court and its Interlocutors"' (1994) 26 *Comparative Political Studies* 510–34.
M Weiss, 'Workers' Participation in the European Union' in P Davies et al (eds) *European Community Labour Law: Principles and Perspectives* (Oxford 1996).
M Weiss, 'Workers' Involvement in the European Company' in M Biagi (ed) *Quality of Work and Employee Involvement in Europe* (The Hague 2002).
HA Winkler, *Von der Revolution zur Stabilisierung: Arbeiter und Arbeiterbewegung in der Weimarer Republik, 1918 bis 1924* (Berlin 1984).
C Woolfson and A Juska, 'A Very Baltic Tragedy' in J Sommers and C Woolfson, *The Contradictions of Austerity: The Socio-Economic Costs of the Neoliberal Baltic Model* (London 2014).

Index

abstentionism, *see also* voluntarism 69, 85, 92–4, 209
Adenauer, Konrad 47, 50, 131–2, 134
Allgemeiner Deutscher Gewerkschaftsbund (ADGB) 18–19, 51
Arbeitsstand 33, 43
arbitration
　and the labour constitution 22, 33–5, 66–7, 213
　Arbitration Decree 1923 33, 40
　Conditions of Employment and National Arbitration Order (Order 1305) 74, 78
　in the Federal Republic of Germany 45–6, 53
　in the UK 75–6, 80, 84, 87
　in the Weimar Republic 26, 28, 40–5
autonomy
　and collective laissez-faire 70–2, 75–83, 89–91, 94
　and the European social dialogue 128, 145–55
　and the labour constitution 8, 23–30, 35, 42–5, 51, 66–7
　of nation states 174, 185–8, 220
　Tarifautonomie 56, 67

Barnes, George 87
BDA, *see* Bundesvereinigung der Deutschen Arbeitgeberverbände
Benelux Memorandum 134
Bercusson, Brian 146–8, 180
Betriebsegoismus, *see* works egoism
Betriebszweck, *see* works objective
Bevin, Ernest 85, 106
BGB, *see* German Civil Code
Blair Governments, *see also* New Labour 101, 108, 110, 116, 122, 203
bourgeois law 16–17, 23, 30–1, 198–9, 213
Bullock Committee 81–2
Bundesbank 56, 63
Bundesvereinigung der Deutschen Arbeitgeberverbände 63
Bürgerliches Gesetzbuch, *see* German Civil Code

capabilities 103–4, 112–16, 203–4
CDU, *see* Christlich Demokratische Union Deutschlands
CEEP, *see* social partners, CEEP
Charter of Fundamental Rights of the European Union (2000)
　adoption 178
　and fundamental rights 161–2, 180–1, 189–92

Christlich Demokratische Union Deutschlands 47–50, 52, 56, 59, 67
citizenship 114, 209, 220
CJEU, *see* Court of Justice of the European Union
Clark, Jon 28–9
class conflict, *see also* conflicts of interest 88, 90, 116, 208–9
　and Polanyi, Karl 195
Clegg, Hugh 77, 79
codetermination
　and the labour constitution 5
　definition 8, 162
　in the EU 162–6, 173, 186
　in the Federal Republic of Germany 48–50, 53–5, 67
　in the Weimar Republic 17
Codetermination Act 1951 46, 50
Codetermination Act 1976 46, 54
Cold War 47, 131
Collective Agreement Act 1949 46, 52–3
collective agreements, *see also* collective bargaining
　and collective laissez-faire 72–80, 83, 86
　and the labour constitution 13, 22–8, 158
　and the law of the labour market 110
　compulsory normative effect 24, 39, 46, 73
　extension *erga omnes* 37, 39, 46, 74, 76
　in the EU 125–6, 129, 139, 142, 174–5, 188–9
　in the Federal Republic of Germany 46, 52, 57–66
　in the Weimar Republic 21, 24–8, 34–41
　opening clauses 58–9, 62
Collective Agreements Decree 1918 21, 27, 36–40, 46, 66
collective bargaining
　and collective laissez-faire 23, 69–70, 72–91, 209–12
　and the labour constitution 19, 23–4, 35–6, 39–42, 51–6
　and the law of the labour market 94–9, 106–11, 114, 119–22, 203
　as a fundamental or human right 175, 180, 183
　decentralization 57–68, 92–3, 153, 189, 192
　European social dialogue as collective bargaining 128, 130, 138, 140, 145–50, 156–7
　international framework agreements, *see* collective bargaining, transnational collective bargaining

collective bargaining (*Cont.*)
  in the EU 162, 178, 192
  in the Federal Republic of Germany 45–6
  in the UK 92–4
  transnational collective bargaining 168–9
collective laissez-faire 3, 9, 23–4, 69–91
  in the 1980s and 1990s 92–9
  today 146, 209–12
collective liberalism 24, 87
collectivism 25–6, 59, 72–3, 75, 78
Collins, Hugh 70, 94–101, 105, 108–10, 122
Commission of the European Union
  and fundamental rights 175–9, 192
  and social dumping 184
  and the European social dialogue 126–30, 151–7
  and the 'information and consultation' Directives 162–6, 168–70, 173, 191
  and the institutionalization of the European social dialogue 135–48, 219
  and the guided social dialogue 148–51
  the 'Troika' 188–90, 192
Committee of Inquiry on Industrial Democracy *see* Bullock Committee
common market, *see also* Benelux Memorandum, Ohlin Report, single market, Spaak Report
  and labour rights 173–5, 180, 182, 186, 218–19
  and ordoliberalism 123
  and the trade union movement 134, 136–8, 140, 156, 167
Community Charter of Fundamental Rights of Workers 1989 138, 161, 174–5, 177–8, 180
company board
  supervisory board 34, 46, 49–55, 67, 164
  worker representation on the company board (EU) 164, 186
  worker representation on the company board (Germany) 8, 33, 46, 49–55, 67, 186
  worker representation on the company board (UK) 81–2
Con Dem Coalition, *see* Conservative Liberal-Democrat Coalition
Conciliation Act 1896 90
Confederation of British Industry (CBI) 83, 130
conflicts of interest
  and collective laissez-faire 81, 84, 208–9
  and the labour constitution 20, 35, 61, 65, 208
  and the law of the labour market 6, 10, 96, 115–16, 121–2, 194
  and works councils 55
  between workers 154, 209, 216
  between management and labour 25, 43, 147
Conservative Liberal-Democrat Coalition 118
Conservative Party (UK) 1, 99, 101, 110

Constitution of the Federal Republic of Germany 46–7, 52–3
Constitution of the Weimar Republic 13, 15, 20–2, 32, 46
  Article 165 20–9, 32–3, 38–9, 42, 45, 66
contract of employment
  and Kahn-Freund 73, 78
  and the crisis of concepts 2, 105, 202, 205, 211
  and the labour constitution 15–17, 21
corporate governance 59, 68, 162, 164, 186, 217
corporatism
  and the European social dialogue 125–30, 137–41, 145, 155
  and the labour constitution 9
  definition 127
  in Germany 44, 54–8, 63–5, 67, 214
  in the UK 93, 110
Council of Ministers of the EU 135–6, 142, 164–6
councils' system, *see* works councils, councils' system
Court of Justice of the European Union 174, 178
  and the Laval/Viking quartet 153, 161, 180–7, 192, 220
  UEAPME case (Case T-135/96) 146
Crouch, Colin 118, 189

Davies, Paul 92–102, 105, 108–10, 119–21, 200–3
Deakin, Simon 102–5, 108–17, 120–2, 177–8, 194, 201–7
decentralization 48, 59–62, 68, 153, 188
Delors, Jacques 138, 154
dependent labour 15–16
Deutsche Gewerkschaftsbund 47–50, 54, 62–3, 131–2, 139
  Düsseldorf Programme 54
  Munich Programme 49
DGB, *see* Deutsche Gewerkschaftsbund
disorganization 9, 59, 62–5, 68, 192–3, 220
Donovan Commission 79–80, 92–3
double movement, *see* Karl Polanyi, double movement

ECB, *see* European Central Bank
economic and monetary union, *see* EU law, economic and monetary union
Economic and Social Committee 135–6, 140, 175
economic constitution:
  and the Webbs 19, 212
  as defined by ordoliberals 4, 123–4, 217
  as defined by Sinzheimer 4–5, 17–23
  as distinct from labour constitution 22, 33–6
  of the European Union 10, 123–5, 158–61, 190, 196, 199–200, 212–13, 216–17

economic sociology 204–5
emancipation 4–5, 17–19, 24, 30–2, 65, 107, 198–9, 213–14
enlargement of the EU, *see* EU enlargement
Erhard, Ludwig 49, 134
Estlund, Cynthia 1
EU enlargement 138, 154, 156, 178–80, 184, 191
EU law
  Acquired Rights Directive 1977 163, 169, 192
  approximation, *see* EU law, harmonisation, upward
  Collective Redundancies Directive 1975 163, 169
  Commission Green Paper, *Employee Participation and Company Structure* 1975 162, 163
  doctrine of direct effect 174, 184
  doctrine of supremacy 174, 184, 186
  economic and monetary union 153–4, 156, 161, 187–90
  European Companies Statute 172
  European Works Councils Directive 1994 129, 164–9, 170, 172
  Fixed-Term Work Directive 1999 128–9
  freedom of association 147–8, 155, 161, 175, 180–92
  freedom of establishment 174, 181, 184, 192
  freedom to provide services 174, 181, 184, 192
  fundamental rights 162, 173–93
  harmonization 11, 124, 158–61, 173, 182, 191–2, 219
    downward 174–5, 179
    upward 136, 143–4, 162–3, 176
  information and consultation 124, 161–73, 217, 219
  Information and Consultation of Employees Directive 2002 129, 169–72
  Laval case (Case C-341/05 *Laval un Partneri*) 180–6, 192, 219
  Parental Leave Directive 1995 128–9
  Part Time Work Directive 1997 128–9
  right to strike 147–8, 150, 155, 173, 185
  Single European Act 1986 123, 138, 143
  Social Action Programme 1974 137, 140, 142–3, 155, 162–3, 217
  Social Action Programme 1989 175–6
  Treaty of Amsterdam 149, 177
  Treaty of Lisbon 151, 191
  Treaty of Maastricht 124–9, 141–7, 155, 187, 191
  Treaty of Paris 130, 132–3
  Treaty of Rome 123–4, 130, 134–7, 142–3, 160–3, 217
  Treaty on the Functioning of the European Union 126, 151–2

Viking case (Case C-438/05 *International Transport Workers Federation v Viking Line*) 180–6, 192, 219
Vredeling Directive 164
Euratom 134
Euro *see also* EU law, economic and monetary union 153–4, 159, 187–8, 218–19
Euro-crisis 153, 187–90, 192, 219
Europe 2020 151
European Central Bank 187–8, 192–3
European Centre of Employers and Enterprises providing Public Services, *see* social partners CEEP
European Coal and Steel Community 130–6, 217
European Economic Community 134–45
European Regional Organisation 133
European social dialogue
  autonomy as a frame of reference 145–8
  autonomous social dialogue 126, 129–30, 148–51, 155
  guided social dialogue 126–9, 155, 157
European social model 127, 151, 162, 180, 189, 193
European social space 138
European Trade Union Confederation, *see* social partners, ETUC
European Works Councils 127–9, 164–70, 172
Ewing, Keith 1, 85

Fairness at Work. White Paper. 100, 116
fascism 26, 29, 45, 75, 80
FDP, *see* Freie Demokratische Partei
First World War 3, 13, 37, 40, 42
Flanders, Allan 77–8, 87–8
flexibility
  flexible employment relations 100, 109, 116, 122
  labour market flexibility 99–110, 116–22, 188, 196, 201–3, 215–16
Fraenkel, Ernst 12, 14, 22, 29, 45, 67
Freedland, Mark 92–102, 105, 108–10, 119–21, 200–3
freedom of association *see also* EU law, freedom of association
  and autonomy 89
  and collective laissez-faire 96, 210
  and the labour constitution 19, 33–5, 43–4
  and the law of the labour market 206
  in the Federal Republic of Germany 46, 51–3
  in the Weimar Republic 41–2
Freie Demokratische Partei 46, 49

German Civil Code 14–15
Greece 173, 188–90
Grundgesetz, *see* Constitution of the Federal Republic of Germany

Hartz Reforms 64
Hayek, Friedrich 103, 114, 120, 194, 204
Hegel, Georg Wilhelm Friedrich 27, 32
Hepple, Bob 177–8
Howell, Chris 87–8

ICFTU, *see* International Confederation of Free Trade Unions
ILO, *see* International Labour Organisation
IMF, *see* International Monetary Fund
In Place of Strife. White Paper. 93–4
industrial action
    in the EU 146, 150, 157, 161, 181, 183, 185, 210
    in the Federal Republic of Germany 45–7, 50–3, 61–2, 66–7
    in the UK 74, 76, 79, 82–6, 93–4, 101, 110, 121
    in the Weimar Republic 20, 22, 25–6, 33, 35, 37, 40–2, 213
industrial democracy 17–19, 81, 140, 162–4, 191, 212, 217
Industrial Relations Act 1971 93–4
inflation, *see also* wages, wage-push inflation 40, 93–4, 96–8, 101
information and consultation, *see* EU Law, information and consultation
international framework agreements, *see* collective bargaining, transnational collective bargaining
International Confederation of Free Trade Unions 131–3
International Labour Organisation 110, 134–5, 185–6, 190
    Committee of Experts on the Application of Conventions and Recommendations 185–6
International Monetary Fund 188, 192–3, 215

Kant, Immanuel 16
Keynes, John Maynard 54, 56, 200
Klare, Karl 213
Kohl, Helmut 64
Kommunistische Partei Deutschlands 38–9, 49
KPD, *see* Kommunistische Partei Deutschlands

labour courts
    labour courts of the Weimar Republic 21–2, 34, 66
    Federal Labour Court 53
    Reich Labour Court 22, 76
Labour Party (UK) 79, 99–103, 106, 108, 119, 122, 203
Langille, Brian 211
Laski, Harold 77–8
Laval case, *see* EU law, Laval case
Lewis, Roy 28, 85
Lisbon Strategy 151, 170, 177

Lo Faro, Antonio 147–50
Luxembourg, Rosa 36–7

Marshall, Thomas Humphrey (TH) 114
Marx, Karl 4, 14–6, 199
methodology 104–111, 199–200, 203–4, 217–18
Milward, Alan 137
Ministry of Labour (UK) 77–8

Naphtali, Fritz 18–19, 51
Nazi Germany 29, 45, 47, 49, 51–2, 73
neo-voluntarism 144–5
Neumann, Franz 4, 14, 32
New Labour 101–2, 119, 122, 203
Nipperdey, Hans Carl 42, 52–3
Nörpel, Clemens 42, 89
November 1918 Revolution 3, 27, 36–9
Novitz, Tonia 182–3

Ohlin Committee and Report 11, 134–6, 159–61, 174, 181–2
opening clauses, *see* collective agreements, opening clauses
order (economic order) 47–8, 82–3, 123–5, 195–6, 212–21
ordoliberal school 4, 123–4, 217

Pelling, Henry 86
Polanyi, Karl 195, 208, 217
    double movement 195, 208, 217
private law, *see also* bourgeois law 12, 14, 16–17, 20, 107, 199, 213
    private law/public law distinction 14–15, 20, 31, 35
privatization 59, 64, 68
property 16–17, 22, 24, 33, 44, 46, 64
public ownership, *see also* state ownership 48, 107, 179

Reagan, Ronald 2
revolutionary workers' and soldiers' councils, *see* workers' and soldiers' councils
right to strike, *see also* EU law, right to strike 34, 52–3, 110, 122
Royal Commission on Trade Unions and Employers' Associations *see* Donovan Commission

Scharpf, Fritz 183–7, 191
Schmidt, Eberhardt 47, 50
Schröder, Gerhard 64, 176
Schuman, Robert 131–4
Second World War 45, 51, 73–4, 106
Sen, Amartya 103–4, 113, 203
shop stewards 78, 92–3
single market
    and labour rights 175, 180, 182, 186, 218–19
    and the trade union movement 134, 136–8, 140, 156, 167

project to complete the single market 162, 165, 173–4
social democracy
  definition 4, 8
  and the labour constitution 29–32, 42, 65, 89, 213
  third way 111–12
social dialogue, *see* European social dialogue
social dumping 11, 173, 177–9, 182, 219
social exclusion, *see* social inclusion
social inclusion 97, 100–2, 108–9, 115, 121–2, 177, 202–3
social insurance, *see* social welfare
social law 13–15, 98, 105–8, 143–4
  as autonomous non-'state' law 24, 35
social partners 124–30, 138–42, 145–57, 169, 171–2
  BusinessEurope 140–2, 150, 154, 164, 169
  CEEP 125, 128, 142, 145
  ETUC 129, 139–46, 150, 154–7, 165–6
social power 16–17, 158, 196, 211
social rights
  and the labour constitution 196, 216, 221
  and the law of the labour market 103–4, 113–16, 119–20, 122
  in the EU 138, 144, 158, 174–8, 180, 191
social welfare
  and the labour constitution 43–5, 63, 66–7, 214
  and the third way 111–12, 117–18
  in the EU 124, 160, 174, 185, 189, 218
    harmonization 11, 144–5, 187, 191
  in the Federal Republic of Germany 8–9, 54–7, 63
  in the UK 101
  in the Weimar Republic 15, 17–18, 27, 42–5
sociology of law 105, 107, 199
Sozialistische Partei Deutschlands 20, 36, 38–9, 49, 51–4
Spaak Committee and Report 11, 135, 160–1, 174, 181–2
SPD, *see* Sozialistische Partei Deutschlands
state
  definition 5
  and globalization 111–15, 117, 207–9, 214–21
state ownership, *see* public ownership
Stinnes-Legien Agreement 27, 37
Streeck, Wolfgang 6, 54–7, 59, 65–7, 144, 154, 157, 167–8, 208
subsidiarity 143, 152, 156, 162, 167, 170
Supiot Report 104

Thatcher, Margaret 2, 63, 96, 98, 101, 175
Third Reich, *see* Nazi Germany
third way 99–104, 111–12, 115–16, 118, 122, 176
trade boards 90
Trade Disputes Act 1906 87, 90
trade unions *see also* collective agreements, collective bargaining
  and the law of the labour market 110–11, 115, 117, 119–22, 201, 206–7
  and the common market 159–62, 166–9, 171–2, 178–81, 188–92
  and the European social dialogue 130–51, 155–6
  in the Federal Republic of Germany 45–65, 66–8, 213–14
  in the UK 69–91, 92–4, 96, 99, 106, 200
  in the Weimar Republic 12, 19–22, 27–9, 34–45, 65–6
  logic of membership, logic of influence 57, 62–5, 68
  recognition 82–3, 88, 110
Trades Union Congress 79, 83, 93–4, 139
'Troika' 188–90, 219, 220
TUC, *see* Trades Union Congress
Tucker, Eric 116–17

Unabhängige Sozialdemokratische Partei Deutschlands 36, 38–9
USPD, *see* Unabhängige Sozialdemokratische Partei Deutschlands

Val Duchesse talks 138, 141
Verfassung
  definition 4
Viking case, *see* EU law, Viking case
voluntarism *see also* abstentionism 23, 69, 87
von Gierke, Otto 14

wages
  internal wage devaluation 154, 188–9
  minimum wages 60, 115, 119, 122, 178
  Posted Workers Directive 183
  wage differentials/wage inequalities 60, 62–3, 134, 178–9, 192
  wage-setting 158, 188–9
    in the Federal Republic of Germany 53–7
    in the UK 85, 87–8, 94, 106–7, 200
    in the Weimar Republic 22, 37, 40, 62–7, 190
    under Taylorism/Fordism 2
  wage-push inflation 93–4, 96, 101
wages councils, *see* trade boards
Webb, Beatrice and Sidney 19, 111, 212
Webb, Sidney 86
Wedderburn, Kenneth William Wedderburn, Baron Wedderburn of Charlton 90, 97, 167–8
Weimar Constitution, *see* Constitution of the Weimar Republic
welfare, *see* social welfare
welfare corporatism 8–9, 54–7, 63, 67
Whitley Committee 90
Wilkinson, Frank 102–5, 108–17, 120–2, 178, 194, 201–3, 206

worker representation on company boards, *see* company boards, worker representation on company boards
workers' and soldiers' councils 17–18, 27, 36–8
   Berlin workers' and soldiers' council 38
works constitution 49, 53–5, 168, 218
Works Constitution Act 1952 46, 53
Works Constitution Act 1972 54
works councils
   councils' system 17, 20, 22, 33, 38, 158, 199, 213
   and the labour constitution 4, 27, 29, 33–4, 36, 158
   in the Federal Republic of Germany 46, 48–50, 53–8, 60, 63, 168
   in the Weimar Republic 21–2, 26, 38–9, 66
   verlängerte Arm 39
Works Councils Act 1920 21, 27–30, 33, 38, 39, 66
works egoism 34, 158
works objective 21–2, 26, 29–30, 82